Midwest Studies in Philosophy
Volume XXI

MIDWEST STUDIES IN PHILOSOPHY

EDITED BY PETER A. FRENCH, THEODORE E. UEHLING, JR.,
HOWARD K. WETTSTEIN

Many papers in MIDWEST STUDIES IN PHILOSOPHY are invited and all are
previously unpublished. The editors will consider unsolicited manuscripts that are
received by January of the year preceding the appearance of a volume. All manuscripts must be pertinent to the topic area of the volume for which they are submitted.
Address manuscripts to MIDWEST STUDIES IN PHILOSOPHY, Department of
Philosophy, University of California, Riverside, CA 92521.

The articles in MIDWEST STUDIES IN PHILOSOPHY are indexed in THE
PHILOSOPHER'S INDEX.

Forthcoming

Volume XXII   1998 Philosophy of the Emotions
Volume XXIII 1999 New Directions in Philosophy

Recently Published Volumes

Volume XVI   1991 Philosophy and the Arts
Volume XVII   1992 The Wittgenstein Legacy
Volume XVIII 1993 Philosophy of Science
Volume XIX   1994 Philosophical Naturalism
Volume XX   1995 Moral Concepts

Midwest Studies in Philosophy Volume XXI

Philosophy of Religion

Editors

Peter A. French
University of South Florida

Theodore E. Uehling, Jr.
University of Minnesota, Morris

Howard K. Wettstein
University of California, Riverside

University of Notre Dame Press • Notre Dame, Indiana

Copyright 1997 by
University of Notre Dame Press
Notre Dame, Indiana 46556

Printed in the United States of America

Library of Congress Cataloging-in-Publication Data

Philosophy of religion / editors, Peter A. French, Theodore E.
    Uehling, Jr., Howard K. Wettstein.
        p. cm. — (Midwest studies in philosophy : v. 21)
    Includes bibliographical references.
    ISBN 0-268-01429-9 (alk. paper). — ISBN 0-268-01430-2 (pbk. :
alk. paper)
        1. Religion—Philosophy. I. French, Peter A. II. Uehling,
    Theodore Edward. III. Wettstein, Howard K. IV. Series.
    BL51.P47 1997
    210—dc21   97-21493
                                                          CIP

The paper used in this publication meets the minimum requirements
of the American National Standard for Information Sciences—
Permanence of Paper for Printed Library Materials, ANSI Z39.48-
1984.

This volume is dedicated to Professor Theodore E. Uehling. Professor Uehling is retiring, and this is the last year of his editorship. His fellow editors wish to express their deep appreciation for Ted's immeasurable contributions to *Midwest Studies in Philosophy* since its inception.

Midwest Studies in Philosophy
Volume XXI
Philosophy of Religion

Midwest Studies in Philosophy
Volume XXI

Symbolic Value

ROBERT MERRIHEW ADAMS

Religious ethical teaching has placed great value on explicit profession of religious belief, and on its explicit expression in ritual and other religiously symbolic behavior.[1] To a modern mentality it may be perplexing that such matters should be thought ethically important. In this essay I shall try to remove some of that perplexity.

1. MARTYRDOM

Let us begin with a puzzle about martyrdom. 'Martyr' is a Greek word for witness, lightly anglicized. An act of martyrdom is an act of testifying to, or standing for, something that one believes. It is distinguished from other sorts of testimony by the fact that the martyr pays a substantial price for her action. The word 'martyr' brings first to mind cases in which the price was death, but I shall not confine my attention to such cases. The costliness of the action, it should be added, is due in some way to other people's opposition to the martyr's cause. Someone who impoverishes himself to build a monument to a hero universally admired is not a martyr.

Martyrdom is praised by many religious traditions, and demanded, in certain situations, by some. The ancient Christian Church was uncompromising in its insistence that Christians must not deny their faith, and must not offer a pagan sacrifice, under any threat or duress whatever. Yet it is not obvious what was the good of martyrdom, in many cases, or what harm would have been done by conforming outwardly to the pagan demand while retaining the Christian faith in one's heart. For the Church demanded a willingness to bear witness that was not conditional on the likelihood that the consequences would be good. The blood of the martyrs may have been the seed of the Church, but the obligation of confessing the faith was not seen as conditional on historical fruitfulness. Without entering into the question whether it was right to regard such a stance as obligatory, we can probably agree that the martyrs command our intuitive admiration. And what I am interested in elucidating is a rationale, presumably not consequentialist, that might lie behind our admiration.

What reason can be offered for being willing to pay the price of martyrdom for no obvious good result? Why wouldn't it be better to stand up for one's beliefs only when the consequences are likely to be good? One possible response to these questions would be an appeal to religious authority. Christians, it may be said, are forbidden to deny Christ, or to worship anyone but God, and therefore must not conform to demands such as the Roman Empire periodically addressed to them. It is hard to rest in this answer, however. For we can hardly help asking why God would want you to be a martyr if it would do no good. And if there is no good reason for God to command martyrdom under such circumstances, that will undermine the plausibility of the belief that it is commanded.

Moreover, the problem can be duplicated in a secular context, in which the appeal to religious authority is not available. Martyrdom over a political issue can seem admirable, if not imperative, to many people of a wide variety of religious and secular persuasions. The following incident comes from the life of a theologian, but I think our feelings about it will not depend on the religious faith of the protagonist. The story is about Dietrich Bonhoeffer, well known as a leader of resistance to Hitler in the Protestant church in Germany, who was put to death by the Nazis towards the end of the Second World War. His friend and biographer Eberhard Bethge records that on the afternoon of 17 June 1940, while he was sitting with Bonhoeffer in an outdoor café at a German seaside resort, the café's loudspeaker, with a sudden fanfare, broadcast the news that France had surrendered.

> The people round about at the tables could hardly contain themselves; they jumped up, and some even climbed on the chairs. With outstretched arm they sang "*Deutschland, Deutschland über alles*" and the Horst-Wessel song. We had stood up too. Bonhoeffer raised his arm in the regulation Hitler salute, while I stood there dazed. "Raise your arm! Are you crazy?" he whispered to me, and later: "We shall have to run risks for very different things now, but not for that salute!"[2]

On Bethge's interpretation, which certainly seems to be confirmed by later events, Bonhoeffer had not gone over to Nazism, or even lost his nerve. Rather he was in the early stages of a change of strategy and personal response, from public protest in the 1930s to conspiracy within the German government during the war—conspiracy that actually involved Bonhoeffer's employment in the German military intelligence service. The epithet 'martyr' is widely, but only very loosely, applied to Bonhoeffer. His public opposition in the 1930s certainly involved some degree of martyrdom. He suffered for it. But he was not killed or even imprisoned for *that*. What he died for was heroic enough, but it was precisely not martyrdom. He was executed for his part in a conspiracy to kill Hitler. That activity was not testimony; it was not publicly acknowledged but secret. It involved much necessary, and in my opinion commendable, deception.

I admire Bonhoeffer, and I would not presume to say that he *ought* to have chosen a different course on the occasion described; but I would *like* his life story better if it did not contain that Hitler salute. On first reading about the incident I shared his friend's apparent shock at Bonhoeffer's action. And even on reflection I do not think it would have been "crazy" to have refrained from the salute, even if it would have involved some sort of martyrdom. This is indeed the first point that I want to use the story to make. Even if we think that Bonhoeffer's path of secret and ultimately conspiratorial opposition was defensible, and maybe heroic, I imagine that most of us, perhaps all of us, will feel that it would also have been admirable to have refused to give the Hitler salute. And this reaction clearly needs no appeal to religious authority to sustain it. It is grounded rather in a conviction, widely shared by people of many religious and nonreligious orientations, that Nazism was a great evil. But it does not rest on a belief, which I do not hold, that an act of silent protest, in Bonhoeffer's situation, would be likely to have had good consequences. So I face the question: What is admirable about a costly and probably ineffective act of protest?

Some may think that this way of putting the question overlooks the effects of the action on the agent. Could the reason for refusing to offer a salute to Hitler, or a pinch of incense to the genius of the Emperor, be that offering it would be harmful to your own moral or spiritual life? I grant that it would be harmful, if you see the act as one of religious disloyalty or abandonment of your moral ideals. But why should you see the act in that way? This is just another version of the original question: What religious or moral value is there in the act of martyrdom?

Our quest for a better answer to this question may begin with the central idea in the concept of martyrdom, the idea of *testimony*. The main thing that is ethically required of testimony, we may think, is *truthfulness*. But we are not likely to find an adequate explanation of the value of martyrdom in the general value of truthfulness. Most of the lies and deceptions that Bonhoeffer was obliged to practice in his conspiratorial activity, for example, are much easier to accept, morally, than the Nazi salute. And if we would admire at all the quixotic truthfulness of someone who would not use forged identity papers to escape from the Nazis because it would involve lying, we would certainly admire that much less than a refusal to give the Nazi salute. This indicates that the value we see in martyrdom is something more than the value of truthfulness.

In particular, the content of one's testimony matters, as well as its truthfulness. Being truthful about one's name and address does not matter in the same way as expressing what one believes about a great moral or religious issue. And I think that is because in the latter case one is testifying, not just *about* something, but *for* or *against* something. The issue in martyrdom is not just one of truthfulness, but also, and more importantly, of what one is for and against. Expressing one's loyalty to Christ in verbal or symbolic behavior is an important way of being for Christ. Refusing to engage in behavior expressive of loyalty to Nazism is an important way of being against Nazism. And it is a major part of virtue to be for the good and against the bad. This I believe to be the main connection between martyrdom and virtue, and the main source of the value of martyrdom.

2. THE MORAL VALUE OF SYMBOLISM

We take it for granted that an action can be good or bad because of what it *causes*, or is meant to cause. I claim that an action can also be good or bad because of what it *symbolizes* or stands for. That is the main idea of this essay, and it deserves some development.

When we think of an alternative to valuing an action for its consequences, we think naturally of regarding the action as *intrinsically* valuable. And no doubt symbolic value could be contrasted as intrinsic with merely instrumental value. But there is another way in which the label 'intrinsic' is not very apt for the sort of symbolic value that most interests me. For in the ancient contrast of *nomos* and *physis,* convention and nature, we associate the intrinsic with the natural; but the symbolism involved in martyrdom is conventional rather than natural.

Theories of signification and communication have long noted that there are natural signs, which are causally rather than conventionally connected with what they signify. And a natural sign is sometimes regarded as a symbol of what it signifies. "The midnight oil," for example, is (or was) a natural symbol of diligence in study. It required no convention to establish this connection, because diligence naturally caused students to burn oil in their lamps late at night.

Natural signs or symbols, like conventional symbols, can be used both to communicate information and to mislead or deceive. For instance, you could leave a light burning on your desk, to give a misleading impression of diligence, when you go to a movie. Many of us customarily leave some lights on in our homes in the evening, whether we are at home or not, to give potential burglars the idea that someone is there. If we are there, what we suggest is true; if we are out, we are trying to deceive.

We may frown on such deception if it causes undeserved harm, or if it amounts to pretending to a virtue that one does not possess. But we do not regard it as lying, and even people who would have qualms about lying to potential burglars normally have no compunction about leaving the lights on. There is no false testimony in misleading natural signs—for the simple reason that there is no *testimony* at all in them. For testimony (like lying) requires *commitment* of a sort that is (logically) possible only within a conventional system of mutually understood intentions, such as a language. It is the conventions that determine that an action is testimony, and what it attests. Lying is a kind of violation of the conventions. And martyrdom, as I have said, is first of all testimony. No doubt we could have conventions by which natural signs would be used to attest what they naturally signify. But that is not the usual case.

This may seem to intensify the problem about martyrdom. We are being asked to value an action not only apart from the value of its consequences but also on the basis of a meaning that does not belong to it naturally, but only in relation to certain conventions. This objection can be overcome, however. What is positively or negatively valued is not raising one's arm or making certain sounds as such; it is expressing commitment or loyalty to a belief or cause. Such expression, I have argued, is good or bad insofar as it is a way of being for or against something good or bad. Expressing love of the good, and opposition to the bad, is naturally and intrinsically good, though the form it takes is variable and conventional.

This is not to say there is a form it could take without any conventions at all. Indeed it is only by virtue of our systems of conventional symbolism that we are able to be "for" or "against" most goods and evils. A dog can desire food, and perhaps can love its mistress. A dog can also be mean or gentle. But if we said that the dog loves gentleness or hates meanness, all we could mean is that it tends to like gentle actions and tends to dislike harsh ones. There is no way that the dog could be in favor of gentleness in general or opposed to meanness in general. How is it that we can be for or against such goods and evils in a way that dogs cannot? Clearly it is by virtue of our ability to make use of conventional symbolism to express explicitly, to others or to ourselves, our allegiance or opposition.

And while it is certainly possible to be for or against a good or evil without expressing that openly, it is not easy. If you express explicitly, sincerely, and openly, to your friends at least, your Christian faith or your hatred of Nazism, you take a stance. You are for Christianity; or you are against Nazism. Now suppose that, under the pressure of persecution, and perhaps justifiably, you suppress all outward expression of your loyalties. After a while you yourself may begin to wonder how much reality there is in your opposition to Nazism. Are you actually opposed to it, or do you only wish you could be? These considerations make clear, I think, the importance of symbolic expression for morality, if moral goodness consists largely in being for the good and against the bad.[3]

Ethical theory has paid little attention to the value that can belong to actions by virtue of their expressing symbolically an allegiance to the good or an opposition to the bad. The value of consequences, by contrast, is a dominant consideration in most ethical theories. If it is not exclusively the consequences of the actions themselves, as in act utilitarianism, then it may be the consequences of adopting certain rules, as in rule utilitarianism or (with somewhat different tests applied to the consequences) in Rawls's theory of justice. Theories of virtue, alternatively, may focus on the consequences of dispositions or traits of character. The tendency to evaluate the way a person lives in terms of consequences is pervasive in contemporary ethical theory.

The value of consequences is certainly important for ethics, but we may well wonder why the symbolic value of actions has been neglected. We take it for granted that the value of what we cause, or at least of what we intentionally cause, is important to the moral quality of our lives. Why should we not assume that the value of what we stand for symbolically is also important to the moral quality of our lives? We sometimes speak of that quality, after all, in terms of the "meaning" of our lives—and there is no reason to suppose that conventional symbolism is irrelevant to meanings!

One reason for the focus on consequences, no doubt, is that ethical theorists have been concerned to show that ethical thinking is *rational,* and an argument from the value of consequences to a prima facie value of the means of attaining them is viewed as the clearest paradigm of practical rationality. There are also reasons for symbolic action, however. I have tried to indicate the most important, which is that symbolic action is a way of being for what one loves and against what one hates. Wanting to find significant ways of being for what one loves and against what one hates is an important part of loving and hating. One therefore has an important reason for giving symbolic expression to one's loyalties. Symbolic action expressing love for the Good and hatred of evils is therefore prima facie rational for those who love the Good.

This may be viewed, however, as a self-regarding reason; and that may be a further cause of the neglect of symbolic value in moral theory. Morality is thought to be concerned with our lives as they impinge on the interests of other people; and the expressive significance of my action as a part of my life does not impinge on your life as clearly, heavily, or inescapably as some of the consequences of my action may. It is for reasons of this sort that the "clean hands" motive for refusing to employ evil means to good ends is often thought to be selfish. And "clean hands," though hardly a matter of conventional symbolism, is a matter of expressing one's loyalties and convictions clearly in one's life.

This objection is not altogether to be dismissed. It would be selfish to give the symbolic, or more broadly the expressive, value of one's life an invariable precedence over the value of consequences. Some aspects of the task of weighing these two types of consideration against each other will be considered in the next section. But the argument that would dismiss all appeal to symbolic value as at best irrelevant to the concerns of morality rests on a misconception of the interests that it is morality's business to protect. If our interest in each other were merely competitive and exploitive, we would view each other only as potential obstacles or instruments, and would not care, at bottom, about the intrinsic quality of each other's lives, but only about their consequences. But those are surely not the only interests for which morality should care. In a morally more desirable system of relationships we care about each other as partners and friends, and therefore have interests in the intrinsic quality of each other's lives. In particular, it matters to us what other people are for and against, as that profoundly affects the possibilities of alliance and social union with them. A morally good person, from this point of view, is not just a useful person, but an ally of the Good and of those who love the Good. And such a person will have reason to perform acts that symbolically express love for the Good, and hatred of evils.

This point applies with special emphasis to theistic ethics. An omnipotent deity can hardly have a *merely* instrumental interest in any creature. The causal consequences of our actions God could secure without our aid, if willing as well as able to intervene in the course of nature. What even omnipotence obviously cannot obtain without our voluntary choice is our voluntary expression of allegiance to God or to the Good. This is a reason for thinking the intrinsic and expressive value of human actions more fundamental in relation to divine omnipotence than their extrinsic and instrumental value.

3. ESCHATOLOGY AND ETHICS

It is not only symbolic action, of course, that expresses our loves and loyalties. Loving the good gives us plenty of reason to care about the consequences of our actions, and striving to produce good consequences can be an expression of such love. Indeed, if the obtaining of good consequences of significant magnitude, or the prevention of bad ones, is a realistic possibility, it commonly will and should seem more important to love for the good to do that than to make a purely symbolic expression. The expressive value of a symbolic act can be undermined if its expected consequences are too costly to the concerns it is supposed to attest.

Whether it would be good to perform an act whose value is mainly symbolic, such as an act of martyrdom, may therefore depend on what other possibilities of action are available in the situation. If Bonhoeffer had a unique opportunity, by pretending to be a Nazi, to assure the success of a conspiracy to overthrow the Nazi regime, then I think it would be irresponsible for him to refuse to give the Hitler salute, despite its moral distastefulness. On the other hand, if there was no realistic hope of successful resistance, conspiratorial or otherwise, to Nazism within Germany, then the symbolic protest of refusing to salute might have been the best available way of being against Nazism. Probably Bonhoeffer's actual situation lay somewhere between those extremes, though closer than he could believe to the more pessimistic one.

This illustrates a more general point which is of great importance for the relation of religion to ethics. What it is reasonable or good, or even makes sense, to do depends on our possibilities of action, and thus on our situation in the world. What that situation is is a largely empirical question; and its details are subject to political, economic, medical, and other sorts of analysis and prediction. Comprehensively, however, and very often in detail, it is subject to great uncertainty. The future is largely unknown to us; and so (in my opinion) are the metaphysical grounds of our existence. These mysteries are a main topic of speculation, faith, and meditation in all religious traditions. And it is very largely because it affects our view of our situation in the world that religion affects ethics.

One way in which this works can be seen in a dispute within contemporary Christian ethics. In the middle of our century the "Christian realism" of Reinhold Niebuhr, with its endorsement of participation in political conflict and its acceptance of some violence as a necessary evil, was the moral theory with the greatest influence, not only on American Christian ethics but probably also on American public life. Some of the most interesting recent work in Christian ethics has criticized Niebuhr sharply from the point of view of what is often called the "Anabaptist" tradition of Christian pacifism. In an unusually systematic presentation of that position, James McClendon has located a major part of his dis-agreement with Niebuhr in the area of eschatology;[4] and that poses the issue I wish to examine.

In traditional theological parlance, 'eschatology' signifies the doctrine of "last things"—death and resurrection, the return of Christ, final judgment, heaven and hell. Beliefs on these subjects have been an obvious part of Christian views of our situation in the world and have played a correspondingly important part in Christian ethics. In my opinion (though not McClendon's) the main point of disagreement between him and Niebuhr in this area is in what has been called "*realized* eschatology."[5]

This term might seem contradictory. How can a claim about what has al-ready been realized be part of a doctrine of last things? The phrase is used in fact to express the claim that part of what has been expected in an earlier escha-tology has already happened. It might be clearer and more accurate to speak here of a theology of history rather than an eschatology. In another way, however, the title 'eschatology' remains appropriate, particularly for ethics. For while we are dealing with a view of history that embraces the past and the present as well as the future (and that has always been at least implicitly true where eschatology is spoken of), there remains, at least for ethics, a special interest in the future. We need and strive to form some opinion about what we can expect or what we should hope for, though for realized eschatology and for ethics the accent may fall on the nearer future. This is true of both Niebuhr and McClendon.

McClendon's pacifism is rooted in his conviction that Christians as such are called to live the life of the Kingdom of God in the midst of this present age, and that the extent to which the Kingdom has already come is sufficient for that attempt to make sense. Accordingly he criticizes "Niebuhr's rejection of the ef-ficacy of the Holy Spirit to make Christians Christ-like, his downplay of the new birth as a real transformation of human life," and "an overemphasis [on sin] that makes of Niebuhr's ethic a strategy for (discriminately) sinful living in an (in-discriminately) sinful world, rather than a strategy for transformed life in a world become new in Christ Jesus." "Niebuhr," he charges, "is too grimly 'realistic' in his assessment of the revolutionary possibilities of Christian community; his re-alism overlooks the new life in Christ."[6]

I agree with McClendon that Niebuhr seriously underrated the possibili-ties of a real spiritual transformation of human life, here and now. But I think history might support Niebuhr in responding that McClendon's view of "the revolutionary possibilities of Christian community" goes too far in the opposite direction. It is one of the lessons of Christian history, as Niebuhr saw it, that the Christian commitment of even the best of Christian communities is itself a standing temptation to spiritual pride, and that all such communities fall from time to time into very harmful sins and errors. This may lead one to doubt that the contrast between church and world can bear the moral weight that McClen-don wishes to lay upon it.[7] And if, with Niebuhr, one finds it less plausible to think that God's grace is at work preeminently in sanctifying a revolutionary Chris-tian community, one may also, with Niebuhr, find it more plausible to seek God's grace in a fairly rough-and-tumble participation in the secular life of one's society.

I incline more to Niebuhr's side in this dispute, but I am not trying to settle it here. My aim is rather to show how differences in what we might broadly think of as eschatology inevitably and appropriately affect views in ethics. This applies to secular as well as theological ethics, though the eschatological assumptions may be less explicit in secular ethics. The dispute between McClendon and Niebuhr finds a clear parallel, indeed, in contemporary moral philosophy.

McClendon's counterparts are those who would devise their ethical theory primarily for an ideal society. Rawls's theory of justice, for example, is offered to us as a "strict compliance" theory, assuming general conformity to the principles of justice. How it is just to respond to widespread injustice, or to other practical obstacles to the implementation of ideal principles, is left to be worked out later.[8] This seems reasonable if we take a fairly optimistic view of our chances of approximating full compliance with the ideal of justice. Those who take a more Niebuhrian view of human sinfulness, however, might expect more guidance from a theory that devoted less attention to ideal conditions of rational agreement and more to the acceptance and limitation of conflict. Derek Parfit's emphasis on "Ideal Act Theory," which says "what we should all try to do, simply on the assumptions that we all try, and all succeed,"[9] puts Parfit, I think, in the same eschatological boat with Rawls, or in a similar one; but I haven't space to develop that point here.

Search for a secular counterpart to Niebuhr might begin with act utilitarians (or "utilitarians," for short). They do not rely on a supposed possibility of any group approximating strict or general compliance with an ideal code.[10] For the utilitarian agent is supposed to do what will probably have the best results, given the *actual* probabilities regarding the behavior of others. If the others are virtuous, the utilitarian takes that into account. If the others are vicious, utilitarian principles apply in exactly the same way, though the best obtainable results may not be so happy.

In another respect, however, utilitarianism is not so Niebuhrian, and may be charged with needing an excessively optimistic eschatology. For utilitarianism is an ethics for people who think they can plan the future. This is not to say that the utilitarian must be able to shape the future to her heart's desire; her lot may be harder than that. But she must have a measure of control over the future; and utilitarianism holds each of us responsible, in principle, for the *whole* future. Two conditions must be satisfied if utilitarian reasoning is to be useful in a situation. One is that we must be able with reasonable reliability to estimate the conditional probability of alternative possible consequences of alternative courses of action. The other condition is that we must have possibilities of action that have a significant chance of substantially improving the outcome as we see it. In many, perhaps most, contexts of choice it is a serious question whether these conditions are satisfied.[11]

This is a question that obviously confronted Bonhoeffer in the situation I described earlier. I suspect that in fact neither condition was satisfied for him; that is, he did not have a significant chance of improving the outcome, and his best estimates of his chances were not reliable. There is a gaping hole in most modern ethical theories, and not just in utilitarianism, at this point. They have nothing to say to us in a situation of helplessness. This has not always been true of ethical theory. Most religions have much advice for the helpless, though some contemporary religious ethics is more exclusively activist. In philosophical ethics, Stoicism is famous for its views about how to cope with outward helplessness.

One reason for the difference may be that many modern theories construe the task of ethics too narrowly, as guidance for *action*. Ethics is not only about how to act well but more broadly about how to *live* well. And whether we like it or not, helplessness is a large part of life. Human life both begins and ends in helplessness. Between infancy and death, moreover, we may find ourselves in the grip of a disease or a dictatorship to which we may be able to adapt but which we cannot conquer. Even if our individual situation is more fortunate, we will find ourselves relatively helpless spectators of most of the events in the world about which we should care somewhat, and many of those about which we should care most, if we are good people. Dealing well with our helplessness is therefore an important part of living well. An ethical theory that has nothing to say about this abandons us in what is literally the hour of our greatest need.

A central part of living well, I believe, is being for the Good and against evils. We face the question, how we can be for and against goods and evils that we are relatively powerless to accomplish or prevent. One of the most obvious answers is that we can give more reality to our being for the goods and against the evils by expressing our loyalties symbolically in action. For this reason acts of martyrdom represent a particularly important possibility of living well for people who find themselves in situations of comparative helplessness—oppressed peoples, persecuted minorities, and inmates of concentration camps, for example. For the same reason, also, sickbeds are rightly surrounded by acts of mainly symbolic value—though the degree of costliness and the context of conflict that would make them a martyrdom is normally lacking. When our friends are ill, most of us are not able to do much about their health. But we can still be *for* them, and that is important to all of us. Sending cards and flowers are ways of being for a sick person symbolically. They may also have the good consequence of cheering up the patient, but that will be because he is glad that his friends are for him. The symbolic value of the deed is primary in such a case.

This line of thought might seem to lead to the conclusion that Bonhoeffer *ought* to have refrained from the Hitler salute in the incident I described, if I am right in suspecting that his real political situation was one of powerlessness. But this inference should be resisted. Martyrdom is a way of being for the Good, and against evils, even when one is helpless, but it is rarely the only way. Pursuing a conspiratorial struggle against an evil regime is also a way of being against it, even when the struggle is hopeless, and even if one knows it is hopeless. I am skeptical of any general rule about *how* to be for the Good in such a situation; it seems to me rather to be a matter of vocation.

4. WORSHIP

These considerations about eschatology (in a loose and extended sense) and the place of symbolic value in ethics apply equally to secular and religious ethics. There are reasons, however, why symbolic action is especially important for religious ethics. One is that there is a tendency for religion to see human life in a framework that emphasizes or even magnifies the place of helplessness in human life, and that consequently enlarges the need for symbolic action. This can be illustrated from the best-loved sacred text of theistic Hinduism, the Bhagavad Gita. A rich and many-stranded poem, rather than the consistent development of a philosophical theory, the Gita presents multiple possibilities of interpretation. But one can hardly deny the centrality of the idea that one ought to engage in action (*karma*) while in some sense renouncing its "fruits." The fruits are the consequences the action will naturally have, both in one's present life, by empirical causal laws, and in future incarnations, by the retributive laws associated with the Indian conception of *karma*. The fruits will certainly follow, except insofar as one is able, through mysticism, to break out of the whole system of *karma;* but one's action should not be for the sake of the fruits. Underlying this idea, I believe, is a mystical intuition of a true Good, unattainable by *karma,* beside which all possible fruits of *karma* pale into insignificance.

Why, then, engage in action at all? This is one of the first questions the Gita considers, and it gives the answer that it is simply impossible to refrain from action. "For no one remains inactive even for a moment. The states of all existence make everyone act in spite of himself" (III, 5). If this is not to be a bondage, one needs a way of acting that is an alternative to acting for the sake of the fruits. Perhaps not the only alternative, but one that is repeatedly proposed in the Gita, is to offer one's actions as a *sacrifice.* "It is true, this world is enslaved by activity, but the exception is work for the sake of sacrifice. Therefore . . . free from attachment, act for that purpose" (III, 9). "Whatever you do, or eat, or sacrifice, or offer, whatever you do in self-restraint, do as an offering to me," says Krishna (IX, 21).[12]

Sacrifice, in the literal sense, is of course a ritual action. Its significance is highly symbolic, and largely conventional. The Gita records a primitive view of sacrifice as instrumentally efficacious (III, 10–16) but emphasizes a different view, in line with the renunciation of the fruits of action. To treat all one's actions as sacrifice, as recommended by the Gita, is in effect to adopt a convention that gives the actions symbolic significance as expressions of one's devotion to God.[13] In this way symbolic value is invoked to fill the place of the instrumental value that has been disparaged.

The devaluation of the consequences of ordinary action in at least a main strand of the Gita may seem extreme from Western points of view; but Western religion has a counterpart in the idea that the most important goods cannot be controlled by our action but depend on God's grace. Where this idea is stressed, it naturally produces an emphasis on the symbolic value of action. The Heidelberg Catechism, for example, asks,

> Since we are redeemed from our sin and its wretched consequences by grace through Christ without any merit of our own, why must we do good works?

and answers,

> Because just as Christ has redeemed us with his blood, he also renews us through his Holy Spirit according to his own image, so that with our whole life we may show ourselves grateful to God for his goodness and that he may be glorified through us. . . .

To be sure, the Catechism goes on, with debatable consistency, to add a consequential bonus, adducing as "further" motives for good works

> that we ourselves may be assured of our faith by its fruits and by our reverent behavior may win our neighbors to Christ.[14]

But the symbolic value of Christian behavior, as an expression of gratitude to God, is clearly given precedence over its instrumental value. The parallel with the Bhagavad Gita, both in the question and in the answer, is striking, especially given the distance that in many ways separates the two religious traditions.[15]

Both of these texts illustrate the centrality of *worship* in theistic ethics. The whole ethical life is clearly assimilated to worship when its value is interpreted in terms of sacrifice or the expression of gratitude to God. The importance of symbolism to religion is nowhere more evident than in the phenomenon of worship, where the significance and value of actions as worship depends heavily, if not entirely, on the conventional significance of symbols.

Something of ethical importance can be done in worship that we cannot accomplish except symbolically. We may or may not think that the Bhagavad Gita and the Heidelberg Catechism underrate the instrumental value of ordinary human activity. But we can hardly deny that our ability to do good, and even to conceive of good and care about it, is limited. Our nonsymbolic activity, perforce, is a little of this and a little of that. Getting ourselves dressed in the morning, driving or riding or walking to work, and then home again to dinner, we try, on the way and in between, to do some good, to love people and be kind to them, to enjoy and perhaps create some beauty. But none of this is very perfect, even when we succeed; and all of it is very fragmentary. I believe that one who loves the good should be *for* the good wherever it occurs or is at stake. But we do not even know about most of the good and opportunities for good in the world, and we cannot do very much about most of what we do know. We can care effectively only about fragments that are accessible to us. Intensively, moreover, as well as extensively, we cannot engage the whole of goodness nonsymbolically. I have an inkling of a goodness too wonderful for us to comprehend, but concretely I must devote myself to getting my essay a little clearer and more cogently argued than the last draft.

Symbolically we can do better. Symbolically I can be for the Good as such, and not just for the bits and pieces of it that I can concretely promote or embody.

I can be for the Good as such by articulating or accepting some conception of a comprehensive and perfect or transcendent Good or goodness and expressing my loyalty to it symbolically. There is no way that I can do it without symbols. It is for this reason, I believe, that when religious thinkers have sought alternatives to the instrumental value of actions, they have tended to focus on symbolic rather than on naturally intrinsic values. My actions can have naturally intrinsic goodness insofar as they imitate or image God. But the relation to the transcendent Good is never as clear in the imitation as it can be in the symbolism. Hence the symbolism provides something for which there is no adequate substitute.

Theists find this value of symbolism supremely in worship. Limited as the extent of my love and beneficence and political influence must be, I can still *pray* "for all sorts and conditions of" people.[16] Qualitatively limited as I must be in the goodness of my life and even in my conception of the Good, I can still name and praise a transcendent Good. And fragmented as my concerns are in dealing with various finite goods, I can integrate my love for the Good in explicit adoration of the one God.

Grave moral and religious temptations attend this symbolic integration. It must not be allowed to become a *substitute* for such nonsymbolic goodness as is possible for us, fragmentary and imperfect as the latter must be. The biblical prophets sternly and rightly denied the value of merely symbolic worship in lives that included no concrete imitation of the divine justice.[17] In most situations symbolic expression by itself does not constitute love for the Good—or for anything. But a genuine love for the Good can find in symbolic expression an integration and completion that would otherwise be impossible. It is perhaps because there is a real need in this area that reformers who have wanted to do away with traditional religious beliefs have sometimes tried to introduce symbolic rituals that would be a functional equivalent of traditional worship.

In view of what I have said about helplessness I cannot find it surprising that the need for worship is felt especially in connection with death. In Jewish liturgy it is striking that the prayer that is most strongly associated with mourning and commemorating the dead, the Kaddish, has hardly anything to say about death or mourning, but is mainly devoted to praise of God. The first sentence sets the theme: "Magnified and hallowed be his great name in the world which he has created according to his will."[18] Precisely because there is nothing we can do about a death that has occurred, we want to affirm the meaning of life in the face of it by expressing symbolically our allegiance to the supreme Good. However little we can do, if we can do anything at all we can worship. As a voice from my own tradition has put it,

> I'll praise my Maker while I've breath,
> And when my voice is lost in death,
>   Praise shall employ my nobler powers:
> My days of praise shall ne'er be past,
> While life and thought and being last,
>   Or immortality endures.[19]

NOTES

This essay has been presented to philosophical audiences on a number of occasions. I should note in particular that it originated as one of a series of Wilde Lectures in Natural Religion delivered at Oxford University in 1989, and was one of the Jellema Lectures delivered at Calvin College in March 1995. I am indebted to many people for their helpful comments and questions.

1. This is not to deny the religious significance of *implicit* attitudes, about which I hope to say something elsewhere.

2. Eberhard Bethge, *Dietrich Bonhoeffer* (New York, 1977), 585.

3. The assumption expressed in this clause deserves emphasis. Some of my hearers have asked if my argument does not depend on the assumption that there is a God, or at least a transcendent good, to be an object of symbolic affirmation. I think not, though I am in fact a theist. The argument depends, not on an assumption about the nature of the good one is for, but on the assumption that it is morally good to be for the good (whether or not one's being for it is effectual). The argument, however, probably does depend on the assumption that moral goodness has a more than merely instrumental value.

4. James Wm. McClendon, Jr., *Systematic Theology*, vol. 1: *Ethics* (Nashville, Tenn., 1986), 320. McClendon claims that Niebuhr lacks an eschatology in the sense that his vision of sin and grace in human history "form[s] a seamless whole without recourse to any future consummation." It should be noted that McClendon prefers, with some reason, to name his tradition "baptist."

5. Ironically, the idea of a future consummation does not play a very fully articulated role in McClendon's own ethics, so far as I can see. See my review of McClendon's book in *Faith and Philosophy* 7 (1990): 117–23, esp. p. 122f.

6. McClendon, *Ethics*, 320, 161.

7. Ibid., e.g., 17f., 234.

8. John Rawls, *A Theory of Justice* (Cambridge, Mass., 1971), 8f. and §39. Rawls acknowledges that the issues thus postponed are "the most pressing and urgent matters" (p. 9) but believes they will be best illuminated by the ideal theory. I am more skeptical of that.

9. Derek Parfit, *Reasons and Persons* (Oxford, 1984), 99. Parfit says that when deciding on a moral theory, "we should first consider our Ideal Act Theory." Such a theory is "ideal" rather than "practical," Parfit agrees, because it is a fact that "[w]e are often uncertain what the effects of our acts will be," and "some of us will act wrongly." (I would add that we are often mistaken about such matters.) Nevertheless he maintains that a moral theory "fails in its own terms" if successful implementation of its Ideal Act Theory would have worse consequences than the successful implementation of some other Ideal Act Theory. Why should this be a decisive test for an ethical theory? We may well be skeptical of Parfit's test if we take a Niebuhrian view of the possibilities of human virtue and moral agreement. The beauty of an unattainable ideal may rightly inspire us when we are thinking about the intrinsic value of an act or a practice. But when we are evaluating an act or a practice on the basis of something so extrinsic as consequences, it would seem to be only the actual or probable consequences that matter, not the consequences that would obtain in an ideal state that will never be realized. If our eschatology is sunnier, on the other hand, at least as regards the nearer future, and if we suppose that reflection on these matters, and on the benefits of a certain ideal practice, might actually lead to sufficiently general conformity with the practice to achieve a good measure of the benefits, then Parfit's test may begin to look more relevant and more reasonable.

10. For this point I am indebted to Lanning Sowden's review of Parfit's *Reasons and Persons* in the *Philosophical Quarterly* 36 (1986): 514–35; see 526.

11. I have not resisted the temptation to take a pot shot at utilitarianism. My larger argument in this essay is not, however, a refutation of utilitarianism. The focus of my argument is on the ethical importance of what we stand for, as distinct from what we cause or try to cause; and I have not tried to prove that symbolic value cannot be accommodated as a special sort of

"utility" in a broadly utilitarian calculus. I do not, in fact, think that such a calculus provides a very natural context for symbolic value; in some of the most interesting symbolic actions, the agent throws such calculations to the winds and simply affirms her values symbolically, and may be quite right in doing so; but that is not the main burden of my argument here. An important recent attempt to incorporate "symbolic utility" in a calculus of utilities is in Robert Nozick, *The Nature of Rationality* (Princeton, 1993), esp. 26–35, 48–49; but I am not sure how similar Nozick's conception of symbolic utility is to my conception of symbolic value. Freudian symbolism plays a prominent part in his account (pp. 26–27, 32) that I think it could not play in mine. Conversely, a value derived from symbolizing a deity or an ethical principle, which is central to my account, does not cohere neatly with the emphasis on (causally evaluated) outcomes and actions in his stipulation that "the symbolic utility of an action *A* is determined by *A*'s having symbolic connections to outcomes (and perhaps to other actions) that themselves have the standard kind of utility" (p. 48)—where the standard kind of utility "is measured in situations that are wholly causal" (p. 48n). Nozick's account and mine agree, however, that symbolic value or symbolic utility need not itself be *causally instrumental* in producing any kind of good (Nozick, p. 48).

12. *The Bhagavadgita: A New Translation,* by Kees W. Bolle (Berkeley, 1979), 39, 41, 109. I have also been helped by the translation and commentary of R. C. Zaehner, *The Bhagavad-Gita* (Oxford, 1969).

13. The convention may of course have been divinely instituted. On Zaehner's interpretation (*The Bhagavad-Gita*, 394), doing one's caste duty counts as an offering to Krishna because Krishna is the author of the system. Here the value of obedience is seen as mainly expressive.

14. Question 86; in *The Constitution of the Presbyterian Church* (*U.S.A.*), Part I: *Book of Confessions* (New York and Atlanta, 1983), paragraph 4.086.

15. To sacrifice and thanksgiving, as categories for the ascription of symbolic religious value to behavior, may be added witness or testimony. Karl Barth, the most eminent twentieth-century protagonist of the tradition represented by the Heidelberg Catechism, claimed that "the essence of [Christians'] vocation is that God makes them His witnesses" (Karl Barth, *Church Dogmatics,* vol. 4, part 3, second half, translated by G. W. Bromiley [Edinburgh, 1962], 575). The meaning of life, or a large part of it, can be found in expressing the truth about God.

16. At this point I have more than once encountered the objection that intercessory prayer is meant to be efficacious. I grant that one who prays, typically, hopes to influence the course of events by influencing God. But it is important to distinguish prayer from magic. Even if God responds to it, prayer is communication with God, not placing one's hands on the levers of the universe. They remain in God's hands. In central cases of intercessory prayer one's action is not based on calculations of expected utility or of probable results. For example, if one starts observing which formulations in prayer "work" in terms of results, and using those that do, one is crossing the line from prayer to magic. In praying, no doubt, one may be *trying* to obtain what one asks, but the attempt proceeds solely by *symbolizing* that one is *for* what one asks. The symbolic value of the prayer is more fundamental than any instrumental value it may have.

17. Amos 5:21–24; Isaiah 1:10–17, 58:1–9; Micah 6:6–8; Jeremiah 6:20.

18. David De Sola Pool, *The Kaddish* (New York, 1964), xii f.; Rabbi Marvin Luban, *The Kaddish: Man's Reply to the Problem of Evil* (New York, 1962), 20f.

19. Isaac Watts, quoted from *Congregational Praise* (London, 1951), 8.

Probabilism

C. A. J. COADY

The ardour of the saints in seeking truth was a waste of time if the probable is the certain.

—Blaise Pascal, *Pensées* 861

I want to reexamine an old theory in moral theology that may have interesting implications for contemporary moral philosophy. These implications are perhaps more directly pertinent to the "applied" movement in moral philosophy, but they also raise broader issues about the nature of morality.[1] The theory is probabilism which was a crucial component in the movement of thought known as "casuistry" that had its heyday in the sixteenth and seventeenth centuries.

Late medieval casuistry arose as a theoretical response to the recognition of the complexity, uncertainty, and need for judgment involved in applying moral principles, rules, etc. to the messy realities of life. The tradition suffered crippling damage from Pascal's brilliant literary skills in his *Provincial Letters,* but it should be remembered that whatever the legitimacy of Pascal's objections to particular excesses or tendencies to excess, his criticisms emerged from a background of struggle between puritan and more humanistic interpretations of a common Christian morality, and that Pascal's puritanism may not be independently all that attractive. Pascal was defending his Jansenist friends against their Jesuit critics, and in his polemic against the Jesuit casuists there was a theological perspective operating that viewed the world in which people labor, rule, manage, love, and raise families as corrupt, or at least profoundly tainted. All Christians believed in original sin and the Fall, of course, but the perspectives on the world that this belief engendered in the contending theological parties, whether within or beyond Catholic Christianity, were widely divergent. The puritan outlook often encouraged a renunciation of that world in favor of uncontaminated pursuits, and, in any event, tended to treat morality as almost entirely within the domain of faith. One of Pascal's comments in his *Pensées* catches the attitude nicely: "All the religions and sects of the world have had natural reason for their guide. Christians alone have been compelled to take their rules from outside themselves and to find out about those which Jesus Christ left to the ancients to be handed on to the faithful."[2] Pascal was torn between rationalism and fideism; the great mathematician and scientist yearned for clarity and exactitude and the passionate believer exalted the heart and urged subjection to God. Since most moral thinking seems equally remote from axiomatization and from special revelation, the reasoning characteristic of such thinking was ill-adapted to treatment by an intellect and temperament like Pascal's.

I do not intend to delve deeply into the history of probabilism or casuistry. This has recently been effectively done by Jonsen and Toulmin in their fascinating book *The Abuse of Casuistry*.[3] I want to abstract from that history a version of the doctrine that is plausible enough to examine and possibly learn from. In my version, the doctrine is concerned with three permanently significant moral issues, all of which have a particular religious resonance, though their interest goes beyond this. These three are:

(1) the degree to which morality, or parts of it, must or can be understood as lawlike;
(2) the viability of the concept of a moral authority;
(3) the problems involved in trying to resolve uncertainties about moral matters.

WHAT WAS PROBABILISM?

In expounding probabilism, the first thing to note is that the theory was developed to deal with moral action in conditions of genuine uncertainty. Where an agent knows what is right or wrong, where there is no serious room for controversy, then there can be no room for the distinctions and recommendations of probabilist theory. Pascal often writes as if the Christian lives in a world where total certainty about all moral matters is available via faith, but, although this outlook has had its adherents, it hardly fits the historical or experiential dimensions of either Christianity or morality. A second clarification is that the term seems sometimes to have been used to denote the whole of casuistry, understood as a method, but more commonly it referred to a particular doctrine propounded by the casuists, and later developed and amended by various moral theologians such as Alphonsus Liguori, who developed a variant on the doctrine that he called equiprobabilism. I am interested in the more particular understanding of the term, and, indeed, most interested in one version of it.

What then is probabilism? Though it is associated with the Jesuits, the explicit origin of the view seems to lie with a Dominican, Bartolomeo Medina, who flourished in the sixteenth century. He gave it the classical (and confusing) formulation: "It seems to me that, if an opinion is probable, it is licit to follow it, even though the opposite opinion is more probable."[4] I want to begin by exploring aspects of Medina's succinct statement. His formulation is confusing, especially to our ears, partly because probability is not being used in (quite) the modern sense. The probabilists were following a medieval usage which shifted significantly during the very period in which their doctrines became so influential. As Ian Hacking has argued (following Byrne), there prevailed at the time a sense of "probable" which amounted to "approval or acceptability by intelligent people," and this usage very naturally gave a considerable weight to the approval of authorities of one kind or another.[5] In the background was the strong medieval distinction, inherited from the classical world, between science and opinion. Demonstrative knowledge derived from first principles was the epistemic correlative of science, and probability was the correlative of opinion. According to Hacking, there was "no clear concept of evidence" available for the realm of opinion, and hence what was probable was merely what was approved by respectable authorities.[6] Gradually, however, the idea arose that there could be natural, nontestimonial support for matters of opinion. This came about partly through the work of empirics, alchemists, and other practitioners of "the low sciences" who interpreted nature as a sort of book which spoke to us through "signs." Nature thus became an authoritative speaker in its own right without the interposition of human speakers, and the idea of a natural probability independent of the vagaries of human authority became established. The older meaning of probability was transformed by these changes in the systematic study of nature and then overwhelmed by the development of the mathematical theory of probability in the seventeenth century with which, of course, Pascal's name is triumphantly associated. The new sciences and the new approach to probability deliberately set their faces against the use of authority, human or divine, and insisted that what was approvable or acceptable was what, on the evidence of events themselves, had a greater chance of being true.

Some parts of Hacking's thesis are more controversial than others. That the medievals explicitly placed more weight than their successors upon authoritative views in matters of "opinion," especially in the areas now covered by the modern sciences, is clearly correct, though the force of this fact needs to be measured against the extensive reliance upon authoritative testimony that still prevails within contemporary science and in common judgment about the workings of the natural world, much of which seldom receives theoretical acknowledgment.[7] It is also clear that the medievals had a much less developed sense of the way in which systematic reasoning and developed evidentiary techniques could apply to the forming of beliefs about the world of contingent events than became possible after the seventeenth century. This is not to say, however, that they had "no clear concept of evidence" for beliefs formed without recourse to authorities. Indeed the very idea that one should resort to the wise to discover what was probable strongly suggested that, at some point, the wise themselves did something in the way of exercising reason other than resorting to the wise.[8] Nor did ordinary folk have to resort to "the wise" to conclude from smoke on the horizon to the presence of unseen fire. It is pertinent that the probabilist tradition itself had employed a distinction between intrinsic and extrinsic probability, which is explained, for instance, by Gabriel Vasquez in the sixteenth century as being between an opinion founded upon the quality of arguments on the one hand and the authority of the wise on the other.[9]

A related distinction is deployed in the seventeenth century by a noted opponent of casuistry, Antoine Arnauld. This is the distinction between the internal circumstances and external circumstances of an event. Arnauld was a Jansenist theologian and philosopher, and a friend of Pascal's. He wrote (or mostly wrote) an influential work of logic, *The Art of Thinking,* commonly known as the Port Royal Logic in honor of its origin in the Jansenist community at Port Royal. The book was originally published in 1662 in the early days of the beginnings of modern probability theory. Discussing our reasons for believing in the occurrence of contingent events, Arnauld says that the event should not be considered in isolation "as a proposition in geometry would be," but in all its circumstances, "both internal and external." He then explains these circumstances as follows: "I call internal circumstances those which belong to the event itself; external circumstances, those which pertain to the persons by whose testimony we are led to believe in the event's occurrence."[10]

Perhaps it is best to conclude that the probabilist tradition was using a concept of probability that placed a great emphasis upon the role of authoritative testimony in the formation of reasonable beliefs about the world, including those that determine action with a moral dimension, but that this concept included reference to the greater or lesser prospect of the beliefs' being true or correct, a prospect that could sometimes be assessed on grounds other than the reliability of the authorities maintaining it.

Against this background, I think we should construe probabilism primarily as the theory that in a situation of genuine moral doubt about what to do, where one cannot resolve the doubt by one's own reflection, one may consult a moral authority (i.e., some person that one reasonably regards as a reliable guide to moral decision making). Further, in so doing, one may confront the situation in which there are a number of such moral authorities of equal standing, and (say) four advise that you should not do X and one advises that you should or may do X. Suppose X is the action of authorizing the withdrawal of life-support, or feeding, for a severely retarded child or a terminally ill elderly person. You are in any case inclined to do X (perhaps by compassion). Probabilism says that you can act on the minority moral opinion, as long as it is genuinely authoritative. I will consider a secondary construal of the theory later.

It is worth noting a historical issue at this point, especially as it has some contemporary echoes. The historical point is that the doctrine was originally developed in a pastoral context where confessors and advisors were seeking help with how they should counsel good people who were confused or uncertain as to their duties. I have presented the theory (and will continue to do so) as if it were concerned with the deliberations of the agent confronting the moral problem, but for the casuists the problem was often at one remove from this. It was the problem the confessor faced where he held one view about the right thing to do but was aware that his view was controversial, in the sense that there was respectable opinion for his view, but also for a conflicting view. The casuists offered probabilism to such confessors as a guide for the advice they could give to the penitent.[11] This point is important, not merely for historical accuracy, but because it has some contemporary relevance to the thinking of those secular advisors who are, in some respects, descendants of the clerical advisors and confessors who were offered this guide. Present day "ethicists," "applied philosophers," and the like are indeed very differently placed from their clerical predecessors; they cannot give absolution, at least not literally, and their "clients" seldom view them as representatives of God. Even more significantly, they themselves have a very different attitude toward the idea of moral authority. To this we shall return, but for now it is enough to observe that, although the problem that called forth the theory of probabilism was at one remove from the usual understanding of it, this is no obstacle to treating the theory as a theory about how individuals (rather than their confessors) are entitled to think and decide in certain contexts. Where such individuals are already aware of the competing views of moral authorities, or discover them after investigation, then, in certain circumstances, what is sauce for the advisor is presumably just as good for the advisee.

To strike a more contemporary note, it would seem that echoes of this ancient and much reviled probabilist doctrine can be found in the workings of the common law (and I suspect in common sense) even today. A case in New South Wales a few years ago makes the point. This concerned a nurse, Sophia Heathcote of Wilcannia Hospital, who appealed in 1991 to the District Court of New South Wales against a suspension of one year by the NSW Nurse Registration Board. Sophia was suspended for failing to perform her duties in caring for an aboriginal patient, Mark Anthony Quayle. Briefly, the facts of the case are that Quayle was brought to Wilcannia hospital in a remote part of NSW by relatives who described him as being "in the dings," which Nurse Heathcote rightly understood to mean that he was suffering from alcohol withdrawal. Although the patient was hearing and seeing things, Nurse Heathcote did not think that he was seriously ill because he was not tremulous or vomiting or complaining of being cold or sweating excessively. After the patient disappeared several times from the hospital, which was only twenty-five yards from a river, the nurse became anxious and called the police, who found him and brought him back to the hospital. The nurse was concerned at her capacity to manage the patient, given her responsibilities for other patients, including two young children. After consulting by phone the director of nursing and the doctor at the Flying Doctor Service Broken Hill, she checked the patient's blood-sugar level and decided that his safety would be best served by his spending the night in the police station. The police reported back to her at 3 a.m. that Quayle was sleeping, but when she visited the police station after her shift ended at 8:30 a.m., she was informed that he had hanged himself in his cell. Her critics claimed that she should have made more checks on the patient's health and should not have released him into the care of the police. In granting her appeal, Mr. Justice Ward said: "It is appropriate to consider also the view expressed by Hutley JA (both judgements being approved by Samuels JA) that, where there exists a reputable, though minority view that conduct in the circumstances is acceptable, 'it cannot be said that one who acts on the minority view is guilty of professional misconduct.' " This consideration was only one amongst many that the judge took into account in upholding the appeal, but I am interested in it because of the similarities between the judicial thinking here and what seems to be involved in probabilism.[12]

Let us return to Medina's formulation. One thing in it that strikes the modern ear as paradoxical is the contention that one should accept the less probable opinion rather than the more probable. If, as Bishop Butler famously advised, we are basing our actions on the guide of probability, then, in the modern sense of that term, we should surely always prefer the more probable course. Indeed, that is what it is to base one's actions upon probability. Just as it is rational to believe what is seen to be more likely to be true, then it is surely rational to act on what is more likely to be true. Yet there is at least some room for fissure between the rationality of belief and that of action. Modern Bayesian decision theory, in the form of expected utility calculations, has taught us to factor into our thinking about how to act, not only probability but the value of the outcome: if some course of action has two possible outcomes one of which confers a small benefit that is highly probable and the other of which brings a total disaster which has only a small probability of occurring, then the size of the disaster combined with its real, though small, probability, may militate against acting to gain the highly probable small benefit. For example, if the proposed action is building a nuclear power station, we might reckon as highly probable benefits slightly cheaper power and somewhat less pollution than other power-generating options, but count on the other side some slight risk of a Chernobyl-style disaster. (The example is mere illustration; many would weight the benefits and probabilities differently for this case, and I intend no commitments on this here.) This shows that probability by itself cannot be the guide to life. Nonetheless, the Medina claim remains paradoxical, because it does not seem to lend itself readily to this treatment.

Consider a problem that must have loomed large in the period when the Catholic Church's prohibition on usury was breaking down. There is some room for interpretation about what the prohibition meant, but it seems clear that it was originally a ban on making a profit from interest charged on a loan.[13] Someone planning to make (or accept) such a loan knows that other reputable people have, increasingly, engaged in the practice, and is in genuine doubt about whether it is wrong to do so. The doubter, who is anxious to make the loan because it is financially advantageous and because it will help the community to have the money used well by the borrower, consults a pious, wise confessor. He in turn knows that there have now developed a variety of theological opinions on the morality of such a loan, some of which turn on conflicting interpretations of the meaning of the prohibition. Most of the reputable authorities hold to the strict line that such a loan would be immoral, but there are a few who treat it as licit.

The confessor following probabilist reasoning advises the doubter that the loan is permissible. Now it is true that there are desirability values involved here as well as probability factors; the agent sees a complex of legitimate goods involved in giving the interest-bearing loan, and against this there is the evil of acting immorally, if indeed the act is wrong. But this way of seeing things cannot make sense of probabilism since the evil is not an outcome of the proposed action in the way that the nuclear meltdown is in the earlier example. The agent who acts to reject the nuclear power station does not deny that certain benefits are thereby very probably lost, just as the agent who thinks it most reasonable to build the nuclear plant still admits as real the remote prospect of disaster. The doctrine of probabilism holds, by contrast, that the agent who sincerely follows the less "probable" course of action runs no risk of hellfire, or at least no more risk than any other poor sinner, and no more risk than if he had acted on the more "probable" opinion. Inasmuch as the "disaster" is read as "acting immorally" then that is no longer a real prospect no matter how remote. We might try recasting the decision matrix in such a manner as to make the risk something like the innocent and unintentional bringing about of the evil that God's law is broken. In this fashion, we might say that the greater probability that God's law is being broken combined with the disvalue of this state of affairs is less than the combined high probability and high value of achieving personal advantage and community advancement by making the loan. But this not only seems an implausible outcome of the calculation, since the bringing about of such an evil is presumably of very great disvalue, but it seems to misrepresent the sort of thinking that probabilism involves.

PROBABILISM UNRAVELED: LAW AND FREEDOM

It seems that there are many different strands in the thread of probabilist thinking. It is time to try to unravel them. One is the idea of morality as a body of laws and the relation of these to the value of an agent's freedom to act; another is that of a threshold of acceptability for moral opinions; and a third is the importance of moral authorities. First, the picture of morality as lawlike. This is currently an unfashionable view, especially outside religious circles (and even sometimes within them), but it has been immensely influential in the history of moral thinking. The Judeo-Christian tradition certainly invokes it, but it has currency outside of that, for not only has what we now call law (in the sense of civic law) evolved historically from societies where it was closely linked, even identified, with morality, but thinkers outside the Judeo-Christian fold have adopted the legal perspective on ethics, most notably of course the Stoic philosophers with their influential concept of Natural Law. (Such thinkers are not of course obliged to equate the moral law with the civic law, indeed the conception of morality as lawlike usually goes with the idea that it represents a standard by which the civic law can be criticized. In addition, such an outlook imposes no necessity to think that the civic law must sanction everything that the moral law condemns.) Moreover, theorists who reject the lawlike approach to morality but preserve concepts like duty, obligation, permissibility, and even certain uses of moral modalities such as "must" and "cannot" seem to employ a picture of morality in which there is the sort of bindingness about many moral conclusions that goes naturally with some idea of law. There are no doubt other explications they can offer for their use of such ideas, but many of them seem to be hardly incompatible with expression in at least quasi-legal terminology. One objection to so doing is the thought that the concept of law is too rigid to capture the necessary ambiguities and fluidities of moral thinking. This is an important objection, because moral thought and moral life are distorted by too mechanical an understanding of them, but (in spite of the connotations of the term "legalist") an account of morality as lawlike need not fall victim to this criticism, for two reasons. First, it is a crucial feature of any form of law that it is not translucent and self-explanatory but requires interpretation and adaptation to changing circumstances. This is clearly true of the civil and criminal law despite the explicit and precise terms in which so much of it is cast, and it will be evident in the prohibitions and strictures of "the moral law." The prohibition on murder, for instance, whether it is framed as "Thou shalt not kill," "Murder is wrong," or "Do not be a murderer" (or in terms closer to virtue ethics), still leaves a great deal up for debate, as it always has in the history of Christianity. Capital punishment, war, personal self-defense, assassination of a tyrant, suicide, abortion, and euthanasia all provide contexts for disagreement about the applicability of the prohibition. Second, the idea that morality is lawlike is not intended to be exhaustive of the distinctive features of morality. This is clear in Aquinas, who seeks to combine a lawlike conception of morality with an Aristotelian-style account of the virtues, and who acknowledges, along with many others in the Christian tradition, a distinction between precepts and counsels. This distinction embodies a contrast between acts that are required by duty and those ("supererogatory") that are good but beyond what is so required.[14]

This is not the place to canvass fully the pros and cons of the conception of morality as lawlike, but it should be said that such a picture goes naturally with the idea of what Robert Nozick has called "side constraints" on the achieving of good outcomes or the prevention of bad ones. Some courses of action, that is, are prohibited as means for achieving such outcomes by the binding force of the moral law. Such prohibitions seriously restrict the agent's liberty to act in pursuit of her goals whether these concern her own good or the good of others or still other categories of good. This is the point of the probabilists' talk of freedom. If we value the agent's freedom, for various reasons, we will not want it restricted needlessly, and, in particular, not by constraints that are dubiously part of the law. Where an agent is genuinely uncertain about whether the moral law prohibits some action, and this uncertainty is reflected in the best understandings of the moral law, there is value in not insisting on the prohibition. Moral theologians sometimes enforce this point by invoking mottos such as "no one may act on a doubtful conscience" or "a doubtful law does not oblige" or "where there is doubt there is freedom." But much traditional discussion around these slogans is distinctly confusing. For one thing, the relations between the sayings are none too clear; the second and third seem to license someone who doubts whether a supposed law applies, to act on his doubtful conscience by choosing freedom, although this seems to conflict with the first maxim. But the first maxim should perhaps be read as a caution against indifference to the determination of one's responsibilities, rather than as an insistence on achieving some level of perfect certainty before acting. So read, we can continue to think of the agent as acting in a context of ambiguity and uncertainty even though she has done her best to come to an opinion settled enough for action. This reading is encouraged by one common explanation offered for the soundness of the first maxim, namely, that someone who acts on a doubtful conscience shows that he "is willing to do it even if it should be wrong."[15] Clearly, this explanation does not apply straightforwardly to conscientious agents who act on the probabilist doctrine, since such people think it will lead them to do what is right. The most that can be said of them is that their recognition that the moral problem they face is controversial should alert them to the possibility that, contrary to their intent, they may be doing what is in fact wrong. This should always be a disturbing thought, but it does not show that the agent is acting wrongly.

Of course, it might be claimed that this commitment to a distinction between the subjective and objective (what is subjectively right may be objectively wrong and vice versa) is here misplaced, because the doubt surrounding the controversial moral matters shows that they are essentially indeterminate. In response, it must be said that the mere existence of doubtful and controversial moral issues at any given time shows nothing of the sort. It may be that there are some moral matters that are essentially indeterminate; if so, the argument for this must invoke more than the existence of the morally debatable throughout the history of ethics, since, apart from anything else, the debate on some of these matters has been decisively settled, as the case of slavery surely shows. There was a fact of the matter, and it was and is that slavery is wrong. Nonetheless, there may be a place for the idea that some moral questions are essentially unanswerable, as would be claimed, for instance, by the advocates of the category of "moral dilemmas." It would be beyond our scope here to pursue that topic, though it is an interesting question whether a moral-law approach to ethics could allow for it. My own suspicion is that we have yet to see the theory of the strict moral dilemma—a dilemma in which the opposed courses of action are both wrong but one must be chosen—sufficiently elucidated to decide the matter. In any case, my present point is only that the problems for which probabilism is invoked need not be contentious in that sort of way.

The slogans "a doubtful law does not oblige" and "where there is doubt there is freedom" serve two functions. The first is to give the benefit of what doubt obtains about the existence of a moral constraint to the conscientious agent. Why should this be? Probabilism at this point sets itself in opposition to what is called in the literature "tutiorism" but is more colloquially known as rigorism. We might put this view as the motto "where there is doubt choose restriction" or "where there is doubt about whether you are bound by a law, assume that you are." Why prefer probabilism (or one of its variants) to this? The probabilists put a high valuation on the freedom of the agent, and it is tempting to see this as foreshadowing modern liberal attitudes to the significance of personal freedom. Perhaps, to some degree, it does, since the probabilists tend to speak of freedom as prior to law and constrained by it, which has something of the flavor of that view of freedom which Sir Isaiah Berlin has characterized as negative liberty and seen as central to the liberal tradition. In religious terms, they might well have seen themselves as faithful to the liberating language of both Christ and St. Paul, who do not reject the Jewish law out of hand but emphasize a certain liberation from it. It was probably equally significant for them that they considered the rigorist view impossible for people to live by. Where moral imperatives were certain, they had to be respected no matter what the cost, and these costs were often high, but the casuists saw no point in imposing costs where the imperatives were not certain; indeed, they thought the effect of doing so was likely to be morally counterproductive.

MORE UNRAVELING: ACCEPTABILITY
AND AUTHORITY

Yet this framework of thought simply makes more urgent the question: why should a law remain doubtful when there is a preponderance of "probability" in its favor and a "lesser probability" against it? Here, I think, we need the notion of a threshold of acceptability or "probability." In terms of the modern concept of probability as degree of chance of being true, the threshold is simply .5, since above that an opinion is probable and its negation improbable. But for the probabilists, the situation looked very different. On many given questions of conduct (and, in terms of the older concept of probability, on many matters of contingent fact) there would be conflicting opinions that were all above a threshold of acceptability. The situation is a bit like that which prevails in an issue of science when the experts are divided about a speculation as yet unamenable to proof. Consider the debate in the 1950s between proponents of the "big bang" and the "steady state" hypotheses about the origin of the universe. The dispute has now moved on and (as I understand it) the "steady state" theory has been discredited by argument and evidence, but at the earlier time both views were intellectually respectable. A layperson in doubt about which to support could be told that, although most scientists (let us suppose) supported the "big bang," several reputable theorists were in favor of "steady state." The layperson would be holding a reasonable view in the circumstances if she adopted "steady state." Of course, there would usually be no pressing reason for such a person to adopt either thesis, and this is a point of contrast with the ethical case where an agent has to act and will usually value her freedom to act in ways that promote various personal and interpersonal goods (as in our example of the loan). On the threshold view, the "probability" of the one view does not mean that the other view is "improbable," since it is reasonable for a layperson to believe either. In the Sophia Heathcote case, the appeal judge was not saying that a nurse who had conducted more investigations on the patient, and inquired more into what the police were going to do with the patient, would have adopted the wrong ("improbable") view of her duties and thus been acting wrongly. Similarly, the person who heeded the majority view about usury and didn't lend the money on interest terms was also acting within reason.

But, it will be objected, the analogy with the scientific example surely shows what is wrong with probabilism. Scientific experts stand contrasted with non-scientific laypeople, and so we can get a sensible story going about how to think about accepting their authority, but ethics is not a specialized science in the same way; there are no moral experts and there is no moral laity to defer to their authority. The theory of probabilism belongs to a world in which morality is not only considered lawlike but in which knowledge of the laws is seen as particularly the province of a caste of clerical experts. These have the authoritative role they do because the moral law is divinely revealed or a public possession or both. No sense can be made of this outlook in a predominantly secular world in which ethics is a matter of autonomous, rational decision by individuals. There can be no doubt that this objection has some teeth. In matters of morality, as in much else, the medieval and early modern world is no longer ours, and this is as true for most contemporary Christians as for unbelievers. The rise of individualism and the values associated with it, most notably autonomy and personal freedom, have had a profound effect upon the modern understanding of morality and, indeed, of knowledge.

I would be the last to decry the importance and value of these develop-ments, but there are several qualifications that need to be made to the common picture of uninterrupted progress towards moral and intellectual liberation that often accompanies our appreciation of these changes. One qualification concerns our image of the past: although authority, tradition, and public control held pow-erful sway over the medieval mind, there were many ways in which independent thought and personal commitment had room to move. Medieval theories of con-science, for instance, provide a surprising degree of freedom and respect for the moral thinking of the individual,[16] and there were many theological controver-sies in the medieval and early modern period where the public authority of the Church gave no verdict, even though the issues were of considerable importance. The controversy over the nature of grace is one example of this latter, and the probabilist debate itself is another, since the Church, while ruling out what were considered the extremes of tutiorism and laxism, made no decision between the other contending theories—probabilism, probabiliorism, and equiprobabilism. Another qualification concerns our image of the present: authority and reliance upon others still play a large and ineradicable role in our lives, both intellectual and practical, even though we are often reluctant to acknowledge it, and this reliance is sometimes strongest where our protestations of individual autonomy are loudest. An important point here is that it is not merely the layperson who must depend, often fairly "blindly," upon the expert in such areas as medicine, law, architecture, transport, science, and technology, but the same or similar re-lations of trust and reliance are involved, and required, amongst the peer groups themselves, whether lay or expert. Ordinary knowledge and scientific advance both involve at deep and surface levels a combination of epistemic trust and individual investigation. The trick in giving a sane account of individual intellectual autonomy is to do justice to these facts without losing sight of what is crucially important in the ideal of autonomy.[17]

In the case of morality, there is no equivalent to the role that science has assumed in our lives for the understanding of the natural order or for the creation of techniques of control, production, and prevention. It is true that some people still see their Church or their Scriptures (or some combination of the two) as powerfully authoritative in moral matters, and this is clearly relevant to the probabilist tradition. Yet such sources no longer receive the widespread deference in morality, even within the respective religious communities, that at least the physical sciences command with regard to the natural order. We should not, however, conclude from this that there is no role for authority in the sphere of morals. Our grasp of moral truth (or its surrogate for those who do not believe that moral thinking aims at truth but want to preserve some degree of rationality and intersubjective acceptability for moral assessments) is not a wholly individual business; we seek communal paths to the resolution of our moral perplexities, and we pay special respect to the opinions of those we regard as possessing moral wisdom and those whose lives embody outstanding moral qualities. Our capacities to learn from discussion and communal judgment, to recognize moral wisdom, and to acknowledge lived goodness are not reducible to formulas but are nevertheless very fundamental to our constitution and evident in our experience. We do not "blindly" bend to such influences, but, like the word of others in matters of fact or theory, they have an authority for our moral thinking and deciding that is, in broad terms, primary rather than derived. This may be part of what Aristotle means when he says that what "appears to the good man is thought to be really so . . . and virtue and the good man as such are the measure of each thing,"[18] and when he insists that "we ought to attend to the undemonstrated sayings and opinions of experienced and older people or of people of practical wisdom not less than to demonstrations."[19] Of course, the three dependencies mentioned—the authority of community discussion, of the morally wise, and of personal example—are different in kinds of ways that we cannot now explore. What I want to draw from consideration of them is merely the point that, in spite of the distance between the contemporary world and the world of the casuists, our own thinking contains less formal and institutional analogues of the moral authority that the probabilists took for granted. Moreover, in the domain of public life, the analogues are a little more formal because in business and the professions we have now developed by processes of discussion, reflection, comparison, and trial and error a considerable body of ethical "case law" which provides a sort of benchmark for interpretation, modification, and analysis within these groups and in the wider community. Codes of ethics, ethics committees, ethical auditors, and so on have proliferated both as evidence of the phenomenon and as a contribution to it. There is no priesthood or caste of theological experts enjoying some privileged association with these developments, though there are often ministers of religion and philosophers on ethics committees or employed as consultants.

SHIFTING PERSPECTIVE
AND SOME REMAINING PUZZLES

This exploration of the different strands in the thread of probabilism suggests a change of perspective on the theory. The change would move us away from the baffling idea that we should adopt views that we know are less likely to be true and towards the idea that an agent's freedom should not be restricted by a rule that is genuinely dubious. The basic thesis that the agent should be given "the benefit of the doubt" about a contentious moral matter so that she is free to act or not on the putative law is preserved by seeing the probabilist position not as a claim about what is actually more likely to be the correct moral view but as providing criteria for determining when a moral rule or prohibition *is* genuinely uncertain. Viewed thus, the structure of the argument looks rather different, for it goes as follows:

(1) Where there is genuine doubt about the morality of some course of action, the agent should be free to do or to refrain from doing the action.

(2) There is genuine doubt when (a) after due reflection on the issues involved, the agent is herself in doubt, and (b) reputable authorities are divided on the matter, even if there is a preponderance of opinion on one side.

The second clause invokes the idea of acceptability discussed earlier but does so for the acceptability of the proposition that the moral status of the prohibition in question (or a particular application of it) is doubtful. Part (a) of the clause makes it a necessary condition that the agent be personally in doubt about the matter because if the agent is confident about the right way to act she should so act. One might think that (a) should also be sufficient, but the requirement to satisfy (b) serves to emphasize both the need for the doubt to be reasonable and its public nature. This fits neatly into the picture of medieval thought discussed above, and coheres with the Catholic insistence on communal authority as against the Protestant resort to "private judgment." But it can also be defended by the weaker theses about the contemporary significance of moral authority maintained above. The first clause acknowledges that we often have to act in situations where we are well short of certainty about what is right and claims for the agent the right to act for what she regards as a good outcome in the circumstances, unhindered by a doubtful side-constraint. This takes very seriously the idea that moral laws, like other laws, restrict freedom to act and such restriction needs a clear justification because the freedom to act is genuinely valuable. From this perspective, an obsession with restricting spontaneity and freedom by a plethora of rules, laws, regulations, and restrictions is a mark of moralism, not authentic morality.

In trying to understand the curious theory of probabilism and to put it in a better light than it has often enjoyed, I have sought to clarify its structure and to remove obstacles to its appreciation, but I don't doubt that there remain problems with it. Let me conclude by rehearsing some of them.

When all is said and done about the ways in which authority continues rightly to play a significant role in moral judgment and decision, it remains true that this insight must be aligned with the important place that individual reasoning and conscientious reflection should occupy in the moral landscape. The errors of an excessive individualism should not obscure the significance of personal, if not "private," judgment in moral matters. When in doubt about moral options, the agent's primary responsibility is to resolve the doubt by thinking through the problem which may, of course, include reference to the opinions of "people of practical wisdom." This will often produce a state of conviction sufficient to make the existence of divergent authoritative opinions on the matter irrelevant, and where such an agent learns of these their existence need have no effect on her conviction. (Where she sees clearly, she may still want to know what reasons could have persuaded others to the contrary view, and she might come to be influenced by these, but that is another matter.) Where doubt and its accompanying indecision persist, then probabilism becomes relevant, though it should also be stressed, as it isn't in the probabilist tradition, that the probabilist route on contentious questions remains available only while the issues remain contentious for the agent. From the fact that one cannot determine at time t whether one is bound by a duty, it does not follow that one cannot determine the matter conclusively at time t_1, indeed it is plausible to hold that one has an obligation to try to settle this matter by further reflection.

These considerations are germane to two further puzzles about probabilism. The first concerns the meaning of "doubt," "certainty," "knowledge," and so on in the context of these discussions, and the second concerns the application of the probabilist mode of thought to the "intrinsic" reasons for moral belief. As to the first, we cannot accept a picture of the moral life in which a moral laity can have no idea of what is right or wrong unless told so by moral experts who are unanimous in their views. Indeed, it is unclear that such a picture has anywhere ever been acceptable, or even accepted. Nonetheless, we are familiar with both personal doubt about what to do and with the idea of the morally controversial. In other words, we can understand what it is to be personally morally perplexed when facing certain choices and what it is for such choice situations to be more generally understood in a broader community as matters on which disagreement is reasonable and legitimate. It is of course a difficult matter to give a satisfactory philosophical account of what is legitimate and reasonable amongst conflicting moral outlooks, as recent debates in political philosophy around such ideas as "public reason" and "reasonable comprehensive doctrines," stemming from the work of John Rawls, clearly demonstrate.[20] Rawls and his critics are, of course, concerned with a very different set of questions to those that

I am raising here; I mean only to draw attention to the way in which his need to characterize, for his purposes, what are reasonable and reputable moral and philosophical outlooks gives rise to difficulties that parallel those facing the probabilist enterprise.

In the case of probabilism, it seems apparent, nonetheless, that there is something genuine to be elucidated, since the complex history of moral thought shows such continuities and discontinuities, persistence and disappearance, decay and development, as to encourage a distinction between what is morally solid and what is morally evanescent and (at the cognitive level) between moral fact and moral opinion. These distinctions cannot be fully defended here, and they will strike some as alarming, but it seems persuasive that across time, and at any given time, there will be much that is for individuals and for communities morally solid and secure and much that is contested and open to debate. There need be no perfect match between individual and social embodiments of these distinctions, and different issues will move in and out of the categories. What is at one time morally controversial, a matter of moral opinion, will become at another time established as moral fact. So it was with voting (and several other) rights for women: in most political societies of a democratic cast this issue moved from the category of moral fact ("no such right") to moral opinion to moral fact ("palpable right").

My classification here is offered partly as sociological observation and partly as normative philosophy. Consequently, the term "moral fact" may be misleading: as will be clear from the example of female suffrage, it is intended to capture the idea of the epistemically (relatively) secure, taken-for-granted datum, but not necessarily what is true or forever fixed. The history of moral thought seems to me to exhibit this sort of structure, but I think it is also true that there is something necessary about it if moral thinking is to take place at all, and, moreover, the degree of flux in the picture should license no relativistic conclusions. The movement of moral judgment in the case of female suffrage exhibits the workings of moral progress from a false (or incorrect) moral appreciation to a true appreciation via a period of moral controversy. Such unsettled controversy is only possible if some individuals are not the least in doubt and are seeking to persuade others by reasoning and example. Yet at any given time there will be many who are in doubt even after (and perhaps especially after) confronting the conflicting arguments. The probabilist thesis may be seen as primarily concerned with such people, and as recommending a way in which they may guiltlessly settle the question of action *pro tem.*

Another problem concerning doubt is raised by an ambiguity in the idea of resolving doubt. The casuists sometimes write as if what is required to end doubt about the right thing to do is decisive knowledge about what is right (or permissible). The changes in understanding of factual knowledge that have accompanied the rise of the natural sciences and the emergence of the modern concept(s) of probability, some of which we discussed earlier, have produced the idea that not only can we be certain of many things concerning the natural order on evidence that is short of offering deductive guarantees, but that the same ap-

plies to the order of practical action. This means that we shall often have sufficient assurance for confident action even where we can acknowledge that things
may turn out other than we now believe. Condition (1) above concerns the doubt
that cannot be so resolved.

I said earlier that I would consider a secondary construal of probabilism,
and this concerns the possibility of applying it to "intrinsic" rather than "extrinsic" probabilities. Can we treat the actual internal arguments for and against the
proposed course of action as analogous to the authorities for and against the
option? I am a doctor in a public hospital and I am uncertain whether to comply
with a patient's wish to die by giving her a lethal injection as requested. I have
thought a lot about this sort of situation and am impressed by both the arguments for and against so acting. I think that they are all above a threshhold of
acceptability though there seem to be more considerations in favor of not complying, so am I free to act upon the promptings of compassion and choose the
"less probable" reasons for complying? Some probabilists have certainly envis-
aged the theory having this sort of implication (though without citing this sort
of example).[21] This seems to me a somewhat precarious application of the theory.
There is indeed some appeal in the idea of a threshold of respectability for arguments so that we can consider some set of arguments for p as rationally respectable and some other set of arguments for not-p as equally respectable, as
may have been the case, for example, in the early days of the debate around the
Darwinian intellectual revolution.[22] Yet in the case of practical thinking, or in
the case of theoretical thinking where we are ourselves theorists, we would have
to take a peculiarly external view of our own thinking and judging. Standardly,
in assessing reasons for acting one way or another, we are not involved in assessing their broad reputability but their cogency for us. As I interpret it, the probabilist strategy is proposed only for the situation where the agent cannot settle
this.

Some supporters of probabilism, perhaps worried by accusations of laxism,
have claimed that it doesn't apply to certain spheres of human activity. Favored
examples are the valid administration of the sacraments and matters affect-
ing human rights.[23] The first example raises special theological issues that I shall
avoid, but the second is more obviously pertinent to our discussion. G. H. Joyce
argues that "probabilism is inapplicable where the rights of another person are
concerned. We are under strict obligation not to wrong our neighbour, and it is
unlawful to put ourselves in danger of so doing."[24] But this, as Joyce sometimes
seems to appreciate, does not provide a sphere of activity to which probabilism
is inapplicable, but merely affirms that it relates only to situations where an obligation is doubtful. There is no reason to hold that claims concerning human
rights can never be legitimately controversial. The confusion here seems to arise
from the idea that we do not want people to be casual about moral matters of
considerable gravity, and certainly where the stakes are high about such things
as harm to others or rights violations we expect an agent to think and act with
due care. Such thinking must advert to levels of risk and will have to weigh the
gravity of what is risked against the degree of risk and the benefits to be gained.

There are certainly contexts in which we have clear duties not to inflict even small risks of great harm to others or of violations of their known rights for trivial gains either personal or communal. Yet none of this seems to restrict the scope of probabilism.

Finally, there are two issues that need further exploration. One is the investigation of whether there are useful criteria for determining when some division of opinion in a community about some question of moral obligation bespeaks the reasonably controversial and when it merely signifies the corruption of some segment of the population, even some segment otherwise exhibiting marks of goodness. The history of slavery and some aspects of the degeneration of Germany under the Nazis would provide interesting materials for developing such an inquiry. The second concerns the degree to which probabilist thinking requires that the perplexed agent needs to be aware of the division of reputable opinion on the issue at hand and acts in the light of it, or whether it is sufficient that her action accords with it, consciously or not. I have tended to treat the discussion in the former terms, but the legal case cited earlier *seems* to be one in which the mere existence of a "less probable" reputable opinion was sufficient to grant blameless freedom of action in its terms to Nurse Heathcote without her having explicitly adverted to it in her thinking. Perhaps a bridge could be built between the two construals by the idea of a background of training or education which is based on the relevant authoritative opinion and which informs the agent's decisions without her explicitly adverting to it.

On my account of probabilism, it is not opposed to the search for truth in morality and so represents no scorning of the ardor shown by the saints in seeking it. Nor is it contemptuous of ethical certainties. On the other hand, it does represent an acknowledgment that striving for the truth takes place in a context of uncertainty, and sometimes against a background of deep differences of moral opinion that are both intelligible and worthy of a certain respect. Where ardor, and other forms of enthusiasm, ignore that, then they can propel us into moralism and even fanaticism.[25]

NOTES

1. One modern theologian, Daniel C. Maguire has invoked probabilism in an interesting discussion of the ethics of mercy killing. See Daniel C. Maguire, "A Catholic View of Mercy Killing," *The Humanist* 34 (1974): 16–18. In their impressive book, Jonsen and Toulmin make an explicit connection between casuistry in general and modern applied ethics. See Albert R. Jonsen and Stephen Toulmin, *The Abuse of Casuistry: A History of Moral Reasoning* (Berkeley, 1988).

2. *Pascal's Pensées,* translated and introduced by Martin Turnell (London, 1962), no. 865, p. 381.

3. Jonsen and Toulmin, *Abuse of Casuistry.*

4. Ibid, 164.

5. Ian Hacking, *The Emergence of Probability* (Cambridge, 1975), 22. See also Edmund F. Byrne, *Probability and Opinion* (The Hague, 1968).

6. Hacking, *Probability,* 22.

7. I have argued a case for the extent of this reliance, and challenged attempts to dismiss or explain away its significance in my book *Testimony: A Philosophical Study* (Oxford, 1992). See also John Hardwig, "Epistemic Dependence," *Journal of Philosophy* 82 (1985).

8. I have criticized Hacking's position in slightly more detail in *Testimony*, 15.

9. See Jonsen and Toulmin, *Abuse of Casuistry*, 167. On these matters, it seems to me that Byrne is a better guide to medieval thinking than Hacking.

10. Antoine Arnauld, *The Art of Thinking* (Indianapolis, 1964), 342.

11. Jonson and Toulmin make this point.

12. Justice Hutley's comments were made in *Qidwai v Brown* (1984), NWSLR, p. 100, which was a case concerning charges of inappropriate surgical procedures. In the Heathcote case, the judge also considered that many of the allegations against the nurse had too many benefits of hindsight and ignored the limited options available to her at the time. The Heathcote appeal was heard in the District Court of NSW by Mr. Justice Ward on April 12, 1991, and was extensively reported in the nurses' journal, *The Lamp* 48 (1991), from which the present account is taken.

13. For a full discussion of the usury controversy in historical context, see John T. Noonan, *The Scholastic Analysis of Usury* (Cambridge, Mass., 1957).

14. For a discussion of the theoretical puzzles around the concept of supererogation, see David Heyd, *Supererogation: Its status in ethical theory* (Cambridge, 1982), and Marcia Baron, "Supererogation," in *Encyclopedia of Ethics,* edited by Lawrence C. Becker and Charlotte B. Becker (New York, 1992).

15. So argues the well-known traditional moral theologian G. H. Joyce in his entry on "Probabilism" in *The Encyclopedia of Religion and Ethics* (Edinburgh, 1918), 349. Joyce goes on to add that such a person is "deliberately exposing himself to the risk of committing a sin" and this itself is sinful. Again, this comment makes it sound as if the conditions of the problem that calls for the probabilist solution are being undermined, since the person who acts on the "less probable" opinion remains aware that the "more probable" opinion has some weight. Presumably, Joyce's position is best construed (as some of his later remarks at least suggest) as depicting the agent who is quite unconcerned with achieving a reasonable resolution of his doubts, rather than the agent who accepts the probabilist solution. The latter is no longer exposed to a risk of sinning, at least according to probabilism, even if there is still a risk that his action is not in fact in accord with the moral law.

16. For further discussion, see, for instance, Eric D'Arcy, *Conscience and Its Right to Freedom* (London, 1961).

17. See my *Testimony: A Philosophical Study.* For a very good discussion of the connections between autonomy and our reliance upon testimony, see Frederick F. Schmitt, "Justification, Sociality, and Autonomy," *Synthese* 73 (1987): 43–85.

18. Aristotle, *The Nichomachean Ethics,* translated by Sir David Ross (London, 1959), Bk. X, Ch. 5, 1176 a 14.

19. Ibid, Bk. VI, Ch. 11, 1143 b 11.

20. For Rawls's own attempts at elucidating such notions, see John Rawls, *Political Liberalism* (New York, 1993), especially Lectures II and VI.

21. See, for instance, Joyce, "Probabilism."

22. See, for instance, Philip Kitcher's discussion of the plausibility of many of the early scientific objections to Darwin's theories in chapter 2 of his *The Advancement of Science: Science without Legend, Objectivity without Illusions* (Oxford, 1993).

23. See Joyce, "Probabilism," C. Williams's entry on "Probabilism" in *The Encyclopedic Dictionary of Religion* (Washington, D.C., 1979), and Brian V. Johnstone's entry on "Probabilism" in *The New Dictionary of Theology* (Wilmington, Delaware, 1988).

24. Joyce, "Probabilism," 350.

25. My thanks to my colleague, Dr. Bruce Langtry, for helpful criticism of an earlier version of this essay.

In Support of Paganism:
Polytheism as Earth-Based Religion

CHARLES CRITTENDEN

It goes without saying that a man's shadow, which looks like him, or his mirror-image, the rain, thunderstorms, the phases of the moon, the changing of the seasons, the way in which animals are similar to and different from one another and in relation to man, the phenomena of death, birth, and sexual life, in short everything we observe around us year in and year out, interconnected in so many different ways, will play a part in his thinking (his philosophy) and in his practices, or is precisely what we really know and find interesting.[1]

'Paganism', in the use I shall be concerned with, refers to the set of polytheistic religions where (typically): the deities have an explicit domain or domains; there are ritual commemorations, for example, of various seasonal events; and practices such as oracles, dream interpretation, and magic are accepted.

Paganism was the religion dominating classical Greece and Rome and also Egypt and many of the Mediterranean countries. It was practiced throughout pre-Christian Europe, e.g., by the Celts and the Germanic and Norse peoples. The indigenous religions of Africa, Australia, the Americas, and much of Asia and the Pacific islands were often pagan or had distinct pagan elements. Contemporary neo-paganism belongs in this classification as well. Obviously there are great contrasts among these varieties of paganism, and not all groups I am calling 'pagan' have *all* the features mentioned or have them in the same way. 'Paganism' is a "family-resemblance" term—groups to which it applies will share many of paganism's characteristic features but not necessarily all of them.[2]

A religion may be pagan on one level, and monistic or even monotheistic at another. Pantheists can be pagans if they accept particular divinities, and pagans can be pantheists but need not be. Hinduism is pagan insofar as it includes cults devoted to a particular figure (Krishna, Kali). At the same time some Hindus would see these deities as manifestations of a single being, Brahman. Some groups within contemporary neo-paganism accept the Goddess as the ultimate divinity while honoring others as well: Isis, Demeter, the Horned God, Pan, Dionysus, Odin, the elements.[3]

In view of paganism's very long history and extensive adoption, it is remarkable that there are practically no modern philosophical discussions of its concepts and principles. Perhaps this reflects the general cultural evaluation of paganism as belonging to a "primitive" stage of religion that more "advanced" religions have outgrown. Paganism, despite its longevity and widespread acceptance, has never been classified among the world's great religions. Indeed one purpose of this classification is to distinguish the favored persuasions from paganism: whatever differences there are among the "great" religions, they are all superior to paganism. In any case, although modern Western philosophers have considered and advocated a large number of positions on religion and the nature of the divine, paganism has almost never been viewed positively by them.[4] My intention in what follows is to make it reasonable to accept one of the central commitments of paganism, polytheism as based on a certain conception of nature and certain attitudes toward it. This will not immediately bear on some of the practices often associated with paganism, e.g., witchcraft or magic; these are not part of paganism proper, as I shall point out later. In any case, polytheism and the attitudes I shall be considering are central to paganism and important enough to be interesting in their own right.[5]

My essay has two sections. Part I offers an account of the origins of pagan concepts and belief, intended not as historical but as elucidating the principles characteristic of pagan thinking. Part II gives the case for paganism, using the principles found in Part I first to construct replies to popular objections and then to offer considerations weighing positively in its favor.

I. THE PAGAN OUTLOOK

Origins: A Thought Experiment

The method I shall use for arriving at the principles of pagan thought will not focus on any specific instance of paganism but will be concerned with principles that plausibly underlie general pagan belief and practice. My procedure is to imagine human beings in circumstances where their dependence on the earth and its processes is quite obvious. In response to this dependence, these people simply find it appropriate and natural to adopt the principles characteristic of paganism. They are acting in accordance with general human tendencies, and so the functions these concepts have for them are clear and their thinking understandable. This is not meant to be an anthropological or historical explanation, since I am not concerned here with the details of how particular beliefs actually came to be accepted. Rather I am trying to show how it is intelligible and natural that human beings living on the earth might arrive at the principles and concepts characteristic of paganism. My procedure will help to clarify the meaning of these principles and concepts, to give plausible motivations for their adoption, and to indicate why the practices associated with them are appropriate. For this purpose it does not matter whether historical human beings actually came to have them in this specific way or not; the point here is conceptual clarification.[6] So my proposals do not compete with empirical hypotheses such as those of Taylor (that religion originates in animism) or Frazer (that religion grows out of magic).[7]

There is, of course, something inevitably speculative in the attempt to reconstruct pagan thought, even if one is familiar with neo-paganism. As I have suggested we can try to clear our own minds of the conceptions of contemporary life by imagining human beings in situations without the trappings of "civilization" and technology and mainstream religion, and then notice what would be impressive and important to respect and celebrate about human life in that situation. So the thought-experiment proceeds by projecting onto the individuals imagined the same general kinds of understanding of nature that we find in ourselves; it shows that the principles that would naturally emerge correspond more or less to actual pagan practice.[8] To make sure of this, I shall introduce various examples from historical paganism. Of course there may be varieties of paganism or other types of earth-based religion that have a different content and stem from different motivations than those I discuss; my account will provide no support for them. The aim here is to show that pagan concepts and practices are entirely in accord with basic human instincts and emotions and ordinary knowledge, and in this sense are natural and reasonable.

Here is the thought-experiment: imagine a group of human beings living in circumstances where they are immediately dependent for food on what they grow, gather, or hunt, and for housing on what they themselves build. They live in a relatively small community that shares many activities. These are normal people living in what we would consider primitive circumstances. The point of starting with such people is that the attitudes I shall ascribe to them will seem more natural in these circumstances than if they bought their food from stores and lived in housing constructed by professional builders using manufactured materials. This is what the thought-experiment is supposed to make clear: it is quite in accordance with general human tendencies for individuals in these agricultural or pre-agricultural circumstances to adopt the principles underlying pagan thought.

Let me start by emphasizing the relation between various features of the conceptual scheme these people have and certain very general facts about nature. First, these individuals will inevitably develop a series of classifications of the things that they find around them in the world: they distinguish such items as trees and rocks, animals, and other human beings. Their having concepts of these types reflects the stability and regularity of their natural world. Of course these people understand themselves to constitute a kind of thing, being like other animate and inanimate things in some ways and unlike them in others, and they realize that they are dependent on these other things in innumerable ways. Thus it is quite reasonable for them to see themselves as part of a larger whole, interacting with other parts and interdependent on them.

It will be inevitable that they recognize their absolute dependence on the earth and its annual cycles; they will recognize this as one of the most fundamental facts about their situation. It will be entirely clear to these people that there are times when plants germinate and grow and when animals mate, followed by periods of plant maturation and animal gestation, and finally times for harvest and birth. Thereafter is an interval of quiet regeneration of the soil, when the cycle begins again. Human beings learn the elements of this cycle and come to understand that they participate in them. Women will be aware of their menstrual cycles, for example, and the stages of pregnancy. People learn to plant at a certain time, to protect their crops and to foster their growth by providing fertilizer and water, and then to harvest their plants and sometimes prepare them for storage. Animals participate in these cycles, mating at certain times and giving birth at others, and often humans must assist. Animals will sometimes be plentiful and sometimes not—to mention two obvious types of seasonal change. It will be evident that natural conditions affect these processes—less rainfall than usual, or long periods of unseasonal weather. These people will inevitably come to see their own activities as interwoven with other natural processes and as dependent on them for their survival and well-being.

The earth is not only a provider of nourishment and materials; it constitutes the solid ground on which we live. It is our home. We are used to being concerned with the reliability of another person or, in today's world, of our car, but our trust in the continued stability of the earth is so profound that it escapes notice. If we felt we could not depend completely on the earth to maintain its stability, common enterprises such as building structures and roads would become questionable. We would have to live in an entirely different way, perhaps dwelling in light and transportable structures and not constructing large buildings to live or work in. The character of our civilization would be drastically affected and would be radically different: without large structures, it would be impossible to carry on many of the activities characteristic of contemporary life. Our absolute reliance on the unchanging state of the earth's surface is fundamental to our basic activities—a commitment we are reminded of by a serious earthquake. Anyone who has been through an earthquake realizes what it is like to have the solidity and constancy of the earth interrupted. The physical effects of such disruption are terrible enough, but the psychological damage may be even more lasting, since one may lose a sense of sureness and reliability that often takes a long time to recover. These consequences show that our dependence on the earth is fundamental to our practical and emotional life.

The individuals we have postulated will be aware of the changes in the seasons and the need for participating in them in various ways, and they will understand that their species is merely one of many in an environment where each relies on others. They will see themselves as related to these other species in certain ways. The dependence of their concepts on the regularities of nature and their assumption of stability in the earth will be less immediately obvious to them. Nevertheless they might well come to have a broad appreciation of the earth: they can see that they must rely on it for nourishment and shelter, and it would be apparent to them that its cycles, which they come to expect, participate in, and enjoy, are essential to their well-being. Similarly they will come to recognize other basic aspects of their existence. They will be impressed by terrifying occurrences such as thunderstorms and the destructiveness and beauty of nature, the phases of the moon, sexuality and the ways humans can be overwhelmingly attracted to and repelled by one another, relations between humans and animals, the terrifying and inspiring qualities of particular places in the forests or mountains, the sense of immense forces beyond their understanding, inexplicable good fortune yet also loss and tragedy, the mysteries of dreams and the messages they seem to convey, and the like.

Having come to experience and appreciate these aspects of their world, these individuals may feel it appropriate to acknowledge them ceremonially. Perhaps these people find it appropriate to have rituals at times of the year and in settings that seem especially fitting to commemorate various aspects of the world around them. At the end of the growing season, it could well seem satisfying to have a festival celebrating the harvest and featuring expressions of thankfulness for nature's bounty. These ceremonies require the aspect of nature being celebrated to be present, and for this purpose it will be appropriate to have this aspect represented in the form of some figure, plausibly human or animal. Even suitable plants or inanimate elements in nature could have a place. Such figures are then introduced into the rituals and ceremonies; and so we have gods and goddesses and animals and other sorts of deity. There could well come to be a group of divinities invoked in harvest rituals, celebrated at the end of the harvest and to whom thanks can be directed. Other seasons will require the participation of other deities representing other aspects of nature: spring will focus on the celebration of new life and so ritual activities and the deities included in them will be different from those to whom gratitude for a full harvest is expressed. Winter could include acknowledging the end of one cycle of change through its various stages to the transition to a new cycle. There will be commemorations of puberty, marriage, victory in war, of death. For these purposes it would be fitting to have a large range of figures each standing for a specific theme in nature or aspect of life: for example, depending on local conditions, a bear could represent strength and wisdom, corn might be central in harvest celebrations. There might be a god of war, a goddess of hunting, a figure symbolizing change and destruction. There need be no limit to the number or kinds of deity or spirit or power appropriately invoked in rituals or ceremonies.

In this schematic and simplified account of the place of the gods, goddesses, spirits, and powers in the thinking of these people, I have written as if there were *first* the sense of the appropriateness of expressing certain attitudes toward nature and *later* the introduction of suitable figures representing the relevant dimensions of nature. But this is a distinction introduced solely for the purposes of emphasis. One need not think that there are two distinguishable processes here, as the attitudes toward nature would more typically be felt *in terms of* symbolic representations of nature. To suppose that there was some moment when an individual consciously introduced a religious figure as a representative of a feature of nature that he or she wanted to celebrate would be, in general, psychologically and conceptually false. Rather, an adherent would have an attitude that was directed toward a particular figure as representing a certain aspect of nature. Thus, a more realistic picture sees these activities in the context of a long-standing tradition that includes not only a series of seasonal festivals and other types of ceremony but also a full set of myths and stories about the deities. These stories contain lessons and insights of different kinds which are understandable to hearers according to their level of maturity. For a child, the stories might be just good entertainment; for older youths they can contain moral teachings; for more mature individuals there are psychological lessons and spiritual insights.[9] Some traditions have temples associated with cults devoted to particular figures: the Parthenon was dedicated to Athena and had a full complement of officials who presided over a variety of ritual activities. Seasonal festivals should be seen as just one sort of activity among many that a fully developed tradition offers. There would be occasions for private rituals (perhaps shrines and altars in individual homes), for religious sanctification of important events (births, marriages, funerals, occasions of state), for spiritual instruction, purification, and personal growth. Well-developed pagan traditions can address a large range of personal, social, and spiritual concerns.

Clarifications: Existence, Proof, and Belief

If this is a plausible picture of how such deities might have come to be introduced, what would be their status? must they be believed to *exist?* This is an issue that must be clarified for a correct understanding of the pagan outlook; certainly it is one that raises initial questions about paganism. First, it is important to notice that, in the account above, these deities are closely bound up with certain evaluative attitudes and ceremonial activities: participants feel it appropriate to express gratitude, for example, which, to be fully displayed in ritual acts, requires a figure to whom the gratitude can be directed. There is also a set of stories about such figures. Adherents of a particular pagan religion come to accept its deities not by being persuaded by a proof of their existence, or by taking a leap of faith; what is prior, one might say, is the sense of the appropriateness of the rituals themselves. Adherents participate in the commemorations of seasonal events and find these expressing their attitudes of thankfulness or self-reflection or sense of new life; or there are ritual activities of other types—marriages, coming-of-age celebrations, community ceremonies—that participants find spiritually fulfilling.

These activities can be satisfying on deep levels: they evoke and provide for the expression of profound emotional responses to the natural world and the place of humans in it, they acknowledge the various aspects of life and offer an opportunity to reflect on them, they foster spiritual growth and personal maturity, they provide a sense of personal identity and community solidarity, and the like. A central part of these rituals is the invocation of specific figures—gods, goddesses, spirits, the elements, animals—that are understood, through the associations conveyed by traditional myths and stories, to be suitable representatives of the aspects of nature commemorated. To continue to participate in such activities is to *accept* these deities; it is this acceptance that is crucial to the maintenance and stability of the tradition. Adherents continue to feel that these deities are appropriately associated with the rituals and commemorations that give life to the tradition: just *these* gods, goddesses, spirits, and powers, representing their specific aspects of life and nature, really do fit the deep emotions that ritual evokes. Succeeding generations have a similar reaction and find the rituals and the figures they include compelling and deeply satisfying.

Let us bring these considerations to bear on the question of existence. It is important to point out that one could participate fully, emotionally, seriously in the rituals, and so achieve, at least to a considerable degree, many of the benefits mentioned, without believing in the actual existence of the deities. Presumably there would be no stage in the learning of this religion or of being accepted into it where there was an attempt to give objective, independent support for its deities or where an explicit commitment to their existence was required. One would learn the religion by participating in it and feeling that it satisfied deep human emotions and, as a result, come to accept its various practices and the divinities they included. As mentioned, what is crucial to the continuation of a tradition is that its adherents continue to find satisfying its rituals and myths: they must participate in ceremonies, take seriously stories about the divinities, and use the conceptions offered by the tradition to describe events in their lives, among other things. For these purposes participants need not have a commitment to the actual existence of the deities. An individual could well find a particular ritual successful and fulfilling, or certain myths profound and instructive, or receive many of the other benefits mentioned, without having a belief about the existential standing of the deities incorporated in the ritual. There could even be practitioners who expressly denied existence: such participants could receive benefits from this participation in finding the rituals powerful and enriching and valuable in the ways described above, ways which cannot be replaced for them by other forms of activity. The appropriateness of the ceremonies and at least some important benefits from them do not require belief in real existence.

This point will be more understandable when we consider the concept of a deity corresponding to the spiritual practices I have been outlining. A divine being can take various forms: that of a male or a female person, sometimes with special bodies signifying their extra powers (the many-limbed deities of Tibetan Buddhism), or of an animal (Ganesha, the Hindu elephant god; or Damballa, the vodoun snake god) or element in nature (fire). Typically there is a set of stories and myths that describe the characteristic powers and interests of the deity. As noted, deities usually have special domains; they are the god or goddess *of* something—Aphrodite is the goddess of love but also the patroness of seafarers, Mars the god of war. These figures represent and personify deep and recurrent aspects of nature and of human life. They are to be invoked or called on as is required— Aphrodite is present in fertility festivals, e.g.—and as such can be asked to provide the appropriate energies or to be present in suitable ceremonies. Or a divinity can be asked for help—to cure an illness, or for aid in warfare. Gods and goddesses are figures who can be thanked or propitiated or called on for various purposes. An adherent feels that there are occasions for interacting with them personally in the sense of directing various emotions toward them or making them the objects of requests and entreaties. One can offer them thanks, or celebrate, serve, and honor them. In this regard the divinities have a special and very important place in the emotional and spiritual life of the practitioner: they are embedded in a particular form of life, to use Wittgenstein's expression, and make it possible.

But a question arises: aren't all these gods and goddesses and other beings really just fictions, created by forgotten authors, and so nonexistent and unreal? I have contended that activities such as invoking the deities in ceremonies and listening to myths about them do not assume the genuine existence of these creatures; but if so, a critic might hold that they are simply invented at some point by human beings. This critic might concede that they do represent major features of life and nature. But if so, then paganism does not look much different from an outlook such as Jungian psychology, which postulates a set of archetypes corresponding to major aspects of human life. Pagan deities can be regarded as personifications of these archetypes, our critic contends. Similarly a Platonist might say that the deities have the function of giving the major Forms, or perhaps complexes of them, a tangible appearance. Under these conceptions paganism may offer a valuable set of practices, yet perhaps it should be classified with certain forms of psychotherapy or aesthetic activities representing metaphysical theories: a particularly dramatic form of psychotherapy. Pagan rituals and myths would have the value of putting the participant in touch with neglected or repressed sides of his or her personality, or of providing the experiences of sharing group ritual activity, for example. But now paganism looks very different from full-fledged religions such as Christianity or Islam, where the deities are believed genuinely to exist and to act in the world.

There is something to this analysis; at one level, one might say, paganism can function in this way, but if this were the *only* type of function it had, then paganism would be essentially a dramatization of Jungian or Platonic theory and not an outlook offering a genuinely alternative worldview. To get clear on all this, it will be helpful to contrast the concept of a deity with that of a fictional character. Fictional characters are typically created as figures in stories by authors whose identity is usually known. Nevertheless we really do refer to and think about these characters, make true and false statements about them, become involved in their adventures, compare them with other such characters, and the like. Yet fictional characters do not exist in any sense; they are merely grammatical or intentional objects, introduced to be read and talked about, but which do not have any existential status whatever.[10] Fictional characters have a different conceptual status from deities: they are not invoked in rituals, not thanked or appreciated or celebrated, not propitiated or supplicated. Nor are they taken to represent aspects of nature or human life or to have domains of concern. The religious practitioner feels it is appropriate to direct emotional and evaluative attitudes to a deity in a way that would not be done toward an individual conceived as purely fictional.[11] Yet this could be questioned: this is an inessential difference, our critic might say; even though deities are treated differently from fictional characters, both are human creations and so unreal. Practices honoring aspects of nature or reflecting seasonal changes can certainly include such figures, but unless these beings are considered genuine existents, then pagan practices have more in common with psychotherapy or aesthetic activities such as dance or theater—or some combination of both—than with religion.

I have already indicated that this analysis represents an incomplete understanding of paganism. Before presenting the major point in response, let me make a relatively minor one. There are *many* forms of religion, from strict monotheism to Hinduism with its gods-as-aspects-of-Brahman conception, to Buddhism (which in some forms is explicitly atheistic) and Taoism and Confucianism, which are not concerned with deities. 'Religion,' like 'paganism,' is a family-resemblance term. So even if one were to grant that paganism is only a ritualistic way of acknowledging important aspects of reality which did not include belief in the actual existence of the deities involved, this in itself would not rule it out as a genuine religion. For surely, even here one could make the case that paganism has enough in common with religions such as Buddhism (atheistic in its initial form) or Taoism to justify classifying it as a religion. The more substantial response, however, is expressed in a passage from a Professor Leuba quoted (with approval) by William James:

> The truth of the matter can be put this way: *God is not known, he is not understood; he is used*—sometimes as meat-purveyer, sometimes as moral support, sometimes as friend, sometimes as an object of love. If he proves himself useful, the religious consciousness asks for no more than that. Does God really exist? How does he exist? What is he? are so many irrelevant questions. Not God, but life, more life, a larger, richer, more satisfying life is, in the last analysis, the end of religion. The love of life, at any and every level of development, is the religious impulse.[12]

Leuba is evidently speaking about divinity as conceived monotheistically, but his comment expresses the pagan perspective very nicely. The idea is that, as far as the basic activities of the religion are concerned, having a belief as regards the existence of the deities or investigating their nature or status would contribute nothing: what is important are the activities and the experiences and benefits they provide. There is no requirement of public acceptance of belief in the actual existence of the deities for participation in ceremonies; there is no period of instruction in pagan theology, at the end of which the aspiring pagan gives intellectual assent to the doctrines proposed and is thereby granted full pagan status. On the contrary, it is more accurate to say that one is admitted into the pagan community simply on the basis of participation in the rites. So, both participants who would explicitly deny existence if pressed, and also those who would definitely affirm existence of the gods, can qualify as fully pagan. A full spectrum of positions on existence could well be represented in a given pagan community.

Here the pagan perspective begins to diverge from that of the Jungian or

Platonist as imagined above.[13] For these positions do not allow genuine existence to the figures taken to represent more abstract entities. Yet it is certainly open to pagans to believe in the actual existence of their gods and goddesses and undoubtedly many have done so. Homer writes of the "immortals" as taking physical part in the Trojan wars, themselves wielding weapons and injuring and killing their opponents. Some might take the *Iliad* as a piece of fiction, but no doubt many citizens of ancient Greece understood it as literal. In the popular literature of Greco-Roman paganism, the gods and goddesses are portrayed as real.[14] Indeed there are certain kinds of activity where it would seem right to say that these cannot be entered into without a belief in the actual existence of the deities included in the activity. A pagan might feel that he or she has a relationship with a deity who responds personally to questions and requests, or one might perform a ritual for the sake of bringing about a particular result and when this occurred feel that a particular deity was responsible. Or, as the term 'immortals' suggests, one might believe that there was a large number of beings, powers, and spirits of various kinds additional to the familiar empirical entities that constitute our commonsense world.[15] Paganism accepts positions ranging from the minimal one of conceiving pagan deities as not actually existing but serving only a symbolic function to the very liberal one of admitting great numbers of real spirits, powers, and divinities. And as indicated earlier, one might even conceive the various deities as aspects or manifestations of a single higher one; different pagan traditions might have different positions on such matters. Considered generally, paganism tolerates many positions on the existence, nature, or situation of the gods. What is central to paganism is simply the admission of distinct deities and participation in the various activities associated with them, which in some circumstances can be public or community ceremonies and rites.[16]

Paganism and Monotheism

The attempt to press the question of the independent existence of the deities is characteristic not of pagan thought but of dominant Western monotheism,[17] where accepting the existence of God is a condition for full membership in monotheistic religion. At a certain stage one must affirm one's belief in God; without this one cannot receive the full benefits of such practices as listening to sermons or participating in Mass or Communion: for a nonbeliever, a sermon would not be seen as indicating the applications of God's word, and Mass or Communion would have no religious significance. Only believers take the sacred texts as having divine authorship, only they can receive religious benefit from participation in ceremonies, and only believers qualify in the afterlife for the rewards of belief. Defenses of monotheism therefore often center around the soundness of arguments for the existence of God or the appropriateness of faith (the ontological, cosmological, and teleological arguments, Pascal's wager, Kierkegaard's leap of faith).

Corresponding to this is the emphasis on *correct* belief: it is essential to accept the One True God as based on a correct understanding of the relevant scriptures. Deviation from accepted belief has even been used to justify inducing belief through force; this is warranted because incorrect belief can condemn the heretic's soul to eternal damnation. From this perspective the Inquisition—admittedly an extreme case and controversial even within Christianity—can be justified as intending to save souls through torture that compels assent. Deviation in belief defines a group as no longer among the real believers, and it can therefore be a reason for war, invasion, domination, or slavery. Belief in the actual existence of God, determination of God's properties, profession by individuals of correct doctrine, community acceptance of sound religious practices, have been crucial to central traditions within monotheism. Consequently there is the need for theology—the attempt to discover by reason the true properties of God and their consequences for humanity. This intellectual enterprise has flourished in many countries dominated by monotheism—and has led to endless disagreements among adherents, resulting in divisions into innumerable sects and groups. The importance of correct belief has also tended to make monotheism hierarchical and authoritarian, with only certain individuals, usually through their institutional position, entitled to pronounce on religious doctrine. These have typically been males, and indeed the image of God the Father is enshrined in basic monotheistic texts; hence monotheism has tended to be patriarchal as well.

Much of this stands in sharp contrast to paganism. Here the basic spiritual motivations are acknowledgment of the primary elements of life and nature and a sense of being part of a larger whole and participating in its processes. To accept a particular pagan tradition is to participate in its practices, to find its rituals satisfying, its stories illuminating and meaningful, and the like. As we have seen profession of belief has no part in this process: one might find the appearance of a particular deity in a given ceremony especially appropriate, but this would not necessarily indicate or require a belief in the independent existence of the deity. If it were important that only existing deities could appear in ceremonies, then one would suppose that at some point in pagan practice there would be an attempt at establishing existence—finding evidence or proof, or sorting out the existing deities from the purely imaginary. Paganism includes no such attempts, however, any more than it requires affirmations of existence from participants: nothing in paganism corresponds to monotheistic proofs for God or a required assent to creeds.

Similarly, rational investigation as to what properties these deities *really* have is not found in pagan practice. Even in the ancient world, where paganism was the dominant religion, and where philosophy also flourished, there was no attempt to discover by reason the actual properties of Pan or Jupiter or Isis.[18] There were no intellectuals working within the framework of a commitment to paganism and attempting to work out a correct pagan doctrine; there were no councils attempting to reconcile differences in pagan belief or to establish orthodoxy. Rather, one just participated in the practices or one did not: there was no pagan theology to determine correct belief.

Corresponding to this was the tolerance of pagan groups for one another. Although in the myths there were occasional contests and conflicts among the immortals, mortal adherents of one deity did not engage in religious wars with the followers of another. Of course there were conflicts between groups belonging to different pagan traditions, and these called on their deities for aid. But such wars did not have a religious motivation, unlike the Crusades, for example. On the contrary, those in the service of one divinity often honored other deities as well.[19] Gods in other provinces or countries were even accepted as local divinities honored under different names.[20] Criteria of identity for gods and goddesses are loose and flexible. Similarly, pagan thought is not centralized and so subject to an authority that overrides local practice. There were, of course, in the paganism of the classical world, major temples and their priests and priestesses. These sometimes provided the model for practice in other places, but there was nothing like a sacred text that all pagans of a given sect must follow, and no group of interpreters were authorized to set the standards for all cult practice.

A natural explanation for all this is that pagans conceived their religious traditions as springing up more or less independently, each a response to a felt appropriateness for community and individual commemorations. Traditions would be understood to have incorporated local elements and commitments, yet to express fundamental attitudes and responses that other pagans would find familiar. Particular divinities would be more or less specific to a tradition, with the qualification that the same deity could appear in different locations under different names, as indicated above. In fact it would be reasonable to suppose that deities can so appear, given common motivations for their appearance in rites; the presumption would be against exclusivity. The model of a religion as introduced at a definite time and place by a particular individual or group, having its authority in a set of sacred texts or sayings, and propagated by adherents, would only distort an understanding of paganism. The motivations for religious activity characteristic of paganism are attitudes basic to human beings generally: the need to express certain attitudes toward nature or to acknowledge recurring aspects of life. Such feelings spontaneously occur to human beings living in different parts of the world, and the expressions of these in ritual, prayer, song, dance, chanting, drumming, and the like spring up independently of each other. Those who have responded to such feelings and developed their own practices reflecting local traditions have no reason not to be tolerant of others. The exclusivity found in monotheism, and the subsequent motive to convert others to it, would find no resonance in paganism.

II. MAKING THE CASE

At this point I have sketched some of the central principles of pagan thought, and in the remaining sections I want to use these principles in making a case for paganism. This is not the only case that can be made. Paganism offers promise in dealing with the problem of evil, as James suggests, and there are other types of support available.[21] Before laying out my case two remarks are in order.

First, in what follows I will be giving considerations of various kinds designed to show the advantages of paganism over other spiritual approaches, particularly monotheism. This is the appropriate religion of comparison because of its historical domination of religion in the West, intellectually as well as culturally. It presents the paradigm of religion, both for intellectuals and spiritual seekers. Whatever their final conclusions, at some point they have had to come to grips with monotheism. Monotheism has set the terms for debates about religion (e.g., theism, atheism, and agnosticism are almost invariably formulated in terms of monotheism's God). That a plausible theistic alternative exists should be of great interest to Westerners: the advantages of accepting the deity as personal can be retained without the liabilities of standard monotheism, and there are attractions that polytheism but not monotheism can offer. Aside from a few remarks, I am not considering Eastern religions here. Some have interesting commonalities with paganism (consider Tibetan Buddhism, Taoism, and Shinto; earlier I have mentioned Hinduism as having a pagan component) which would be interesting to examine. My discussion is intended to take Western thought as context; the struggle between paganism and Christianity has been one of the major themes of Western history and I wish to make a contribution to this debate.

Second, something must be said about the kind of argument I shall be making: supporting one religion over others. Religions are complex, and when evaluating them one needs to take many considerations into account. If it were possible to prove the existence of the monotheistic God in some final and unproblematic way, then this would go a long way in settling the issue in favor of monotheism. But among philosophers and intellectuals who deal with such matters, the consensus is that such proofs are not conclusive; on the whole they are irrelevant or insignificant to actual religious belief. And on the pagan side there is no question of trying to *prove* in some rationalistic way, analogous to the familiar arguments attempting to prove the existence of God, that some set of deities exists. What can be done, however, is to *make a case* for polytheism. My case recalls the emotional and spiritual attitudes that arise in certain conditions; it requires seeing polytheism as a part of a whole set of practices, a "form of life," to use a Wittgensteinian term. When seen as reflecting these attitudes, the practices characteristic of paganism, including its polytheism, seem attractive and appealing—so my argument goes. To make this out I shall consider a whole range of factors. I shall point out negative aspects of the dominant monotheism: its intellectual difficulties and the undesirable consequences of its attitudes and values, as well as problems inherent in its institutional organization. The form of life broadly flowing from monotheism is relevant as well; matters of practice as well as purely intellectual issues have a bearing. Since this way of defending polytheism requires seeing it as closely associated with a set of attitudes and practices, it cannot consider beliefs independent of practice, as arguments for the existence of God typically do. So attitudes and practices associated with monotheism come into consideration too. In this way my support for polytheism requires a defense of a set of religious practices, adopted in various degrees by different forms of historical paganism. But let me make it clear that I am supporting these historical religions only to the extent that they include the attitudes and practices pointed out in the thought-experiment earlier. Historical pagans have engaged in all sorts of ritual and other activities that have no connection with these attitudes; such activities get no backing from the analysis here.

Presumably there will be no one issue that, in itself, will be decisive in this evaluation. Rather, I hope to make paganism attractive by considering *many* issues; the cumulative result of this analysis will depict paganism favorably. The comparison is with a court trial: a lawyer presents the case for her client, rebuts the case of the opposition, tries to meet its arguments against her own case, and then summarizes the whole debate—where this reasoning is intended to be balanced and responsive to the relevant facts. Nevertheless it is clear that there is plenty of room for analyzing the various issues in different ways, with different emphases and from different perspectives, and for giving different evaluations to various concerns. So one might feel that certain issues ought to be analyzed or judged differently than is done here, or that there are other elements or perspectives that deserve consideration. Inevitably there is an appeal to one's judgment, which will be colored by all sorts of personal considerations. This is related to James's idea that in the absence of decisive considerations one simply has the right to believe what one is inclined to believe.[22] In any event, it seems to me important to present the factors that weigh in favor of the kind of polytheism outlined above; their final evaluation will depend on an individual's own situation and commitments. That such a case can be made at all might be surprising considering today's intellectual climate, where the typical poles of religious discussion are monism in one form or another on the one hand, and skepticism on the other.

Paganism: Objections and Replies

Let us begin by meeting objections raised against paganism. First, there is the question of how reasonable it is to accept *many, limited, morally flawed* deities when there is the possibility of belief in a single, perfect, and unlimited God. It seems implausible to affirm deities having restricted powers or faculties when contrasted with the infinite ones ascribed to God; why accept a god or goddess being *partly* good or powerful or knowing? Even less reasonable is to adopt a deity who has committed acts for which humans would be morally condemned, and to accept many such deities is still worse. Surely, one might say, the most advanced conception of a deity is that of a single, supreme being who has infinite powers and is not morally flawed. Only such a God is worthy of epithets such as the "almighty" and "most high" and has the majesty and perfection worthy of worship. The idea of many deities, each having limited powers and moral weaknesses, seems immature and spiritually flawed, far less developed than the ideal expressed in classical monotheism.

There are several points to be dealt with here. Let us start with the concept of a deity implicit in this objection and the assumption that what is central in a religion is its divine being. On these principles, the most elevated religion is the one that contains the most morally and spiritually perfect divinity, who is the central focus of thought, emotion, liturgical practice, and the source of morality—nothing else will have comparable status and authority. If one makes the further assumption that the virtues of authoritative males are superior, then this divinity becomes masculine, all-powerful, and a judge of human actions and life. This deity is obviously far removed from human weaknesses and inabilities, and the fitting attitudes toward him are therefore ones such as veneration, worship, abasement, and unworthiness, and a sense of extreme distance from the divine. The believer can only hope that strict obedience to God's rules will make him or her worthy of the removal of the profound deficiencies inherent in the human condition. The concept of a deity in paganism, however, is not guided by the idea of a perfect being. Pagan deities represent important dimensions of immediate, experienced life and nature, and they are bound up with ceremonies and rituals that acknowledge them. Paganism is not a belief system centering around a highest being, to which appropriate practices are added, but has its motivation in the recognition of deep, impressive, recurrent, and pervasive aspects of the world in which we immediately live. Because of their association with these aspects, and not because of their perfect or infinite powers, these deities are seen as figures to honor, celebrate, and serve. Consequently, there need be no limitation on the number of divinities the tradition accepts; in fact it is fitting that there should be many deities, so that nature and life in all their manifestations can be fully represented. Limiting the attitudes of worshipers to a single remote divinity makes it impossible to acknowledge directly the variety and depth of the experienced dimensions of nature.

There is another aspect to the issue of the nature of divinity. Monotheism postulates a single, perfect deity, one having all the perfections (as Anselm put it). There is a serious question whether the notion of a being having every perfection is coherent. Some kinds of goodness are categorially distinct from other kinds, and to suppose that there is one entity that could have all kinds of goodness seems nonsensical. Can something have the qualities of a good knife (be sharp and long-lasting, handle well) and of a good piano sonata (be moving, inventive, well developed)? If the reply is that only human perfections are meant, then there is the question of why only these are relevant, and again, how they are to be selected. The ideal weight of a ballet dancer is very different from that of a heavyweight boxer. If the perfections be limited to moral ones, then this leaves out some of the traditional ones (omniscience, omnipotence) and raises the question of which model of a moral individual is to provide the list of virtues. The knight has different virtues from the saint, the warrior from the diplomat, and it seems questionable that some one individual could possess all these sets of excellences: could some one individual be both ready to fight to the death for his cause and simultaneously willing to compromise? These considerations suggest that it is incoherent to conceive one individual as possessing *all* the virtues and arbitrary to select any one type of individual as possessing the only important ones.[23] Paganism avoids these problems by admitting many deities, allowing for different types of moral ideals to be represented. Aphrodite represents sexuality and physical enjoyment, Artemis withdrawal, solitude, and chastity. From the perspective of paganism both aspects of life need to be honored and given their place in the spiritual life but can hardly be made the essential characteristics of a single figure. The pluralism inherent in polytheism reflects the many sets of values and ideals appropriate for practical life.

The monotheist may claim that only something deserving the designations 'Almighty' or 'Supreme Being' is worthy of worship and veneration. But pagans have a different set of feelings reflecting their distinctive worldview. They see their religion as one where they as well as the spiritual powers are participants in a common world and consequently are subject to similar kinds of problems and temptations. Consequently their religion is not hierarchical but egalitarian and participatory. Indeed the very flaws imputed to the deities may contribute toward their effective participation: we can take more seriously the weaknesses we find in ourselves when our deities exhibit them too. This does not make those weaknesses acceptable in ourselves; it shows that they represent tendencies that are a real part of the human condition and so must be confronted with great seriousness. We can feel closest to deities that have had our experiences and suffered from the weaknesses we have known; these are the individuals we want to address in our poetry and to whom we can express our human feelings. They can guide and instruct or heal us as we enter into the areas that are their special domains. Such divinities are nearby, local, and ready to be called on, rather than exalted and removed from the imperfect life that we actually live. Worship and veneration of a remote and perfect being, self-abasement and deep expressions of humility, are suited to religions where there is a large gap between worshiper and worshiped. Monotheists may feel that these attitudes have important spiritual value, but paganism expresses a different spirituality: celebration of important personal or civic events, desire to honor and participate in changes in the seasons, an offering of thanks to a specific deity for his or her perceived intervention, or, perhaps especially, the expression of awe and wonder about the mysteries of nature and gratitude to the earth for its sustenance and bounty. Pagans see themselves as having their own inherent value and as playing an important role in a much larger whole; notions of worthlessness and "original sin," humanity as needing "salvation," of abasement before the "Almighty," are not part of their outlook: being natural creatures, we share in the basic goodness of nature. The sacred is not something remote or located only in special human structures or in an afterlife; it is found around us everywhere on the earth and is to be respected and honored in daily activities. Obviously monotheism does not lack such inclinations, and some monotheistic traditions—notably certain versions of mysticism—would emphasize them. But pagan spirituality makes them central and does not accept the separation between a remote divinity or holy realm and a desacralized everyday world, a separation that can very easily attend the notion of a 'Supreme Being' existing apart from nature.

A second objection sees paganism as based on ignorance of the regularities of nature and originating as an attempt to control them. Paganism appears in societies without developed empirical science and so unaware of the causes of disease or the growth of crops. Therefore it postulates spirits as causal agents; control over them is then sought by propitiation and ritual. Such "superstitions" arise out of ignorance and fear, and are primitive attempts to achieve what science has provided so successfully, an understanding of the real causes operating in nature and thus the means to control it.

Now it may be a historical fact that some pagan practices began with a background of ignorance of natural causality and were intended to control nature, and certainly in ancient paganism sacrifice was common as a means of encouraging the deities to grant favors. But it is unfounded speculation to assume that this is the only or even a basic motive behind paganism. The fact that at present many sophisticated, highly educated individuals accept paganism suggests that this motive is not a strong one. Evidently such individuals do not fear basic natural processes and have no need to control them through ritual; despite their awareness of the achievements of science they value their pagan practices.[24] Indeed if the analysis earlier is correct, paganism has a quite different sort of appeal than the objection here assumes. Pagans have been more interested in acknowledging the deep aspects of nature and expressing their attitudes toward it than in controlling it. In any case, I am not concerned to analyze historical paganism but to point out a different kind of motivation plausibly underlying pagan practice; if other motives have been sometimes in effect, then this does not discount the strength of the purposes that I have pointed out. Nevertheless, the objection raises the question of the relation between paganism and science. What are the consequences for paganism of our present scientific understanding of nature?

In the way that there is room in paganism for different positions on the issue of the real existence of the deities, there is also latitude for a variety of standpoints on the relations between science and paganism. Someone who takes the deities as symbolic only and not real has no reason to think that science does not give a complete account of physical reality. Gods, goddesses, and other figures would symbolize important aspects of nature, but they play no causal role. This does not detract from their importance or from the value of paganism generally. Clearly, on this conception there is no conflict between a physical account of the natural world and paganism. Of course, one should not think that this conception implies that the scientific account is really the true and hence most important one, and consequently that the pagan view merely adds an imaginary dimension to the literal and realistic explanations of science. A spiritual conception of things has its own important functions. It is connected with the kinds of activity, emotion, and experience mentioned earlier that reflect a deep part of the human psyche. The ways of thinking and acting that are fostered and expressed by pagan practices constitute a very important part of a mature and balanced outlook on life. Science and religion may serve different purposes and be connected with different interests, but there is no reason to privilege the former above the latter since they are not in competition. Science has added immeasurably to human knowledge, but religion has allowed the psyche to venture into mysteries and to achieve a kind of development far beyond anything scientific understanding can provide.

Paganism will have this kind of importance no matter what an adherent's beliefs about the reality of gods and goddesses. Nevertheless, if one believes in the reality of the deities and accords them more than symbolic status, the question of the relation between spiritual and physical entities arises. One response is this: science deals essentially with the empirical realm, what can be observed and inferred or postulated to exist on the basis of observed data, where this includes not only what is available to the human senses but to its extension by instruments such as electron microscopes, cloud chambers, and radio astronomy. The spiritual beings and powers that pagans of this type acknowledge are beyond these sorts of detection and measurement: the gods are not assumed on the basis of a need for accurate predictions. Religious belief would be comparable to scientific theory in being about actual causal forces, only it would refer to ones different from those science acknowledges and would not rely on normal scientific techniques. Such a conception might be acceptable to someone like William James, who accepts dimensions of reality other than those available to the ordinary senses. Notice that on this view pagan belief does not result from fear or ignorance but from a presumed insight into elements of reality and their relationships beyond the reach of standard science.[25] Still, even with this realistic understanding of the divinities, paganism would not have the purpose of essentially providing causal explanations couched in nonphysical terminology; its beliefs would rather be associated with the kinds of reactions to nature and the ritual and personal experiences discussed above. Paganism provides a view of reality that incorporates spiritual entities and powers, and sees them as active in the world. It also has a place for scientific theory as successfully explaining a specific type of reality, but it conceives of science as limited to this level of reality, valuable as its explanations might be.

Although paganism can admit these nonempirical entities, it does not, as paganism, attempt outright control over them. That is the province of magic and witchcraft, and there is a distinction between religion and magic.

> Historians, theologians and anthropologists seem to be in general agreement upon a distinction between the two. Religion consists of an offering up of prayers, gifts and honor to divine beings who operate quite independently of the human race and are infinitely more powerful than it. Those actions may be aimed at obtaining favor or merely at maintaining the existing order, but whatever the inspiration of the worshiper, the decision as to whether or not any response will be made lies entirely with the deity or deities concerned. Magic, by contrast, consists of a control worked by humans over nature by use of spiritual forces, so that the end result is expected to lie within the will of the person or person working the spell or the ritual.[26]

Further,

> All the literary sources for European paganism also make plain that magic of any kind was not connected with the worship of deities. Whether courtly

or rural, learned or traditional, benign or malignant, it was an art or science, not part of a religion.[27]

The consequence is clear:

> Thus, magic of any kind cannot, strictly speaking, be described as 'paganism.'[28]

Those who perform magic are to be distinguished from ordinary practitioners of the religion and their leaders:

> The distinction in pre-Christian society between a priestess or priest and sorcerer or witch was usually plain.[29]

Sorcerers and witches might operate within the worldview of paganism, calling on the spirits and powers that a particular version of paganism might admit. In so doing they would be using what were considered to be "the morally neutral forces of nature, which could be turned to good or bad effect just like the physical natural world."[30] But one could belong to the religion and not practice magic.[31] The pagan worldview, like those of most religions, allows for the possibility of magic and sorcery, but, as in other religions, these are phenomena distinct from its more typical and central practices.[32]

In Favor of Paganism

Having addressed some of the main objections to paganism, I can now set out a positive case. First, the grounds for pagan practice that I have been emphasizing lie in the recognition of elementary facts about human life, and of adopting a worldview that is very natural, given certain aspects of human experience. Human beings whose way of living requires close participation in the earth's cycles will feel deeply involved in these processes; they can easily see themselves as one element in the larger web of nature and as interdependent with other parts. They will think of their lives as bound up with the rhythms of nature and wish to commemorate them symbolically and ritually. They will also notice the very general elements of life, the facts of birth, maturation, and death, human relations with each other and with nonhuman animals and plants and other elements of the environment, the sun, moon, and stars and their cycles, and the like. They will want to celebrate and commemorate these aspects of life and to acknowledge the other powers whose presence they feel. These are motivations we can at least partly understand and respect, even if our society, with its highly developed science, technology, and predominantly urban lifestyle, shields us from the kinds of participation in nature's cycles and contact with the earth that our ancestors knew. For we, no less than earlier human beings, are entirely dependent on the earth and its provisions, even if it is difficult for us to remember this because of the commercialism and technology so central in contemporary Western society. Pagan conceptions of the earth, and our relations to it and other aspects of nature, are understandable and attractive, even if they clash with the prevailing beliefs that the human species is set off from the rest of nature and that the natural world has value only because it provides resources for human use.

The foundational concepts of paganism can be the basis for the development of a highly diversified tradition in which many types of valuable human service flourish. Participating in shared rituals and other spiritual activities can be moving, empowering, deeply satisfying, and fulfilling. A tradition incorporating these practices can offer many kinds of service for its participants. It would, for example, include means of dealing with the personal issues that inevitably arise in life, provide for the education of young people and the continued spiritual growth of members of the community, encourage artistic expressions of various kinds, offer various kinds of physical and mental healing. Paganism as a religious practice, as well as a world-outlook, need be no less personally rich and fulfilling than any other religious perspective.

Second, consider the relations between paganism and other forms of religion. Monotheism has been dominant in many parts of the world for almost two millennia and its prima facie difficulties are well known; I list some of them without commenting on the many attempts to meet them. The problem of evil is both intellectually and psychologically damaging. What theoretical explanation can monotheism have for evil? How can a being with the immense powers ascribed to God allow the amount of suffering endured by both humans and nonhuman animals, and that on monotheistic theory he has foreseen and, as creator of the world, actually produced? How can one ever worship or praise a being that allows and has even created such immense evils? Second, patriarchialism and authoritarianism are ingrained in the texts of monotheism and its practices. It is a religion of textual authority, and so there must be individuals to give us God's divine word or to transmit His messages. These have traditionally been male, and indeed at many points the texts indicate the superiority of males over females. Accordingly, males generally occupy positions of institutional power and doctrinal authority within monotheistic institutions. God himself is described in masculine terms; feminine elements are at best subordinated and must appear indirectly. Further, I have noted the tendency in monotheism to remove divinity from nature, locating it strictly in God or in Heaven, or perhaps within the constructed spaces of churches and temples, and thus denying direct sacredness and value to the natural world in which we actually live. This is to be cared for only insofar as it is necessary to human purposes and perhaps as God's creation, not because of its own sacredness. Animals do not have souls and so are radically different from human beings, who alone have ethical standing and deserve religious consideration. Gratitude and respect are due to the earth and the various elements of nature not because they are inherently worthy, but because the physical world is created by God. Our time on the earth is merely preparation for eternity in heaven or hell; life here is a "vale of tears" and not the focus of our real emotional and practical activity, which is our afterlife state. All of this conflicts with our spontaneous feelings about the importance and beauty of nature, but God the Father does not have Mother Earth as his wife and monotheists cannot offer direct thanks to such a being. Let me say again that there is much to be said about each of these issues, and different traditions within monotheism have their responses; I am not suggesting that matters are simple and easily settled. But on the face of it the problems inherent in monotheism are substantial, and whatever one's judgment about the issues raised, it is certainly reasonable to take the alternatives seriously.

It is interesting to consider Western society from the perspective of the pagan cultural contents it contains. Even in the West, where monotheism has long been dominant, many of the conceptual elements of paganism have survived. Stories about legendary and mythical figures have always been a part of the culture and have functioned to give a vision that offers an alternative to the official monotheistic and scientific conception of the natural world. In this literature, there are spirits and demons, mythical beings, strange forces, heroic men and women, powerful animals, and impressive natural settings. These figures exhibit mysterious abilities and perform amazing deeds; in fact, these are just the sorts of figures and deeds that appear in the narratives that were the basis of paganism. Of course this literature is not now connected with religious practice in the way that it was in antiquity, and so it is not classified as religious. Nevertheless, it has kept alive the sense of the mysteriousness and depth of nature and of the strange powers that can easily be seen in it. In this way even mainstream Western culture has always had a place for the characteristically pagan attitudes toward the natural world. So despite dominant intellectual and religious beliefs, the potentiality for paganism has always remained strong in the West. Many Westerners might not find that the adoption of paganism as a spiritual practice requires so great a change in their outlook as they might have expected. Indeed, as environmental issues become more pressing, it will seem right to have a perspective honoring nature and expressing humanity's interdependence with it—a role paganism is highly qualified to play.

What is the appropriate reaction of paganism toward the monotheism that has dominated Western religion? From an intellectual and spiritual perspective, monotheism presents simply another religious practice, not to be honored or dishonored more than any other. The cosmological writings of monotheism offer an account that differs in some ways from comparable pagan ones: the world is the work of a single being, produced by an act of will; it does not result from a process requiring cooperation among many creatures, often including animals. Paganism can accept various monotheistic narratives as having the same status and functions as pagan stories: to entertain and enlighten on various levels, to delineate the basic elements of reality, to offer examples for ethical reflection, and the like. Monotheistic accounts are no more but no less true than similar ones in pagan traditions and they have the same kinds of importance and value. Paganism can see monotheism as another form of religion, one following a set of spiritual intuitions and emotional reactions that are importantly different in some but not all ways. There is no reason not to tolerate monotheism and learn from it where this is in accord with basic pagan principles.

Third, the particular intellectual outlook that paganism offers can help to deal with another tendency encouraged by scientific and technical thinking: that of reducing nature to elements postulated by scientific theory. Much has been written about the "disenchantment of nature," the inclination of intellectuals to describe the essential qualities of nature in terms of the findings of chemistry or physics. This reductionism is only strengthened by removing divinity from nature and making it merely God's product: if the natural world itself were the location of the spiritual, it would be wrong to think that the physical sciences have discovered the essential qualities of things. Such physical descriptions leave no room for anything sacred or even valuable except its usefulness to human beings. But, as I have argued elsewhere, the framework of the physical sciences is a secondary one, parasitic practically and logically on everyday commonsense thought: everyday concepts are required to teach and explain technical conceptions found in both science and religion.[33] I have emphasized the profound influence that attitudes of appreciation for our existential situation can have on the development of religious thought; this contrasts with the attitude of curiosity about nature and a desire to manipulate it, motivations that are typical of technical science and engineering. As suggested earlier, religion and science represent different human interests and have different types of legitimacy; these two systems of concepts have very different functions, operate on different types of subject matter, and have different standards of success.[34] Accordingly, the pagan will not be in conflict with scientific theory, since it is consistent with pagan principles to hold that scientific explanations concern just *one* type of entity and need not be taken as authoritative for what exists generally. Spiritual systems of thinking are appropriate in their own ways and their postulations satisfy their own standards of justification. The pagan will be able to think scientifically about those issues where scientific concepts and procedures are appropriate, and to think in spiritual terms where this is appropriate. One has just as much right to think of the world as mysterious, rich, and magical, as to think of it in terms of quantitative laws ranging over the entities of the physical sciences; or, for many purposes, to think of it in *both* ways.

Finally, something should be said about the forms that paganism employs. To the Western intellectual it may seem a deficiency that paganism offers no creed, includes no theology, gives no proofs for its divinities. This is to be explained, I have argued, through the origins of paganism in the attitudes of appreciation and wonder. The point here is not historical, that paganism originated among preliterate peoples among whom intellectual disciplines had not yet developed. Rather it is inherent in the nature of the pagan outlook. A pagan can claim, along with such philosophers as Hume, Kant, James, and Wittgenstein, that theological and philosophical attempts to arrive rationally at conclusions about the nature of divinity go beyond the boundaries of knowledge. Even if one should accept the reality of these deities, there is no possible way of achieving genuine knowledge about them. Our faculties are too limited, our powers of reasoning too weak, the information given us too fragmentary and elusive. In principle, one cannot have reliable knowledge of transcendental beings, even if one wants to hold that they are somehow there. Paganism respects this boundary; in this way the absence of a pagan theology is in accordance with reason. One might say that in not violating the limitations of thought by attempting to investigate the unfathomable, it conforms to reason's best dictates. But pagans are not skeptics or positivists; they do not believe that there is nothing to be acknowledged or expressed in the realm of the spiritual. Nature contains forces and powers that are overwhelmingly impressive and meaningful to us and that we can barely grasp; we can try to represent them only by using modes of expression that reflect our deepest emotions. This inevitably takes us beyond the limitations of rationality and literal statement. Paganism responds to the inclination to transcend the limits of language by expressing nonverbally our most profound feelings about the world; its means can only be myth, poetry, ritual, song, music, and dance. Only in such ways can human beings try to express what is ultimately inexpressible. Paganism can be regarded as tacitly acknowledging a limit to evidence, knowledge, and literal understanding but as attempting, nevertheless, to respect our intuitions about the deeply mysterious presences we sense in the world around us.[35]

NOTES

1. Ludwig Wittgenstein, "Remarks on Frazer's *Golden Bough*," reprinted in *Ludwig Wittgenstein: Philosophical Occasions 1912–1951,* edited by James C. Klagge and Alfred Nordmann (Indianapolis, 1993), 127–29.

2. For the notion of a family resemblance term, see L. Wittgenstein, *Philosophical Investigations,* 3rd ed., translated by G. E. M. Anscombe (New York, 1958), secs. 66–67.

3. For discussion of neo-paganism in the United States, see Margot Adler, *Drawing Down the Moon: Witches, Druids, Goddess-Worshipers, and Other Pagans in America Today,* revised and expanded edition (Boston, 1986). *Paganism Today,* ed. C. Hardman and G. Harvey (London, 1996), has scholarly articles on various aspects of contemporary paganism.

4. One possible exception is William James: the only obvious escape from the problem of evil, he writes, "is to cut loose from the monistic assumption altogether, and to allow the world to have existed from its origin in pluralistic form, as an aggregate or collection of higher and lower things and principles, rather than an absolute unitary fact" (*The Varieties of Religious Experience,* in *William James: Writings 1902–1910* [New York, 1987], 125). Later James explicitly refers to this conception as "polytheism" (p. 468). But James does not consider polytheism as related to the attitudes toward nature and everyday life that are central to paganism as I see it. Gustav Fechner, however, does offer a polytheistic view including such attitudes; his polytheism culminates in monism. See, e.g., W. James, "Concerning Fechner," *A Pluralistic Universe,* Lecture IV, pp. 690–710, in ibid.

In antiquity, the situation is more complex. Plato is usually considered to be a monotheist but there are polytheistic elements in his thought (e.g., in *Statesman* 272e he speaks of "the gods of the provinces, who had ruled under the greatest god" [*The Collected Dialogues of Plato,* edited by Edith Hamilton and Huntington Cairns (Princeton, 1961), 1038]). Similarly there are passages in Aristotle that can be interpreted as favoring polytheism. In *Metaphysics* XII Ch. 9 he calculates that there are either fifty-five or forty-seven unmoved movers, and then remarks that "our forefathers in the most remote ages have handed down to their posterity a tradition, in the form of a myth, that these bodies are gods and that the divine encloses the whole of nature" (1074b 1–3, *The Basic Works of Aristotle,* edited by Richard McKeon [New York, 1941], 884). Aristotle goes on to call this an "inspired utterance" (1074b 10–11, p. 884). There were ancient philosophers who explicitly worked out accounts of the gods. Epicurus believed that they existed and were sometimes seen (e.g., in dreams), and that they lived in the empty regions of space between the worlds. Plutarch developed a comprehensive system that incorporated the various types of being accepted in popular religion (see for example *Isis and Osiris*).

5. My topic is *paganism* rather than more broadly *polytheism* because paganism, at least the form I want to discuss, is a form of polytheism that is intimately associated with certain distinctive reactions toward nature. So it is only polytheism as having this basis that is under consideration. There may be other ways of supporting polytheism, e.g., as a solution to the problem of evil (as James suggests), but I shall not take them up here.

6. This method is inspired by concepts found in Wittgenstein. First there are his examples of "primitive language games" that are supposed to illustrate basic facts about language (see *Philosophical Investigations,* 3rd ed. [New York, 1958], secs. 2, 8). Second, in *On Certainty* he indicates that there are "extremely general facts of nature" that are background for certain kinds of concepts. For example: "Certain events would put me into a position in which I could not go on with the old language-game any further. In which I was torn away from the *sureness* of the game. Indeed, doesn't it seem obvious that the possibility of a language-game is conditioned by certain facts?" (*On Certainty* [New York, 1969], sec. 167; see also *Philosophical Investigations,* Part II xii, p. 230). Here Wittgenstein is alluding to general regularities such as the stability of physical objects as the basis for terms for natural kinds (words referring to kinds of physical thing—'lemon,' 'cat'). What I want to suggest is that the "primitive language-game" of basic paganism, as it might be put, can be regarded as stemming from a recognition of the "extremely general facts of nature" of the broad and important factors of life, prominent among them being our relation to the earth and the processes of nature. A third Wittgensteinian idea is that of a "common spirit": pagan practices, so conceived, are intelligible to us because we share the basic emotions and reactions that I am describing as characteristic of paganism; insofar as this is the case this outlook offers a spiritual perspective that is natural and attractive.

7. Cf. Wittgenstein: "we are not doing natural science; nor yet natural history—since we can also invent fictitious natural history for our purposes" (*Philosophical Investigations,* 230).

8. Cf. Wittgenstein: "All these *different* practices show that it is not a question of the derivation of one from the other, but of a common spirit. And one could invent (devise) all these ceremonies oneself. And precisely that spirit from which one invented them would be their common spirit" ("Remarks on Frazer's *Golden Bough,*" 151).

9. For more on the functions of myths and stories in spiritual traditions, see my "Myths, Stories and Existence: Spirituality Without Belief," in *Myths and Fictions,* edited by Shlomo Biderman and Ben-Ami Scharfstein (Leiden, 1993), 161–83.

10. For elaboration, see my *Unreality: The Metaphysics of Fictional Objects* (Ithaca: N.Y., 1991).

11. The possibility that a fictional character should become a deity should not be entirely ruled out. There would have to be some genuinely spiritual reason for changing the conceptual status of an acknowledged fiction from created character to deity: from treating this individual as something merely to be read about and as the object of literary interest, to treating him or her as appropriately worshiped, honored, propitiated, and the like. The qualities of the fiction would have to make the transition appropriate—the character would have to be spiritually powerful in some way, charismatic one might say. This change would certainly not be right for normal fictions, but one can imagine cases where a reader would feel that what is clearly a standard fictional character embodies the attributes of divinity. More plausible is the transition from a *legendary* figure—one thought of as historical but whose qualities have perhaps been embellished through imaginative extension—to deity. Legendary figures are not attached to specific authors or creators even though their qualities may be supposed to owe something to the imagination. They might be thought actually to have existed and to have had extraordinary ("legendary") powers; the gap between legendary character and deity is not as wide as between literary fiction and deity.

12. W. James, *Varieties of Religious Experience,* 453. James is quoting from Leuba's article, "The Contents of Religious Consciousness," *The Monist* 11 (July 1901): 536.

13. I do not mean to ascribe the positions outlined to anyone; the historical Jung may well have believed in spirits, as a Jungian therapist tells me.

14. For example, in Apuleius' *The Golden Ass,* Isis appears to Lucius in a dream and tells him what to do to regain his human form (he has been magically changed into a donkey). Lucius follows her directions and all transpires as she predicted. Clearly Isis is depicted as real and able to bring about real changes. See *The Golden Ass of Apuleius,* a new translation by Robert Graves (New York, 1951), chap. 17, "The Goddess Isis Intervenes."

15. Indeed William James comes close to adopting this outlook: "The whole drift of my education goes to persuade me that the world of our present consciousness is only one out of many worlds that exist, and that those other worlds must contain experiences which have a meaning for our life also . . . " (James, *Varieties of Religious Experience,* 463).

16. "What marked out the Christians [among classical Romans] . . . was that unlike Jews they did not accept the validity of the competition for glory and honour within the context of city-state society . . . " ("Polytheism, Monotheism, and Religious Co-existence: Paganism and Christianity in the Roman Empire," Thomas Wiedemann, in *Religious Pluralism and Unbelief: Studies Critical and Comparative,* edited by Jan Hamnet [London, 1990], 73). For Christians, supporting civil society by making donations for public purposes for the sake of honor and glory was worldly and vain; not only did Christians fail to participate in the (pagan) civic ceremonies but they withdrew from the system on which public welfare depended and offered a set of values antithetical to it (ibid., 74). Since Roman paganism was the state religion, Christianity offered not simply a religious challenge but one to the state. Similarly charges against intellectuals such as Anaxagoras (banished from Athens for publishing his theory that the heavenly bodies were not gods but stones) or Socrates (convicted of teaching the young to believe in new deities instead of the gods the state recognized) were serious because the activities in question were potentially politically subversive, not simply because they conflicted with current religious belief.

17. My discussion concerns principal tendencies in Christianity and to some degree in Islam. An important difference between Judaism and Christianity as regards paganism appeared in the previous footnote, and Judaism retains many of the characteristics of a tribal religion— membership is chiefly through birth and is retained through continued participation in the ceremonies rather than through adopting a creed to which one continues to assent, for example—and many of the comments in what follows do not apply to it. Of course even in Christianity and Islam there are traditions rejecting or deemphasizing some of the principles on which I focus, and there are elements in these religions which could well be called 'pagan' (e.g., in Catholic Christianity the veneration of saints, who have many of the features of pagan deities: domains of special interest, the capacity to intervene in human life, etc.).

18. It is true that sometimes *philosophers* speculated on the general status of deities. As noted earlier, Epicurus, for example, held that the gods lived in the interstices between the worlds. But these are philosophical speculations and do not belong to religious belief or practice. They played no role in the religion itself, in the way that Aquinas's theology has deeply influenced Catholic Christianity, or Luther's or Calvin's thought Protestantism.

19. "Examples abound of ministrants of one sort or another erecting an altar or a plaque or themselves signing some honorific inscription, in worship of a god other than the one they served. The practice can be observed without distinction of honor and, whether Roman, traditional Greek, Oriental, or Celtic . . . " (Ramsay MacMullen, *Paganism in the Roman Empire* [New Haven, Conn., 1981], 93).

20. See, e.g., MacMullen, *Paganism in the Roman Empire,* 91. It is sometimes said that increased travel led to the comparison of one religious viewpoint with another and so to the desire to find out by rational means what true religious belief was. This is certainly not the ordinary reaction, which was typically one of tolerance and accommodation: "Given the pilgrims, traders, tourists, and above all, soldiers and civil servants [who] moved about from province to province, comparison of cults was inevitable; and the conclusions inevitably enriched the praises of this or that deity as being really (so worshipers believed) one and the same beneath a dozen local faces" (ibid.).

21. To mention just two: in *The New Polytheism: Rebirth of the Gods and Goddesses* (New York, 1974), David Miller mentions cultural, religious, and psychological factors supporting polytheism. And postmodernists sometimes describe their work as "pagan" (e.g., J.-F. Lyotard, "Lessons in Paganism," in *The Lyotard Reader,* edited by Andrew Benjamin [Oxford, 1991], 122–54). Lyotard is not concerned with the kind of spiritual issue on which I have focused but is more interested in principles he thinks are associated with classical paganism, e.g., the absence of a canonical narrative, ethical principles applied locally, a style of discourse. This suggests an emphasis altogether different from mine: paganism as a mode of thinking, applicable in political and ethical as well as spiritual contexts.

22. See "The Will to Believe," in *William James: Writings 1878–1899* (New York, 1992), 457–79. James, however, was concerned to show that one had the right to believe when lacking sufficient evidence; he did not specifically discuss matters typical of *cases:* mixed evidence bearing on complex issues with no clearly decisive considerations, and where reasonable people could analyze matters differently.

23. These considerations are marshaled against the ontological argument in my "The Argument from Perfection to Existence," *Philosophical Studies* (1968): 123–32.

24. For an anthropological discussion of present-day witchcraft, see T. M. Luhrmann, *Persuasions of the Witch's Craft: Ritual Magic in Contemporary England* (Cambridge, Mass., 1989).

25. I say "standard science" because of the possibility of nonstandard sciences—e.g., parapsychology—developed to study such supposed non-normal, or "paranormal," dimensions of reality. These investigations are scientific in attempting to apply rigorous techniques of investigation but adjusting them to the special subject-matters in question. Recall James's attempts to investigate what he considered to be unrecognized dimensions of reality through the examination of mediums such as Mrs. Piper, and his support of the Society for Psychic Research. There are also J. B. Rhine's careful studies of telepathy and other psychic phenomena. But even if such paranormal sciences were successful, one could hold that there are limits to this kind of investigation and that there are justified claims about other dimensions of reality not based on the techniques that even paranormal science employs: about dreams, for example.

26. Ronald Hutton, *The Pagan Religions of the Ancient British Isles—Their Nature and Legacy* (Oxford, 1991), 289–90.

27. Ibid., 291.

28. Ibid., 292.

29. Ibid., 291.

30. Ibid., 290.

31. This distinguishes ancient paganism from the contemporary variant called 'Wicca,' which, as Hutton notes, "deliberately blurs the distinction between religion and magic" and which draws most of its practices from the latter (ibid., p. 335). Hutton goes on to list a number of differences between the practices of ancient paganism and Wicca, and then concludes, "All told, the paganism of today has virtually nothing in common with that of the past except the name" (ibid., p. 337). This is unjustified. First, Wicca is only one version of contemporary paganism, many of which do not employ the methods characteristic of Wicca. More importantly, Hutton's comment ignores the motivations characteristic of paganism generally and so common to ancient and contemporary forms: the wish to acknowledge immediate areas of life and to celebrate nature and its cycles and processes. Present-day paganism can be regarded as an attempt to recapture this outlook and to implement it through means that seem appropriate today even if these may differ significantly from ancient practices.

32. This is not to imply that there is nothing positive to be said about the value and effectiveness of magic. I think there is, but this is a large issue distinct from the topic here.

33. See "Transcendental Arguments Revived," *Philosophical Investigations,* vol. 8, no. 4 (October 1985): 229–51.

34. This is certainly true for the physical sciences and pagan thought; some of the purposes and methods of psychology, on the other hand, may overlap with the goals and techniques of pagan spirituality. There are also attempts to unify the concepts and principles of the physical sciences with those of religion. These, however, have to be undertaken very carefully since

it is extremely easy to conflate considerations belonging to distinct conceptual levels—another large topic that must be set aside here.

35. Fortunately I have had the help of many people on this essay. Elise Wolf introduced me to contemporary paganism, theoretically and practically, and our conversations have been valuable sources of ideas. I am indebted in various ways also to John Billigmeier, Laurie Calhoun, Narayan Champawat, Chris Crittenden, James Goss, Heather Lind Greyville, James Kellenberger, Robert Kirchner, Christine Korsgaard, Linda Lam-Easton, Kristi Maki, Delia Morgan, James Peterman, Avilynn Pwyll, Renee Rothman, Elizabeth Say, John Schroeder, Diane Teagarden, Bergeth Tregenza, and Mark Whitaker. Discussion of an earlier version by the Religious Studies Department at California State University, Northridge, was very helpful. Susannah LeBaron's editorial comments and suggestions on the penultimate draft have improved the essay considerably.

MIDWEST STUDIES IN PHILOSOPHY, XXI (1997)

Praying for Things to Have Happened

THOMAS P. FLINT

"O. J.: I'm Praying That You Didn't Do It"
Sign seen outside the house of O. J. Simpson shortly after the murder of his former wife.[1]

According to the notion of providence common among traditional Christians, God is to be thought of as intimately involved with the lives of his creatures.[2] God not only creates, but also cares for all of those whom he brings into being. Part of this care is made manifest by God's speaking to us through prophetic utterances, inspired writings, infallible papal or conciliar pronouncements, and the like. But, of course, creatures are not solely the *recipients* of communication bridging the gap between the creator and the creature; often enough, we are the *initiators,* and God (we hope) is the recipient.[3] To put this in less academic language: We pray, and God (we trust) both hears us and fashions his overall providential plan in light of our prayers.

Prayer, of course, comes in a wide variety of forms. At times our prayer is simply an expression of praise, an explicit articulation of and celebration in God's glory. At other times, we pray to thank God, either for the general gifts of life and love which we constantly enjoy, or for more specific blessings which we feel God in his providence has bestowed upon us. And we often pray that God forgive us for what we have done, or what we have failed to do. Sometimes, though, we pray to ask God for certain things. It is this type of prayer—petitionary prayer—which will be my focus here.

Prayer of any form raises a number of interesting questions, and this is especially true with respect to petitionary prayer. We might ask, for example, for what is it appropriate to pray? Should we pray for specific goods, or only for di-

vine blessings of whatever sort God thinks best? If specifying goods is acceptable, may we pray for what we might call *external* (or *material* or *temporal*) goods,
such as health or wealth? If so, is it appropriate to pray for such goods both for
oneself and for others? Or is it proper, or at least better, to seek such goods only
for others? And what about (arguably) less important external goods? Is praying that one's favorite football team win their upcoming game acceptable? Or is
praying for *any* sort of external or material good, regardless of its significance,
somehow misguided? Should our prayer rather be directed toward *internal* or
spiritual goods, e.g., the development of virtue, the gift of grace, final salvation, and the like? Furthermore, to whom should our prayers for goods (of whatever sort) be addressed? To God? To Christ? To the Virgin Mary? To angels and
saints?[4]

These are but a few of the questions which arise when we begin to think
carefully about the topic of petitionary prayer. Theists, of course, would not answer all such questions with a single voice. Indeed, even among Christians, there
would be considerable disagreement over the questions listed above. Some of
these disputes, I suspect, are utterly irresolvable. Others may be adjudicable (to
a greater or lesser degree), but only by appeal to evidence and arguments that
are largely nonphilosophical in character. To expect philosophers to contribute
significantly to most of these debates is to expect far too much.

Still, I think there are at least a couple of issues relating to petitionary prayer where those philosophers who embrace what is commonly called the
Molinist picture of divine providence may well be able to shed some light. First,
why is it that our petitions so often appear to go unanswered? And second, does
it make sense to pray for things to have happened? The second of these questions
will be my concern in this essay. I will attempt to show that, given the Molinist
picture, praying for things to have happened is often a perfectly reasonable practice.

1. THE PROBLEM

Generally, petitionary prayer is *future*-oriented. Though we may thank God for
what he has done for us in the past, and praise him for what he is in the present,
we usually ask God to help us in the future. We ask God that marriage vows newly
made be kept; that this child being baptized have a rich and fruitful life; that this
loved one approaching death be granted eternal life in heaven. Sometimes, of
course, the future dimension of the object of our petition shades over into the
present. In praying that God give me strength against a particular temptation, I
may well be seeking such aid not only for the long-term or even near-term future
but for the very moment of prayer as well. Nevertheless, that our petitions are
usually directed at future events seems fairly clear.

Sometimes, though, it *seems* natural to pray concerning, not future or even
present events, but *past* events. Think, for example, of the mother whose (rather
foolhardy) child is late one Sunday night returning from a (rather foolhardy)
mountain-climbing expedition. Suppose this mother, whose preoccupation with

more rational activities (say, attending Philadelphia Phillies baseball games) had filled her weekend, hears on the Sunday evening news that the area in which her child was climbing was hit by a record-setting blizzard Saturday morning, and that there is great concern for the survival of those who were outdoors at the time. Would it not be natural for her to pray for the safety of her daughter? And would it not be natural for her to phrase this petition in the form of a prayer that certain things not *have happened?* ("Oh God, please let my daughter not have been harmed by the storm!")[5]

Such a prayer, an instance of what Michael Dummett calls *retrospective prayer,*[6] would not strike most Christians as odd or unusual. Indeed, most of us who are Christians have probably offered such a prayer at one time or another ourselves, and not felt philosophically indisposed in doing so. Of course, were we certain concerning the occurrence of the past event in question, things might be different. (Praying that World War III be prevented, most of us would agree, is beyond reproach; praying that World War I be prevented would surely raise more than a few eyebrows.)[7] Where we are genuinely unsure whether the prayed-for event occurs, though, praying often seems appropriate, whether the event be in the future or in the past.[8]

Yet, when we look at the matter more critically, we can easily begin to wonder whether this indifference to tense is so innocent as it seems. Most of us believe that the future is open in a sense that the past is not. Actions we perform now can have a causal impact upon what happens in the future. The past, however, is closed; it's over and done with; it's completely immune to any interference by our current activities. As philosophers, of course, we will be cognizant of the distinction between hard facts and soft facts, and thus realize that certain propositions which appear to be about the past—"It was true five years ago that I will vote in the presidential election of 2012"—may really be as much or more about the future, and thus are arguably not exempt from our causal impact. But the kinds of past facts concerning which people are inclined to pray are not at all the "funny" kind of facts which have given rise to the hard/soft distinction. They seem to be facts (such as that child's surviving the blizzard) which are about as hard as they come. Perhaps our prayers can have an impact on the future, but isn't it preposterous to think that they can causally affect the (hard) past? In short, however natural retrospective prayer may appear, isn't such activity essentially irrational?

2. MOLINISM TO THE RESCUE?

Most of us will no doubt feel some force to such an objection. Still, there may be at least one way to rescue retrospective petitionary prayer from the fate of the philosophically incorrect. If the Molinist picture of providence alluded to previously is accepted, an avenue of defense for retrospective prayer would appear to be open.

What is this Molinist picture? For present purposes, the following brief summary will have to suffice:

In essence, Molina attempted to fashion the strongest notion of divine providence compatible with genuine human freedom. He argued that, for any person who does or might have existed, God (being omniscient) would know, prior to any creative act on his part, what that person would freely do in any situation in which that person might be created and left free.[9] Given his commitment to libertarianism, though, Molina also argued that the truths God would thus know—truths of the form "If person P were to be placed in circumstances C, P would freely do A"—would not be truths over which God had any control, despite the fact that such conditionals would be only contingently true. For if libertarianism is correct, God could not just decide or causally determine which such propositions (which will be called *counterfactuals of creaturely freedom*) would be true; rather, their truth would have to be independent of the divine will. Molina saw such truths as constituting the most important segment of what he called God's *middle knowledge*—knowledge of contingent truths which are true independent of any free act of the divine will. Middle knowledge, Molina argued, would allow God to exercise sovereign control over his world, for it would inform him as to precisely what kind of world would result from the activity of any set of free creatures and circumstances he might decide to create. By consulting this knowledge, then, God would know which creative actions on his part would lead to the kind of world he desires. Hence, the whole world is indeed in God's hands; things are as they are because God knowingly decided to create such a world.[10]

A couple of clarifications concerning this much-disputed Molinist picture will aid in our discussion of retrospective prayer. First, Molinists typically have argued that the circumstances mentioned in the antecedents of counterfactuals of creaturely freedom are to be thought of as *complete*—i.e., as including the entire history (or at least the entire causal history) of the world prior to the time specified by the consequent, along with whatever influences are acting on the agent at that time. Antecedents less rich than this would yield counterfactuals which were not only less evidently true or false ("If Richard Nixon had been born in Rome, he would have decided to employ John Dean") but also not so evidently action-guiding for God, for counterfactuals with impoverished antecedents can differ in truth-value from their enriched analogues.[11] What God needs to know, one might think, and what he would base his providential activity upon, is what one of his creatures would do (so to speak) *all* things considered. Molinists needn't *deny* that there are true counterfactuals with incomplete antecedents, or that God has middle knowledge of them, but the experienced Molinist will recognize that endorsing the claim that God has "all things considered" counterfactual knowledge assures one of enough philosophical challenges for one lifetime, and hence will see no reason to harbor incomplete counterfactuals which can't be derived from full-fledged counterfactuals of creaturely freedom.

The second point is of more immediate relevance to our questions concerning retrospective prayer. As the Molinist sees it, our actions should be seen as having a causal impact neither upon God's knowledge nor upon God's will. God's creative decisions as to which beings he is to create in which circumstances are based upon his middle knowledge. If that middle knowledge were causally dependent upon our actions, then God's creative decisions would be similarly dependent. But that, of course, simply can't be; rather, our actions are causally dependent upon God's decision to create us in the circumstances in which those actions are performed. So we don't cause God to know what he knows by middle knowledge. But then, neither do we have any causal effect upon God's will, given that his decision as to who to create in what circumstances is based upon his middle knowledge. Hence, nothing that we do can have any causal effect upon what God knows or what God wills.

Of course, while denying such *causal* impact, the Molinist will insist that there are all sorts of *noncausal* connections between what we do and what God wills or knows. I may not be able to cause God to know what he knows, but if I'm free, then I do have the power to do things such that, were I to do them, both God's middle knowledge and his simple foreknowledge would have been other than they in fact were. Following Hasker's terminology, we might say that, though lacking *causal power* over God's knowledge or will, I might well have *counterfactual power* over them.[12]

The potential relevance of this distinction to our problem with retrospective prayer is easy to see. For if the Molinist is right, then *no* petitionary prayer of *any* sort has *any* causal effect upon God. If I pray that some future event occur (say, that the Phillies win the World Series next year), my prayer has no causal impact upon God whatsoever. It might still make a difference, but if so, that difference needs to be explicated in terms of middle knowledge and divine decisions which are causally prior to my praying. But if this is the account the Molinist offers of *prospective* petitionary prayer, why not offer the same account of *retrospective* petitionary prayer? Why not say that prayers concerning the past are efficacious in the same noncausal way as are prayers concerning the future? Why not, in brief, claim that prayer may afford us, not *causal,* but *counterfactual* power over the past?

Molinism thus appears to open the door to a solution to our problem. But whether it is a door we can enter safely remains to be seen. To suggest that I have counterfactual power over the past would be to assert that there is some true proposition strictly about the past and some action I now have the power to perform such that, if I were to perform that action, that proposition would not be true. The counterfactual involved in such an assertion is what is generally referred to as a back-tracking counterfactual, and the claim that there are true conditionals of this sort is viewed by many philosophers as suspect at best.[13] While a wholesale skepticism concerning such counterfactuals seems to me unwarranted, it might be prudent for the Molinist to grant that, given the strength of our intuition regarding the fixity of the hard past, the burden of proof in this case lies with the advocate of counterfactual power over the past.[14] Our question, then, is this: Can one build a strong case from a solid Molinist foundation for the claim that we have the type of counterfactual power over the past which would justify retrospective prayer?

3. ALVIN'S ANTS

The suggestion that we may have counterfactual power over the past is one which has been put forward in recent days by Alvin Plantinga, in a paper entitled "On Ockham's Way Out."[15] While denying that we have causal power over the past, Plantinga contends that there is no obstacle to thinking of ourselves as having counterfactual power even over hard facts about the past. Plantinga's example concerns Paul (who may or may not be related, perhaps even by identity, to Jones the Mower made famous by Nelson Pike[16]) and a certain army of arthropods:

> Let's suppose that a colony of carpenter ants moved into Paul's yard last Saturday. Since this colony hasn't yet had a chance to get properly established, its new home is still a bit fragile. In particular, if the ants were to remain and Paul were to mow his lawn this afternoon, the colony would be destroyed. Although nothing remarkable about these ants is visible to the naked eye, God, for reasons of his own, intends that the colony be preserved. Now as a matter of fact, Paul will not mow his lawn this afternoon. God, who is essentially omniscient, knew in advance, of course, that Paul will not mow his lawn this afternoon; but if he had foreknown instead that Paul *would* mow this afternoon, then he would have prevented the ants from moving in. The facts of the matter, therefore, are these: if Paul were to mow his lawn this afternoon, then God would have foreknown that Paul would mow his lawn this afternoon; and if God had foreknown that Paul would mow this afternoon, then God would have prevented the ants from moving in. So if Paul were to mow his lawn this afternoon, then the ants would not have moved in last Saturday. But it is within Paul's power to mow this afternoon. There is therefore an action he can perform such that if he were to perform it, then the proposition
>
> (A) That colony of carpenter ants moved into Paul's yard last Saturday.
>
> would have been false. But what I have called 'the facts of the matter' certainly seem to be possible; it is therefore possible that there be an agent who has the power to perform an action which is such that, if he were to perform it, then (A) would have been false. . . . [17]

The central argument which Plantinga is presenting here might be expressed as follows. Since God is omniscient, it follows that

(1) Paul mows → God foreknows that Paul mows,

where the single-line arrow stands for counterfactual implication. Given God's intention that the colony of carpenter ants be preserved, it's also true that

(2) God foreknows that Paul mows → God prevents the carpenter ants from moving in.

But, of course, if God prevents the ants from moving in, then they didn't move in last Saturday. So,

(3) God prevents the carpenter ants from moving in → ~(**A**).

And from (1) through (3), Plantinga claims, we can infer

(4) Paul mows → ~(**A**).

Therefore, Paul has the power to do something—namely, mow his lawn—such that, were he to do it, then something which as a matter of fact *is* a truth about the hard past—namely, (**A**)—would *not* have been a truth about the past. In other words, Paul has *counterfactual power* over the past.

If this idea of counterfactual power over the past makes sense, then so does the idea of praying for things to have happened. Suppose that we alter Plantinga's example just a bit. Suppose that Paul's wife Paula, while away from home last weekend (searching for that benighted mountaineering daughter), hears on the news that there was a massive carpenter-ant invasion in parts of her hometown on Saturday. Knowing that their lawn is in bad enough shape as it is (or was), Paula considers praying that their lawn was one of those spared. She *considers* doing so—but that's all; no actual prayer for the safety of her lawn comes forth from Paula. Foreseeing this failure to pray by Paula, God allows the ants to enter their yard. However, had he foreseen that Paula *would* pray, God in his goodness would have seen to it that the ants avoid Paul and Paula's property.

Using this altered example, we can construct an argument parallel to Plantinga's to show that Paula's prayer would have made a difference with respect to the ants' having invaded her lawn. Given God's omniscience, it follows that

(5) Paula prays that their lawn have been spared → God foreknows that Paula prays that their lawn have been spared.

As we've described the case, it's also true that

(6) God foreknows that Paula prays that their lawn have been spared → God prevents the carpenter ants from moving in.

But, of course,

(3) God prevents the carpenter ants from moving in → ~(**A**).

So, from (5), (6), and (3) we could derive

(7) Paula prays that their lawn have been spared → ~(**A**).

Paula, then, has counterfactual power over the past; i.e., she has the power to do something (pray) such that, were she to do it, a fact about the past (that the ants moved in) would not have been a fact about the past. Paula's decision not to pray, then, can appropriately be seen as making a difference with respect to **(A)**'s having been true. Thus, her praying that the carpenter ants not have invaded would have been anything but irrational.

If the notion of this type of counterfactual power over the past makes sense, then, our problem seems solved: Retrospective prayer turns out to be philosophically beyond reproach. And since Plantinga's story and our variation on it make the notion of counterfactual power over the past seem plausible enough, at least for one with Molinist sympathies, one might think that we are indeed out of the woods on this one.

4. COUNTERFACTUAL POWER: SOME CAUSES FOR CONCERN

My fear, though, is that these woods are darker and deeper than our discussion thus far has acknowledged. For, despite its surface plausibility, Plantinga's argument for the conclusion that Paul could have counterfactual power over the past should give a Molinist concern for at least three reasons.

First, the argument as presented offers a picture of divine action which appears misleading from the Molinist perspective. On that perspective, recall, God's activity in the world is guided by his middle knowledge, while his foreknowledge, which simply follows from that activity and middle knowledge, plays no action-guiding role whatsoever. As Plantinga presents things here, though, foreknowledge at least appears to be that upon which God is relying in reaching his creative decisions, while middle knowledge seems to be entirely absent from the process. Consider again (2). What it seems to be telling us is that God's decision to prevent the carpenter ants from moving in would have followed from his foreknowledge that Paul would mow. And this, the Molinist will insist, is mistaken; it's middle knowledge, not foreknowledge, which guides divine activity.

This first concern needs to be taken seriously, for it is not unknown for philosophers to give to foreknowledge the role which, if Molinism is correct, is properly ascribed only to middle knowledge.[18] Still, it's important to note that Plantinga's argument, though silent regarding middle knowledge, need not be seen as rejecting it. At first glance, (2) may *appear* to place foreknowledge in a role the Molinist would deny it, but the simple affirmation of such a counterfactual need not have so dire an implication. For despite its appearance, (2) needn't be seen as a conditional which displays God's *reason* for acting. Couldn't (2) be a truth which simply *follows* from other counterfactuals of freedom, both creaturely and divine?

Plantinga's argument, then, is not necessarily weakened by the fact that middle knowledge doesn't play a starring role in that argument, for it could conceivably hold an essential, though off-screen, position. Molinists may prefer that God's middle knowledge be given top billing in arguments which rely upon it, but they ought not inflate such presentational predilections into substantive objections.

A second cause for concern centers on the fact that Plantinga's argument appears to rely upon a fallacious rule of inference. For that argument is most plausibly read as suggesting that (4) follows directly from (1) through (3) via transitivity. Since transitivity is not a valid rule of inference for counterfactuals, it follows that the argument Plantinga offers is invalid.

This second concern, like the first, points, I think, to a genuine expository infelicity in Plantinga's discussion. But, as in the first case, we ought not assume that this weakness of presentation points to a serious weakness in the argument. Though Plantinga makes it look as though (4) is derived via transitivity, one can in fact derive it in perfectly legitimate ways. For example, since what God foreknows cannot be untrue, it follows that

(8) God foreknows that Paul mows → Paul mows.

From (1), (8), and (2), it follows via the valid inferential principle *If $(X \to Y)$, $(Y \to X)$ and $(Y \to Z)$, then $(X \to Z)$* that

(9) Paul mows → God prevents the carpenter ants from moving in.

But then, since (3) is not only a truth, but a necessary truth—i.e., since

(10) □[God prevents the carpenter ants from moving in → ~**(A)**]

is true—we can derive (4) from (9) and (10) via the valid inferential principle *If $(X \to Y)$ and $□(Y \to Z)$, then $(X \to Z)$*. So, appearances to the contrary notwithstanding, Plantinga's line of reasoning is not in fact invalid.[19]

A final concern the Molinist might have is that Plantinga's argument obscures the fact that actions are always performed in a specific set of circumstances. As we've seen, Molinists believe that the antecedents of counterfactuals of creaturely freedom specify such circumstances, which are to be thought of as including the complete causal history of the world prior to the time in question, along with all simultaneous exercises of causal power by other agents. In Plantinga's argument, though, Paul's mowing appears to be taking place in a circumstantial vacuum. There is no mention in any of the premises, or in the conclusion, of the circumstances conditioning Paul's action.

Now, one might feel that this was a mere oversight on Plantinga's part, and that we could, if we so desired, simply plug the relevant circumstances into the premises and conclusions with no adverse effect. When we try to do so, though, we quickly discover that things are not so simple. Let C stand for the circumstances in which Paul found himself. As usual, C is to be thought of as including the complete causal history of the world prior to the time in question. Were we simply to include reference to C in the premises and conclusion of Plantinga's argument, we'd end up with the following:

(1*) (Paul mows in C) → (God foreknows that Paul mows in C).

(2*) (God foreknows that Paul mows in C) → (God prevents the carpenter ants from moving in).

(3) God prevents the carpenter ants from moving in → ~**(A)**.

∴ (4*) (Paul mows in C) → ~**(A)**.

Though superficially similar to Plantinga's actual argument, this line of reason suffers from the malady of being palpably unsound. C, recall, is supposed to include all exercises of causal power prior to the time of Paul's action. But then C includes the fact that the ants moved in last Saturday. So C by itself entails that **(A)** is true. Hence, (4*) could be true only if it were impossible that Paul mow in C. Since it isn't, something is obviously amiss with this argument.

The source of the problem is easy to pinpoint: since (1*) and (3) are both necessary truths, it must be (2*) which is mucking up the works. And so indeed it is; (2*) is not only false, but necessarily false. For if God foreknows that Paul mows in C, then, given that C includes the fact that the ants moved in, God foreknows that Paul mows in the wake of the ants' moving in. But then God knows that the ants did move in, and so will hardly act so as to bring it about that they didn't move in.

If we wish to incorporate reference to the circumstances of action in Plantinga's argument, then, it can't be reference to the complete set of circumstances which *actually* obtained, but rather to some other set of circumstances. If these circumstances were to include the ants' having moved in, though, we would have made no progress, for our conclusion would still be clearly false. So, we might think, the circumstances need to include the statement that the ants *didn't* move in. Indeed, if our replacement for (2*) is to come out true, one might argue, the circumstances need to entail that God prevented their moving in. Perhaps, then, there is some such set of circumstances C^* entailing the falsity of **(A)** which will do the trick. If so, our circumstance-incorporating variation on Plantinga's argument would look like this:

(1**) (Paul mows in C^*) → (God foreknows that Paul mows in C^*).

(2**) (God foreknows that Paul mows in C^*) → (God prevents the carpenter ants from moving in).

(3) God prevents the carpenter ants from moving in → ~**(A)**.

∴ (4**) (Paul mows in C^*) → ~**(A)**.

This argument has the advantage of being both valid and sound. Given the restrictions we set up for C^*, each of the three premises is not only true but necessary; and since transitivity holds for strict implications, it's clear that the derivation of (4**) is indeed valid. Unfortunately, this argument fails to show that Paul has counterfactual power over the past. For Paul is actually in C, not in C^*. The fact that he could do something in circumstances which don't actually obtain which would counterfactually imply that **(A)** is false no more shows that Paul has counterfactual power over **(A)** than the fact that I could buy the Sears Tower, had I inherited a billion dollars last year, shows that I have counterfactual power over my not owning the Sears Tower.

If we wish to leave the reference to the complete circumstances in the argument, we clearly need to supplement the argument if it is to be used to support the possibility of our having counterfactual power over the past. One, and perhaps the only, way to do this would be to add a premise at the start of the argument stating that, had Paul mowed, C^* would have been the circumstances in which he was mowing, i.e.,

(11) Paul mows $\rightarrow C^*$.[20]

When combined with (1**) through (3), this would allow us to derive

(4) Paul mows $\rightarrow \sim$**(A)**

as our conclusion, and this conclusion, of course, would allow us to say that Paul has counterfactual power over **(A)**.

The problem with this supplemented argument, though, is that it appears perilously close to begging the question. The point of the argument, after all, is to *show* that it's possible that an agent such as Paul has the power to do something such that, were he to do it, the past would have been different than it in fact was. But if we use (11) as a *premise* in our argument, then we're simply *assuming* that which we were attempting to show. For to assume both that (11) is true and that Paul has the power to mow just is to assume that Paul has the power to do something such that, were he to do it, the past would have been different than it in fact was (C^* rather than C would have obtained). So I don't think we make any headway in demonstrating the possibility of counterfactual power over the past by bringing (11) into the discussion.

The ramifications of this result should not be minimized. Making no reference to the complete set of circumstances in which Paul acts, which at first appeared to be merely an accidental oversight by Plantinga, now at least appears to be essential to his argument's viability. In a sense, this should not surprise us; after all, *many* back-tracking counterfactuals can be held true only if their antecedents are not held to be complete. Still, to the Molinist who feels that reference to circumstances cannot be so easily dismissed, and who grants that the sort of controversial counterfactuals required for counterfactual power over the past should be endorsed only insofar as we can see them as grounded in full-fledged counterfactuals of creaturely freedom, the fact that the argument Plantinga actually presents seems resistant to such grounding should lead to a significant degree of dissatisfaction with it.

5. AN ALTERNATIVE TO COUNTERFACTUAL POWER OVER THE PAST?

To the extent that one is dissatisfied with Plantinga's argument concerning Paul, of course, one will also be dissatisfied with our parallel argument concerning

Paula, and consequently still skeptical about the practice of praying for things to have happened. A natural strategy to blunt such skepticism would be to find some other way of arguing for the possibility of counterfactual power over the past, and this is a strategy I will in fact pursue in the next section. But before I do so, it might be instructive to consider whether there might not be another way for the Molinist to proceed. Is there, perhaps, an *alternative* to counterfactual power which allows a connection between our current activities and past events sufficient to make retrospective prayer reasonable?

One possibility is suggested by Freddoso in a footnote to the introduction to his translation of Molina.[21] Let C continue to stand for the set of circumstances in which Paul (in Plantinga's story) finds himself, a set of circumstances which *includes* the fact that the ants moved into his yard last Saturday. Since we are looking here for an alternative to counterfactual power over the past, let us assume here that Paul lacks such power, and hence assume that were Paul to mow, he would do so in C. In other words, let us assume that the counterfactual *Paul mows* $\rightarrow$ *Paul mows in C* is true. Now, if Paul were to mow in these circumstances, then clearly the counterfactual of creaturely freedom stating that he would mow if in C would be true. Thus,

(12) (Paul mows in C) $\rightarrow$ ($C \rightarrow$ Paul mows).

So, given that Paul is free either to mow or not to mow in C, and given that, were he not to mow, ($C \rightarrow$ Paul mows) would have been false, it follows that Paul has counterfactual power over this counterfactual of creaturely freedom. But God, of course, has middle knowledge of all true counterfactuals of creaturely freedom. So we also know that

(13) ($C \rightarrow$ Paul mows) $\rightarrow$ [God has middle knowledge that ($C \rightarrow$ Paul mows)].

Indeed, since (13) is *necessarily* true (because it's impossible that God be ignorant of a true counterfactual of creaturely freedom), we can conclude from (12) and (13) that

(14) (Paul mows in C) $\rightarrow$ [God has middle knowledge that ($C \rightarrow$ Paul mows)].

Of course, Paul doesn't actually mow in C, and since ($C \rightarrow$ Paul mows) is in fact false, God doesn't have middle knowledge of it. Hence, we are justified in concluding that Paul has counterfactual power over God's middle knowledge. That is, he has the power to perform an action such that, were he so to act, then God's middle knowledge would have been different than it in fact is. Even if counterfactual power over the past were dubious from a Molinist perspective, counterfactual power over God's middle knowledge would be undeniable.

Now in Plantinga's story, recall, God wants the colony of carpenter ants to survive. Had he known by middle knowledge, then, that Paul would mow if placed in C, God would presumably have seen to it that Paul is not placed in C. There are various ways in which he might have done this, but one way would be to prevent the ants from moving in last Saturday. So it may well be true that

(15) [God has middle knowledge that $(C \to$ Paul mows)] $\to$ God prevents the carpenter ants from moving in.

Since, as we've already seen,

(3) God prevents the carpenter ants from moving in $\to$ ~(**A**)

is true, and (more importantly) necessarily true, we could deduce from (15) and (3) that

(16) [God has middle knowledge that $(C \to$ Paul mows)] $\to$ ~(**A**).

So the truth of (**A**) depends counterfactually upon what it is God knows via middle knowledge.

Now, one who questioned our working assumption in this section (that we have no counterfactual power over the past) might think that from (14) and (16) one could reach the kind of conclusion Plantinga reached. That is, one might be tempted to propose the following argument.

(14) (Paul mows in C) $\to$ [God has middle knowledge that $(C \to$ Paul mows)].

(16) [God has middle knowledge that $(C \to$ Paul mows)] $\to$ ~(**A**).

∴ (4*) (Paul mows in C) $\to$ ~(**A**).

But this, of course, would be to make the mistake once again of thinking that the counterfactual relation is transitive. Nor can we derive (4*) via use of the valid inference schemes we suggested warranted Plantinga's derivation of (4) from (1) through (3).[22] Indeed, there *can* be no way in which we can properly get to (4*), for, as we noted in our earlier discussion of Plantinga's argument, (4*) is quite evidently false. Since C includes the fact that the carpenter ants *did* move in last Saturday, Paul's mowing *in C* will in fact *entail* that (**A**) is *true*. So (4*) is not simply false, but necessarily false. Hence, we *shouldn't* be able to derive it from two truths such as (14) and (16).

Looking at the matter from this decidedly Molinist perspective, then, seems to offer us no reason to question our working assumption that Paul has no counterfactual power over the past. What we seem justified in saying, rather, is only this: Paul has the power to do something (mow in C) such that, were he to do it, God's middle knowledge would have been different; and had God's middle knowledge been different in that way, God would have prevented the ants from moving in, thereby both rendering (**A**) false and changing the situation in which Paul as a matter of fact found himself.

Now, were one so inclined, one might still think of Paul as having a kind of power over the past, though a kind even weaker than the counterfactual power Plantinga has in mind. Following a hint from Freddoso, one might even distinguish between *strong* and *weak* counterfactual power.[23] Strong counterfactual power would be what we have heretofore been calling simply counterfactual power, the type of power Plantinga is ascribing to Paul. This kind of power, one might say, can be understood in the following way:

> S has *strong counterfactual power* over truth V iff for some X,
>> (i) S has the power to cause it to be the case that X, and
>> (ii) $X \rightarrow \sim V$.

Weak counterfactual power, on the other hand, would refer to the kind of relationship between Paul and the ants' entry which we have suggested Molinists should endorse. More formally, we might say:

> S has *weak counterfactual power* over truth V iff for some Y,
>> (i) S has strong counterfactual power over Y, and
>> (ii) $\sim Y \rightarrow \sim V$.

As Molinists, then, even were we to deny that Paul has strong counterfactual power over the past, we ought still to affirm that he has strong counterfactual power over God's middle knowledge. And if he does, then he may well have weak counterfactual power over the past.

Many Molinists (myself and Freddoso included) might well be somewhat perturbed by the language involved here. After all, if the ants would still have moved in no matter *what* Paul were to do, isn't it (at best) misleading to speak of him as having *any* sense of power over the truth of (A)? But suppose we put our stylistic qualms to the side and agree to abide by the terminology introduced above. The important question seems to be this: Is weak counterfactual power over the past enough to justify the practice of praying for things to have happened?

I'm not sure, but I fear that it is not. Consider again the case of Paula, Paul's wife, who considers praying that their lawn have been exempt from the carpenter ant invasion. If our suspicion that there is no strong counterfactual power over the past is correct, then our earlier way of justifying her past-directed prayer can no longer be maintained. For

> (7) Paula prays that her lawn have been spared $\rightarrow \sim$(A)

would no longer be tenable. And if (A) would have been true *whether or not* Paula prayed, it's at least difficult to see her failure to pray as making any difference.

This, of course, is not to say that the Molinist should reject the notion of weak counterfactual power. Indeed, given the reasoning outlined above, a Molinist denial of our weak counterfactual power over the past seems simply indefensible. Furthermore, there may well be contexts in which it is valuable to point to the distinction between weak and strong counterfactual power. My suspicion, though, is that this is not one of those contexts. If we have *only* weak counterfactual power over the past, the practice of praying for things to have happened appears insupportable.

6. STRONG COUNTERFACTUAL POWER RESURRECTED

If we are to defend this practice, then, it seems that we need to find some way to justify the claim that we can have strong counterfactual power over the past. But how, we might wonder, can we do so? Plantinga's argument, as we saw, seems difficult to formulate once we try to incorporate reference to the circumstances of action in it, while our Molinist successor to his argument warrants only the claim that we have weak counterfactual power over the past. Is there a way to resuscitate one or both of these arguments?

Perhaps. In each of these arguments, we suggested, the circumstances in which an action occurs ought not to be ignored. Furthermore, we argued, circumstances are to be thought of in the rich Molinist sense as including the complete causal history of the world, for only counterfactuals which include such complete circumstances in their antecedents qualify as counterfactuals of creaturely freedom. Though both of these points seem to me nonnegotiable, perhaps they have blinded us to a fact which is easy to forget: middle knowledge is not *simply* knowledge of counterfactuals of creaturely freedom. *Any* contingent truth not under divine control will be part of God's middle knowledge, and some of these truths (e.g., contingent truths entailed by counterfactuals of creaturely freedom) will not themselves be counterfactuals of creaturely freedom. In particular, middle knowledge can include counterfactuals with *incomplete* antecedents—antecedents which specify only a *part* of the circumstances in which a free action is performed. Perhaps what we need to do is see if focusing upon conditionals of this type can help us justify the possibility of strong counterfactual power over the past and thereby undergird past-directed prayer.[24]

Consider once again the case of Paula's failing to pray that her lawn have been free of the ants—i.e., failing to pray that **(A)** be false. Paula's situation, we noted, is one of uncertainty concerning **(A)**. Indeed, though many factors play a role in her free decision not to pray—her existing, her being free, her desire to have an ant-free lawn, her belief that there is a God who sometimes answers prayers, her having developed a degree of laxity concerning prayer, her uncertainty concerning whether her lawn was invaded, and the like—**(A)**'s being true or false does not seem to be such a factor. **(A)**, we know, is actually true—the ants *did* move in—but Paula, unaware of this fact, considers praying that it be false before deciding not to do so. Had **(A)** been false, there is no reason to think Paula's action would have been different in the slightest.

Suppose, then, that we divide the circumstances in which Paula finds herself into two categories. First, consider only that subset of the circumstances which are *counterfactually relevant* to her free activity. Paula's beliefs about God, her desire for a healthy lawn, her laziness, and so on, are plausible candidates for membership in this subset (call it *S*), for it's reasonable to think that her activity wouldn't have been exactly the same had they not been present. Second, consider all those parts of the circumstances which are *counterfactually irrelevant* to Paula's freely acting as she does. Facts such as that someone in China lit a cigarette five seconds prior to the time in question, or that a certain iguana 8,000 miles away from Paula is opening its eyes at the time of her action, would presumably be part of this subset (call it T). And, as we've seen, so (apparently) would the fact that the ants moved into Paula's yard last Saturday. **(A)**, then, is presumably also in T.

Together, S and T make up the complete set of circumstances in which Paula was placed. As we know, this was a set of circumstances in which she decided not to pray that God spare her lawn. So

(17) [(Paula is in S) and T] → Paula doesn't pray that their lawn have been spared

is a true conditional with a complete antecedent; hence, God would know (17) by middle knowledge. Suppose, though, that T *hadn't* obtained. Would

(18) [(Paula is in S) and $\sim T$] → Paula doesn't pray that their lawn have been spared

also be an element of God's middle knowledge? It seems to me that it would. T could have failed to obtain in many different ways. It would not have obtained had that Chinese smoker not lit up, or had that iguana not opened its eyes, or had the ants not moved into Paula's yard last Saturday. But whichever way T failed to obtain—i.e., whichever non-T way we choose to supplement S so as to form a complete set of circumstances for Paula—it seems that Paula still would not have prayed, given our assumption that T includes only circumstances irrelevant to her action.[25] So there are, it would seem, infinitely many harmonizing counterfactuals of creaturely freedom which together entail (18). Hence, (18), then, would also seem to be part of God's middle knowledge.

If (17) and (18) are both part of middle knowledge, though, a solution to our problem finally appears in sight. For (17) and (18) together entail

(19) (Paula is in S) → Paula doesn't pray that their lawn have been spared.

Since (19) is a contingent truth entailed by two elements of God's middle knowledge, it too must be part of God's middle knowledge. Suppose that we henceforth abbreviate (19) as

(19) S → Paula doesn't pray.

As we've seen,

(20) (S → Paula doesn't pray) ⇒ [God has middle knowledge that (S → Paula doesn't pray)],

where the double-line arrow stands for entailment (i.e., for strict implication). Suppose, though, that (19) had been false. Suppose it had been the case that Paula *would* have prayed had she been in S—i.e., that

(21) S → Paula prays

had been true. Presumably God would have known (21) had it been true. And, had it been true, it presumably would have followed from a group of harmonizing complete counterfactuals of creaturely freedom, just as we've seen that (19) does actually so follow. So we seem justified in asserting that

(22) $(S \to$ Paula prays$) \Rightarrow$ [God has middle knowledge that $(S \to$ Paula prays$)$].

Of course, we also know that

(23) (Paula prays in S) $\to$ $(S \to$ Paula prays$)$.

And from (23) and (22) it follows that

(24) (Paula prays in S) $\to$ [God has middle knowledge that $(S \to$ Paula prays$)$].

Now, if God had known that Paula would pray if placed in S, perhaps he would have seen via middle knowledge that much good would result were he to place her in S and answer her prayer by seeing to it that the ants avoided her lawn. That is, it might well be true that both

(25) [God has middle knowledge that $(S \to$ Paula prays$)$] $\to$ Paula prays in S

and

(26) [God has middle knowledge that $(S \to$ Paula prays$)$] $\to$ God prevents the carpenter ants from moving in.

But (24), (25), and (26) together entail

(27) (Paula prays in S) $\to$ God prevents the carpenter ants from moving in.

Since

(3) God prevents the carpenter ants from moving in $\to$ ~**(A)**

is a necessary truth, it would then follow from (27) and (3) that

(28) (Paula prays in S) $\to$ ~**(A)**.

And (28), of course, is precisely the type of conclusion we need. For it tells us that Paula has strong counterfactual power over the past: there is an action Paula has the power to perform (namely, pray) in the (incomplete) circumstances she is in (namely, S) such that, were she to perform that action, the ants would not have moved into her yard. Paula's retrospective prayer, then, would really have made a difference with regard to how things went last Saturday.

Let us briefly consider two objections to this line of reasoning. The first of these objections contends that the argument offered above for (28) is faulty, while the second objection grants the soundness but questions the relevance of the argument.

Our first objection goes as follows. The argument offered for (28) depends upon the claim that **(A)** is counterfactually irrelevant to Paula's activity. But, one might ask, couldn't this claim be false? Might there not be some bizarre counterfactual connection between the ants and Paula such that, had they *not* moved in last Saturday, she *wouldn't* have acted as she in fact did? If so, then **(A)** would have to rank as one of the relevant circumstances—as part of S—and so the argument to (28) would be blocked.

We Molinists, of course, are in no position to deny the possibility of bizarre counterfactual connections. So we have little choice but to concede the possibility that **(A)** is counterfactually relevant to Paula's action. It seems to me, though, that such a possibility does little to undermine the case being made here for the legitimacy of retrospective prayer. For even if the counterfactuals concerning Paula and the ants were bizarre in the way described, she would surely be ignorant of this fact. Only if one knew, or reasonably believed, that one's counterfactuals were bizarre could one know, or reasonably believe, that one's retrospective prayer could make no difference. Since hardly anyone can know, or reasonably believe, this about themselves, the rationality of such prayer seems untouched by this first objection.

Our second objection grants that the argument for (28) succeeds, but denies that its success establishes the rationality of retrospective prayer. Since (28) makes reference only to *in*complete circumstances, it doesn't change the fact that Paula is actually in *complete* circumstances, circumstances which would have obtained no matter what she had done. Hence, attempting to influence the past via prayer remains irrational even if the argument for (28) is accepted.[26]

As I see it, this objection amounts to little more than begging the question, for it asks us to assume that circumstances which are complete are ipso facto beyond one's counterfactual power. Furthermore, the assumption in question is in fact untenable if, as the objection grants, the argument for (28) is sound. For, in the case of Paula, that assumption would lead us to say that, had Paula prayed, she would have prayed in C, the complete set of circumstances composed of S and T. Consider, then, what follows if we make this assumption:

(29)	Paula prays → Paula prays in C	[assumption for *reductio*]
(30)	Paula prays in C ⇒ Paula prays in S	[necessary truth]
(31)	Paula prays → Paula prays in S	(29), (30)
(32)	Paula prays in S → Paula prays	[necessary truth]
(28)	Paula prays in S → ~**(A)**	[argument in text]
(33)	Paula prays → ~**(A)**	(31), (32), (28)
(34)	~**(A)** ⇒ ~(Paula prays in C)	[necessary truth]
(35)	Paula prays → ~(Paula prays in C)	(33), (34)

Given that it's possible that Paula prays, (29) and (35) cannot both be true. But the only contingent premises needed to derive (35) were (29) itself and (28). So (29) and (28) cannot both be true. Now the objector, we have been supposing, grants that we have a solid Molinist argument for (28). On the other hand, we have no real argument for (29). So, unless some problem with the argument for (28) can be uncovered, we have good reason to reject (29). In other words, one who accepts our argument has no choice but to grant that completeness does not entail fixity; had Paula prayed, the complete circumstances in which she prayed would have been different from those which in fact obtained.

7. CONCLUSION

Praying for things to have happened, then, seems to be defensible. Of course, the argument we have given for this conclusion depends essentially on Molinist assumptions concerning God's middle knowledge. So perhaps our conclusion should be stated more as a hypothetical: *If* Molinism is defensible, then so is the practice of praying for things to have happened. Some with Geachian qualms concerning retrospective prayer will no doubt see this as but one more reason to steer clear of Molinism. But, as I noted at the start of our discussion, I think that few believers find universal skepticism regarding such prayer to be attractive. For those in the majority here, the fact that Molinism allows us to justify such activity will surely count as a point in its favor. For those already convinced of the truth of Molinism, its ability to defend praying for things to have happened will most likely be seen as but one more illustration of the theory's fecundity.[27]

NOTES

1. Reported on National Public Radio on June 22, 1994. Curiously, the NPR commentator interpreted the sign as part of an endeavor to *change* the past, and thus as an indication of the irrationality which was surrounding this case. My thanks to Trenton Merricks for calling this report to my attention.

2. In speaking (here and throughout the essay) of the Christian belief in providence, my intent is not to imply either that Christians alone hold God to be provident or that non-Christian conceptions of providence are fundamentally different from that notion common among Christians. The issues and problems I will examine are ones of obvious interest to Christians, and hence I will discuss them from a traditional Christian perspective, but many people who do not share that perspective may surely find those issues and problems of interest.

3. To speak of ourselves as initiators would be misleading if we were to think of our prayers as arising solely from ourselves. Most reflective Christians would surely concede that the very impetus toward prayer is of divine origin. Insofar as this impetus is nondetermining, though, speaking of ourselves as initiating acts of prayer is probably harmless—at least, as long as we remind ourselves that our action, in this as in every case, is essentially reactive.

4. It should come as no shock to readers to hear that many of these, along with other, questions are discussed with characteristic ingenuity and insight by Aquinas. See especially *Summa Theologiae,* 2a2ae, question 83.

5. Michael Kremer has pointed out to me that such prayers could be interpreted as disguised prospective ones; e.g., the mother might really be praying that she see her daughter alive and well again. Such interpretations, though perhaps appropriate in certain contexts, seem to me generally strained and often utterly implausible. Suppose that the mother in our example were to discover that her daughter had indeed died in the storm. Could her subsequent prayer,

"Oh God, please let her not have suffered long," seriously be interpreted as directed toward the *future?*

6. Michael Dummett, "Bringing About the Past," in *Truth and Other Enigmas* (Cambridge, Mass., 1978), 335.

7. If I'm convinced that something *did* happen, praying that it *not* happen seems odd. But what about praying that it *did* happen when I'm convinced that it *did* happen? Things seem less clear here. At the end of Book Nine of the *Confessions,* Augustine asks his readers to pray for the repose of the soul of his mother. Are those of us who know her as *Saint* Monica, and thus are convinced of her having received the beatific vision, absolved of all responsibility to do as Augustine asks? Is it perhaps possible that Monica attained sanctity at least in part as a result of the prayers offered for her in response to Augustine's entreaty, including prayers offered by those who already believed in her sanctity? Monica's prayers are often, and I think rightly, viewed as partly responsible for her son's salvation; might it not also be true that the prayers of her son and his readers are partly responsible for her salvation? These questions deserve much more space than I can allot them here. (So do other, closely related ones—e.g., Is *all* prayer for the dead properly understood as prayer that the dead *have been aided* in a certain way *while still alive,* and hence is all such prayer reasonable only insofar as retrospective prayer more generally is reasonable?) What seems obvious, though, is that the answers are not as obvious as one might have thought.

8. For much-discussed presentations of this view, see both the Dummett piece cited above and C. S. Lewis, *Miracles* (New York, 1947), 185–86. For an oft-cited and vigorous attack upon the view, see Peter Geach, "Praying for Things to Happen," *God and the Soul* (London, 1969), 86–99.

9. In speaking of God's having knowledge of persons who might have existed, we are speaking a bit loosely. One way to tighten up our discussion here would be to see God as having prevolitional knowledge, not of persons, but of individual essences.

10. Thomas P. Flint, "Prophecy, Freedom and Middle Knowledge," in *Our Knowledge of God,* edited by Kelly James Clark (Dordrecht, 1992), 158–59. For more on Molina's position and his criticisms of the alternatives, see Luis de Molina, *On Divine Foreknowledge: Part IV of the Concordia,* edited and translated by Alfred J. Freddoso (Ithaca, N.Y., 1988), especially Disputation 52. For further elaborations of the Molinist position, see Freddoso's Introduction to his translation; my "Two Accounts of Providence," in *Divine and Human Action,* edited by Thomas V. Morris (Ithaca, N.Y., 1988), 147–81; and my "Hasker's *God, Time and Knowledge,*" *Philosophical Studies* 60 (1991): 103–15. Robert Adams and William Hasker have emerged as among the most insightful critics of the Molinist account. For the former, see "Middle Knowledge and the Problem of Evil," *American Philosophical Quarterly* 14 (1977): 109–17, and "An Anti-Molinist Argument," *Philosophical Perspectives* 5 (1991): 343–53; for the latter, see William Hasker, *God, Time and Knowledge* (Ithaca, N.Y., 1989), chapter 2, and "Response to Thomas Flint," *Philosophical Studies* 60 (1991): 117–26.

11. See Freddoso, "Introduction," 50. The notion of the causal history of the world—basically, the conjunction of all the "hard" facts—also comes from Freddoso; see p. 59.

12. See Hasker, *God, Time, and Knowledge,* chapter 6, especially p. 103.

13. For the principal reasons for such skepticism, see David Lewis, "Counterfactual Dependence and Time's Arrow," *Nous* 13 (1979): 455–76, reprinted, along with three postscripts, in both David Lewis, *Philosophical Papers,* vol. 2 (Oxford, 1986), and Frank Jackson, ed., *Conditionals* (Oxford, 1991).

14. For a persuasive argument to this effect, see Linda Trinkaus Zagzebski, *The Dilemma of Freedom and Foreknowledge* (New York, 1991), 98–106.

15. Alvin Plantinga, "On Ockham's Way Out," *Faith and Philosophy* 3 (1986): 235–69. Reprinted in *The Concept of God,* edited by Thomas V. Morris (New York, 1987), 171–200. Page references are to this reprint. Readers should note that, though the *concept* of counterfactual power over the past is clearly one which Plantinga is endorsing, the *terminology* stems not from him but from William Hasker. See note 12.

16. Nelson Pike, "Divine Omniscience and Voluntary Action," *Philosophical Review* 74 (1965): 27–46.

17. Plantinga, "On Ockham's Way Out," 189–90. What I have labelled **(A)** is (34) in Plantinga's essay.

18. See, for example, Dummett, "Bringing About the Past," 336–38.

19. One might also validly derive (4) by thinking of the antecedents of (2) and (3) as tacitly including the statement that Paul mows. Plantinga has informed me that this is, in fact, how he thought of the argument as proceeding.

20. Strictly speaking, (11) should be stated as "Paul mows $\rightarrow C^*$ *obtains.*" To simplify the presentation, I will generally refrain from writing the "obtains" in such cases.

21. Freddoso, p. 59, n. 80.

22. Were it the case that

(15*) [God has middle knowledge that (C $\rightarrow$ Paul mows)] $\rightarrow$ Paul mows in C,

(4*) would follow from (14), (15*), and (16) via the valid inferential principle *If $(X \rightarrow Y)$, $(Y \rightarrow X)$, and $(Y \rightarrow Z)$, then $(X \rightarrow Z)$.* But (15*) isn't true if (16) is. For the latter tells us that **(A)** would have been false had God known by middle knowledge that (C $\rightarrow$ Paul mows). But if **(A)** would have been false, then C, which includes **(A),** wouldn't have obtained, so Paul, of course, wouldn't have mowed in C. Similarly, were (16) a necessary truth, then (4*) would follow from (14) and (16) via the valid inferential rule *If $(X \rightarrow Y)$ and $\Box(Y \rightarrow Z)$, then $(X \rightarrow Z)$.* But (16) surely is *not* a necessary truth. Given his middle knowledge that (C $\rightarrow$ Paul mows), God surely could have achieved his purposes by doing many things other than prevent the ants from moving in. (For instance, he might simply have prevented *Paul* from moving in; indeed, he might have decided not to create Paul at all.) So we can't get to (4*) in this way either.

23. See again p. 59, n. 80. It should be noted that Freddoso does not commit himself to the claim that we have only weak counterfactual power over the past. Furthermore, Freddoso himself uses the terminology of weak and strong *counterfactual dependence,* not weak and strong *power.*

24. In a paper cited in note 10, I suggested that focusing upon counterfactuals of this incomplete variety allows the Molinist to see divine prophecy as guided by middle knowledge. See "Prophecy, Freedom and Middle Knowledge," 151–65.

25. If counterfactual irrelevance is thought of in the most straightforward way—as what we might call *individual* irrelevance—then (18) could conceivably be false even though (17) was true. To say that, for example, the iguana's eye opening is *individually irrelevant* to Paula's action is to say that, had the iguana *not* opened its eyes, but everything else remained the same (as much as possible), Paula still wouldn't have prayed. If T is thought of as containing circumstances which are irrelevant only in this sense, then (17) clearly does not entail (18). For it's possible that, if Paula were in S and T had not obtained, then *no* element of T would have obtained. And it's also possible that, if Paula were in S and *no* element of T had obtained, then Paula *would* have prayed. But then, of course, it follows that (18) could have been false.

There are two responses one might make here. The first would be to leave the concept of irrelevance alone, concede that (18) could be false though (17) was true, but note that, since the counterfactuals involved in such a scene are clearly rather bizarre (e.g., Paula *wouldn't* have prayed if the iguana hadn't opened its eyes, *wouldn't* have prayed if the Chinese smoker hadn't lit up, but *would* have prayed if the iguana hadn't opened its eyes *and* the Chinese smoker hadn't lit up), Paula would have no reason to suspect that they were true, and hence no good reason (assuming the soundness of the rest of our argument) not to engage in retrospective prayer. The second response would be to tinker with the concept of relevance so as to guarantee the move from (17) to (18). We might, for example, say that a circumstance Y was *collectively irrelevant* to Paula's action just in case (i) Y is individually irrelevant to Paula's action (in the sense noted above), and (ii) for any set of circumstances $Z_1, \ldots, Z_n$, if each of Z_1 through Z_n is independently irrelevant to Paula's action, then $(Y \vee Z_1 \vee \ldots \vee Z_n)$ is independently irrelevant to her action. If we specified that T includes only those circumstances which are collectively irrelevant to her action, then (18) could hardly be denied.

26. I am indebted to William Ramsey for pointing out to me the significance of this type of objection.

27. This essay is based upon a chapter of a someday-to-be-completed book which attempts to explicate, defend, and apply the Molinist picture of providence. An earlier version of the essay was presented at a departmental colloquium at the University of Notre Dame; I am especially grateful to Bill Ramsey, who served as commentator at the colloquium, for his insightful remarks. Special thanks are also due to Scott Davison, Fred Freddoso, Al Howsepian, Trenton Merricks, and Alvin Plantinga.

In Defense of Petitionary Prayer

JEROME I. GELLMAN

I wish to defend the practice of petitionary prayer against the charge that, given God's nature, a prayerful request of God cannot be efficacious in bringing about a prayed-for state of affairs. More specifically, I want to examine two arguments formulated and discussed by Eleonore Stump which aim to show that petitionary prayer cannot make a difference to what God will do. Stump herself replies to these arguments by presenting what she takes to be a plausible theology of petitionary prayer, an explanation of why God would want to relate to His creatures by way of such prayers. I will not be evaluating Stump's response to these arguments nor criticisms that have been made of her proposal.[1] Rather, I aim to show that there is good reason to reject these two arguments independent of our ability to come up with a plausible theology of petitionary prayer.

In defending the "efficacy" of petitionary prayer, I mean to defend no more than the efficacy of the *practice*. I take it that the practice has a point even if not all prayerful requests, or even most, are actually granted. It is sufficient that one's requests can make a difference to what is going to happen and that it be reasonable to assume they will make a difference often enough to make the practice worthwhile.

In stating and examining the arguments formulated by Stump, I will be making the assumption that God is the omnipotent, omniscient, and perfectly good creator of the world. For the sake of ease of presentation I will be assuming as well that God is mutable, insofar as petitionary prayer can change His mind about what He is going to bring about in the future. But the validity of my points does not depend on God's being mutable. The same points can be made if we assume that in the first place God creates the world in a certain way because He knows in advance what will be prayed for, and so sets up the world beforehand in response, as it were, to what He knows will be prayed for. So in what follows, wherever I talk as though God is mutable and thus changes His mind as the result of being prayed to, a similar point can be made assuming God's immutability.

ARGUMENT I

The following is the essence of the first argument formulated by Stump:[2]

(1) God never makes the world worse than it would otherwise be and always makes the world better than it would otherwise be.

(2) What is typically requested in petitionary prayers is or results in a state of affairs the realization of which would make the world either worse or better than it would otherwise be.

(3) If what is requested in a petitionary prayer is or results in a state of affairs the realization of which would make the world worse than it would otherwise be, God will not fulfill that request. (from (1))

(4) If what is requested in a petitionary prayer is or results in a state of affairs the realization of which would make the world better than it would otherwise be, God will bring about that state of affairs even if no prayer for its realization has been made. (from (1))

(5) Therefore, what is typically requested in petitionary prayers either will not come about or will come about whether or not the request is made. (from (1), (2), (3), and (4))

(6) Therefore, typically petitionary prayer can effect no change of the sort it is designed to cause.

In this argument, "than it would otherwise be" means "than the world would have been had he not brought about or had omitted to bring about the state of affairs in question."

Premise (1) is ambiguous between two different claims. Let us say that the *exclusive* value of the world at a time t_1 is determined by the value of the world at t_1 without reference to the relationship between the state of the world at T_1 and any past or future state of the world. And let us say that the *inclusive* value of the world at T_1 is determined by considering as well the past from which the world has come and the future toward which the world is heading. Hence, if a person is undergoing a painful operation at t_1 which will bring it about that at t_2 she will be cured of her illness, the *exclusive* valuation of the world at T_1 will include the negative value of the present pain but not the good state of affairs toward which the pain contributes. The *inclusive* valuation will consider both. And if a person at t_1 contributes a large sum of money to charity, but gained the money in immoral ways, the inclusive valuation of the world at T_1 will consider the latter fact while the exclusive won't.

I am confident that the distinction between inclusive and exclusive valuations is intuitively clear enough for my purposes and that it could be made as rigorous as it need be if someone took the time to do so.

Given the distinction, (1) can be given two different readings:

(1a) At any time t_1, God will never make the world to have a degree of *exclusive* value at T_1 which is less than He could cause it to have at t_1, and will always make the world to have a degree of *exclusive* value at

T_1 which is more than any other *exclusive* value He could cause it to have at t_1.

or:

(1b) At any time t_1, God will never make the world to have a degree of *inclusive* value at T_1 which is less than He could cause it to have at t_1, and will always make the world to have a degree of *inclusive* value at T_1 which is more than any other *inclusive* value He could cause it to have at t_1.

There are good reasons to reject (1a). God could allow the world at t_1 to have an *exclusive* value less than He could cause it to have at t_1. And that is because the state of the world, S, at t_1 may be necessary for a greater *inclusive* value for the world than would be achievable were God to bring about some other state of affairs with a greater exclusive value than S at T_1. The existence of the greater inclusive value might entail S. Or, it may be that humans have free will and that God is justified in creating them with free will, and that S is required in order to bring about an exclusive value which is both justified and obtainable within the workings of human free will. God can sacrifice a temporary, exclusive value for the sake of achieving a greater inclusive value than would otherwise be obtainable.

An entirely different objection that might be raised against (1a) is that at any given time there seems to be no upper limit to the exclusive value the world could have at that time. God could, it seems, always create just one more person than he has, and bring it about that at T_1 that person is in a positively valued state. In that case, to require that God bring about a state of affairs having an exclusive value not less than God could bring about at that time would be to charge God with an impossible task. But if (1a) requires an impossible task of God, then it should be rejected.[3]

Turning to (1b), it is equivalent to the assertion that God (supposing He creates a world) creates a world such that He cannot create a world better than it. This is because the *inclusive* value of the world at any time includes the value of the world as a whole, past, present, and future, and because (1b) applies to the very first moment of the world. Hence, when God goes about creating a world, He must, on (1b), create a world with an inclusive value such that there is no greater inclusive value that He can cause it to have at the very first instant of its existence. And the inclusive value of a world at any time is its inclusive value at all times.

We can therefore rewrite (1b) as follows:

(1c) God creates a world, W, such that there is no possible world, W_1, which He could create which is better than W.

(1c) is not equivalent to the assertion that God creates *the* best possible world, or *the* best possible world that God can create. It only states that whatever world God does create, He could not have created a better world than it. But maybe there are other worlds as good as the one He did create which He could have created instead.

At least two objections may be raised against (1c). It could be argued that there is no upper limit to the inclusive value of a world that God could create. No matter what world God creates He could always have created a better. Or it could be argued that God has no obligation to create a world than which He can create no better, but only to create a world in which each creature which is in fact created is better off having been created rather than not and in which it is at least as happy on the whole as in any other possible world in which it could have existed.[4]

If either of these objections is acceptable, then it turns out that neither of the readings of (1) which suggest themselves is acceptable, and (1) falls, and with it the argument.

In what follows, however, I am going to suppose that (1c) is true, because there are theists who have held beliefs either equivalent to or entailing (1c), and it will be worthwhile to pursue the argument further. If there are theists who have held something equivalent to or entailing (1a), what I say below on the basis of (1c) can be applied, *mutatis mutandis,* to them on the basis of (1a). But I myself will not pursue that line of reasoning.

Sticking now with (1c), I turn to premise (2), which can be interpreted in three different ways:

(2a) What is typically requested in petitionary prayers is or results in a state of affairs which would be better to be than not to be or which would be worse to be than not to be, *everything else being equal.*

or:

(2b) What is typically requested in petitionary prayers is or results in a state of affairs the realization of which will make the world either *in fact* exclusively worse at some time or *in fact* exclusively better at some time, than it *in fact* would be were that state of affairs not to obtain.

or:

(2c) What is typically requested in petitionary prayers is or results in a state of affairs the realization of which will make the world either *in fact* inclusively worse or *in fact* inclusively better at some time, than it *in fact* would be were that state of affairs not to obtain.

(2a) is true of the practice of petitionary prayer. Typically, petitionary prayers involve requests for salvation, moral strength, the saving of a life, health, wisdom, relief from poverty, and the like. With regard to all of these, they are requests for or would result in a state of affairs which would be better to be than not to be *everything else being equal.* Hence, (2a) is true of what is typically requested in petitionary prayers.

For (2a) to combine with (4) to yield (5), (4) must be read as:

(4a) If what is typically requested in petitionary prayers is or results in a state of affairs which would be better to be than not to be, *everything else being equal,* then God will bring about that state of affairs even if no prayer for its realization has been made.

So read, (4a) does not follow from (1c). (1c) obligates God to create a world such that He can create no better. Let's call such a world a "theistic optimal world," or a "TOW." In a TOW it is false that any state of affairs which would be better to be than not to be, *everything else being equal,* is such that God would bring that state of affairs about even were it not prayed for. This follows from the fact that not all such states of affairs are logically compatible with one another. And it also follows from the fact that a particular such state of affairs just might not fit into God's plans for the particular TOW He has in mind to realize. So everything will not be equal. So for any TOW there will be states of affairs which would be better to be than not to be, *everything else being equal,* which God would not bring about if not prayed for. Suppose God has decided that world TOW_1 will be actualized. And suppose TOW_1 does not include a state of affairs, S, which it would be better to be than not to be, *everything else being equal.* If S were prayed for, it would be false that God would have brought about S even if it hadn't been prayed for. So (4a) does not follow from (1c). Neither do there seem to be any other premises from theistic belief that would yield (4a) as a conclusion.

I turn to the second way of reading (2):

(2b) What is typically requested in petitionary prayers is or results in a state of affairs the realization of which will make the world either *in fact* exclusively worse at some time or *in fact* exclusively better than it *in fact* would be were that state of affairs not to obtain.

In order to engage (2b) in order to yield (5), (4) must now be read as:

(4b) If what is requested in a petitionary prayer is or results in a state of affairs the realization of which would make the world *in fact* exclusively better at some time than it would otherwise be, then God will bring about that state of affairs even if no prayer for its realization has been made.

But (4b) does not follow from (1c), for reasons similar to those for rejecting (4a). Not all states of affairs the realization of which would make the world *in fact* exclusively better at some time than it would otherwise be are compatible with one another, and some of them may just not fit into God's plans for the particular TOW He has in mind in realizing. So God's having to create a TOW, as (1c) asserts, does not mean that (4b) is true. And there does not seem to be any other way of deriving (4b) from standard theistic beliefs.

Finally,

(2c) What is typically requested in petitionary prayers is or results in a state of affairs the realization of which will make the world either *in fact* inclusively worse or *in fact* inclusively better at some time, than it *in fact* would be were that state of affairs not to obtain.

(2c) is unsupported. For all we know, what is requested in petitionary prayer is such that were the prayer to be granted the world would be no better and no worse when considered *inclusively* than it otherwise would be. And that is because God could arrange matters so that in answering the prayer the world would be the same in overall inclusive value as it would have been had the prayer been denied. As the result of the prayer, God could bring about a different TOW than the one He had been planning to bring about, a TOW containing the prayed-for state of affairs. And of course the same applies for instances in which God denies a prayer. We cannot know that the world would be any different when evaluated inclusively than it would have been had the prayer been granted.

Suppose *S* prays that he become wealthy and use his wealth for the service of God. Call the state of affairs prayed for, *W.* We cannot know in advance what God would do instead and what the world would be like were *W* not to obtain. For all we know, were *W* not realized the world would neither be a better nor a worse place than if *W* were realized, because we cannot know what God would do and how the world would be were *W* not to obtain. Maybe if *S* remains poor he will be purer in soul and not given to pride and will devote his life to helping people in other ways than by distribution of wealth. And maybe God knows or would bring it about that the result of doing so would yield the same value that would obtain were *W* to be realized. And this may be true of petitionary prayer in general. In addition, we do not know what offsetting circumstances might come about as the result of the realization of *W.* Perhaps *S* will grow haughty and prideful, and although his wealth will be used in the service of God, maybe, but afterwards, by his own free will *S*'s wealth will be usurped to the service of the devil. And perhaps the net value of *W* not being realized will be the same as that of *W*'s being realized. And this may be true of petitionary prayer in general.

It is implicit in the practice of petitionary prayer that the pray-er wants her prayer to be answered without that diminishing the overall inclusive value of the world. And if this is too much to suppose, we can at least say that it is religiously improper to pray a "selfish prayer," one in which the person wants a request to be met no matter what the consequences will be for the inclusive value of the world. A selfish petitionary prayer may indeed be theistically incoherent. A proper prayer is one in which God is beseeched, at least implicitly, to "work things out" so that what is prayed for be included in the inclusive value God is after in the world. Undoubtedly some prayers cannot be answered on that basis, and will be denied for that reason. But it makes sense to think that in many cases God could bring about a different TOW than He had been planning to bring about, a TOW including the prayed-for state of affairs. And that is enough to ground the *practice* of petitionary prayer.

So none of the readings of (2) together with (4) yields a valid argument with plausible premises. I conclude that Argument I fails to show that petitionary prayer cannot be efficacious in bringing about a prayed-for state of affairs.

It might be asked, however: if God has in mind to realize a certain TOW, why should someone's praying for something bring it about that God realizes a different TOW instead?

Insofar as this is merely a question, we do not yet have a reason for thinking that the practice of petitionary prayer is incoherent from a theistic point of view. After all, it should not be a condition of the coherence of petitionary prayer that we mere mortals understand God's reasons for relating to creatures by way of such a practice. It is good theistic teaching that God often works in deep ways beyond our understanding. So even if we were not to know *why* God works through petitionary prayer, it can make perfectly good sense to believe *that* He does. This need be no different from there being no problem in believing that God has a good reason for allowing innocent children to suffer, even if we mere mortals do not know *what* the reason is.

If the question, "Why does praying sometimes change God's mind?" is to threaten the coherence of petitionary prayer it must be backed up by a reason for thinking that praying should not be able to change God's mind. The second argument formulated by Stump attempts to do just that. I now turn to Argument II.

ARGUMENT II

The essence of the second argument formulated by Stump is as follows:[5]

(1) If the prayer of a person S for a state of affairs, A, is efficacious, then God brings about A as a reply to S's prayer for A.

(2) If God brings about A as a reply to S's prayer for A, then God is influenced to bring about A by S's prayer.

(3) What is prayed for in petitionary prayer is generally either a bad or a good state of affairs.

(4) If A is a bad state of affairs, God will not allow Himself to be influenced to bring A about just because it has been petitioned.

(5) If A is a good state of affairs, God will bring A about just because it is good and not because of having been influenced to do so by someone's having petitioned for it.

Therefore:

(6) What is prayed for in petitionary prayer is generally such that God will not be influenced by the prayer to bring it about. (from (3), (4), and (5)).

Therefore:

(7) What is prayed for in petitionary prayer is generally such that God will not reply to the prayer. (from (2) and (6))

Hence:

(8) Petitionary prayer is not efficacious. (from (1) and (7))

Stump thinks that a reply to this argument requires an explanation as to why God would "let the prayers of human beings make a difference to his actions."[6] So in her reply Stump offers what is in effect a theology of petitionary prayer, an explanation for why God would want to relate to His creatures by way of such a practice.

However, a reply to this argument does not require our understanding why God would "let" Himself be influenced by the practice of petitionary prayer. And the argument can be turned back, I believe, independently of our being able to provide a theology of petitionary prayer. A cogent reply to Argument II is to be found elsewhere.

My reply to Argument II begins with an excursion into the moral status of *requests*, requests that one person makes of another. Geoffrey Cupit has argued for the claim that requests, made by anyone of anyone, create an obligation in the requestee to fulfill the request.[7] Let's be clear about what Cupit's thesis is.

First of all, the claim is not that just any request whatsoever creates an obligation in the requestee, but only sincere, non-frivolous requests. If a request is cynical or frivolous, no obligations are created on the part of the requestee to fulfill it. Secondly, it is not being claimed that the obligations created by requests are always or necessarily *overriding* obligations, but, rather, obligations that can be overridden by other relevant considerations. Let's call these "defeasible" obligations. So what is claimed is perfectly consistent with the feeling that with regard to many or even most requests we do not have to fulfill them. The consistency comes from the fact that indeed many or even most requests are overridden by stronger counter-considerations. Thirdly, when we hear of requests creating "obligations" we need not think of requests always or necessarily putting powerful claims on us. Obligations needn't pack a wallop. Requests may sometimes create quite weak obligations, rather than strong ones, which would account for why so many request-obligations are in fact overridden by other relevant considerations.

But Cupit does wish to maintain that sincere, non-frivolous requests do always create defeasible obligations on the part of the requestee. Cupit has an interesting argument for why it is that requests create obligations.[8] In essence, he argues that when a person makes a request of another, the requestor is treating the requestee as a person who is "not cold, uncaring, unloving, disregardful." In short, the requestor in making the request expresses the belief that the requestee is to be trusted. Indeed, the request is an expression of that trust. Hence, if the requestee were not to fulfill the request, she would be degrading the requestor, by "making a fool" of him. The requestor thought that the requestee was the type of person who would care, and turning one's back on the requestor would degrade him, making him foolish for having thought the requestee was a caring soul. One has an obligation, says Cupit, not to degrade a fellow human being. So the requestee has an obligation not to turn aside the request.

Now it might be asked why the requestee should be responsible for the belief the requestor has about her? Why should that be the *requestee's* problem? Cupit's answer is that, had the requestor refrained from making the request on the grounds that the requestee was not expected to grant it, that would have been for the requestor to risk paying an injustice to the requestee. It would have been be to treat the potential requestee as cold and uncaring. And that would have involved the requestor's degrading of the requestee. So the request comes about, partly at least, as the result of the requestor's obligation not to do an injustice to the person who is, subsequently, approached with the request. Hence, in turn, the requestee has an obligation not to degrade the requestor by making a mockery of the latter's trust, since the requestee was approached in the first place because of the requestor's obligation not to degrade the requestee. In this dialectic way, says Cupit, requests create obligations.

Cupit wishes his argument to apply equally to cases where a request is for the doing of an immoral or bad act. In such cases, he avers, the obligation to comply with the request is always overridden by the consideration of the immorality of doing so. This application of Cupit's thesis can be questioned. But for my purposes it will not be necessary to go into this question. In what follows it will be my implicit intention to be discussing only requests that involve no asking of immoral or bad behavior on the part of the person asked.

Even with this restriction, Cupit's argument is dubious when applied to two people who are total strangers or only casually acquainted. In such cases it is gratuitous to suppose that the requestor is making the assumption that the potential requestee is a trusting and caring soul. I would have thought that the requestor would be making the request solely because he needs something, and hopes the person he is about to approach might help him, *having no reason to think otherwise.* That is different from assuming that the person approached is a kind of person who *will* help. It hardly seems right that the requestor by making the request means to be conferring upon the requestee the status of a kind, considerate, helping soul. He might *pretend* that, but that's another matter. So there is no reciprocation called for on the part of the requestee, and Cupit's dialectic just doesn't work to show that in general requests create obligations.

Cupit's argument aside, there is some evidence for his thesis from our own behavior in the face of requests. When we do not wish to comply with a request we typically find ourselves giving reasons or excuses, to ourselves or to others, for *why* we are not complying with the request. We say things like, "I can't afford it," or: "Why should I give him money if he's too lazy to work," or: "You had the car last night, and now it's her turn." The best explanation of this behavior is that we believe that requests create obligations. If we did not think that requests created obligations it is not easy to see why we should think we are called upon to cite reasons *not* to grant a request when we didn't wish to do so. It should be sufficient to simply ignore the request. It will not do to reply that our excuses only show that requests provide "a reason to act" in a certain way, but not obligations. I can rationally fail to act in a certain way even though I have a reason to act in that way for no greater reason than that I do not wish so to act. I can safely ignore a reason to act without having to explain, either to myself or others, why I am not acting in that way.

The fact that we tend to cite reasons for not meeting requests seems good evidence that we really do think that requests create obligations. Now strictly speaking this shows only that we *think* requests create obligations, not that requests do create them. But I will simply assume that our basic moral judgments are true, and that therefore if we believe that requests create obligations, then we can assume they do.

In making my way to a defense against Argument II, however, I do not need Cupit's strong thesis that sincere, non-frivolous requests create defeasible obligations on the part of *all* requestees. Instead, I will make do with the weaker thesis that requests create obligations when the requestor and requestee are in a good, close, personal relationship; the closer the relationship the stronger the obligation, everything else being equal. Cupit's dialectical argument for requests creating obligations seems right when restricted to two people who have a good, close relationship. For in entering into, allowing, and contributing to a good, close relationship, each person in the relationship is indicating to the other that she is for the other a source of care, trust, and kindness, and is not cold and uncaring. If then, one person makes a request of another in such a relationship, she does so not only because she has no reason to think the person will *not* care, as is the case when the requestor is a stranger or only a casual acquaintance of the requestee, but because she has good reason to believe that the potential requestee *will* care about her troubles. The requestee herself has encouraged and nurtured the impression that she *does* care for the requestor, and the requestor is taking her up on that impression. The requestee has encouraged the other to think of her as compassionate and caring about the other. So in this case the requestee is indeed responsible for the requestor's belief about her, and is to that extent obligated to fulfill the request, everything else being equal, in order, at the least, not to degrade the trust that the requestee herself has encouraged. To refuse the request would be to degrade or do an injustice to the requestor.

There is yet another side to the obligation when the requestor and requestee are in a good, close, personal relationship. In such a relationship, when one person makes a request of the other, that act itself expresses an acknowledgment of the relationship. When a person comes to another for help in that way, the request for help can be as much of an expression of love as is the help that is subsequently offered. Furthermore, the request signals a readiness and intention on the part of the requestor to maintain her own part of the relationship and do what she can, in turn, for the requestee. In making the request, therefore, the requestor enters into a risk, risking the investment of her self into the relationship, a relationship which the requestee has done her part to create and sustain. Hence, to disregard the request would be, in this additional way, to degrade and even to violate the requestor.

Finally, the obligation of the requestee to the requestor gains in proportion to what we can call the "appropriateness" of the request to the specific relationship that has come to be between the two of them. That is to say, the relationship between the asker and the asked might be such as to have given the asker a reason to believe that the requestee would help, especially with regard to petitions of a certain kind. If my friend is a physician who in the past has initiated on her own the giving of medical advice and counsel to me in the context of our friendship, then that fact increases the obligation of my friend to help me out if I go to her with a medical request. After all, it is precisely with regard to such problems that she has demonstrated worry and care in the past on her own initiative. Hence, that type of request, being appropriate to the relationship, generates more of an obligation than otherwise.

I conclude that to the extent to which two people, S_1 and S_2, have a good, close, personal relationship, and to the extent to which a request is appropriate to the relationship, to that extent if S_1 makes a sincere, non-frivolous request of S_2, for help in bringing about a state of affairs A, S_1's request creates a defeasible obligation for S_2 to bring about A.

It follows from this truth, together with beliefs about God in Western religious traditions, that God is under a defeasible obligation to answer the prayers of those who petition Him for help. God has created us and sustains us in existence, in love and grace. He has informed us of His care for us and has encouraged us to come to Him in a close, personal relationship, through faith, good works, and adoration, and has made promises to us in turn. God has created the impression that He does care for His creatures with an infinite care. And God's relationship to us is sometimes compared to that of a father to a child, a personal relationship of an especially obligating kind.

God calls us to goodness and faith, creating an impression that He cares for our welfare and for our moral and religious goodness. A prayer for our welfare or for moral goodness is thus perfectly *appropriate* to the nature of God and to the nature of the relationship to Him which He encourages and nurtures.

In addition, petitionary prayers are prayed in the context of the close, personal relationship of the pray-er with God.[9] In the Hebrew Scriptures, petitionary prayers are regularly preceded by an address to God of the nature of "My God," "Our God," "God of my fathers," "My rock," "My strength," "God of our salvation," and the like, invoking the intimate relation between the petitioner and God, as a ground of trust. And the central prayer of the Christian canon, the Lord's Prayer, opens with declaring God as "Our Father."

It is clear, then, that the petitioner is not simply petitioning God on the chance that God might answer, *having no reason to think otherwise*, but that the appeal to God is predicated upon the intimate relationship that exists between God and the pray-er.

Additionally, biblical petitions to God are regularly accompanied by allusions to God's nature and character. Petitionary prayers juxtapose declarations of God's being just, faithful, merciful, and the like, with the request. We may safely assume that this is done not in order to remind God what His nature is, in case He has forgotten. Rather, the purpose of doing so, at least in part, is to *ground* the petition upon God's character as God Himself has revealed Himself to us within the personal relationship He has sought.

In the Hebrew Scriptures, petitionary prayers are regularly accompanied by declarations of God's past saving help. This feature too grounds the *appropriateness* of now praying to God for help. God Himself has provided good reason for thinking that He cares to the utmost both for our welfare and goodness and for the intimate relationship between Himself and us.

And in the Lord's Prayer, God is said to be our Father "who art in Heaven." It is plausible to think that this is said at this point not only in order to stress God's transcendence. Instead, saying that God is in Heaven acknowledges God as the supreme source of all that transpires here below, and thus further grounds the *appropriateness* to pray to God, "Our Father," for, amongst other things, our daily bread.[10]

The biblical prayers, both of Hebrew Scriptures and of the Christian canon, are paradigmatic for all prayers in the Jewish and Christian traditions.[11]

When God is addressed with an appropriate, sincere, non-frivolous request in petitionary prayer, it follows, therefore, that there is thereby created an obligation on God's part to fulfill that request. The closer the relationship between God and the person praying, the stronger is the obligation upon God to meet the request. Some prayers will be cynical, others insincere or frivolous, and God may have no obligation at all to answer them. But knowing the hearts of creatures, God will be able to detect even the slimmest component of sincerity and genuinely felt closeness in a prayer and thus be under some, however slight, obligation to fulfill it. Whether weak or strong, in any case God's obligations can be overridden by other considerations.

That petitionary prayers create obligations on God's part helps explain a few features that the practice of petitionary prayer is thought to have in religious traditions. It helps explain why the prayers of saints are considered more efficacious than those of the nonsaintly. This is because saints have a closer personal relationship to God than do others. And it helps explain why God might grant a wish only after it has been prayed, even though God, if omniscient, would know of the wish prior to the prayer. The answer is that, until prayed-for, a wish gives God only a reason to act but not an obligation to do so. Reasons to act are much weaker moral motivators than are obligations. It is only when prayed that the wish creates an obligation. And, finally, that prayers create obligations in God the way they do helps explain the efficacy of persistence in making a request of God. The person who returns to God with the same request, again and again, is expressing both his dependence upon and his trust in God's commitment to him as well as investing more and more of himself in the relationship he has with God. This can be insincere, of course but, when sincere, it increases the obligation upon God.

Now in writing of petitionary prayers creating obligations on God's part, I do not mean to be presenting a theology of petitionary prayer, an explanation of why God should choose to relate to His creatures by way of the practice of petitionary prayer. There is surely much more to petitionary prayer than God's obligation. I mean to argue only that whatever the right theology of petitionary prayer may turn out to be, it is a fact that petitionary prayers as conceived of in religious traditions indeed do create defeasible obligations on God's part to answer the prayers. And this fact is sufficient to turn back Argument II.

Consider this premise of Argument II:

(5) If A is a good state of affairs, God will bring A about just because it is good and not because of having been influenced to do so by someone's having petitioned for it.

We can now see that (5) is false. It can be the case that A is a good state of affairs but that its goodness is not yet a sufficient reason for God to bring it about. Yet when A is prayed-for there may now be a sufficient reason for God to bring A about, because in addition to A's goodness God now has a (defeasible) obligation to bring A about. In many circumstances, this can now morally obligate God to bring about A. A's goodness itself may not be sufficient reason for God to bring it about, because there may be another state of affairs, B, as good as A and incompatible with it, which God has decided to bring about. Or, B's goodness may even surpass the goodness of A's coming about. In either case the fact that A has been prayed-for can now cause God to bring about A instead of B. This is clear for the case where A and B are of equal goodness. If God has a choice between bringing about A or B, which are of equal goodness, but God has an obligation to bring about A but has no obligation to bring about B, God should bring about A and not B. But even in the case where B is a greater good than A, the fact that God has an obligation to bring about A can still make it morally incumbent upon God to bring about A in place of B. Up to a certain point, obligations deontologically overrule considerations of the goodness of the consequences. Hence, within bounds, the fact that God has an obligation to do A will win out over the fact that B is a greater good than A. God's obligation to bring about A is defeasible, but obligations are overridden only by appreciable increments of goodness accruing from alternatives. Up to a point, mere surplus of goodness in an alternative will not tip the scales in its favor against an obligation.

To put the point slightly differently, let "A^*" be the state of affairs of God bringing about A in response to a sincere, non-frivolous, appropriate prayer. It may be the case that A's goodness is not sufficient for God to be required to bring it about. But A^* is, everything else being equal, a better state of affairs than A. That is because it is a very good thing that God, like anybody else, fulfill His obligations if He possibly can. Hence, while A may not warrant actualization by God, A^* might. Hence, the fact that A has been prayed for may now make it the case that A^* is a/the best state of affairs that God can now bring about. But of course, if God brings about A^* He brings about A. So, it can be the case that while A is not good enough to be brought about by God until prayed for, A^* is now good enough to be brought about by God. So God will now bring about A. So (5) is false.

Of course, it may be the case that even if A is prayed for, not everything will be equal. Even after the added increment from A's having been prayed for, A^* might still not be "good enough" for God to now want to bring A about. It could be that the prayer was not sincere enough or that B is just too good to be overtaken by A^*. But this is not a problem for the *practice* of petitionary prayer. It is no part of that practice to believe that every prayer is accepted. There is no magical quality to prayer. A petitionary prayer is prayed out of the conviction that it *can* and often does make a difference. God is beseeched, in His infinite wisdom, to consider our pleas and to answer them in light of His perfect goodness. This may not be true of what we have earlier called "selfish prayer," in which the person beseeches God to answer her request, everyone else be damned. But a selfish prayer need not be condoned in the practice of petitionary prayer. A defense of petitionary prayer against Argument II need only show that there is a good enough chance, for all we know, for our prayers to be answered in order to make the practice worthwhile.

I have argued that Argument II can be answered by attending to the moral status of requests and the obligations they generate. There are features of petitionary prayer which, I acknowledge, are not well explained by reference to God's obligations to us. But I have not set myself the task of explaining all features of petitionary prayer. It has been my task to do no other than defend the practice of petitionary prayer from the two arguments formulated by Eleonore Stump, without having to provide a theology of petitionary prayer. I trust I have fulfilled that task in an adequate way.[12]

NOTES

1. Her discussion can be found in Eleonore Stump, "Petitionary Prayer," *American Philosophical Quarterly* 16 (1979): 81–91, and Eleonore Stump, "Hoffman on Petitionary Prayer," *Faith and Philosophy* 2 (1985): 30–37. A reply to Stump's first paper is Joshua Hoffman, "On Petitionary Prayer," *Faith and Philosophy* 2 (1985): 21–29. See also Michael J. Murray and Kurt Meyers, "Ask and It Will Be Given to You," *Religious Studies* 30 (1994): 311–30, and David Basinger, "Petitionary Prayer: A Response to Murray and Meyers," *Religious Studies* 31 (1995).

2. See Stump, "Petitionary Prayer," 83–84.

3. For more on this type of argument, see George Schlesinger, *New Perspectives on Old-Time Religion* (Oxford, 1988).

4. Robert Adams argued in this way that God does not have to create *the* best of all possible worlds. The same reasoning shows, if correct, that God does not have to create a possible world than which there is no greater. See Robert Merrihew Adams, "Must God Create the Best?" *Philosophical Review* 81 (1972): 317–32.

5. See Stump, "Hoffman on Petitionary Prayer," 35–36.

6. Stump, "Hoffman on Petitionary Prayer," 36.

7. See Geoffrey Cupit, "How Requests (and Promises) Create Obligations," *The Philosophical Quarterly* 44 (1994): 439–55.

8. See Cupit, "How Requests," 448–55.

9. I have learned much about the form of biblical petitionary prayer from Patrick D. Miller, *The Cried to the Lord, The Form and Theology of Biblical Prayer* (Minneapolis, 1994). That work should be consulted for a more complete treatment of the topic than I give here.

10. See Miller, *They Cried to the Lord,* chapter 10, on the Lord's Prayer.

11. It is true that there is a second, different theme to be found in these religions. I have in mind the idea that we are to pray only that God's will be done, and not pray for anything for ourselves. This is clear in the Christian depiction of Jesus at Gethsemane as offering a prayer which is no less than a submission to God's will, rather than a request for God to act so as to save Jesus from his impending fate. This is also reflected in the Lord's Prayer when it in prayed, "Thy will be done." And in Judaism, the submissive prayer became paramount in thor early teachings of the Hasidic movement, where it was taught that one should not pray for one's own needs, but only that God's name be "completed" and "made whole" in the indwelling

Divine Presence. (For the conception of petitionary prayer in early Hasidism, see Rivka Schatz Uffenheimer, *Hasidism as Mysticism* [Princeton, 1993], chapter 6]). At the same time, though, these traditions continue to acknowledge the religious appropriateness of petitions addressed to God other than that God's will be done.

12. I am grateful to Tziporah Kasachkoff and John Kleinig for discussions we had which helped me clarify my views on the relation between requests and obligations.

Nature, Awe, and the Sublime

PHILIP J. IVANHOE

A number of influential modern Western thinkers with quite different attitudes toward religion have developed distinctive views concerning how human beings do or should respond to the rest of the natural world. Some of these thinkers are strong and sincere advocates of a particular faith, others hostile "debunkers" of religion. Their conceptions of the form and character of our response to Nature differ considerably. Some see our response to Nature as the foundation for religious belief, others as a symbol or representative of our moral and religious sensibility, while yet others regard it as an infantile and largely debilitating illusion best banished from awareness or rendered impotent in ordering and motivating our beliefs and actions. I will present and discuss the views of three thinkers: Immanuel Kant (1724–1804), Sigmund Freud (1856–1939), and Abraham Heschel (1907–1972). I choose Kant first because his views have had such a profound influence, both direct and indirect, not just on Freud and Heschel but on all modern thinkers. In addition, his views on the sublime present a middle way when contrasted with the scientific reductionism of Freud and the devotional theism of Heschel. I will note the differences, similarities, and clear cases of direct influence among our three thinkers wherever these serve to deepen or refine our appreciation of their thought. By way of conclusion, I will draw upon their views, taking as reliable insights some of their central claims, but also criticizing some of their characteristic assumptions and conclusions and modifying or adding to the points they make. My aim is to offer a more adequate and complete account of how human beings tend to and should respond to Nature and to show how this can provide a foundation for environmental concern.

As will be clear in the following sections, my description of and comments on the various views I shall examine come out of a set of specific interests and are directed toward a particular, some might even say a peculiar, end. These are not intended as complete or definitive statements of the philosophies I am exploring. This is not to say that those features I focus on are not representative or important aspects of each thinker's thought, only that they are partial and in some sense idiosyncratic. I feel the force of these qualifications with exceptional poignancy in the case of our first thinker, Kant, as his views on Nature and the sublime are not only parts of a larger philosophical account of the aesthetic but this work in turn is but a movement within the grand project of the three *Critiques*. As his ideas are the most complex and detailed and, as noted above, exert a profound influence on both Freud and Heschel, my presentation and discussion of his views are more developed than with either of the other two thinkers I shall discuss.

KANT ON THE SUBLIME

Kant was not directly interested in providing an account of the relationship between human beings and Nature. We will explore what he has to say on this topic in regard to his analysis of aesthetic judgments.[1] We can begin to understand Kant's account of aesthetic judgments by appreciating his insight that when we judge a given thing to be beautiful we seem to mean more than simply that we find that thing *agreeable* to us. The agreeable is what we take a particular interest in, but the beautiful is beautiful regardless of what our particular interests might be. To judge something beautiful is therefore to make a judgment of "taste." In making such judgments, we both expect and in some sense can demand that others will agree; we presuppose a "common sense" in such matters. Thus, Kant argues, the beautiful must attract and delight us in a special way. True judgments of taste must be pure—not empirical—judgments; we must delight not in contingent particulars but in certain universal, *formal features* of the object.

Judgments of taste are reflective and are not based merely upon sensations, as are our judgments about the agreeableness of a particular flower or color. Nor are such judgments connected with explicit concepts such as the judgment, "*x* is a rose." While numerically singular, a judgment of taste is not specific, it does not entail any direct interest in its object per se, either in the object's existence (which would involve sensation) or in its purpose (which would involve conceiving of it under some determinate concept). Judgments of taste concern only the general *form* of an object. Specifically, they concern what Kant calls a "harmony" between our powers of imagination and understanding (i.e., empirical cognition). This harmony arises with the free play of imagination under the general notion of an object and consists in an awareness—*felt,* not *conceived*—of this unspecified purposiveness, "a purposiveness without a purpose."

These general features of judgments of taste lead Kant to see a broad analogy between our appreciation of beauty and our respect for morality. Just as our appreciation of beauty does not depend on any interest or purpose beyond our contemplation of the beautiful object (the source of our notion of "art for art's sake"), our respect for morality does not depend on some further particular purpose but rather arises from the very nature of morality (the inherent goodness of the moral will). Beautiful objects, whether of human or natural production, appear to us as products of the free and spontaneous exercise of imagination.[2]

Thus they are *like* the freedom and creativity of the moral will (practical reason) which fashions individual moral acts. As noted above, beautiful objects are not conceived in terms of specific concepts but are experienced under the notion of an object in general. That is, they are not conceived (or produced) under any specific empirical concept (this would constitute mere imitation or craft). This is analogous to the way the moral will conforms to the nonempirical and general notion of what it is to act from a sense of duty. Finally we are attracted—not compelled—to the beautiful in the same way we are drawn—not compelled—to perform moral actions. In both cases, we do and must submit freely.[3]

Based upon these and other strong parallels between judgments of taste and moral judgments, Kant claimed that the former are *symbols* of the latter. The exact sense in which beauty is a symbol of morality is quite elusive, but Kant seems to mean that beauty shares many characteristics of morality (as we have seen above), that it therefore can represent morality through analogical association, and perhaps that being a more *palpable feeling* it can serve to evoke the fully rational moral sense. This last feature makes the aesthetic sense lower in value than our moral sense, for it arises from a *felt* harmony among our powers of imagination and understanding and not from reason alone. This leads us to the topic of central importance for the present essay, Kant's notion of the sublime.

The sublime is a feeling that, for clear reasons, Kant valued above the aesthetic yet below that of morality itself. It is a feeling we experience most often and most clearly in our contemplation of certain aspects of Nature. This feeling is also important for Kant's understanding of religion, for only such a "sublime mental attunement . . . intrinsically distinguishes religion from superstition."[4]

Judgments of the beautiful and the sublime share several similar characteristics. Both are reflective judgments, and in both our liking depends not on sensations or determinate concepts but on a *felt* harmony between imagination—our "power of exhibition"—and our "power of concepts" (understanding and reason, respectively).[5] We like such experiences for their own sake, and these judgments, while numerically singular, claim universal validity. But despite such similarities, there are important differences between the two kinds of judgment. While both concern indeterminate concepts, beauty is connected with the understanding while the sublime concerns reason.

> The beautiful in nature concerns the form of the object, which consists in [the object's] being bounded. But the sublime can also be found in a formless object, insofar as we present *unboundedness,* either [as] in the object, or because the object prompts us to present it, while yet we add to this unboundedness the thought of its totality. So it seems that we regard the beautiful as the exhibition of an indeterminate concept of the understanding, and the sublime as the exhibition of an indeterminate concept of reason.[6]

These dissimilarities result in distinctive and morally significant differences in our liking of beauty and the sublime. The former elicits a this-worldly, happy, and playful feeling, the latter points to what is beyond the senses and elicits a feeling of respect and reverence.

> For the one liking ([that for] the beautiful) carries with it directly a feeling of life's being furthered, and hence is compatible with charms and with an imagination at play. But the other liking (the feeling of the sublime) is a pleasure that arises only indirectly: it is produced by the feeling of a momentary inhibition of the vital forces followed immediately by an outpouring of them that is all the stronger. Hence it is an emotion, and so it seems to be seriousness, rather than play, in the imagination's activity. . . . [7]

Thus the sublime is characterized by a kind of inherent unruliness and a recalcitrance to both imagination and understanding. As a result, our experience of the sublime directs our attention not out toward the objects in nature but rather inward upon the power of reason. We might say that in our experience of the sublime the starry Heavens above *call forth* the moral law within:

> we express ourselves entirely incorrectly when we call this or that *object of nature* sublime, even though we may quite correctly call a great many natural objects beautiful; for how can we call something by a term of approval if we apprehend it as in itself contrapurposive? Instead, all we are entitled to say is that the object is suitable for exhibiting a sublimity that can be found in the mind. For what is sublime, in the proper meaning of the term, cannot be contained in any sensible form but concerns only ideas of reason, which, though they cannot be exhibited adequately, are aroused and called to mind by this very inadequacy, which can be exhibited in sensibility.[8]

But it is not simply the chaotic restlessness and rulelessness of Nature that summon forth feelings of the sublime, there must also be an incomprehensibility of scale: "it is . . . in its chaos that nature most arouses our ideas of the sublime, or in its wildest and most ruleless disarray and devastation, *provided it displays magnitude and might.*"[9]

Nature's displays of magnitude and might constitute two basic types of sublime experience: the *mathematical* (regarding "magnitude") and the *dynamic* (concerning "might"). Kant begins his account of the mathematically sublime by saying, "We call sublime what is absolutely [schlechthin] large."[10] Such phenomena present an experience that stretches and ultimately breaks free of the power of both imagination and understanding (i.e., conception under a determinate concept). While we can think of any number of things as large, the sublime is connected only with the *absolutely large:* "That is sublime in comparison with which everything else is small."[11] It is a feeling that arises through a kind of imaginative vertigo; more precisely, through the reestablishment of order and control brought about by the power of reason when we confront the sensibly incomprehensible. It is the respect and dignity we feel when reason restores sense and hope in the face of the infinite and overpowering, "Sublime is what even to be able to think proves that the mind has a power surpassing any standard of sense."[12] The sublime gives pride of place to reason and its ability to face and

master the realm of sense, even at the limit of the insensible, and so such feelings
are of greater moral value than our appreciation of beauty:

> our imagination strives to progress toward infinity, while our reason de-
> mands absolute totality as a real idea, and so [the imagination,] our power
> of estimating the magnitude of things in the world of sense, is inadequate
> to that idea. Yet this inadequacy itself is the arousal in us of the feeling that
> we have within us a supersensible power; and what is absolutely large is not
> an object of sense, but is the use that judgment makes naturally of certain
> objects so as to [arouse] this (feeling), and in contrast with that use any
> other use is small.[13]

The connection between sublime feelings and the dignity of reason is even more
vividly evident in cases of the dynamically sublime, "[w]hen in an aesthetic judgment we consider nature as a might that has no dominance over us."[14] In order
to experience such feelings we must at the same time, "consider an object *fearful*
without being afraid *of* it"[15] in the way that "a virtuous person fears God without
being afraid of him."[16] In other words, as in the case of the beautiful, we must
take a disinterested interest in what we confront. Moreover, as in the case of the
mathematically sublime, our liking is indirect (i.e., it arises out of our appreciation of reason's ability to face what overwhelms our sensible powers) and directed inward (i.e., toward our own reason):

> consider bold, overhanging . . . threatening rocks, thunderclouds piling up
> in the sky and moving about accompanied by lightning and thunderclaps,
> volcanos with all their destructive power, hurricanes with all the devasta-
> tion they leave behind, the boundless ocean heaved up, the high waterfall
> of a mighty river. . . . Compared to the might of any of these, our ability to
> resist becomes an insignificant trifle. Yet the sight of them becomes all the
> more attractive the more fearful it is, provided we are in a safe place. And
> we like to call these objects sublime because they raise the soul's fortitude
> above its usual middle range and allow us to discover in ourselves an ability
> to resist which is of a quite different kind, and which gives us the cour-
> age [to believe] that we could be a match for nature's seeming omnipo-
> tence. . . . though the irresistibility of nature's might makes us, considered
> as natural beings, recognize our physical impotence, it reveals in us at the
> same time an ability to judge ourselves independent of nature, and reveals
> in us a superiority over nature. . . . This keeps the humanity in our person
> from being degraded, even though a human being would have to succumb
> to that dominance [of nature]."[17]

Kant goes on to consider the objection that such a view seems to suggest that the
human mind is superior to God's wrath, as manifested in the overwhelming natural powers which He commands, and points out that, "it would be both foolish
and sacrilegious to imagine that our mind is superior to the effects produced by
such a might, and is superior apparently even to its intentions."[18] This last remark
in turn might be taken to imply that the only proper response to God's might is

"prostration, worship with bowed head and accompanied by contrite and timorous gestures and voice."[19] But Kant emphatically rejects this implication, for such a frame of mind is incapable of appreciating the sublime nature of true religion.

> The frame of mind [needed] to admire divine greatness . . . requires that we be attuned to quiet contemplation and that our judgment be completely free. Only if he is conscious that his attitude is sincere and pleasing to God, will these effects of might serve to arouse in him the idea of God's sublimity, insofar as he recognizes in his own attitude a sublimity that conforms to God's will, and is thereby elevated above any fear of such natural effects.[20]

In *Religion within the Limits of Reason Alone,* Kant relies upon this very distinction to distinguish religions of "ingratiation" or "mere worship" from true, "moral religion." This will be an important distinction to keep in mind in connection with Freud's views, discussed below.

Throughout the following sections, I will have occasion to refer back to this and other features of Kant's rich analysis of aesthetic judgments, but I want to conclude this section by pointing out that according to Kant any finite, free, and rational being would share not only our moral views but our judgments of both the beautiful and sublime as well. Such judgments are not directly connected with our particular physical constitution, and so agreement would not require close physical similarity between us and these other creatures. None of these judgments depend on the innate sensible powers of human beings but only on certain relationships among their powers of imagination, understanding, and reason.[21] In this respect at least, Kant's views are not in any strong sense anthropocentric and thus are distinctive among those we shall examine.

FREUD'S OCEANIC FEELING

In two of his mature works, *The Future of an Illusion* (1927) and *Civilization and Its Discontents* (1930), Freud explores the bases of both civilization and religion. This leads him to make a number of claims regarding the relationship between human beings and Nature, the feelings we characteristically have when contemplating our place in Nature and the significance of such feelings in the good human life. Freud starts out by saying,

> Human civilization, by which I mean all those respects in which human life has raised itself above its animal status and differs from the life of beasts . . . presents . . . two aspects to the observer. It includes on the one hand all the knowledge and capacity that men have acquired in order to control the forces of nature and extract its wealth for the satisfaction of human needs, and on the other hand, all the regulations necessary in order to adjust the relations of men to one another and especially the distribution of the available wealth.[22]

We will be focusing our attention on the first of these "two aspects," which can be understood as consisting of two distinct functions: *protection* and *satisfaction*.[23] Civilization protects human beings from the dangers of Nature and allows them to draw upon Nature to provide for the satisfaction of their needs.

According to Freud, religion and civilization share this first aspect as a common lineage, for our motivation to fashion both arises out of our fear of Nature's awesome power: "religious ideas have arisen from the same need as have all the other achievements of civilization: from the necessity of defending oneself against the crushingly superior force of nature."[24] When we consider this quote carefully, we see that it only supports the claim that religion shares the *first* of the two functions distinguished above, the protective function. In the later *Civilization and Its Discontents,* Freud appeals to something like the second function as well, for he argues that religion is motivated by a desire to maintain our infantile impression of an all-embracing bond between ego and the world. But in the end, Freud rejects this immature wish and does not recognize any legitimate need that religion—or anything like it—might satisfy. The clearest candidate for such a need is what he describes as the "oceanic feeling" we sometimes experience in our contemplation of Nature, and this feeling will be the focus of much of the discussion below.

According to Freud, religion's deep and fatal flaw is that it can neither protect us nor can it fulfill even our infantile wishes, because it is predicated on a debilitating illusion whose costs far exceed any material benefit or psychological consolation it might afford. An illusion differs from a simple error in two ways: illusions are derived from human wishes and they are not necessarily contrary to reality.[25] Moreover, while some illusions prove harmful, others can be beneficial both to oneself and others. Indeed, some illusions, such as art, seem indispensable in a rich and fulfilling human life. Illusions resemble psychiatric delusions in being derived from wishes, but delusions are more complex and it is part of their essence that they conflict with reality and prove harmful to oneself and others. Religious teachings "are illusions, fulfillments of the oldest, strongest and most urgent wishes of mankind."[26] These wishes concern the desire for protection that arises out of our early, terrifying feelings of utter helplessness and that remains and is reinforced throughout our lives by the threat of Nature's "crushingly superior force."

> the terrifying impression of helplessness in childhood aroused the need for protection—for protection through love—which was provided by the father; and the recognition that this helplessness lasts throughout life made it necessary to cling to the existence of a father, but this time a more powerful one. Thus the benevolent rule of a divine Providence allays our fear of the dangers of life; the establishment of a moral world-order ensures the fulfillment of the demands of justice, which have so often remained unfulfilled in human civilization; and the prolongation of earthly existence in a future life provides the local and temporal framework in which these wish-fulfillments shall take place.[27]

Freud's account of the origin of both civilization and religion shows some similarity to Kant's views regarding the sublime: both see the fearfulness of Nature as a critical feature of the characteristic human response. Since Freud believes Nature indeed is dangerous, religious beliefs are not completely contrary to reality and thus are illusions (albeit harmful ones), not delusions. Moreover, both Kant and Freud agree that a timid acquiescence in the face of Nature's power does not constitute a true religious sense.

> Critics persist in describing as "deeply religious" anyone who admits to a sense of man's insignificance or impotence in the face of the universe, although what constitutes the essence of the religious attitude is not this feeling but only the next step after it, the reaction to it which seeks a remedy for it. The man who goes no further, but humbly acquiesces in the small part which human beings play in the great world—such a man is, on the contrary, irreligious in the truest sense of the word.[28]

But such similarities should not obscure the profound differences between these two thinkers. Freud regards the raw fear of natural dangers as a primary and direct source of all cultural phenomena, including religion. Kant explicitly denies this possibility (such fear could give rise only to superstition, not to true religion) and regards the sublime as a complex reflective judgment involving our powers of imagination and reason and resulting in reverence. But in this last respect, some similarity between the two again appears, and their common commitment to the enlightenment project is revealed. For in his own way Freud thought our natural fear of Nature should elevate our commitment to moral community and the status of rational, scientific thinking:

> Against the dreaded external world one can only defend oneself by some kind of turning away from it, if one intends to solve the task by oneself. There is, indeed, another and better path: that of becoming a member of the human community and, with the help of a technique guided by science, going over to the attack against nature and subjecting her to the human will.[29]

In both Kant and Freud we see a movement from the contemplation of Nature back to the human capacity to reason. For Kant this allows us to feel a quiet yet determined dignity and confidence in the face of the most overwhelming phenomena and to appreciate a true sense of God's sublime will. In Freud's more stark universe, our fear of Nature drives us to renounce many of our deepest desires for individual satisfaction and to band together with others to "attack nature" and subjugate it to human (not divine) will. But neither thinker sees any deep connection between human beings and Nature. Kant's views about how Nature lends itself to our appreciation does present a picture in which human beings are reasonably "at home" in the world. But at the same time, Nature is very much other and inferior to rational human beings. Freud's view of Nature is even more alienated and antagonistic.

At one point, Freud raises a possible objection to his rejection of religion. For if religion does indeed satisfy existing human desires which cannot be satisfied through science, why then would he seek to remove this consolation? Freud poses this question to himself:

> Countless people find their one consolation in religious doctrines, and can only bear life with their help. You would rob them of their support, without having anything better to give them in exchange. . . . Man has imperative needs of another sort, which can never be satisfied by cold science; and it is strange—indeed it is the height of inconsistency—that a psychologist who has always insisted on what a minor part is played in human affairs by the intelligence as compared with the life of the instincts—that such a psychologist should now try to rob mankind of a precious wish-fulfillment and should propose to compensate them for it with intellectual nourishment.[30]

Freud offers a concise and decisive response to his own question: "civilization runs a greater risk if we maintain our present attitude to religion than if we give it up."[31] He goes on to present a wide-ranging argument in support of this central claim, what we might call "Freud's Wager." This aspect of Freud's position relies upon a remarkably provincial and unflattering conception of religion. He nowhere explores the views of non-Western religious traditions, many of which are nontheistic, nor does he consider the possibility of there being forms of Western theism that might avoid many or perhaps all of the shortcomings he describes. But apart from the question of the overall utility of religion, the passage quoted above suggests that Freud entertained the possibility of there being some unique human needs or desires that could be satisfied only through religion. The problem with religion, then, would be not that it was without basis but simply that it was not worth the costs. This possibility leads us to our more modest concerns: Freud's view of Nature and its significance for human beings. He discusses these in regard to a different possible explanation of religious sensibilities: the "oceanic feeling." This idea was first suggested to Freud in a letter from a friend who had recently read his *Future of an Illusion,* and Freud's discussion of it is cast as a response to this suggestion.[32]

> It is a feeling which he would like to call a sensation of "eternity," a feeling as of something limitless, unbounded—as it were, "oceanic." This feeling, he adds, is a purely subjective fact, not an article of faith; it brings with it no assurance of personal immortality, but it is the source of the religious energy. . . . One may, he thinks, rightly call oneself religious on the ground of this oceanic feeling alone, even if one rejects every belief and every illusion.[33]

Freud attempts to describe the nature of this feeling (all the while denying he has ever felt anything like it and complaining how difficult and improbable a concept it is). At one point he settles on a definition that informs much of his further discussion: "it is a feeling of an indissoluble bond, of being one with the external world as a whole."[34]

Freud shows considerable resistance to the idea that such a feeling is an innate and active inclination:

> this seems something rather in the nature of an intellectual perception, which is not, it is true, without an accompanying feeling-tone. . . . The idea of men's receiving an intimation of their connection with the world around them through an immediate feeling which is from the outset directed to that purpose sounds so strange and fits in so badly with the fabric of our psychology that one is justified in attempting to discover a psycho-analytic—that is, a genetic—explanation of such a feeling.[35]

This is precisely what Freud then goes on to do. He first likens the oceanic feeling to the "unusual" though not "pathological" state of being in love: "At the height of being in love the boundary between ego and object threatens to melt away. Against all the evidence of his senses, a man who is in love declares that 'I' and 'you' are one, and is prepared to behave as if it were a fact."[36] We can assume that Freud *has* this kind of experience and he finds it less than "improbable," merely "unusual." Human beings have a legitimate and usually nonpathological *need* for love. Love may entail a certain level of illusion, indeed it may require a certain level of illusion, as does art, but that does not necessarily detract from its value. Freud regards the appreciation of art, a classic case of illusion, as one of our most profound consolations.[37] Despite what Freud suggests, it is not at all clear that something very much like the oceanic feeling necessarily involves beliefs contrary to reality; if it does not require such beliefs it clearly does not constitute or tend toward delusion and may well represent an illusion that is beneficial both to the self and to others.

But Freud quickly abandons the analogy with love and prefers his genetic explanation; the oceanic feeling is understood as a vestige of an infantile view in which the world is intimately connected with the self:

> Our present ego-feeling is . . . only a shrunken residue of a much more inclusive—indeed, an all-embracing—feeling which corresponded to a more intimate bond between the ego and the world about it. . . . In that case, the ideational contents appropriate to it would be precisely those of limitlessness and of a bond with the universe—the same ideas with which my friend elucidated the "oceanic" feeling.[38]

Freud concludes his consideration of the oceanic feeling by acknowledging that many people do indeed experience it (which requires that he not only can *comprehend* what it is but believes that it exists), but he insists that his genetic account provides the most plausible explanation of its source. He remains unconvinced that this feeling can "be regarded as the source of religious needs," for a feeling can only be a "source of energy if it is itself the expression of a strong need."[39] In his final remarks on the subject, he speculates that the "oceanic feeling" was not the source of religion but that it came to be connected with religion later on in an attempt to console us and deny "the danger which the ego recognizes as threatening it from the external world."[40] This is characteristic of Freud's loudest complaint about appeals to the oceanic feeling, not only as the source of religion but as a legitimate human need. He believes that such feelings can only lull us into complacency and thereby expose us to the myriad, active dangers in the world. The oceanic feeling can only serve to obscure the "crushingly superior force" of Nature—the true source of religion. It is a dangerous illusion, tending toward a pathological delusion.

HESCHEL'S AWE OF NATURE

As is the case with our two earlier thinkers, Heschel's views on Nature were not developed as freestanding positions but rather as part of a larger project. For him, this larger project was gradually to move people to faith in God and to devoted observance of the commandments. This movement begins with a feeling of awe and wonder that Heschel believes all human beings experience whenever they view Nature in the proper way. But this is not the end of the journey, for as Arnold Eisen says, "Once we have begun to sail, Heschel believes awe and wonder will take us all the way to God."[41] While Heschel is a deeply religious thinker, he is not trying to *prove* the existence of God or the truth of Judaism; he takes these as given and moreover would admit that they are not amenable to anything like definitive proof. His mission is to evoke a latent religious sentiment, which he believes lies behind such beliefs, and orient it toward the practice of his tradition.[42] Given this project, Heschel's first task is to point out and lovingly describe the overlooked and underappreciated evidence for this underlying sense in our common and ubiquitous experience of the natural world.

In his account of our experience of Nature, Heschel employs a largely phenomenological approach. This leads him to draw, as most phenomenologists do, a sharp contrast between his work and that of science. While he pays tribute to the accomplishments of science, he holds the religious point of view in much higher esteem. Moreover, he claims that the scientific approach has a tendency to dominate and distort a true and complete perception of reality.

> Behavioral sciences have enriched our knowledge of psychological, biological, and sociological facts and patterns of behavior by observation and description. However, we must not forget that in contrast to animals man is a being who not only behaves but also reflects about how he behaves. . . . Empirical intemperance, the desire to be exact, to attend to "hard" facts which are subject to measurement, may defeat its own end. It makes us blind to the fact behind the facts—that what makes a human being human is not just mechanical, biological, and psychological functioning. . . . The more refined and accessible the avenues to the study of behavioral facts become, the greater the scarcity of intellectual audacity in probing what is imponderable about human being. Our understanding of man is dangerously incomplete if we dwell exclusively on the facts of human being and disregard what is at stake in human being.[43]

One can discern another important and related theme in the above passage, the universal search for meaning. Heschel has strong views on what we need in order to find life meaningful. He begins by claiming that we are meaning-seeking creatures, again revealing his debt to phenomenology. But this very quest lands us in a paradox, for the search to find meaning in the world leads to an awareness of "what is imponderable"—to mystery and a further sublime sense of a transcendent meaning beyond the mystery.

> Is there meaning beyond all conventional meanings? The Greeks discovered [the] rational structure of the given, yet beyond the given and the rational they sensed dark mystery—irrational fate or necessity that stood over and above men and gods, a mysterious power which filled even Zeus with fear . . . beyond all mystery is meaning. God is neither plain meaning nor just mystery. God is meaning that transcends mystery, meaning that mystery alludes to, meaning that speaks through mystery.[44]

One can see in this aspect of Heschel's thought vestiges of Kant's claims concerning our sense of the sublime. For Heschel's sense of mystery and awe, like Kant's feeling of the sublime, arises out of a feeling of incomprehensibility—an awareness that our powers of imagination, understanding, and (for Heschel) reason are overwhelmed. For Kant, though, this experience differs from our aesthetic appreciation of beauty; it requires displays of "magnitude or might" and results in respect for reason. Heschel here explicitly parts company with Kant. He insists that we can experience what he calls the sublime when contemplating the beautiful or even the everyday; it does not require any display of "magnitude or might," just the proper frame of mind:

> The sublime is not opposed to the beautiful, and must not, furthermore, be considered an aesthetic category. The sublime may be sensed in things of beauty as well as in acts of goodness and in the search for truth. . . . The sublime is that which we see and are unable to convey. It is the silent allusion of things to a meaning greater than themselves. It is that which all things ultimately stand for. . . . The sublime, furthermore, is not necessarily related to the vast and the overwhelming in size. It may be sensed in every grain of sand, in every drop of water. Every flower in the summer, every snowflake in the winter, may arouse in us the sense of wonder that is our response to the sublime.[45]

The reasons for these differences can be found in the character of what each thinker regards as incomprehensible and in how they view our purported "natural" response. For Kant, our sense of the sublime arises when imagination is overwhelmed and reason restores order; hence our respect for reason's power. For Heschel, the incomprehensibility arises in the course of our quest for meaning. When we exhaustively attempt to understand what some given thing means, to contemplate its essence, its place, its relationship to ourselves and even the very act of perceiving it, we are led to what he calls "radical amazement"—the "mystery" of why anything exists at all and how we ourselves come to be, perceive, and think:

> Radical amazement has a wider scope than any other act of man. While any act of perception or cognition has as its object a selected segment of reality, radical amazement refers to all of reality; not only to what we see, but also to the very act of seeing as well as to our own selves, to the selves that see and are amazed at their ability to see. . . . We do not have to go to the end of reasoning to encounter it. Grandeur or mystery is something with which we are confronted everywhere and at all times. Even the very act of thinking baffles our thinking, just as every intelligible fact is, by virtue of its being a fact, drunk with baffling aloofness.[46]

This helps us to understand some of Heschel's more dramatic claims, for example, "The world's mystery is . . . either absolutely meaningless or absolutely meaningful, either too inferior or too superior to be an object of human contemplation."[47] It also helps us to see why he says that "the sheer being of the universe . . . calls forth the question about meaning."[48] Such a call emanates from every corner of the world and can be seen in each facet of existence. "The divine seeks to be disclosed in the human. Silence hovers over all the mountain peaks. The world is aflame with grandeur. Each flower is an outpouring of love."[49] This "call" of the "question of meaning," like Kant's notion of the sublime, is universal and accompanied by a sense of awe. But unlike Kant's notion of the sublime, it is not a reflective judgment nor a harmony among innate human powers but rather a direct, sensed intuition. It is closer to a perception than a judgment, something we might ignore or shut our eyes to but something which thrusts itself upon consciousness:

> The awareness of transcendent meaning comes with the sense of the ineffable. The *imperative of awe* is its certificate of evidence, a universal response which we experience *not* because we desire to, but because we are stunned and cannot brave the impact of the sublime. It is a meaning wrapped in mystery. It is not by analogy or inference that we become aware of it. It is rather sensed as something immediately given, logically and psychologically prior to judgment, to the assimilation of subject matter to mental categories; a universal insight into an objective aspect of reality, of which all men are at times capable."[50]

Freud claims that a raw and potentially debilitating fear is our most characteristic response to Nature, while Kant argues that in feelings of the sublime we gain a sense of respect for the moral law within us, God's sublime will. But Heschel claims that the proper response to Nature is to sense another presence *behind* the incomprehensible world, a greater, caring power. "Standing face to face with the world, we often sense a presence which surpasses our ability to comprehend. The world is too much for us. It is crammed with marvel."[51]

Heschel seems to agree with Kant when he says that our sense of the sublime is a "sign of the inward greatness of the human soul."[52] But such agreement is only apparent. For Kant, our response to the sublime in Nature calls us to respect the moral law within us, which is God's sublime will. But for Heschel, the sublime is not a real and inherently valuable aspect of reality, it is rather a sign for that which is truly real and valuable—God:

> the sublime is but a way in which things react to the presence of God. It is never an ultimate aspect of reality, a quality meaningful in itself. It stands for something greater; it stands in relation to something beyond itself that the eye can never see. The sublime is not simply there. It is not a thing, a quality, but rather a happening, an act of God, a marvel.[53]

Thus Heschel's notion of the sublime is a *symbol* of God—the hidden agent behind observable phenomena—in much the same way that Kant claimed the beautiful is a symbol of morality.

CONCLUSION

One of the most striking and distinctive features of the views we have examined is their common emphasis on the awesomeness of Nature. Nature's unruly power poses a prominent threat to human beings and so is an appropriate object of awe. Kant argued that this should lead us to respect for reason and a profound appreciation of God's sublime nature. Freud thought Nature's terrible power had the unfortunate result of giving rise to religion but that it could lead to solidarity with society and a greater respect for "scientific" forms of thinking. Heschel shows a more mystical inclination, one that leads him toward religion, not reason and science. For Heschel the awesomeness of Nature is not restricted to cases of what Kant called "magnitude or might"; we can experience awe in the presence of the beautiful and commonplace as well.[54] Such "awe" is the feeling we experience in the face of the profound inscrutability of existence itself. It gives rise to "wonder" and "radical amazement" and a sense of the hidden agent behind the myriad phenomena of the world.

Many of us will find it difficult to accept aspects of one or perhaps all of these accounts of Nature's awesome power. But these views converge on a claim that would be most *unreasonable* to reject: Nature is worthy of respect, the kind of respect a rational person affords to any dangerous and unpredictable thing. The respect or awe we feel is grounded in the objective fact that Nature is dangerous and much more powerful than creatures like us. Such an emotional response is well warranted. I agree with Ronald de Sousa, who describes how the appropriateness of emotional reactions to what he calls "formal objects"—a second-order property that supervenes on some other property or properties, e.g., something being frightening because it is dangerous—should serve as the standard to judge the rationality of all emotions.[55] There is nothing at all irrational about acknowledging a certain level of respect for Nature. As Bernard Williams says, "we have a healthy respect for mountainous terrain or treacherous seas."[56] Such respect for Nature is "healthy" in that it is essential to the task of successfully navigating through the world. This is the first type of response we do and should have toward Nature. It helps us to appreciate certain simple truths about the world that are critical to our functioning successfully within it.

Another response we do and should have toward Nature is an appreciation of its beauty. Again we see this concern represented, in different ways, by Kant and Heschel and to some extent Freud. Freud places the least amount of emphasis on this aspect of our response to Nature but he does occasionally remark that the beauty "of natural objects and landscapes . . . can compensate for a great deal."[57] This lack of emphasis on the profound satisfaction one can derive from the contemplation of natural beauty is odd when one considers the degree to which Freud valued art in general.

There are good reasons to believe that our enjoyment of Nature operates on a number of different levels, often simultaneously. These include but probably are not exhausted by the sense of awe we experience when gazing across Yosemite Valley from Glacier Point or the feeling of comfort and peace we experience when looking down from a gentle hilltop on an open pasture with a pond, bordered by trees.[58] Our enjoyment can be visual, olfactory, auditory, and tactile. When out in Nature we can feel these simultaneously, and that is why *this* kind of experience is thought to possess a particular kind of value in itself.

There are other ways in which certain of our most basic responses to Nature are of value. For example, in his discussion of his notion of "wonder" Heschel quotes Plato and Aristotle on how a sense of "wonder" "is the prelude to knowledge."[59] Our response to Nature not only guides us away from certain genuine sources of danger, it leads us on to discover and invent as well. Heschel also offers his account of wonder as a cautionary tale about the objectification and disenchantment of the world and the dire consequences that can result. One could accept much of what he is claiming here in terms of a warning against a kind of Promethean arrogance. As a source of a healthy degree of humility and skepticism, such a feeling serves a useful and rational purpose. We have often been overly optimistic in our ability to understand and foresee the effects our technological prowess will have on the greater environment. This is not a denial of the wonders or value of science, only a call for greater care and doubt: two intellectual virtues that seem central to the scientific spirit itself. Because it inspires us to investigate and can serve as the source of the intellectual virtues of humility and skepticism, we should accept and encourage a sense of wonder in the face of Nature.

The final response to Nature which I would like to describe and advocate has a great deal in common with Freud's "oceanic feeling," though my conclusions regarding the worth of this feeling are contrary to Freud's view. As we saw earlier, Freud regards the oceanic feeling as a dangerous illusion. I will argue that a certain conception of it is not only beneficial but may be indispensable for a healthy, rich, and fulfilling life. I am not concerned with refuting or endorsing Freud's genetic explanation of the oceanic feeling. For my purposes, the source of this feeling is largely irrelevant. I take it as a fact, one that Freud himself admits, that many people do experience a feeling of "an indissoluble bond, of being one with the external world as a whole."

First, despite what Freud claims, there is nothing about such a feeling that necessarily entails beliefs contrary to reality. A great deal, of course, turns on how one conceives of being "one" with the world. Clearly it is contrary to reality for me to think of myself as one with the world in the sense of an *identity* between self and world (i.e., in the way that Batman is "one" with Bruce Wayne). But it is not at all irrational to see myself as part of the world; perhaps not quite in the way my arm is part of my body but surely in the way that the Nile is part of the ecosystem of a large portion of northeastern Africa. It is clearly contrary to reality to believe we are *not* part of the larger ecological systems that constitute the biological life on this planet. It is precisely such false beliefs that result in highly irrational and threatening behavior including, among other things, a dangerous rate of population growth and the wanton degradation of ecosystems. Because the oceanic feeling, properly understood, reinforces the belief that we are part of the larger ecosystems that constitute this planet, and this belief is both true and helps us to avoid such dangerous and irrational behavior and work to repair its harmful consequences, it seems perfectly reasonable to both accept and encourage such a feeling.

Since the oceanic feeling is fully consistent with these higher-order rational beliefs and their beneficial results, we are perfectly within our rights to *enjoy* it not only for these good results but also in itself, i.e., in the same way we enjoy other aesthetic experiences. As noted above, Freud himself admits that our aesthetic appreciation of beauty, including the beauty of Nature, offers us considerable consolation and that such experiences are much more varied and complex than they might at first seem. Why then can we not enjoy the special pleasure of an expansive and intimate feeling of oneness with Nature?

Finally, the oceanic feeling may give rise to and support a certain more abstract conception of our place in nature which fulfills a deep human need to belong to our greater environment. Such a need would be similar to our need to justify ourselves to our fellow human beings. If something like this is true, then there is considerable sense to Heschel's focus on the relationship between our experience of Nature and the search for meaning.[60] It does not seem unreasonable to believe that self-conscious and reflective creatures will sooner or later recognize that they are not only in human communities but in a greater natural environment as well. In order to find meaning among human beings, we need an understanding of our lives that not only *we* find meaningful but that others regard as worthy of respect as well. Perhaps once we become aware that we are embedded in the world at large, we feel a need for a parallel understanding of how we fit into this greater pattern. Having a reasonable view of our place, one that sees us as in some sense at home in Nature, can offer a kind of metaphysical as well as aesthetic consolation.[61] Moreover certain conceptions of how we fit into the world can offer concomitant benefits as well. For example, if one respects Nature and seeks a harmonious balance between human needs and Nature's well-being, such attitudes can help develop a general character that respects and seeks harmony with people as well.[62]

I have argued that there are many good reasons to accept and advocate certain responses to Nature. These fall into two, not wholly unrelated, categories. The first category concerns more basic responses to Nature. These include our respect for nature's power, our appreciation of the many forms of Natural beauty, and the inspiration, humility, and skepticism that can result from a sense of wonder in the face of Nature. The second set of reasons are associated with a particular conception of the oceanic feeling. I have argued that this feeling helps us to appreciate more complex truths about our relationship to the world which in turn can help us to avoid irrational and ultimately self-destructive behavior. This feeling of oneness with the world provides a distinctive and profoundly satisfying aesthetic experience as well. I have further suggested that it can give rise to and support a view of our place in Nature which offers us a kind of metaphysical consolation, a way of understanding ourselves as "at home" in the world, and that this in turn may help support certain more generally recognized ethical traits of character.

Thus there are a wide range of clear objective reasons for accepting and cultivating certain attitudes toward and understandings of Nature and in particular a certain conception of the oceanic feeling. It may well be that in order to be committed to some or perhaps all of these views about Nature and our place within it, in order to consistently make the sacrifices necessary to live according to these beliefs, we need the inspiration and support of the oceanic feeling—a sense of oneness with and love of Nature. If this is true, then while the oceanic feeling may not lead us to perceive God's sublime nature or God's presence behind the myriad phenomena of the world, it would prove critical to leading a reasonable, rich, and fulfilling life.

NOTES

My thanks to Bryan W. Van Norden and Robert B. Louden for helpful comments and suggestions on earlier drafts of this essay.

1. For a remarkably insightful study and critical evaluation of Kant's aesthetic views, see Paul Guyer, *Kant and the Claims of Taste* (Cambridge, Mass., 1979).

2. The sense in which natural beautiful objects appear to us as products of free creativity is connected to Kant's idea of Nature's "subjective purposiveness." Kant argues that Nature does not display a distinct purpose in its production of objects; i.e., Nature does not produce any given thing (or all things) in order to realize some predetermined end. Rather Nature displays an indeterminate purpose, a regularity that allows us to cognize it. The things Nature produces lend themselves to our perception and appreciation and thus manifest a "subjective purposiveness."

3. I owe this last observation to Ted Cohen. See his "Why Beauty Is a Symbol of Morality," in *Essays In Kant's Aesthetics,* edited by Ted Cohen and Paul Guyer (Chicago, 1982), 234.

4. Immanuel Kant, *Critique of Judgment,* translated by Werner S. Pluhar (Indianapolis, 1987): 123; Ak. 264.

5. Kant, *Judgment,* 97; Ak. 245.

6. Ibid., 98; Ak. 245.

7. Ibid.

8. Ibid., 99; Ak. 246.

9. Ibid., 99–100; Ak. 246–47, emphasis added.

10. Ibid., 103; Ak. 248.
11. Ibid., 105; Ak. 250.
12. Ibid., 106; Ak. 250.
13. Ibid.
14. Ibid., 119; Ak. 261.
15. Ibid.
16. Ibid., 120; Ak. 261.
17. Ibid., 120–21; Ak. 261–62.
18. Ibid., 122; Ak. 263.
19. Ibid.
20. Ibid., 122–23; Ak. 263–64.
21. I mean of course that our particular and contingent physical constitution is not the reason we (or any other possible creature) experience the distinctive nature of beauty, the sublime, and morality; not that our physical constitution does not determine the particular range of phenomena that we can appreciate in these different ways.
22. Freud, *The Future of an Illusion,* translated and edited by James Strachey (New York, 1961), 6. See page 19 for similar comments concerning how the fearfulness of "majestic, cruel and inexorable" Nature motivates the renunciations necessary for the rise of civilization.
23. Freud does not explicitly draw this distinction though it is well-attested here and throughout his works.
24. Freud, *Illusion,* 26–27.
25. For a revealing discussion of the differences between illusions and delusions, see Lee H. Yearley, "Freud as Creator and Critic of Cosmogonies and Their Ethics," in *Cosmogony and Ethical Order*, edited by Robin W. Lovin and Frank E. Reynolds (Chicago, 1985), 381–413. See especially pp. 390–92.
26. Freud, *Illusion,* 38.
27. Ibid.
28. Ibid., 41–42. For Kant's views, see the discussion above. This kind of blanket claim about what constitutes the true essence of religion is now largely recognized as in most cases deeply misguided. Daoism seems to present a clear counterexample to this particular claim of Freud's.
29. *Civilization and Its Discontents,* translated and edited by James Strachey (New York, 1961), 27.
30. Freud, *Illusion,* 44–45.
31. Ibid., 45.
32. The expression occurs only eight times in Freud's writings; all are in *Civilization:* 11 (4x), 15 (2x), 20 (1x), and 21 (1x). The friend was Romain Rolland.
33. Freud, *Civilization,* 11.
34. Ibid., 12.
35. Ibid.
36. Ibid., 13.
37. See Freud, *Illusion,* 17; Freud, *Civilization,* 31 and 45. Freud expresses similar approval for the "play" of creative writing, which shares much of the formal structure of the oceanic feeling, i.e., it is often based on early childhood experiences, awakened in present circumstances, and fulfills a wish. See "Creative Writers and Day-Dreaming" in *The Standard Edition of the Complete Works of Sigmund Freud,* translated and edited by James Strachey, vol. 9 (London, 1959): 141–53. Yearley raises a similar question when he asks, "Why, for example, is it acceptable to enjoy and be consoled by Dante's art, but unacceptable to believe in Dante-like cosmogony?" (See above, p. 391.)
38. Freud, *Civilization,* 15.
39. Ibid., 20.
40. Ibid.
41. Arnold Eisen, "Re-reading Heschel on the Commandments," *Modern Judaism,* 9, no. 1 (February 1989): 5.
42. For a helpful and succinct discussion of the nature and method of Heschel's work, see

Jakob J. Petuchowski, "Faith as the Leap of Action: The Theology of Abraham Joshua Heschel," *Commentary,* 25, no. 5 (May 1958): 390–97.

43. Abraham J. Heschel, *Who Is Man?* (Stanford, Calif., 1965), 9–10. As we shall see, Heschel believes a proper sense of awe is necessary in order to discern the objective, divine nature of the world. See his *God in Search of Man* (New York, 1955), 75.

44. Heschel, *Who?* 76–77.

45. Heschel, *Search,* 39. On this and the preceding page, Heschel outlines Kant's views on the sublime and contrasts them with his own.

46. Ibid., 46.

47. Abraham J. Heschel, *Man is Not Alone* (New York, 1951), 31. My understanding of this aspect of Heschel's thought has benefited from my reading of James M. Hyman's dissertation, "Abraham Heschel: Theology and Meaningfulness," Stanford University, 1996.

48. Heschel, *Who?* 76.

49. Ibid., 77.

50. Ibid. Heschel's views on feelings of awe are quite distinctive. He describes awe as what we might call a mode of perceiving, something like "appreciating the world as divine creation." He says, "Awe is more than an emotion; it is a way of understanding" (*Who?* 88; *Search,* 46, 74). Moreover, it "calls" on us to act in certain ways, "Religion is not a feeling for the mystery of living . . . but rather the question *what to do* with the feeling for the mystery of living, what to do with awe, wonder or fear . . . wonder is not a state of aesthetic enjoyment. Endless wonder is endless tension" (*Who?* 110). Awe is also inherently attractive: "Awe, unlike fear, does not make us shrink from the awe-inspiring object, but, on the contrary, draws us near to it. This is why awe is compatible with both love and joy" (*Search,* 77).

51. Heschel, *Who?* 90.

52. Heschel, *Search,* 36.

53. Ibid., 40.

54. Heschel repeatedly insists that the awe he describes is not restricted to or a particular characteristic of the fearfulness and terrible power of Nature. Yet his examples, particularly those drawn from the Hebrew Bible, are almost always of precisely this kind. For example, see Job 37:14–22 or Psalms 8:4–5, which he quotes on pp. 47 and 48 of *Search.*

55. See his *The Rationality of Emotion* (Cambridge, Mass., 1991), 122–23.

56. From "Must a Concern for the Environment Be Centered on Human Beings?" in *Reflecting on Nature: Readings in Environmental Philosophy,* edited by Lori Greun and Dale Jamieson (New York, 1994), 51. Williams argues that there are two legitimate concerns we should have for Nature: the feeling of respect mentioned in the quoted passage (which he also calls "Promethean fear"—cf. my notion of Promethean arrogance below) and an appreciation of the beautiful or sublime (he seems to use these two terms interchangeably). As will be clear, I agree with both of these concerns and see them as deriving directly from the earlier thinkers whose thought we have explored. However, I also see additional legitimate concerns we should have for Nature.

57. Freud, *Civilization,* 33.

58. Edward O. Wilson has claimed that human beings possess "biophilia," an "innate tendency to focus on life and lifelike processes." See *Biophilia* (Cambridge, Mass., 1984), 1. This claim is explored in a series of essays in *The Biophilia Hypothesis,* edited by Stephen R. Kellert and Edward O. Wilson (Washington, D.C., 1993). See in particular the essays by Roger S. Ulrich and by Judith H. Heerwagen and Gordon H. Orians which argue for an innate preference for savanna landscapes like that described here.

59. Heschel, *Search,* 46.

60. Charles Taylor has argued that human beings are meaning-seeking creatures in a way not wholly unlike Heschel, though with significantly different conclusions. See his *Human Agency and Language: Philosophical Papers 1* (Cambridge, 1985), *Sources of the Self* (Cambridge, Mass., 1989), and *The Ethics of Authenticity* (Cambridge, Mass., 1991). I propose that just as we feel a need to justify ourselves to others in order to find meaning for ourselves, we

need to have a conception of our place in the greater scheme of things which is both consistent with our other beliefs and makes sense of our lives.

61. I have argued that the early Chinese Confucian philosopher Xunzi proposed something like this vision as part of his justification of the Confucian view of self and society. See my "A Happy Symmetry: Xunzi's Ethical Thought," *Journal of the American Academy of Religion* 59, no. 2 (Summer 1991): 309–22.

62. David Wong argues that our deep capacities for appreciating qualities such as harmony in music or in conceptions of our place in Nature may play an important role in moral education. See his "Xunzi on Moral Motivation," in *Chinese Language, Thought and Culture,* edited by Philip J. Ivanhoe (LaSalle, Ill., 1996), 202–23.

Creation without Creationism

NORMAN KRETZMANN

1. AQUINAS'S NATURAL THEOLOGY

In my view a great deal—not all—of theology's traditional subject matter is really continuous with philosophy's subject matter and ought to be integrated with it in practice.[1] Most philosophers who lived before the twentieth century would share that view, and no substantive developments in the last hundred years should have obscured it. In the first three quarters of the twentieth century it surely was obscured, but we have recently been witnessing a development in which that view is no longer so hard to find among philosophers: as late-twentieth-century theologians have been moving away from their traditional, doctrinal subject matter, philosophers have been moving in.[2] And natural theology, a branch of philosophy, interests me especially because it provides the traditional and still central means of integrating (some of) theology with philosophy.

For a concise, general account of natural theology's nature and status, independent of my particular concern with Aquinas's work, I couldn't do better than to present William Alston's view of the discipline in this passage: "*Natural theology* is the enterprise of providing support for religious beliefs by starting from premises that neither are nor presuppose any religious beliefs. We begin from the mere existence of the world, or the teleological order of the world, or the concept of God, and we try to show that when we think through the implications of our starting point we are led to recognize the existence of a being that possesses attributes sufficient to identify Him as God. Once we get that foothold we may seek to show that a being could not have the initial attributes without also possessing certain others; in this manner we try to go as far as we can in building up a picture of God without relying on any supposed experience of God or communication from God, or on any religious authority."[3] The view Alston takes in this passage is broad by comparison with the more familiar notion of natural theology, which limits it to attempts to argue for (or against) the existence of God.[4] His view here could serve well as a sketch of Aquinas's undertaking in Book I of *Summa contra gentiles* (SCG), which Aquinas himself describes as covering "matters associated with God *considered in himself*" (I.9.57),[5] i.e., the subject matter of what might fairly be called classical natural theology: the existence of something whose inferred nature constitutes a prima facie basis for identifying it as God, and the further aspects of God's nature that can be inferred in working out the implications of that starting point.

But an even broader view of natural theology is called for if it is to include the topics Aquinas goes on to develop in SCG II and III—a view almost as broad as the one Alston takes up soon after presenting the one we've been considering: "This characterization of natural theology [the one quoted above] sticks closely to the classically recognized 'arguments for the existence of God', but it need not be construed that narrowly. It also includes attempts to show that we can attain the best understanding of this or that area of our experience or sphere of concern—morality, human life, society, human wickedness, science, art, mathematics, or whatever—if we look at it from the standpoint of a theistic . . . metaphysics" (p. 289). The idea of a natural theology that goes far beyond arguments for God's existence is one Alston shares with Aquinas, as can be seen in detail in SCG II and III. I think it's quite likely that Aquinas believes, too, that the explanatory capacity of natural theology is in theory universal—as Alston suggests with his "or whatever." But the idea Aquinas puts into practice in SCG is less broad than the one Alston outlines here. Aquinas does take up some of the broad topics Alston lists, and a few more besides. But he expressly excludes the concerns of natural science from the scope of the project he's engaging in, and he shows no signs of having thought about including art or mathematics. Still, Alston's implied characterization of natural theology as theistic metaphysics is very like what Aquinas seems to have had in mind generally.

Aquinas devotes SCG II to creation, "the emergence of created things from [God]," and SCG III to providence, "the ordering and directing of created things toward [God] as their goal" (I.9.57). As even Aquinas's short descriptions of the three parts of his natural theology may suggest, it is intended to integrate a great many topics that would ordinarily be treated separately, and differently, in other branches of philosophy—branches recognizable both in the Aristotelian philosophy he knew best and in the philosophy of the late twentieth century, including, e.g., metaphysics, philosophy of mind, epistemology, and ethics.[6] Integrating all those topics by means of natural theology involves developing within this particular branch of philosophy some of the subject matter specifically associated with theology as it developed outside philosophy in the three great monotheisms, in the form of "revealed" or "dogmatic" theology, based on scriptural exegesis. That, of course, is what makes this branch of philosophy natural *theology:* investigating, by means of analysis and argument, at least the existence and nature of God and, in this fuller development, the relation of everything else—but especially human nature and behavior—to God considered as reality's first principle.

But developing parts of that subject matter within philosophy of course requires forgoing appeals to any putative revelation or religious experience as evidence for the truth of propositions, and taking for granted only those few naturally evident considerations that traditionally constitute data acceptable for philosophy generally.[7] That's what makes it *natural* theology.

Aquinas's natural theology does, however, make a restricted, philosophically tolerable use of propositions he considers to have been divinely revealed. Often at the end of a chapter in SCG I–III, after having argued for some proposition in several different ways, each of which scrupulously omits any reference to revelation, he will cite Scripture by way of showing that what has just been established by unaided reason agrees with what he takes to be revealed truth.[8] (For example, in Book I, Chapter 20, after having presented ten arguments to show that God is not in any way corporeal, he observes that "divine authority concurs with this demonstrated truth," citing three biblical passages, including John 4:24: "God is a spirit . . . " [188].) On those occasions he certainly does not take himself to be introducing a revealed text in order to remove doubts about natural theology's results; they are, after all, the results of "natural reason, to which *everybody* is *compelled* to assent" (I.2.11). "Divine authority" is never invoked as *support* for any proposition occurring as a premise or a conclusion in the logical structure of SCG I–III.[9]

Scripture's systematic contribution to Aquinas's natural theology may be construed as primarily an aid to navigation, showing him his destinations and practicable routes to them in a rational progression. From any one of the propositions previously argued for in the systematic development of his natural theology, reason could, in theory, validly derive infinitely many further propositions. But Aquinas's systematic natural theology, like the presentation of any well-defined subject matter in a series of connected arguments, is more expository than exploratory.[10] It is designed to show, primarily, that reason *unsupported* by revelation could have come up with many—not all—of just those propositions that constitute the established subject matter of what he takes to be revealed theology. But that design requires that reason be *guided* by what he takes to be revelation. Whatever may be said of natural theology generally, Aquinas's version of it certainly is, as Alston puts it, "the enterprise of providing support *for religious beliefs* by starting from premises that neither are nor presuppose any religious beliefs."[11] So Aquinas needs Scripture in these circumstances as providing the chart that guides his choice of propositions to argue for as well as a list of specifications that can be consulted to see, first, that it is indeed one and the same "truth that faith professes and reason investigates" (I.9.55) and, second, "*how* the demonstrative truth is in harmony with the faith of the Christian religion" (I.2.12). But his distinctive, primary aim in the first three books of SCG is the systematic development of that demonstrative truth, *up to* the point at which the theism being argued for begins relying on propositions that are initially accessible to reason only via revelation and becomes *distinctively* Christian.

As I see it, then, SCG I–III is Aquinas's most unified, systematic contribution to the project of arriving at a thoroughly rational confirmation of perfect-being theism generally, of showing the extent to which what had been revealed might have been discovered, the extent to which "the invisible things of God from the creation of the world" might be "clearly seen, being understood by the things that are made" (Romans 1:20). As such it is addressed to every open-minded, reasoning person.[12]

2. FOR ALL THINGS THE CAUSE OF BEING

Very broadly speaking, the topic of both SCG II and SCG III is God's transeunt action—action that has overt effects outside the agent. As Aquinas explains at the beginning of Book II, in Book I's investigation of matters concerning God considered in himself, the only divine action investigated was the immanent action of intellection and volition. Consequently, "for the complete consideration of divine truth we still have to investigate the second [i.e., transeunt] kind of activity—the one through which God produces things [Book II] and governs them [Book III]" (II.1.856). In II.6–14 he investigates the producing of things, the only divine transeunt activity I'm considering here, as regards its source in God; in II.15 as regards its terminus in everything else. After these essential preliminaries, Aquinas is ready to undertake the direct examination of the activity itself, a project to which he devotes the next six chapters (II.16–21).

He begins by delineating this divine activity as a species of production, which is itself a species of transeunt action (II.16). Delineating a species, or constructing a real definition, involves identifying its differentia, the characteristic or set of characteristics that differentiates that species from all others in its genus. The differentia Aquinas identifies for God's universal production reveals that this activity can correctly be classified as production or even as transeunt action only on the basis of Aquinas's relational method for adapting ordinary terms to the purposes of making true statements about God.[13] In this case the method prescribes omitting from the definition of God's universal production some elements of the standard definitions of production and of transeunt action—those elements that are incompatible with absolute perfection. In II.17–19 Aquinas examines more closely the omission of one particularly important set of those elements. Having in that way delineated the peculiar character of this activity, he reasons from it to the sort of agent it entails (II.20–21), concluding that universal production must be the action of God alone.

(I'm postponing regular use of the established, familiar name for God's universal production only because in SCG II Aquinas himself seems careful to avoid using the verb *creare* [or the noun *creatio*] until the very end of Chapter 16, where he introduces it in special circumstances we'll be looking at. Nowhere in Chapters 6 through 15 does he speak explicitly of "creating" or of "creation." Even in the introductory Chapters 1 through 5 there is only one stray occurrence of the verb, and that one is in an example.[14] And although in Chapters 1–16 he often uses the associated noun *creatura* [which I'm translating as 'created thing'], he is plainly treating it not as a technical term but just as a generic designation for any natural thing considered in the way required by his purposes in Book II—i.e., in its relation to God. As he says elsewhere, "every being that is not God is a created thing (*creatura*) . . . " [ST Ia.5.3, sc].)

That God is the producer of everything else was established in Chapter 15, which Aquinas himself titled "God is for all things the cause of being."[15] However, even the title of the chapter shows that extensional universality isn't all that's at issue. The causal claim isn't merely 'God is for all things the cause'. If it were, there'd be no good reason not to read it simply and broadly as 'God is the cause of all things'. That God is for all things the cause of being is a narrower and immeasurably stronger claim.

When you make a salad, you are the (efficient) cause of the salad. And since without you that particular salad would not have been, it might seem right, if a little stilted, to say that you are for that salad the cause of being. But putting it that way does exaggerate your role, which would be described more accurately as your being for that salad *a* cause of being. In the case of an artificial thing, such as a salad, characterizing you as a cause of being for it means simply that without you there would not have been that result of your altering and moving natural things: in this case (leaves of) lettuce, (slices of) tomato, (shreds of) carrot, etc. You've given certain natural things a new inessential (accidental) form: what were unassociated, particular, whole vegetables have been transformed into a new, artificial, particular thing that was not before. You might even have been the gardener who grew those vegetables from seed, in which case it would be right to say that you are for that head of lettuce (and the rest) a cause of being. If you had left that seed unplanted, that head of lettuce wouldn't exist at all. But neither you nor any other ordinary agent is for *lettuce* the cause of being. An ordinary artificial production can be analyzed along the same lines, in terms of altering and moving pre-existing stuff that is ultimately natural.

The pattern of this analysis can be obscured in cases where the strata of artifice are many and go deep. When you compose a poem, you're making English sentences that have never been made before; you are for those sentence-types and for that poem a cause of being, through giving their constituent words a new arrangement. Now the making of the poem is unlike the making of the salad because the things that you the poet are combining in novel ways—the words—are themselves not natural but artificial. And even the particular, mostly complex vocal sounds that long ago became words of English also originated in deliberate human actions. Nonetheless, neither you, nor the first speakers of English, nor the first users of language are for *sound* (or even for *human vocal* sound) the cause of being. All the strata of artifice, however many they may be, are always supported on the bedrock of nature.

Ordinary production that is artificial—i.e., involving at some stage human intellect and will—makes up only a tiny fraction of ordinary production, of course. A seed's production of a plant, the plant's production of a flower, the flower's production of a fruit, the fruit's production of a seed—all of those, like countless other, widely divergent processes, are instances of ordinary *natural* production. And, again, while that flower on this plant can be correctly described as for this fruit a cause of being, neither it nor any other ordinary producer can be identified as for *fruit* the cause of being.

No one should imagine—looking ahead just a little—that considerations of these sorts will be called on to support a hypothesis of some extraordinary individual producer that is for sound, or for fruit, the direct cause of being. The natural sciences have given us good reasons to believe that variously linked cosmological, physical, chemical, biological evolutionary processes operating within the stuff of the universe in accordance with natural laws can account for the being of galaxies, stars, and planets; of light, heat, and sound; of hydrogen, helium, and uranium; of viruses, plants, and animals. If in that context we take seriously the thesis that God is for *all* things the cause of *being*, that God's productive action is the ultimate explanation of the existence of whatever else exists, artificial as well as natural, then we are supposing that God's productive action is the cause of being for (at least) all the primordial stuff of the universe and the dispositions natural to that stuff (the natural laws), and that God is in that way (at least) the cause of being for *everything* other than God. "Everything there is besides God is from God as its *first* source" (*Summa theologiae* [ST] Ia.7.2, sc).

So in Chapter 15 Aquinas is explicitly out to show both that God's production is extensionally universal, and that God's production is absolutely fundamental, or *intensionally* universal. I think that the second of those two claims is less effectively argued in Chapter 15 than the first.[16] In Chapter 16, however, intensional universality emerges more clearly and is argued effectively.

3. OUT OF NO ANTECEDENT MATTER

The thesis of Chapter 16 is contained in its first sentence, which deserves to be examined as a whole: "But on that basis it is apparent that God has produced things as regards their being out of no pre-existing [subject], as out of matter (*Ex hoc autem apparet quod Deus res in esse produxit ex nullo praeexistente sicut ex materia*)" (932).

The first words of the sentence, "But on that basis it is apparent that . . . ," show that Aquinas takes this thesis to follow readily from the result of Chapter 15, as it surely does. Besides God himself, there can't be anything at all that exists *before* "God is for *all* things the cause of being," any pre-existing stuff *out of* which God produces *all* things as regards their being (as you produce things out of vegetables or out of words, the matter of your salad or of your poem). The fact that Aquinas nonetheless provides eleven arguments in support of the chapter's thesis suggests that he wants to accomplish more here than simply to establish that "God has produced things as regards their being out of no pre-existing [subject], as out of matter." We'll be looking at additional results of that sort in some of those arguments.

The first part of Chapter 16's thesis, "God has produced things as regards their being," is clearly intended to be a version of the thesis established in Chapter 15. And so, I think, it can justifiably be emended to read "has produced *all* things." With that emendation Chapter 16's thesis is, of course, even more apparent on the basis of Chapter 15. But the version of Chapter 15's thesis embedded here—"God has produced [all] things as regards their being"—is more awkward than the original: "God is for all things the cause of being." I would ordinarily have translated *in esse produxit* less clumsily as "has brought into being," which is in any case what the Latin means. But I want the translation here to preserve the fact that in this thesis Aquinas is refining the notion of God's "producing" everything else, which has been his explicit topic through Book II so far.

The refining is encapsulated in the last words of the thesis: "out of no pre-existing [subject], as out of matter." Anyone who has any acquaintance with the concept of divine creation will recognize this as a wordy surrogate for the famil-iar, elegant "out of nothing" (*ex nihilo*). Even the medieval scribe responsible for giving Chapter 16 its title reverts to that simple formula: "*Quod Deus ex nihilo produxit res in esse.*" Aquinas himself, however, studiously avoids it throughout the chapter, always using a more detailed expression, like the one he uses here, in the first statement of the thesis.[17] And since in those expressions he is present-ing what he takes to be the differentia that specifies creation within the genus of production, in our investigation of Chapter 16 it is only sensible to stay with his less elegant, more careful formulations.

Besides, these more complicated formulations suggest that Aquinas has some particular purpose for using them here, since he is in general certainly not opposed to characterizing creation as *ex nihilo.* On the contrary, "it must be firmly maintained that God can, and does, make something out of nothing (*ex nihilo*)," as he insists in a later work (*Quaestiones disputatae de potentia* [QDP] 3.1c). And in his commentary on the *Sentences,* written before SCG, he distin-guished three ways in which "the thing that is said to be created" can rightly be said to be "out of nothing": (1) "because it is not out of anything pre-existing"; (2) because in any created thing not-being is "*naturally* prior" to being, by which he means that "the thing has being only from the influence of a higher cause" and "if left to itself" reverts to not-being; (3) because in the created thing not-being is not just naturally but also *temporally* prior to being, "so that it is said to be out of nothing because it is temporally after nothing" (In Sent. II.1.1.2c). Re-garding (3), Aquinas says "in *that* way creation cannot be demonstrated, nor is it granted by philosophers. It is, however, supposed through faith" (ibid.). So it can't be in this third way that creation could be said to be *ex nihilo* in Aquinas's natural theology in SCG II, in which he is out to argue for creation in a way that will be acceptable to philosophers. Of (1) and (2), on the other hand, Aquinas says "if these two suffice for the defining conception (*ratio*) of creation, then in that way creation can be demonstrated. And it is in that way that philosophers have posited creation" (ibid.). Sense (2) does have relevance here, especially in light of considerations that show that God's role as first cause has as much to do with sustaining as with producing, with keeping things in existence as with bring-ing them into existence in the first place. However, the formulations Aquinas uses in SCG II.16 clearly show that it is only (1) that is explicitly at issue in this chap-ter. And perhaps it is just because he is concerned here with only one of the three senses he had already distinguished for *ex nihilo* that he prefers to avoid that expression in favor of less familiar, unambiguous formulations.

At the end of Section 2 above I referred to the "absolutely fundamental, or *intensionally* universal" character of God's production. I mean that in this species of production the producer is not merely a cause of the product that results from the producer's engaging in a process of moving and changing pre-existing stuff, as in all other, *ordinary* species of production. Instead, God is for any created thing considered just as such the ultimate cause of its being *at all*. On the basis of even these preliminary considerations of Chapter 16's thesis we are entitled to conclude that this characterization of God's production is entailed by the production's being absolutely independent of antecedent matter (and, therefore, devoid of any operation on any pre-existing stuff). The no-antecedent-matter differentia also tends to support the claim that God is the ultimate producer of everything else, since the species of production that depends on nothing will be what produces the stuff for all ordinary species of production (unless there is some basic cosmic matter that is entirely unproduced, existing independently[18]). Ordinary production, all of which does depend on antecedent matter, is neither universal in this way—extensionally—nor, of course, can it ever be universal intensionally, in the sense that it accounts for the *whole* product. This intensional universality of God's production of things depends even more clearly on the no-antecedent-matter differentia. Aquinas brings out this consequence in replying elsewhere to the question "Is creating making something out of nothing (*ex nihilo*)?": "we have to consider not only the emanation of a particular being from a particular agent, but also the emanation of the whole of being (*totius entis*) from the universal cause, which is God. And it is this emanation that we designate by the name 'creation'. . . . [S]o if we are considering the emanation of the universal whole of being (*totius entis universalis*) from the first source, it is impossible that any being be presupposed for that emanation. But 'nothing' is the same as 'no being'. Therefore, . . . creation, which is the emanation of the whole of being (*totius esse*), is out of the non-being that is nothing" (ST Ia.45.1c).

As it has emerged so far, then, the no-antecedent-matter differentia of this species of production seems to have several interrelated consequences; but they can conveniently be reduced to these two: God's production of things is (A) extensionally universal and (B) intensionally universal. God is (A) for *all* things (B) the cause of *being*.

And, as I suggested earlier, what differentiates divine production also distinguishes it from all ordinary transeunt activity, especially because of (B). Even Aquinas's introduction of the notion of transeunt activity indicates this, when he describes it at the very beginning of Book II as activity "that goes over into an external thing (*in exteriorem rem transit*)—e.g., heating, cutting, and building—and is a completing of the result that is established (*constituitur*) through that very [first kind of] activity"—i.e., immanent activity (1.853). His careful formulation—"goes over into an external thing"—leaves room for characterizing God's doubly universal production of things out of no antecedent matter as transeunt activity. But, as his (Aristotelian) examples show, all ordinary transeunt action must be action on some pre-existing stuff. And so in ascribing transeunt action to God, the natural theologian using the relational method will have to omit transeunt action's dependence on antecedent matter, because dependence on anything indicates something less than absolute perfection in the agent. God's productive transeunt action is like the ordinary kind in that the agent brings some other thing into existence, and different from the ordinary kind in that the agent achieves that result absolutely independently of any pre-existing stuff. If, as the reader of SCG already has some reason to think, for God to produce something is simply to will its existence,[19] then this transeunt action of God's will turn out to be a special case of his immanent action of intellection and volition.

4. NOT EVEN PRIME MATTER

The eleven arguments of Chapter 16 present an embarrassment of riches.[20] Since, as we've been seeing, the chapter's thesis really is apparent on the basis of Chapter 15's result, these arguments are less important as providing support for the no-antecedent-matter differentia than for their exploration of some of its ramifications. Several of the arguments are worth investigating; I will limit myself to just two. These two are, I think, especially clear in themselves, they focus on concepts central to Aquinas's theoretical account, and they involve no technicalities extraneous to our considerations here.

The argument I want to consider first focuses on *prime* matter, the only element of Aquinas's account of nature that even a friendly critic might well suppose could not be included within the extensional universality of divine production.[21] One could argue for its exclusion along these lines, for instance: "Some actuality is the terminus of every action, just as the action also proceeds from some actuality; for every agent acts insofar as it is in actuality, and every agent does something like itself in nature. But *prime matter is pure potentiality.* Therefore, the action of creating cannot terminate in it. And so not all things are created by God" (QDP 3.5, obj. 3). Everything that is taken for granted in this objection is a principle or definition that is basic to Aquinas's own (Aristotelian) metaphysics, including the crucial definition of prime matter as pure potentiality.[22] And so this is a formidable argument against including prime matter within the otherwise universal scope of God's production. How could even an omnipotent agent produce pure potentiality? It's true that producing the world's primordial stuff with all its built-in natural dispositions would necessarily involve producing natural potentialities also. But not even those distinguishable, natural potentialities—such as water's potentiality to be converted into steam—are produced in their own right or numbered among existent things.

In his rejoinder to the objection against including prime matter within the ranks of created things, Aquinas acknowledges that it's true that pure potentiality, considered just as such, really cannot be created: "That argument does prove that prime matter is not created *per se*. But from this it does not follow that it is not created *under a form;* for it is in that way that prime matter has being in actuality" (QDP 3.5, ad 3). "For that reason,"[23] as he helpfully puts it elsewhere, "it is more *con*created than created" (ST Ia.7.2, ad 3)—i.e., it is created only as the theoretically necessitated concomitant of the form that gives it actuality.[24] Even these brief introductory remarks provide enough background against which to assess this eleventh argument of Chapter 16, which I'll label PM for its use of the notion of prime matter.

> Prime matter *is,* in a way, since it is being in potentiality (*ens in potentia*). But God is the cause of *all* that are (*omnium quae sunt*), as was shown above [II.15]. Therefore, God is the cause of prime matter. *No* [matter] is pre-existing [matter] for *it.* Therefore, divine action does not require a pre-existing nature. (16.943)

What I've been saying about prime matter so far has certainly not cleared up all the difficulties in the notion, but nothing about it could be clearer than the crucial claim in PM's fourth sentence: there couldn't be any pre-existing matter out of which *prime* matter could be produced. So if the claim that "God is the cause of prime matter" is justified, it will indeed follow that "divine action does not require a pre-existing nature" out of which to produce its products. However, the justification offered in argument PM itself for that causal claim in the third sentence strikes me as dubious and unnecessarily weak, partly because of the overly generous existential claim with which PM begins, but even more because Aquinas then cites the *extensional* universality of divine production (in the first two sentences) where an appeal to its *intensional* universality would have done the job more effectively. He shows this, I think, in a parallel discussion in ST: "Therefore, that which is the cause of things *insofar as they are beings* must be the cause of things not only insofar as they are *thus-and-so* through accidental forms, or insofar as they are *these* [things] through substantial forms, but also as regards *all that pertains to the being of those things in any way at all.* And it is on that basis that we have to posit even prime matter as created by the universal cause of beings" (Ia.44.2c). How exactly prime matter does pertain to the being of things will be explored by Aquinas in later chapters of Book II—e.g., 39–45. For present purposes it seems enough to recognize that he can justify his claim that even prime matter must be included among the products, or among at least the by-products, of God's universal production, although the justification he offers in argument PM is not the strongest sort available to him. We can also see that, as argument PM claims, the production (or by-production) of prime matter is paradigmatically production out of no antecedent matter.

5. NOT THROUGH MOVEMENT OR CHANGE

Chapter 16's fourth argument is the other one I want to consider. I'll call it MC, for its rejection of movement and change as features of God's universal production.

Acting only through movement and change is unsuited to the universal cause of being, for it is not through movement and change that a being is made out of *absolute* non-being. Instead, [through movement and change] *this* being is made out of *that* non-being. But God is the *universal* source of being, as has been shown [II.15]. Therefore, it is not suited to God that he act only through movement or through change. Neither, therefore, is it suited to God to need pre-existing matter in order to make something. (16.936)

Part of the description of ordinary production in argument MC (second sentence) is perfectly obvious. Since all ordinary production is out of antecedent matter, all ordinary producing must involve doing something to that stuff: moving or changing it in some way—either substantially (as in generation and corruption) or accidentally (as in artificial production). As Aquinas observes in the immediately preceding argument, "everything that cannot produce things as regards their being (*producere res in esse*) except out of antecedent matter acts only by moving and transmuting (*transmutando*), for making something out of matter occurs through some kind of movement or change (*mutationem*)" of that matter (935).

But ordinary production is also described (in the second sentence) as making "*this* being . . . out of *that* non-being." Of course, in ordinary production "that *non*-being," the antecedent matter that the ordinary producer moves or changes in order to make "this *being*," is more readily recognized as some other, pre-existing *being* or *beings*. The antecedent matter out of which you make an omelette is ordinarily thought of as eggs rather than as the particularized non-being of that particular omelette, though it can be thought of in that way, too—with a little effort. Aquinas is thinking of it in that way here because he is contrasting ordinary production in this respect with God's universal production "out of *absolute* non-being" (*ex non ente simpliciter*) (first sentence). Anyone who does think of creation as involving change will take it to involve the change from nonbeing to being and will liken it in that respect to ordinary production, which involves a change from *that* non-being to *this* being. But in the unique case of creation there is nothing at all, not even prime matter, that can be identified as that non-being. Every *change* is a move from that to this, or has two extremes. Creation, though, has only one.[25]

Argument MC's descriptions of God as "the universal cause of being" (first sentence) and "the universal source of being" (third sentence) are plainly to be interpreted here as picking out *intensional* universality. What's at issue in MC isn't that *every* thing owes its being to God, but that everything owes to God the fact that it is *at all*. It's only on that basis that Aquinas can argue (as he does in the first sentence) that "movement and change is unsuited to the universal cause of being" just because "it is not through movement and change that a being is made out of *absolute* non-being."

Notice, however, that what is "unsuited to the universal cause of being" is "acting *only* through movement and change" (first sentence), and that "it is not suited to God that he act *only* through movement or through change" (fourth sentence). Moreover, MC's conclusion is that it is not "suited to God to *need* pre-existing matter in order to make something" (fifth sentence). (The conclusions of all the other arguments of Chapter 16 are relevantly like this one, as can be seen in n. 17.) The plain implication is that although God's doubly universal production necessarily involves no pre-existing matter and thus no movement or change, there may be *other* divine transeunt action that *does* involve the moving or changing of pre-existing matter. For instance, a miracle, conceived of as a divine intervention in natural processes, would presumably qualify as transeunt action of that sort—e.g., the parting of the Red Sea. But miracles are no part of Aquinas's concern here, where he is developing his natural theology, detached from the data of revelation. More relevantly, since in Aquinas's usage every particular natural thing is a "created thing" (*creatura*), a divinely produced thing, there must be perpetual, ubiquitous transeunt action in which God does act through moving or changing pre-existing matter. If there is some sense in which God is the producer of the maple tree now growing in my backyard, then he has produced it not out of nothing but out of pre-existing matter: a maple seed, dirt, water, air, sunlight, etc. And if all the galaxies are results of the Big Bang, then they, too, are things God produces out of antecedent matter through movement and change. If God's production of things is extensionally universal in the sense that every natural particular is one of its products, then it will have to involve all the innumerable modes of natural generation actually going on in the universe. But, of course, in none of those modes will natural generation be production out of no antecedent matter. That sort of doubly universal production—creation—must be distinguished, strictly speaking, from natural generation, as Aquinas will explain later in Book II.[26]

This emerging picture of a perpetually busy divine producer occupied with unimaginably many, unimaginably tiny details of natural production is by no means the only one discernible here, however. On the basis of what Aquinas has been arguing for so far, it's also possible, and much more attractive, to view the entire universe—all the stuff there is, with all its natural dispositions—as the sole immediate product of God's doubly universal production out of absolute non-being. One way of combining the extensional and intensional universality of God's production of things is to view the universe, the-whole-of-what-there-is-other-than-God, as its single immediate product. In this holistic interpretation of God's doubly universal production of everything else, everything in the universe, down to each particular generated in keeping with its natural laws, will then be viewed as entirely and ultimately dependent on God for its being at all, for its coming into being and for its remaining in being as long as it does. In producing the universe out of no pre-existing matter and so without engaging in any movement or change, God is ultimately the producer also of this maple tree. And this maple tree counts as a created thing—as a thing for which God is the cause of being—even though it is rightly viewed as directly produced out of antecedent matter through a process of movement and change in accordance with natural laws.

This holistic interpretation is not the whole story, but it is the crucial beginning of it, the part that most clearly manifests the intensional universality of God's production of things in a way that can be read as implying also its extensional universality. Perhaps this interpretation is adumbrated already in the first chapter of Book II, where Aquinas says that by the phrase "the works of your hands" in the passage from Psalms (142/3:5) that he uses as a motto for the book, "we understand the heaven and the earth, and all the things that come into existence from God as handiwork comes from an artisan" (857). If "the heaven and the earth" is interpreted (plausibly) as the universe, and "all the things that come into existence from God as handiwork comes from an artisan" is interpreted (plausibly) as the natural particulars that are produced immediately out of antecedent matter through a process of movement or change in accordance with natural laws, then even that introductory observation suggests the interpretation I'm proposing.

In Chapter 16 itself, the passage that most dramatically suggests the holistic interpretation is also focused on a verse of Scripture, Genesis 1:1, the only verse Aquinas quotes as confirmation of his claims in this chapter: "Now Holy Scripture confirms this truth, saying 'In the beginning God created the heaven and the earth'." Aquinas then takes this verse, with its use of the verb 'create', to provide him with the occasion on which, finally, to introduce the technical term he will freely use from this point onward in Book II: "For *to create* is nothing other than to produce something as regards its being without antecedent matter" (944). All that warrants his reading this verse as depicting producing something as regards its being without antecedent matter is the phrase "In the beginning," but taking the very first words of Scripture strictly enough to provide that warrant is not unreasonable. And the something that is produced in that way is "the heaven and the earth," which, as is especially clear regarding the very beginning, is the-whole-of-what-there-was-to-begin-with-other-than-God.

6. SOMETHING OUT OF NOTHING

Besides the confirming allusion to Genesis 1:1, the postscript to Chapter 16 contains Aquinas's correction of what he characterizes as an ancient philosophical mistake. "Now on this basis"—i.e., Chapter 16's establishing no-antecedent-matter as the differentia for creation—"we refute the mistake of the ancient philosophers who claimed that there is absolutely no cause for matter. [They claimed this] because they observed that there is always something antecedent to action where the actions of particular agents are concerned. From that observation they derived the opinion, common to all, that nothing is made or comes about out of nothing (*ex nihilo nihil fit*). As regards *particular* agents that is of course *true*. But they had not yet arrived at a cognition of the *universal* agent, which is productive (*activum*) of the *whole* of being, [the agent] for whose action it is necessary to presuppose *nothing*" (945).

The "opinion common to all" that is at issue here—*ex nihilo nihil fit* (ENNF)—is powerful and broad enough to look like a universal first principle.[27]

In acknowledging its truth as regards particular agents, Aquinas is indeed accepting ENNF as a universal first principle *of nature,* which applies correctly to the productive activity, natural or artificial, of any and every created thing. The ancient philosophers' mistake is not their having adopted ENNF, which they correctly derived from their observation of particular agents, but their having maintained on the basis of ENNF that "there is absolutely no cause for matter." For that reason Aquinas will, later in Book II, recognize ENNF as a principle indispensable to the work of the natural philosopher rather than as just a superseded stage in the history of philosophy.[28] And it is, after all, natural philosophers to whom Aristotle attributed ENNF.[29] But Aquinas's present concern is not with nature but with the metaphysics of creation. And creation, the intensionally universal production of things that here constitutes the sole exception to ENNF, is the business not of the natural philosopher but of "the metaphysician, who considers universal being, and things that exist or occur apart from movement" (*philosophum primum, qui considerat ens commune et ea quae sunt separata a motu*) (II.37.1130*e*).

However, Aquinas's account of creation as it's been developed so far may seem to be compatible with ENNF. Although creation is production out of no antecedent matter, it is also the act of God's intellect and will. For just that reason it may seem drastically misleading to consider it as the unique counter-instance to ENNF, as the unique instance of production out of *nothing.*

I think we're inclined to read ENNF simply as "nothing from nothing," and when it's read that way it seems not at all in conflict with creation *ex nihilo,* just because although what is created is *something,* it's *from God.* As Aquinas reads ENNF, however, in Latin, it does look incompatible with creation *ex nihilo.* Interpreted most strictly, the combination of the verb '*fit*' and the preposition '*ex*' in '*ex nihilo nihil fit*' means 'is made out of', or 'is produced out of'; and the account of creation Aquinas is arguing for could be summarized this way: the universe *is produced* by God *out of* nothing. And the universe is not nothing. So he does have to treat creation out of no antecedent matter as the exception to ENNF: 'nothing is produced out of nothing'.[30]

Taking ENNF to be a universal first principle of nature, as Aquinas does, means taking seriously the possibility that from the special standpoint of natural philosophy the existence of the natural world entails beginningless matter, an infinite regress of natural causes, or both. (Aquinas will consider this possibility in detail in Chapters 31–38 of Book II.)

7. MOVEMENT AND CHANGE CONSIDERED MORE CLOSELY

Once Aquinas has explicitly introduced the notion of creation, at the end of Chapter 16, he uses its terminology freely. Even the titles of Chapters 17 through 21 all contain either the noun 'creation' or the verb 'create'.[31] In the first three of those chapters Aquinas examines more closely one set of elements found in the standard definitions of production and of transeunt action but omitted from his account of creation because they are incompatible with absolute perfection. Chapters 17 through 19 variously emphasize and refine Aquinas's denial that creation, God's doubly universal production of things, could be characterized as some sort of movement or change—a denial we have already seen him develop and defend in Chapter 16's argument MC (16.936). This particularly close dependence of the new material on (one of) the results of Chapter 16 warrants his introducing Chapter 17 by remarking that its thesis is "*obvious,* once *that* has been shown."

In Chapter 17 Aquinas is out to show that "the action of God's that is without antecedent matter and that is called creating is neither movement nor change, strictly speaking" (946). The only features of this thesis that we haven't seen before seem not to mark a clear advance over Chapter 16. First, Aquinas notes that the technical term 'creating' is now in use. Second, and more interestingly, he seems to be softening the denial that creating is either movement or change, by suggesting that the denial applies only in a strict sense. But that suggestion isn't developed in the arguments of Chapter 17, which bear on it merely in sharpening the concepts of movement and change, thereby delineating the strict sense. It isn't until Chapter 18, as we'll see, that Aquinas introduces the broader sense in which creating might, after all, be considered movement or change.

If we then appropriate the first and temporarily ignore the second new feature of Chapter 17's thesis, and if we leave to one side the by now well-established no-antecedent-matter differentia, we're left with a simple claim that seems to add nothing but the term 'creating' to the results of Chapter 16, or even just to the results of argument MC: The action of God's that is called creating is neither movement nor change. After all, MC already contains the claim that "it is not through movement and change that a being is made out of absolute non-being," and making a being out of absolute non-being is what creating is. Nor does the fact that the thesis focuses on creation as an *action* of God's count as a novel contribution, for MC already contains the premise "*acting* only through movement and change is unsuited to the universal cause of being" and the subconclusion "it is not suited to God that he *act* only through movement or through change." Those propositions from MC, with their talk of its being *unsuited* to God to act *only* through movement and change, may look weaker than the thesis of Chapter 17. But, as we've seen, that appearance is a consequence of MC's leaving room for divine transeunt action *other than* creation, and the thesis of Chapter 17 is expressly concerned just with creation.[32]

Still, there is an aspect of God's action in creation that hasn't yet been examined and that might well seem to raise new questions about change. For in cases of ordinary production the movement to which the matter is subjected, and the change effected in the matter, begin as some sort of movement or change *in the agent*—e.g., deciding to make a salad now—and it may not be obvious that God's creating out of no antecedent matter is compatible with God's absolute immutability, even if God's creating X involves no more activity on his part than his merely willing (efficaciously) that X be now. But, although some of what

Chapter 17 accomplishes is relevant to such considerations, Aquinas doesn't mention them anywhere in the chapter.

So it isn't easy to say just how Chapter 17 advances the discussion. As far as I can see, the particular contributions of Chapter 17 to the investigation of creation are that it focuses tightly on the nature of the action itself, leaving aside any considerations of the agent such as shape the conclusions of all the arguments of Chapter 16,[33] and that it sharpens one's understanding of what is involved in the omission of movement and change. Both these contributions appear plainly in all four of Chapter 17's arguments, but especially in the last one, which I'll call MT, for its attention to movements and their termini:

> The movement or change must temporally (*duratione*) precede that which is brought about through change or movement, since [its] having been brought about is the beginning of rest and the end of the movement. That's why every change must be a movement or the terminus of a movement, which is successive. And, for that reason, what is being brought about *is* not. For as long as the movement lasts, something is being brought about and *is* not; while at the very end of the movement, at which rest begins, something is already not *being* brought about but *has been* brought about. In connection with creation, however, this cannot be the case. For if the very act of creating (*creatio ipsa*) preceded [its result], like movement or change, some subject would have to be established prior to it—which is contrary to the defining characteristic of creation. Creation, therefore, is neither movement nor change. (950)

We can think of the change involved in the building of a barn either as (M) the process—the barn's being built—or as (T) the final result—the new barn's having been built: "every change must be [M] a movement or [T] the terminus of a movement" (second sentence). And, of course, the change in the M-sense must precede the change in the T-sense (first sentence). As long as the barn is still being built, it isn't yet built—i.e., the new barn as yet is not (third and fourth sentences). The instant at which the last nail has been hammered home is the first instant of the barn's existence (fourth sentence).[34] And the same analysis applies in all cases of ordinary production, even when the process is so fast that it's ordinarily unnoticed, as in turning on a flashlight: the light's having been turned on is preceded by the pressing of the button and the consequent activating of the current, first in the batteries and then in the bulb.

"In connection with creation, however, this cannot be the case" (fifth sentence). For if the distinction between (M) the process and (T) the result were applicable to creation, in *what* could the movement or change associated with the process occur? Not in God, who is absolutely immutable. Not in the universe, which doesn't exist *before* it exists, so as to be changed by *beginning* to exist: "when the whole substance of a thing is produced as regards its being, there cannot be any same thing that is first one way, then another, because that would be not produced but rather presupposed by the production" (949). And so argument

MT shows how the no-antecedent-matter differentia rules out the possibility of a process of creation.

It looks as if a contemporary controversy may have led Aquinas to emphasize that movement and change are entirely absent from creation. He devotes Chapter 18 to explaining how to reply to those who, taking creation to be a kind of change, "attack creation [as Aquinas conceives of it] with arguments drawn from the nature of movement or change" (951). And, as he has argued in Chapters 16 and 17, creation cannot involve movement or change. "Nonetheless," he must admit, "from a purely conceptual standpoint creation does *seem* to be some sort of change—I mean, insofar as our intellect takes one and the same thing as first not existing and afterwards existing" (953), although, of course, there can't really *be* one and the same thing first not existing and then existing.[35] That's evidently why the thesis of Chapter 17 claims that "creation is neither movement nor change, *strictly speaking*" (946). But, as Aquinas explained in Chapter 17, "in every change or movement there must be something that is one way now and another way earlier, for this is what the very name 'change' indicates" (949), and this is precisely what is ruled out by the no-antecedent-matter differentia.

So, appearances to the contrary notwithstanding, "creation is *not* change but, rather, the very dependence of created being on the source by which it is established" (18.952). In making this pronouncement Aquinas intends to be reestablishing creation in the category of *relation*, which, as we've seen, is what he thinks it must be classified as in reality. But what he says here also suggests the absence of any fundamental natural distinction between creation and conservation.

8. NO SUCCESSIVENESS IN CREATION

Chapter 19 is the third in the trio of chapters that seem designed to drive home the general point argued for in Chapter 16's argument MC and to explore the ramifications of Aquinas's denial that creation could involve movement or change. Chapter 19's thesis—"all creation is without successiveness"—can be established very easily on the basis of MC and the material in the two immediately preceding chapters, especially Chapter 17's argument MT. It really needs no more additional support than Aquinas provides for it in Chapter 19's first, very short argument: "For successiveness is proper to movement. But creation is not movement, nor is it the terminus of movement, like a change [II.17, esp. 950].[36] Therefore, there is no successiveness involved in it" (956). In the strict usage developed by thirteenth-century logicians in their analysis of the concepts of beginning and ceasing, *successive* things or states are those that can exist or occur as such only over a temporal interval, not at a single instant.[37] Local motion is, naturally, the paradigm of a successive state, but the claim that "successiveness is proper to movement" applies much more widely. It means that successiveness and movement (or change) of any kind are essentially linked together. Any single instant within the period during which a body is moving from one place to another is, of course, an instant of the body's local motion; but at that instant the body can only be located at a point. And, for all that the instantaneous location indicates, that point could quite as well be a point at which the body is at rest. So local motion, like every other sort of movement, occurs as such only during a period of time, not at a single instant.

But Aquinas here in Chapter 19's first argument characterizes as successive not only the process of a thing's changing but also its acquisition of the changed state, as he did in the earlier argument MT: "That's why every change must be a movement or the terminus of a movement, which is successive" (950). Medieval logicians tended to classify the *terminus* of a movement, the *acquisition* of a changed state, not as successive but as *instantaneous:* a state that could occur only at an instant (and that was therefore not to be confused with the *persistence* of that state). No matter how long it takes X to get from A to B, and however long X remains at B, X's arriving at B occurs at an instant.[38] By the Principle of the Excluded Middle, there can't be any time during which X has neither arrived nor not arrived, and, by the Principle of Noncontradiction, there can't be any time during which X has both arrived and not arrived.

Still, I think Aquinas is right to see the *terminus* of a movement as successive, too—conceptually. The instant at which X arrives at B has to be understood as an instant immediately *before* which X's state was not what it is at that instant *for the first time.* So, in terminology allowable outside the logical analysis of successiveness as a feature of extramental reality, both the movement and its terminus, the acquisition of the changed state, can helpfully be viewed as successive conceptually. And so, since "creation is not movement, nor is it the terminus of movement, like a change . . . , there is no successiveness involved in it" (956).[39]

Aquinas's scriptural confirmation of Chapter 19's thesis in the chapter's last paragraph depends on a very stringent interpretation of Genesis 1:1: "And that is why divine Scripture declares the creation[40] of things to have been effected at an indivisible [instant],[41] saying 'In the beginning God created the heaven and the earth'. Indeed, Basil explained this beginning as the beginning of time, which, as is proved in *Physics* VI [3, 233b33–35], must be an indivisible [instant]" (961). The Latin "*In principio*" may invite this interpretation more than "In the beginning" seems to do, because it can be read (and by a thirteenth-century Aristotelian would be read) as '*At* the beginning'.[42] And since Aquinas here is making use of the (unsurprising) Basilian line about this beginning's being also the beginning of *time*,[43] and since the very beginning of any temporal interval, including all of time, must itself be not a (divisible) temporal interval (which must have its own beginning) but an absolutely indivisible instant, the first two words of the Vulgate text of Genesis 1:1 *can* be read as strong support for the view that the creation of the heaven and the earth was *durationless, instantaneous*—utterly without successiveness.

But would that be enough to show that "*all* creation is without successiveness"? The rest of the first chapter of Genesis provides the account of what is ordinarily referred to as the six days of creation, an account that certainly appears to involve *successiveness,* however those "days" are interpreted. Of course, Aquinas won't be taking them into account here in SCG II, where he's doing natural theology. He needn't even mention them in this context, since the story of the six days is a particularly clear instance of revealed rather than natural theology, in Aquinas's view as well as ours. But, as we've seen, developing a natural theology that will be *compatible* with revelation is essential to his project in SCG I–III. How, if at all, is his account of creation without successiveness compatible with the rest of Genesis 1?

Chapter 19 itself provides a part of the answer to that question, though not the most important part. Even if there were successive acts of creating, one after another, *each one* of them would have to be without any successiveness within the act itself. And in that respect—in the intensional universality of the creative act—each successive act of creating would be different from ordinary productive acts.[44] To set the stage for displaying this part of the answer, the original statement of the chapter's thesis—"*omnis creatio . . .* "—could be read, a little less naturally, as "*every* creation is without successiveness" instead of as "*all* creation is without successiveness." Against that background, this part of the answer is presented especially clearly in the chapter's fourth argument: "there can be successiveness in movement, or in any making, insofar as that in association with which the movement occurs is divisible, either quantitatively (as in local motion and increase), or in terms of intensification and diminution (as in alteration). . . . However, the very substantial being of a created thing is not divisible in the way just mentioned, because substance does not admit of more and less [*Categories* 5, 3b33–34]. . . . It remains, therefore, that there cannot be any successiveness involved in creation" (959)—because, as we've seen, creation's product must be "the very substantial being of a created thing," the *whole* being of the brand new thing.[45] In this way Aquinas's denial of successiveness in creation does rule out the possibility of successiveness in any one act of creation, and in this way that denial is entirely compatible with the story of the six days.

But it seems to be Aquinas's considered view that the work of the six days, as revealed in Genesis, is *not* creation, strictly speaking. I take his considered view on this topic to be the one he develops in ST Ia.65–74, a set of ten questions sometimes called "The Treatise on the Work of the Six Days."[46] In his preface to this treatise he says that in connection with the production of corporeal created things the first chapter of Genesis "mentions *three* works: the work of *creating* (when it says 'In the beginning God created the heaven and the earth', etc.), the work of *distinguishing* (when it says [1:4] 'God divided the light from the darkness' and [1:7] 'divided the waters which were under the firmament from the waters which were above the firmament', [etc.]), and the work of *furnishing* (when it says [1:14] 'Let there be lights in the firmament', etc.)." Strictly speaking, then, he takes the creating of the heaven and the earth to occur, utterly without successiveness, *before* the first of the six days. The work of distinguishing he assigns to the first three days,[47] and the work of furnishing to the last three.[48]

I'm not now interested in defending the details of Aquinas's account of the work of the six days. Although I think there's something to be said in support, or at least in appreciation, of "distinguishing" and "furnishing" and of their relation to each other in the development of the physical universe, what's important here is the fact that those post-creational operations *are* instances of the movement and change of antecedent matter, even if their agent is God himself.[49] This fundamental division between instantaneous creating to begin with, and successive distinguishing and furnishing thereafter, is an essential and attractive feature of Aquinas's account of the beginning and early development of the universe. The distinguishing and furnishing that give rise to the physical universe as we experience it are only the development of what is already entirely available in potentiality at the first instant. For creating is, as we've been seeing, not only intensionally but also extensionally universal, as can be seen again in SCG II.21.979*a*, where Aquinas once more cites only the very first verse of Genesis as providing scriptural confirmation of God's having created "*all* things," again (of course) leaving the six days entirely out of account. And even in ST, where he *is* developing a detailed account of the work of the six days, he is careful to say that "Therefore, in order to show that *all* bodies were created by God *immediately,* Moses said, 'In the beginning God created *the heaven and the earth*'" (Ia.65.3c).[50] Nonetheless, "the *forming* of corporeal created things was effected through the work of *distinguishing.* But confusion [in the sense of being mixed up together] is opposed to distinguishing, just as formlessness is opposed to forming. Therefore, if formlessness temporally preceded the forming of matter, it follows that at the beginning there was a *confusion* of corporeal created things, the confusion that the ancients called 'chaos'" (Ia.66.1, sc).[51] Distinguishing, then, is the successive process of sorting out the product of the primordial, instantaneous creation of the heaven and the earth, the product in which elements, species, and individuals exist *potentially.*[52]

Although Scripture assigns the works of the six days directly to God, there seems to be no reason in principle why "distinguishing" and "furnishing" could not be natural processes, the divinely overseen development of dispositions built into the instantaneously created heaven and earth: "Nature produces an effect in actuality from a being in potentiality, and so in the working of nature a potentiality must temporally precede the actuality, and formlessness must temporally precede forming. God, however, produces a being in actuality out of nothing [i.e., in creating], and so he can [in that way] produce a complete thing at once, in keeping with the magnitude of his power" (Ia.66.1, ad 2).

Taking alternative hypotheses of this sort seriously is not out of keeping with Aquinas's own approach, even within the bounds of revealed theology. It requires observing the relevant Augustinian rules Aquinas applies when the story of the six days strikes him as presenting very difficult claims, as in its account of the work of the second day: "In connection with questions of this sort [i.e., Was the firmament made on the second day?] two [rules] must be observed, as Augustine teaches [*De Genesi ad litteram* I, chaps. 18, 19, 21]. First, of course, that Scripture's truth be maintained unwaveringly. Second, since divine Scripture can be interpreted in many ways, [the other rule to be observed is] that a person should not adhere to any interpretation so absolutely that, [even] if it is established by undoubted reason that what he believed to be the meaning of Scripture is false, he may be so presumptuous as to assert it anyway. [This second rule should be observed] so that Scripture may not be made the laughing-stock of unbelievers, and so that the way of believing should not be closed off to them. . . . " (Ia.68.1c).[53] A Christian is bound to maintain Scripture's *truth,* but just because "Scripture can be interpreted in many ways" it will not always be obvious which among the many possible interpretations conveys the truth. Moreover, some of the possible interpretations may be proven false. So, observing the first of these two rules requires the responsible open-mindedness enjoined in the second rule. Abandoning Scripture's truth is ruled out. But it is important to see that insisting on interpreting Scripture in a way that seemed right but turns out to be incompatible with what has been irrefutably (*certa ratione*) shown to be true is one way of abandoning Scripture's truth.

9. NO BODY CAN CREATE

The thesis of Chapter 20, that "no *body* can produce anything by way of creation," is so obvious at this point in the development of the notion of creation that it seems to need no special support. In fact, the possibility that the original source of corporeal things must *itself* be "some sort of body" is one of the ancient mistakes Aquinas dismissed at the outset of Book II, rejecting this one in particular on the adequate grounds that a body is obviously the sort of thing "that can exist only on the basis of something else" (3.865)—e.g., some other body or bodies— and is therefore incapable of being a *first* principle of anything. Nor does this thesis acquire any special interest in virtue of its apparent association with *natural* explanations of the origin of the universe, since no one contemplating such an explanation would dream of employing the technical notion of *creation* as the causal mechanism at the heart of the explanation. But every one of Chapter 20's five arguments in support of its negative thesis depends on taking 'creation' in the strict sense that has been developed for it in the immediately preceding chapters.[54]

I think Aquinas's reason for including this apparently unnecessary denial at this advanced stage in his development of the concept of creation shows up in the chapter's final paragraph, where we're told that what has prompted this explicit, argued denial is a later, more detailed version of the simple, ancient mistake he has already dismissed—"the falsity of the position of some who say that the substance of the heavenly bodies is the cause of the matter of the elements. For since matter is the *first* subject of movement and of change, matter cannot have a cause except that which acts by creating" (20.968).

10. CREATING BELONGS TO GOD ALONE

In several respects, Chapter 21 is like Chapter 20. First, its thesis seems to be already well-established by this stage of the investigation: "creation is an action proper to God, and creating belongs to him alone" (969). And so it seems not to need nearly all the support Aquinas supplies for it in the chapter's nine arguments. Some of those arguments are just as short and familiar as we might expect them to be—e.g., "Again, that God creates things has been shown on this basis, that there can be nothing besides him that is not caused by him. But that can belong to no other, since nothing else is the universal cause of being. Therefore, creation is suited to God alone, as his proper action" (971).

Second, Chapter 21 is also motivated by Aquinas's recognition of a prevalent mistake that needs correcting, one that emerges in the chapter's final paragraphs, where 979 presents, with Aquinas's approval, John Damascene's rejection of the theory of *creation by angels,* which was almost certainly an outgrowth of the Neoplatonist *emanationism* Aquinas rejects in 980. It's clearly the existence of such competing *theistic* theories rather than any competition from a *naturalistic* cosmogony that drives him to include this elaborate, otherwise unnecessary, chapter. But because those competing theories introduce the notion of subsidiary, instrumental agents of creation, Chapter 21 also includes more complex arguments that do add something to the concept of creation—e.g., "An instrument is applied because of its suitability for what is caused [by means of its application], so that it is a medium between the primary cause and what is caused, and is in touch with both of them. And in that way the [causal] influence of the first reaches what is caused by means of the instrument. For that reason, in that which is caused by means of the instrument there must be something that receives the [causal] influence of the first. This is contrary to the defining characteristic of creation, for it presupposes *nothing.* It remains, therefore, that nothing else besides God can create, neither as the principal agent nor as an instrument" (974).[55]

NOTES

1. This essay is a version of Chapter 3, "Creation as Doubly Universal Production," in my forthcoming book, *The Metaphysics of Creation: Aquinas's Natural Theology in* Summa contra Gentiles II.

2. Perhaps the fullest, clearest evidence of this development can be found most conveniently in the thriving journal *Faith and Philosophy,* founded in 1984 and associated with the Society of Christian Philosophers.

3. William P. Alston, *Perceiving God: The Epistemology of Religious Experience* (Ithaca, N.Y., 1991), 289.

4. See, e.g., Alvin Plantinga's discussion of natural theology in "Reason and Belief in God" (pp. 16–93 in *Faith and Rationality,* edited by A. Plantinga and N. Wolterstorff [Notre Dame, Ind., 1983]), which begins by identifying it as "the attempt to prove or demonstrate the existence of God" (p. 63).

5. My references to SCG are in this form. The initial Roman numeral indicates a book of SCG: I, II, III, or IV. (Since the vast majority of my references in this essay are to SCG II, that Roman numeral will often be omitted from the references.) The two subsequent Arabic numerals, preceded by periods, indicate the chapter and then the section as numbered in the edition of the Latin text that is best for practical purposes: *S. Thomae Aquinatis, Doctoris Angelici, Liber de Veritate Catholicae Fidei contra errores Infidelium seu "Summa contra Gentiles"* (Textus Leoninus diligenter recognitus), ed. C. Pera, O.P., with the assistance of P. Marc, O.S.B., and P. Caramello, O.S.B., in three volumes (Turin and Rome, 1961–67). In this essay all quotations from Aquinas in English are my translations, and those taken from SCG are based on that Marietti edition.

6. "For human philosophy considers them [i.e., natural things] in their own right" rather than as advancing and enhancing natural theology's investigation of God, "which is why different parts of philosophy are found corresponding to different kinds of things" (II.4.871).

7. Throughout SCG Aquinas freely introduces as premises of his arguments not only propositions he has argued for earlier but also many propositions he treats as *principles,* as needing no support within this project itself. As might be expected, Aquinas gets these principles almost entirely from Aristotle. No doubt he takes some of them to be self-evidently true, and surely he's sometimes within his rights to do so—e.g., "A conditional proposition with an impossible antecedent can be true," or "Substance does not depend on accident, although accident depends on substance." I believe that he takes all the others to have been successfully argued for by Aristotle. For instance, when he invokes the Aristotelian thesis of the incorporeality of the human intellect, something he hasn't even discussed in the preceding chapters of SCG I, he justifies doing so by pointing out that "*it has been proved* that intellect is not a corporeal power" (I.20.183)—which must be an allusion to Aristotle's own arguments to that effect in *De anima* III (an allusion of a sort that his thirteenth-century academic contemporaries would have had no trouble picking up). Since the natural theology Aquinas is developing evidently has, by his own lights, the status of a science subordinate to metaphysics proper, to *Aristotelian* metaphysics, there's every reason why he should—indeed, must—help himself to Aristotelian first principles and argued theses in developing his subordinate science.

8. My references to *unaided* reason in connection with Aquinas's natural theology are intended as short for 'reason guided but unsupported by revelation'.

9. James F. Anderson gives a different, and misleading, impression in the Introduction to his translation of SCG II (Notre Dame, Ind., 1975): "Assuredly, there is a metaphysics—a straight philosophy—of creation contained in Book II of the *Summa Contra Gentiles,* but the Book is not merely a metaphysics of creation. . . . St. Thomas uses arguments purely natural in character, *as well as arguments appealing to the revealed word of God*" (p. 13, emphasis added). Although Anderson gives no example of the latter sort of argument at that point, the only such example he does give, later in the Introduction, is clearly not what he thinks it is: "St. Thomas, as we shall see, does not limit himself to the so-called purely rational order. He proceeds to argue [in II.92], on Scriptural as well as rational grounds, that such [separated] substances are exceedingly numerous. . . . Scripture itself bears witness not only to the existence but to the very great number of separate substances: 'Thousands of thousands ministered to Him, and ten thousand times a hundred thousand stood before him' (Dan. 7:10). Certainly there are rational and natural considerations. . . . But it is the Word of God which is fully conclusive in this matter" (p. 19). In fact Aquinas introduces the passage from the Book of Daniel only at the end of the chapter, after having produced all his arguments for the chapter's thesis, in just the way he handles biblical passages generally in his natural theology: "Now Sacred Scripture bears witness (*attestatur*) to these things, for in Daniel 7[:10] it says . . . " (92.1794). Bearing witness to or confirming the conclusions already argued for is very different from being "fully conclusive in this matter."

10. In this respect as in others it seems likely to have been intended to approximate the idea of an Aristotelian science. "Aristotle does not pretend to be offering guidance to the scientist—or, for that matter, to the historian or the philosopher—on how best to pursue his researches or how most efficiently to uncover new truths. . . . Rather, it [Book A of the *Posterior Analytics*] is concerned with the organization and presentation of the results of research: its aim is to say how we may collect into an intelligible whole the scientist's various discoveries— how we may so arrange the facts that their interrelations, and in particular their explanations, may best be revealed and grasped. In short, the primary purpose of [Aristotelian] demonstration is to expound and render intelligible what is already discovered, not to discover what is still unknown" (Jonathan Barnes, "Introduction," in *Aristotle's Posterior Analytics,* translated with notes, Clarendon Aristotle Series, edited by J. L. Ackrill [Oxford, 1975], x–xi).

11. Alston, *Perceiving God,* 289, quoted more fully above; emphasis added.

12. For what clearly deserves to be the last nail in the coffin of the stubborn tradition that Aquinas wrote SCG as a manual for Dominican missionaries to Jews and Arabs, see Gauthier's

"Appendice: La Légende 'Missionaire'," in René-Antoine Gauthier, *Saint Thomas d'Aquin: Somme contre les gentils, Introduction* (Paris, 1993), 165–76.

13. On the relational method, see SCG I.29–36.

14. "But the believer considers only those aspects of created things that are associated with them insofar as they are traced back to God—that they have been created by God, that they are subject to God, and things of that sort" (4.872*a*).

15. In SCG II the titles of only the following chapters can be found in the autograph, the surviving part of the original manuscript in Aquinas's own handwriting: 11–13, 15, 18–28, 30–31, 34–35, 39–44, 47–48, and 50–60. (See the editors' n. 1 on p. 114 in vol. 2 of the Marietti edition.) Among the lost parts of the autograph is the one that contained SCG II.61–III.43 (see Gauthier, *Saint Thomas,* 8–10).

16. All seven of the chapter's arguments are unmistakably intended to show extensional universality, that God is for *all* things the cause of being. The first four of them—15.923–26—are, I think, directed more clearly than the last three—927–29—at showing also that God's universal production is absolutely fundamental, that God is for all things *the cause of being.*

17. "God in producing his effects does not need antecedent matter from which to work" (933); "in his action he requires no antecedent matter" (934); "it is not impossible to bring things into existence without antecedent matter" (935); "it is not suited to God to need pre-existing matter in order to make something" (936); "God does not require antecedent matter for his action" (937); "he does not require antecedent matter in order to produce an effect" (938); "God does not require antecedent matter from which he acts of necessity" (939); "he does not require matter of necessity" (940); "if any matter is found proportioned to divine action, God himself is the cause of it" (941); "matter is not presupposed of necessity for his action" (942); "divine action does not require a pre-existing nature" (943).

18. See Section 4 below.

19. See SCG I.75: "God in willing himself also wills other things" and 76: "God wills himself and other things in a single act of will."

20. One of those arguments is misprinted in the Marietti edition. The phrase *non potest esse effectus materiae,* which appears on p. 300, column b, lines 2–3 of the Leonine edition of II.16, has been omitted from line 13 of 16.941 (the ninth argument) in the Marietti edition.

21. In Aquinas's Aristotelian metaphysics prime matter is an essential theoretical component of all material things, one that seems easiest to identify as the terminus of a thorough analysis of any material thing: this page is the result of the imposition of certain forms on ink and paper; this paper is the result of the imposition of a certain form on cellulose; that cellulose is the result of the imposition of certain forms on carbon, hydrogen, and oxygen; ...; ... is the result of the imposition of a certain form on pure potentiality. 'Matter' as it's been used earlier in this chapter means not prime matter but absolutely any antecedent, pre-existing thing or stuff considered as receptive of any substantial or accidental form—matter considered relatively rather than absolutely (as in 'prime matter'). All physical matter, right down to quarks and even beyond, is matter considered relatively.

22. See, e.g., ST Ia.115.1, ad 2: "But this is prime matter, which is pure potentiality just as God is pure actuality ... "; also *Quaestiones disputatae de spiritualibus creaturis* [QDSC] 1c: "that is commonly named prime matter which is in the genus of substance as a kind of understood potentiality, beyond every species and form, and even beyond privation, [but] which is nonetheless capable of taking on both forms and privations [of forms]. ... "

23. The reason provided in the immediately preceding sentence is that "Prime matter does not exist in nature on its own (*per seipsam*), since it is a being not in actuality but only in potentiality."

24. See also ST Ia.84.3, ad 2: "Prime matter has substantial being through a form, and so it must be the case that it would be created under some form. Otherwise it would not be in actuality. However, while existing under one form, it is in potentiality to others. ... "

25. In Chapter 19, however, Aquinas does acknowledge that "being and non-being ... are, *so to speak,* the extremes of creation" (*Inter esse autem et non esse, quae sunt quasi extrema creationis, non potest esse aliquid medium*) (957). See also Section 7 below.

26. See, e.g., II.42.1189: "there are many things that cannot come into being except through creation—e.g., all those that are not composed of form and matter that is subject to contrariety. For things of that sort must be incapable of being generated, since all generation is from what is a contrary [of what is generated], and out of matter. . . . Therefore, we have to maintain that all *such* things have acquired the beginning (*principium*) of their being from God *directly* (*immediate*)." See also II.22.982.

27. See, e.g., ST Ia.45.2, obj. 1: "According to the Philosopher in *Physics* I [4, 187a26–29], ancient philosophers accepted as a common conception of the mind that nothing is made or comes about out of nothing. But God's power does not extend to the contraries of first principles—e.g., [it is impossible] that God bring it about that a whole not be greater than its part, or that an affirmation and its negation be true at the same time. Therefore, God cannot make something out of nothing, or create."

28. See II.37.1130e, quoted in part just below.

29. Aristotle describes ENNF as "the common opinion of the natural philosophers" (*Physics* I 4, 187a26–29).

30. Could God's "ideas" be considered as something out of which God creates? After all, Aquinas's account of God's intellect presents God's knowledge as causative and God's ideas as the patterns of divine production. But, of course, the divine ideas are the *formal,* not the *material* cause, of created things. And they're not like our ideas, or even Aristotle's or Shakespeare's ideas, because all human ideas arise out of experience and so have material causes of their own. See Eleonore Stump and Norman Kretzmann, "God's Knowledge and Its Causal Efficacy," in *The Rationality of Belief and the Plurality of Faith*, edited by T. D. Senor (Ithaca, N.Y., 1995), 94–124; esp. 115–17.

31. The titles of Chapters 18–28 are Aquinas's own.

32. In the Leonine and Marietti editions the first sentence of Chapter 17 reads "*Hoc autem ostenso, manifestum est quod Dei actio, quae est absque materia praeiacente et creatio vocatur, non sit motus neque mutatio, proprie loquendo.*" The punctuation of this passage, like the punctuation found in printed medieval texts generally, has been added by the editors. But reading this passage with the editors' second and third commas converts what should be a modifying clause into a clause in apposition, which requires the thesis to be read this way: 'God's action, which is without antecedent matter and is called creating, is neither movement nor change, strictly speaking'. (Anderson's translation reads this way in Anderson SCG, p. 54.) But the arguments of Chapter 16 make it very clear that creating is not God's only (transeunt) action, and that God's transeunt action other than creation may indeed involve antecedent matter, movement, and change. And so, it seems to me, the relative clause must be read as modifying '*Dei actio*', and the editors' second and third commas must be deleted.

33. See n. 17 above.

34. On the medieval analysis of change in terms of first and last instants, see my "Incipit/Desinit," in *Motion and Time, Space and Matter,* edited by P. Machamer and R. Turnbull (Columbus, Ohio, 1976), 101–36.

35. See also n. 25 above.

36. I.e., argument MT, quoted and discussed in Section 7 above.

37. See Kretzmann, "Incipit/Desinit," esp. 110.

38. A and B can, of course, be states as well as locations; X's getting from A to B can be a leaf's turning from green to brown as well as its falling from the twig to the ground.

39. Even stronger versions of this conclusion (the thesis of Chapter 19) are drawn in other arguments in the chapter, e.g., "It is, therefore, impossible that there be successiveness in creation" (958); "It remains, therefore, that creation takes place at an instant. And so anything *while being* created *has been* created, just as anything while being illuminated has also been illuminated" (960).

40. The Marietti edition has *creatione* in line 42, where it should have *creationem.*

41. The nominalized adjective *indivisibile* is often used by medieval philosophers to mean either an instant or a point, depending on the context.

42. *In* is the Latin preposition used by logicians and other medieval philosophers to indi-

cate temporal location *at* a durationless instant (*in instanti*), or spatial location *at* a dimensionless point (*in puncto*), contexts in which the use of the English preposition 'in' would be mistaken.

43. See also, e.g., ST Ia.46.3c; 66.4, ad 4.

44. As can be seen in 19.960, quoted in n. 39 above, Aquinas takes the ordinary act of illuminating to involve no successiveness, but that's only because he, like all his contemporaries, takes the propagation of light to be instantaneous; see, e.g., ST Ia.67.2c, "*Secundo.* ... " He also maintains, plausibly enough, that thinking something and having that thought are simultaneous: "*simul formatur verbum in corde et formatum est*" (Ia.45.2, ad 3).

45. See also In Sent. II.1.1.2, ad 3; ST Ia.45.2, ad 3.

46. That Aquinas considers the doctrine of the six days to be a part of revealed theology only is shown by several features of this treatise, among them the fact that many of the passages introduced *sed contra* in its twenty-nine articles are simply citations of the relevant passages in Genesis and, in five cases, no more than this general observation: "The authoritative passage of Scripture to the contrary suffices."

47. See, e.g., ST Ia.67, preface: "Next we have to consider the work of distinguishing in its own right: first, the work of the first day; second, the work of the second day; third, the work of the third day."

48. See, e.g., ST Ia.70, preface: "Next we have to consider the work of furnishing: first, as regards the individual days in themselves; second, as regards all six days in general. In connection with the first of these two, we have to consider, first, the work of the fourth day; second, the work of the fifth day; third, the work of the sixth day. ... " Aquinas provides a helpful survey of creating, distinguishing, and furnishing in Ia.70.1c.

49. See, e.g., Ia.70.1c.

50. See also Ia.65.3, sc; 68.1, ad 1; 73.1, ad 3.

51. See also Ia.66.1c for a full and very useful discussion of the creation of matter and the imposition of forms. Also Ia.68.1c: "the production of *the substance* of the firmament belongs to the work of *creation,* but some *forming* of it belongs to the work of the second day."

52. See, e.g., Ia.74.1, ad 1: "it can be said that the work of distinguishing and furnishing implies some changing of what is created (*creaturae*), which is measured by time. The work of creating, on the other hand, consists in the unique divine action of producing the substance of things at an instant. And that is why each work of distinguishing and furnishing is said to be carried out *in a day,* while creating is said to be carried out *at the beginning,* which means something indivisible." Also Ia.74.2, ad 1: "[when] God created the heaven and the earth, he also created every plant of the field—not *actually,* but 'before it grew in the earth' [Gen. 2:5], i.e., *potentially*"; also ad 2 and ad 4.

53. In the Leonine and Marietti editions, the third sentence of this passage reads this way: "*Secundo, cum Scriptura divina multipliciter exponi possit, quod nulli expositioni aliquis ita praecise inhaereat quod, si certa ratione constiterit hoc esse falsum, quod aliquis sensum Scripturae esse asserere praesumat. ...* " The Leonine editors ordinarily register few variants, but they list many for this sentence. The fathers of the English Dominican Province, who can usually be counted on for a literal translation, seem to have given up on this text, presenting what they take to be its sense in words that do not match the text: "The second is that since Holy Scripture can be explained in a multiplicity of senses, one should adhere to a particular explanation, only in such measure as to be ready to abandon it, if it be proved with certainty to be false." The most significant of the variants listed by the Leonine editors they attribute to *Editiones aliquae,* one of which is the Migne edition (1860): "*Secundo, cum Scriptura ... , ut si certa ratione constiterit hoc esse falsum quod aliquis sensum Scripturae esse credebat, id nihilominus asserere praesumat. ...* " (I'm grateful to Winthrop Wetherbee for calling my attention to the Migne text.) This edition of course has no authority as a source for the text, but its sensible wording clearly brings out the evident sense of the corrupt passage, and my translation of it here follows this Migne text.

Here are some of the relevant passages in Augustine on which Aquinas is drawing: "In matters that are obscure and far beyond our vision, even in such as we may find treated in Holy

Scripture, different interpretations are sometimes possible without prejudice to the faith we have received. In such a case we should not rush in headlong and so firmly take our stand on one side that, if further progress in the search of truth justly undermined this position, we too fall with it. That would be to battle not for the teaching of Holy Scripture but for our own, wishing its teaching to conform to ours, whereas we ought to wish ours to conform to that of Sacred Scripture" (*De Gen. ad litt.* I.18). "Now it is a disgraceful and dangerous thing for an infidel to hear a Christian, presumably giving the meaning of Holy Scripture, talking nonsense on these topics. . . . The shame is not so much that an ignorant individual is derided, but that people outside the household of faith think our sacred writers held such opinions . . . " (op. cit., I.19).

54. While all five arguments serve their common purpose well enough, the fourth of them may be most important in the grand scheme of Aquinas's natural theology, since it picks up the argument for the infinity of God's power that Aquinas developed in detail in I.43, and shows (again) how the capacity to produce something on the basis of absolutely nothing is what defines infinite power.

55. The account of primary and instrumental agent causes in this (fifth) argument is developed further in the fourth and sixth arguments (973 and 975).

I'm grateful to Scott MacDonald and Eleonore Stump for their helpful comments on an earlier draft of this essay.

Ecumenical Movements and Truth

ALAN MONTEFIORE

There is a perhaps oversimple but at least briefly straightforward version that may be given of the main theme of this essay. There will also, of course, be a variety of more complex and more sophisticated versions, some of which may emerge in its further elaboration. We may start, however, with the basic version.

There was a time within the history of the Christian tradition when believers who nevertheless recognized a certain human value or even merit in those who were of different religious persuasions than their own, and who might even be in favor of cooperation with (at least certain among) them, would support their stance by arguing in favor of toleration. Virtuous adherents of other religions might be mistaken in matters of faith and theological commitment, but that need not stop Christians from appreciating and perhaps working with them, so long, of course, as the Christians in question are not deflected from their own proper hold upon the truth. Toleration of those whose beliefs or practices are different from one's own is not so common a virtue that its worth should ever be underrated. Nevertheless, contemporary ecumenical movements tend to demand something more from their participating partners than mere mutual toleration of difference. What is required is, rather, reciprocity of equal respect. Anyone who takes seriously this demand as one whose imperative must underpin any genuinely ecumenical movement of today has, it would seem, to acknowledge that each participating religion—not necessarily every religious tradition that may be recognizable as such but certainly all that may be recognized as partners within the ecumenical movement—can in principle provide their own adherents with their own equally valid path to religious fulfillment. It would thus seem that within such a movement there can be no room for serious missionary or proselytizing competition. But, it would also seem, those who take seriously their commitment to their own religious tradition are called upon to accept its account of the nature of God and of human beings' relation to Him as essentially true; and also, most importantly, that acceptance of this truth *matters*—that it matters so much, indeed, that those who are not yet persuaded of it must always benefit by being brought to a proper understanding of its force and importance and hence to its acceptance.

Questions of the following sort have then to be faced. Is the truth of one's own faith really compatible with the apparently very different "truths" that are taught by the other traditions with whom one may find oneself in ecumenical partnership? If so, why *should* it matter whether anyone should accept any one version of these truths—or better, perhaps, any one version of what at bottom must be held to be one and the same truth—rather than any other of the versions on offer within that partnership? If not, what is the meaning of that allegedly equal respect which one is ecumenically committed to accord to those who, although they may indeed be one's partners, have to be seen as in some sense at a serious disadvantage in respect of their grasp of religious truth? Taken together, these constitute a potentially not very comfortable set of questions. If they are not simply to be evaded, however, it would seem that those concerned must *either* settle for viewing their ecumenical partnership as being after all no more than one of mutual toleration, of a (perhaps steady) working alliance between those who have common interests in the face of common threats, but who, if ever the threats are faced down, must return to some form of mutual competition; *or* they have indeed to accept that the apparently conflicting claims of the different religions within the ecumenical partnership are but so many different reflections of the one true light, a light that is never visible to direct human view, but is to be seen only through the diffracting prism of humanity's historically variable capacity for religious understanding. In which case, they have, then, to reassess, possibly even to recast, the status or maybe the content of some of what have they have been used to regard as among the most fundamental claims of their own religious traditions—something which the more orthodox members of the traditions in question can never find easy to do. The basic themes of this essay are to be found, then, in a somewhat closer look at the nature of these tensions and in a certain speculation as to the direction in which a resolution might one day be sought.

There are, of course, other and more external perspectives from which the problem of the truth of religious claims may be posed. Nobody, of course, with any knowledge of the world and its history could fail to take religion seriously as a phenomenon of profound human influence and significance. (This must be so whatever the problems in the way of determining appropriate criteria on the basis of which a system of belief and practice is to be accounted a religion.) But this is an altogether different matter from being bound to take seriously the claims of religion, and more particularly what may be called its truth claims. Here the seemingly most obvious difficulty may lie in the apparently straightforward mutual incompatibility of most of these claims together with the total absence of any agreed procedures for adjudicating between them. There are those, no doubt, who would find some or all of them simply too fantastic (or at best too unsubstantiatable) to carry credence. But however that may be, nobody could, in simple logical consistency, actually accept all of them at their face value. If some are true, others must be false. But given that there are no agreed procedures for adjudicating between them, what possible reason, so it is often objected, could there be for accepting the apparently arbitrary truth claims of any one of them?

This line of argument is, however, notoriously inconclusive. From the fact that a given number of theories or theses are mutually incompatible it clearly follows that they cannot all of them be true; but nothing follows as to the falsity of any one of them. Nor does the fact that no reason can be given for a thesis show that thesis actually to be false. In any case, it is the exception rather than the rule for the followers of religious traditions to claim that their commitment is in the last resort based upon demonstrative reason rather than upon, say, revelation, the conviction acquired from conversion, traditional teaching, or simple faith. These sorts of issues have, moreover, been argued backwards and forwards ad infinitum. So let us put them aside for the present to concentrate rather on such problems as may properly, even must, present themselves to those who, being themselves of one religious persuasion, find themselves, or would wish to find themselves, in contemporary ecumenical partnership with members of other religious persuasions than their own.

There are, it would seem, three avenues worth exploring by those who, while fully committed to their own religions in and on the terms according to which they have been handed down by tradition, are yet no less serious in their commitment to the equal mutual respect demanded by contemporary ecumenical partnership. They might, as we have already noted, try to work out some appropriate interpretation of the notion of truth such that two very different accounts of the nature of God (or the Gods, or of a not explicitly Godlike spirituality) might each be properly accountable as true without thereby necessarily contradicting the other. Or they might insist, following Johann Martin Chaldenius, that "If an account which we hold to be true, as the author would have it, seems to contain things which contradict another account also purported to be true, then we still do not understand either one of the two or both of them completely. We will show in the following that a true account can appear to contradict another one. The fault of the apparent contradiction is to be found in the person who feels that the narrative does not present the nature of things the same way as he perceives it. From this one can conclude that we either read too much or too little into the words and, therefore, do not have the correct concepts which the words should call forth. We consequently still do not fully understand the history."[1] Or, on the third and very different hand, they might try to see whether full mutual and noncompetitive respect might not after all be possible between people who nevertheless persisted in believing each other to be genuinely mistaken (and not simply confused or possessed of an inadequate understanding) on matters of what Hume might have called "the very last importance."

Truth, one may suppose, will be of greater concern to a religion which emphasizes doctrinal affirmation or belief than to one which lays comparatively greater stress on forms of ritual or social practice and which, therefore, might be expected to attach relatively greater importance to fidelity of observance. It would not seem easy, for instance, to be a Christian in any traditional sense of the term, if one was unable to accept as true any of the central doctrines relating to the life and peculiar status of Jesus of Nazareth. To quote Dr. George Carey, the present Archbishop of Canterbury: "You mustn't think that being an Anglican means you can believe in anything as long as it's not too definite. We have a coherent set of beliefs in the Creed. We have got the articles of our faith which is a clear Anglican tradition."[2] Jews and Moslems have, by way of apparent relative contrast, mainly to obey the relevant rules of behavior insofar, for example, as observing the dietary laws or fasting during specified periods are concerned. This way of marking the comparison is, of course, a highly selective and loaded one. Judaism and Islam are, certainly, well known to be relatively more law-based and less doctrinally based religions than, at any rate, most forms of Christianity; nevertheless, it is, obviously, not the case that neither of them possesses any doctrinal tenets of its own. Moreover, it will always be possible to ask whether it is really true that I, having been born a Jew or a Moslem, ought not to eat pig or that I ought to fast during a particular period. If this is construed as being in the first instance a question about the nature of Jewish or Islamic Law, then, although the answers may indeed be contested by those who may not even be agreed among themselves as to who are or are not to be taken as properly relevant authorities, the points at issue may be regarded as turning on matters of fact concerning the nature or status of the Law. Beyond this, however, it must always be possible to raise the further question as to whether it is indeed true that the Law and its claims derive from God or the Prophet; indeed, in today's world there will almost always be those who will raise it—just as it is yet another and separate question which (if any) ordinances or injunctions of the Law are to be regarded as addressed to all human beings as such or whether they are to be taken as applying only to adherents of the religions in question.

It is, indeed, such questions of truth that mark the boundary between problems of religious ecumenism and those more general problems that today tend to be labeled problems of "multi-culturalism." Communities of different traditions that, for one reason or another, find themselves living together within the same overall social space may find it more or less easy, more or less difficult, to do so depending on how far faithful obedience each to their own tradition may in practice lead them to getting in each other's way. If, for instance, one lives next door to people of a traditionally reserved and private way of life, one will hardly be able to celebrate one's own more overflowing festivals in the manner that one's own tradition demands without intruding on what others may well regard as their rights; any more, indeed, than they will be able to insist on observance of their rights without thereby imposing constraints on those whose traditions have included rights to more publicly exuberant festivities. Such practical collisions are not necessarily easy to resolve. They do not, however, present any difficulty of principle to the demands of equal mutual respect. If space and/or transport were freely and unproblematically available (as in practice they rarely are), then it should in principle be possible to sort out such problems to each party's own entire satisfaction. If not, and provided always that the active will to equal mutual respect is truly there, there will be a clear need (again not always satisfied) for considerable mutual tolerance and a common willingness to look for perhaps ingenious compromise. In other words, respect for the other may in practice commit one to a readiness to modify the practical manifestations of one's own tradition; but this does not amount to a commitment to admit, whether to oneself or anyone else, that it must have been in some way mistaken. To have to put up with inconvenience, or even compromise, in one's way of manifesting one's fidelity to one's own tradition is a wholly different matter from having to admit that it must have been in some way mistaken.

Certain precepts of traditional (religious) Law may give rise to more problematic conflicts, whose resolution may raise issues of principle as well as of practical difficulty. For example, different religions prescribe different arrangements for the regulation of marriage and divorce. This can, of course, lead to a variety of complications when members of different religions seek to or actually do marry each other, or when the laws of a given land are tied to those of its dominant religion. No one should underestimate the importance of such conflicts or the difficulties that they can present to those seeking to engage in ecumenical partnership (or, indeed, the analogous difficulties that they may present to the political authorities responsible for the direction of a multicultural polity). Even if those committed by their own religious identity to an ideal of lifelong monogamous marriage are happy to acknowledge the equal validity of some other ideal for those of a different religious persuasion, difficulties are bound to arise if and when individuals seek to marry across traditional boundary lines. In many cases such difficulties may be resolvable on the basis of negotiable agreement and convention; that, for example, the man should accept the marriage traditions of his wife's religion, or vice versa; but whether this is possible or not will depend on the nature of the principles embodied within the traditions in question and on how they are interpreted. In the end the question that has to be faced in all such cases is strikingly analogous to that faced by those committed ecumenists who seek to establish partnerships of equal respect in spite of their divergent doctrinal commitments: why after all should it matter whether any given individuals, whatever the facts of their birth or their upbringing, should change to some other doctrine or follow some other practice within the overall framework of the ecumenical or social partnership, if indeed it is one of genuine mutual respect?

There are, no doubt, many possible answers to this question. One, which in itself has nothing to do with religion as such or with the truth of its tenets, is to be found in the importance accorded by its core members to the historical survival of the relevant group together with those traditions which, as they see it, are essential to its identity. Clearly, if "the next generation marries out" in significant numbers, where "marrying out" does not function as a way of bringing new members into the group and where there is no commitment to bringing up any resultant children as members of the group, its very existence as a group will be threatened. That the ongoing existence of their primary reference group or groups, the group of what they think of as their identity—their family, their tribe, their language group, their nation, or whatever—is likely to matter to people is readily understandable. Many may find it almost impossibly hard to accept that others, who are also or who once were of their group, should set greater store by other concerns. Such dissent may easily be experienced as betrayal; it may also be seen and felt as constituting more than one sort of threat to one's own very "identity." In cases where the historical existence of a group is closely bound up with the adherence of all or most of its members to a particular religion, their conversion to some other religious belief and practice will inevitably be regarded as constituting just such a betrayal and threat. Nevertheless, even such a passionate attachment to the values represented by the continuance of one's own group identity is *in principle* compatible with participation in an ecumenical movement based on equal respect for the similar attachments of one's partners to the values represented to them by the traditions of their respective groups, provided always that it is possible to work out mutually acceptable arrangements for dealing with such potential boundary disputes as those to which intermarriage is so capable of giving rise.

It is at this point, however, that we are brought back to the issue of truth. The losses involved in the conversion of a member of one religious group to the beliefs and practices of another, or the bringing up of children in beliefs and practices other than those of the mother or the father, may well present themselves as a potential threat to the ongoing existence of the "original" group. Nevertheless, so long as these other beliefs and practices can be seen as providing the basis for an equally good way of life and, as it may be, an equally valid way of relating to whatever or Whomever may go under the name of God, then relationships of equal ecumenical respect may still be relatively unproblematic, so long as no group goes out of its way to solicit such conversions from its partners. If, however, one believes, or is committed to the belief, that everyone's best hope of virtue and/or salvation (however exactly *they* may be understood) must depend on the doctrinal nature of their religious commitment, one is bound to find a prima facie difficulty in the way of according equal respect to the commitments of those whose doctrines or practices one believes to be in some way mistaken. If I believe that my tradition provides the only true account of the nature of God and of what He requires from His creatures, it would be strange indeed if I did not also believe that it was of vital importance to others that they should come to accept that account—strange, though not, perhaps, logically inconceivable. I may, for example, believe that my view of the chemical composition of the atmosphere of some distant planet is the only correct one, while not supposing that anyone might be in any way better or worse off for accepting or rejecting it, or for simply remaining ignorant of the matter; I may not even care very much whether other specialists agree with my view or not. It would be a strange sort of religion, however, which left it open to its adherents to regard its central doctrines as having a purely cognitive significance, and knowledge of what it claimed to be its truths as valuable only for the satisfaction of a certain type of intellectual curiosity. Certainly, those religions which are currently most actively and prominently engaged in the ecumenical movements of today do not typically regard their tenets in such a detached intellectual light.

We have already noted that some religions seem to attach a greater importance, to give a more evidently central role, to the explicit affirmation of a credo than do others. But we have also noted that so far as the great religions of the Judaic-Islamic-Christian tradition are concerned at any rate, the distinction remains a relative one. It is true that the criteria on the basis of which it may be plausible to attribute a belief to anyone (including oneself) are so complex that there is in general more latitude for constructive attribution in cases where one has, for the most part, only nonverbal behavior to go on. After all, it is not always absurd or even unreasonable to attribute to people beliefs that they might not recognize or even be ready to acknowledge themselves as holding. Given, then, that it is possible to disagree over the proper analysis of what actually constitutes the content and possession of a given cognitive belief, it must be even more possible to disagree as to the proper criteria on the basis of which to attribute it to any given individual. Nevertheless, if there are inevitably intermediate zones of undecidability or indetermination, there must also be areas away from these frontiers where unclarity is at a minimum. It would be perversely implausible, if not simply impertinent, for a Catholic to attribute to a devout Muslim, however admirable a human being he might find him, a secret or unconscious belief in the divinity of Jesus Christ, or for the same Muslim to attribute to his however saintly Catholic friend hidden belief in the special status of the prophet Muhammad. Similarly, devout Jews and Christians may recognize in each other a spirituality which they take to be as deep and pure as their own; but they would be stretching plausibility beyond all defensible limits if they sought to maintain that, despite whatever they themselves might say to the contrary, their partners in ecumenical good will "really" held the same beliefs as their own.

So what becomes of the belief, to which orthodox Catholics at any rate were traditionally committed, that *extra ecclesia, nulla salus*—that outside the Church there can be no salvation? Or to the many functionally equivalent analogues of this belief? And if one gives up such a belief, what becomes of the view that there is something of special importance in the acceptance of the tenets of one's own faith, whichever it may be, and in fidelity to its traditional practices?

One response which would not seem to be satisfyingly available to religious traditionalists, is that of the traditional empiricist for whom there must always be at least some degree of theoretical uncertainty attaching to any truth-claiming affirmation whose claim is not based on the logical necessities arising from the accepted meanings of the terms employed in its formulation. For even if, *qua* empiricist, he has to accept that there must always remain some degree of logically possible doubt as to the truth of the apparently factual claims to which his own religion commits him, just as there must always remain a similar doubt concerning the discrepant claims of any of his ecumenical partners, he can scarcely accept, *qua* traditionalist, that their common logical status amounts to an equalization of their claims to acceptance as religious truth. Nor is it easy for the adherents of a religion rooted in a particular version of history to accept any of those logically reassuring reassessments of the status of religious discourse which re-present it in one noncognitive style or another. It is true that, insofar as such re-presentations tend towards the construal of such claims to truth as differing forms of religious discourse may contain as, in effect, so many claims to the success of a certain kind of performance, they may indeed be understood as rendering them logically compatible very much in the way in which the success of one stage production is compatible with the equal success of another very different one of the same play. The price of any such reconstrual, however, is to make it very difficult to retain any firm grip on the notion that such performances are to be understood as having any determinate cognitive content.

The ecumenist who finds himself committed, as a matter of religious self-respect, to affirming the doctrinal or cognitive truth of the centrally distinguishing claims of his own faith, just as he is committed by the spirit of contemporary ecumenism to equal respect for those among his partners whose own religious self-respect commits them to affirming the putative doctrinal or cognitive truths of their own faiths, may try to work this equation by way of a suitable distinction between respect for others as believers and respect for their beliefs as such. After all, he may say, members of opposing football teams need find no difficulty in respecting the other team even as they seek to defeat it; indeed, in sport as in war, a healthy respect for one's opponent may often constitute a virtually necessary condition for defeating him, just as, after the battle, the assurance of mutual respect between combatants, victors and vanquished alike, makes for a less debilitating outcome all round. So too political opponents of different or even opposing views and commitments may respect each other as men or women of integrity even as they reject and actively struggle against each other's views and commitments. There is no doubt that such respect can and does in fact exist between some, if not all, members of radically opposed political beliefs and parties. I remember, for instance, a former British prime minister recommending the nomination of one of his leading political opponents to sit on a committee of some social, if not directly political, importance with the words "His views, of course, I regard as unacceptable and absurd; but a nicer and more honourable man it would not be possible to find." Or to take another and perhaps more problematic example, I remember a Marxist philosopher, at that time, I believe, still a member of the Central Committee of the Communist party of his country, speaking of his satisfaction at the way in which a conference between him and his colleagues and their opposite numbers drawn from among the order of Jesuits had turned out. He said that there had been a very wide measure of agreement between them and, when I expressed some surprise at this, he explained that they had agreed at the outset that, out of respect for each other, neither side would attempt to bring into question the most fundamental principles of the other, but that absolutely everything else should be regarded as wide open to discussion. This, he said, had resulted in a most harmonious and fruitful debate!

The analogy of sporting competition is, no doubt, an inappropriate one for the relations between what we may call the rival partners in the ecumenical enterprise. For different reasons, so is that of armed combat, however honorable the rules by which the combatants strive to defeat their opponents. This is not, of course, to deny that it has quite frequently happened that different parties have gone to war with each other, each of them equally convinced that their

Gods—or even just the one God—was with them in their fight; men have even fought each other in defense of their Gods, as they have understood the matter. Mutual respect between such opponents may be understood as respect for each other's integrity as human beings of valor and sincere conviction and of fidelity each to their own traditions, be they national, familial, tribal, or religious. There is, however, no sense in which partners in contemporary ecumenical movements would see themselves and each other as engaged in mutual struggle the object of which might be understood as that of bringing about the other's defeat. Respect for an ecumenical partner is not simply to be understood as respect for a worthy opponent.

On the first face of it, the political analogy may seem to carry a promise of greater relevance. Members of different political parties are, clearly, opposed to each other in electoral terms, in the policies which, as members of their respective parties, they are committed to pursuing and, presumably, in their personal beliefs concerning the best running of their common society. But, with the exception perhaps of members of parties of the outer fringes, they would typically recognize each other as belonging all to one and the same society and in such cases as that to which I referred above would regard each other as mistaken, even honorably if hopelessly mistaken, rather than deliberately malevolent. To say in such a context that one respects one's opponents' beliefs is in effect to acknowledge them as being held in good faith; and this in turn is in effect to respect the believer rather than his belief. But, in the political case it very evidently carries with it no suggestion of a commitment not to try and argue him out of it or not to try and persuade his political allies and followers of the wrongness, perhaps moral as well as intellectual, of their position. As in the case of philosophical disagreements, I may hold my colleague in the utmost personal respect even while regarding him as wholly mistaken in his professional views; nor will the respect in which I hold him in any way prevent me from trying to convince our common students of the rightness of my own views on the issues in question, and hence of the fallaciousness of his.

There is, of course, another dimension of mutual respect which is indispensable to all democratic, or at any rate all liberal democratic, politics; that is, the institutional framework of respect within which all parties, whatever their disagreements over social, economic, or international policy, accept the fundamental desirability of allowing each other free access to the political arena and potentially at least to governmental power itself. This is closely linked to a basic respect for the right of groups with recognizably different interests to those of one's own to defend and advance their interests by all mutually recognized political means. The issue here is not so much one of respect for members of different political parties or persons of different political views from one's own as one of a common institutionalized respect for the values of political pluralism as such.

That which distinguishes and separates different political parties and sets them in opposition to each other, even if within a framework of agreement as to the rules of the political game, are differences of policy, typically based on or reflecting certain conflicts of interest or ideological commitment. Different systems of religious belief and institutionalized practice may indeed carry with them very different implications of social and, therefore, political policy, but to the extent that it is not really very plausible to represent the differences between such different belief systems simply on the model of different policy commitments, it would seem at first sight that it is the more personal aspect of the political analogy, that of genuine mutual respect between members of opposing political parties, which carries the more ecumenical relevance for relations between adherents of different religious allegiances. Given certain crucial, but not necessarily very noticeable, assumptions, both the importance and possibility of such respect may seem essentially unproblematic and, indeed, admirable. But it does take for granted that one can make such an acceptable distinction between the believer and his belief as to allow one to show unambiguous respect for the mistakenly believing person together with an utter lack of respect for his or her actual beliefs. In general this is likely to be easier in cases where the grounds for acceptance or rejection of the belief are sufficiently complex or in some other way uncertain for it to be plausible that even those who are well-informed and reasonably intelligent should arrive at different judgments in such matters; or, again, in cases where the beliefs in question, however implausible they may appear to the uncommitted outsider, carry with them all the persuasive weight of the tradition in which they are embedded and to which the believer in question is committed by virtue of his or her upbringing or by subsequently acquired solidarity. Politicians, and even more so philosophers, perhaps, will know how difficult it can be to keep these distinctions effectively clear even in contexts where all concerned are conceptually fully equipped to do so. Indeed, a philosopher whose students are convinced by the arguments of a colleague that their teacher's views are not just mistaken but palpably absurd, may very well feel that, despite all his colleague's protestations to the contrary, he himself is being somehow diminished in their eyes.

There are two different kinds of reason why this may be so. In the first place he may feel that his intelligence, his professional philosophical acumen, is being belittled. Most people in most circumstances are likely to find it hard enough to make such a clear distinction between, let us say, themselves as persons and their own capacity for considered judgment as to be able not to experience an attack on the latter as constituting an attack on themselves *in propria persona;* those whose whole professional role and standing are crucially bound up with their presumed intelligence and judiciousness, and most of whose social relations are, moreover, largely dependent on recognition of their role, are very likely to find any such distinction essentially unreal. This can be so quite independently of the intrinsic importance that they may or may not attach to the beliefs in question. But there are also cases, more often, no doubt, where issues of moral or political philosophy or philosophy of religion are concerned than cases of disagreement over matters of technical logic, where the disputed beliefs themselves, and a philosopher's attachment to them, may constitute so crucial a part of the tradition to which he belongs and of the way in which he sees himself, so much a part of

his own self-identity, that he cannot but experience an attack on them as constituting an attack on himself and on all those who, belonging to the same tradition,
accept the same beliefs as himself. In the case of serious religious beliefs, moreover, it is peculiarly implausible to construe the concept of "adherence to a belief" in such would-be "purely intellectual" terms as to present such adherence
as consisting in nothing more than the readiness to recite, on appropriate public
or private occasions, whether out loud or to oneself, the consecrated formulas of
the belief in question. Just how far belief is to be analyzed in dispositional terms,
and just what sorts of behavior are to be taken in this context or in that as manifesting the relevant dispositions, are in general properly debatable questions
within the philosophy of mind. But religious beliefs at any rate are characteristically so tightly bound into a whole web of ritual and other social practices
that it becomes in principle extremely dubious whether it makes any clear sense
to try and draw any determinate line between them—and, therefore, any determinate line between respect for someone's religious beliefs, respect for their religious and associated social practices, and respect for the person himself or herself. To quote Dr. Carey once again: "My form of Christianity is that belief and
behaviour go together through our lives."[3]

This returns us fairly and squarely to our opening questions. Are the beliefs
constitutive of one's own faith really compatible with the apparently very different beliefs that are constitutive of the faith of one's ecumenical partners? If
so, why should it matter whether anyone should accept the truth of one of these
sets of beliefs and the practical commitments that they may be held to involve
rather than any other? And, if not, what sense may be given to that allegedly
equal respect which one appears to be ecumenically committed to accord to
those who, although they may indeed be one's partners, have to be seen as in
some respect seriously disadvantaged in respect of their religious beliefs and
commitments? It seems that something has to give here. By this I do not, of
course, mean that in contingent reality all those sincerely committed *both* to their
own religious faiths *and* to unqualified mutual respect within the framework of a
thoroughgoing ecumenical movement may not continue more or less indefinitely
in a state of blessedly nonperspicuous failure to recognize the tensions within
their own positions. Nor am I even suggesting that the practical benefits of such
a state might not on occasion substantially outweigh those of a greater clearsight-
edness. Nevertheless, the concepts of belief, knowledge, and truth (and, indeed,
meaning) are so interrelated that it is hard to see how anyone could set out to
teach or to preach the articles or beliefs of their own faith, whichever it might
be, without affirming or at any rate implying that such beliefs were true—with
the further logically inescapable, if perhaps only implicit, implication that any
such doctrines as might be genuinely incompatible with them must be false.

If, then, full and equal respect for one's ecumenical partner implies a recognition that their own spirituality and their own "way to God" is as religiously
valid as one's own, one may have in all consistency to accept the prospect of
having to revise certain of one's own basic and long-standing beliefs. (The same
will, of course, be true for one's partners as well.) It is not likely to be easy for

all those concerned to admit that their ecumenism harbors within it an acceptance of the principle that there may be more than one equally valid expression of the recognition of God, more than one equally acceptable form of His worship, more than one superficially incompatible but in fact equally valid diffraction of the one hidden Truth, but this, it does seem, must in the last resort be the inner sense of any really serious contemporary ecumenical movement. Just what sorts of doctrinal (and liturgical) revisions may be called for on the part of one or another of the partners concerned is hardly something to be guessed at a priori; on the contrary, it is likely to involve much complicated, sustained, and potentially controversial work, work not only of an intellectual nature, moreover, but much work in the institutionalized practice of lived religious relations both within and between different traditions. But if it would indeed be frivolous to try and make any sort of an a priori guess at what the living detail of such work might turn out to be, it may nevertheless be possible to catch a speculative glimpse of the broad outlines that it might have to follow.

An ecumenical partnership is, of course, only possible, and will, indeed, only be seen as desirable, between and by partners who recognize in each other a similarly deep concern for what they see to be common moral and spiritual values. Most typically those who come together in such would-be ecumenical partnership will be representatives of the different branches of Christianity together with those of the different forms of Judaism and Islam, those other two members of the great biblical tradition. In the increasingly multicultural world of today, however, they may be joined by, for example, Sikhs, Hindus, or Buddhists, or indeed by members of other major religious or spiritual traditions. It would be hard and probably not very helpful to try and lay down in advance any rigid criteria of what exactly are to be accounted such traditions; the practical issues must be less those of theoretical definition than of effective mutual recognition. The differences between the partners in any such ecumenical movement may be seen, then, as amounting to differences in their understanding of how best to conceptualize or to symbolize the ultimate source of what they recognize to be their common values, and in their diverse traditional practices, highly institutionalized as they may very well be, of acknowledgment and recognition of the ultimate authority of this ultimate source. It is because these linked practices and symbolizations are so closely tied in with the mutually discrepant doctrines and affirmations to be found in the different associated creeds, affirmations which prima facie certainly present themselves in the form of would-be statements of fact, that contemporary ecumenists find themselves faced with the problems of the reconciliation of equal mutual respect with fidelity to the truths of their own faith as they have received them, with which this essay has been concerned. Their ecumenical commitment would seem, then, to include the perhaps initially hidden further commitment to the search for a new framework of discourse of God, a framework in the sense that it would somehow have to allow for, or make persuasively intelligible, an account of "God's" necessary intervention in the ongoing contingencies of human history as having taken place at more than just one place and time and in more than just one way; if "God" is really to make Himself known, one might say, then it is not only natural but no doubt inevitable that He should do so within the contingently different terms of different human traditions. From this perspective, the analogy with the essentially democratic respect for the values of political pluralism may be seen as having more telling relevance than was apparent earlier on. For, so one might be led to argue, the diversity of Divine self-revelation and of consequent religious formations may be seen as "God's" most appropriate response to the historically contingent diversity of the development of human societies with their different cultures and traditions.

For the most part, again, those who find themselves brought together in working ecumenical cooperation will almost inevitably be representatives of different religious institutions and in all probability role-holders within their respective institutions. It is, however, well known that different traditions, different cultures, provide for very different ways of seeing the relationships between the communities concerned and their individual members; and that within some traditions a person's religion or spirituality, along with so many other aspects of his or her life, may be seen as very much a matter for that person alone. But even in the most individualistic communities, the prevailing values of individualism are, of course, rooted in the common culture of the community concerned. It is indeed one of the most powerful themes of much recent and contemporary thought, whether philosophic, sociological, or psychological, that people only come to self-awareness in and through interchange with others. Thus even at this highly individualistic pole of the spectrum, religion remains very much a matter of how a person relates to what he may identify under the name of God, not only in his own direct terms but also in the expression of that relationship through each of his further relationships within and across the generations with fellow "children of the Divine." Within such a perspective one can well envisage an ecumenical theology insisting on the natural inevitability of God's self-revelation taking different historical forms within the necessarily contingent particularities of this social tradition or that. Why, within such a perspective, should the maintenance of any one particular tradition be so important or should it matter that people stick in general with the religion of their forebears? Because, one can envisage the answer, the continuing life, and hence ready availability, of religion depends on its place within the fabric of an ongoing social tradition. Traditions, once undermined, are not easily recreated; nor is it in general possible for individuals to make up their own traditions as they might wish them to be or to swap them at will. To move from one tradition to another, to convert from one religion to another, is no light or easy thing; it involves the transformation of a whole way of life and of all one's relations with others, and of their relations with oneself in turn. It is not surprising that all the great religions lay great stress on their committed ritualized concern with how their adherents should order the making and breaking and, above all, the maintenance of their family relationships and structures; for these, in all their further ramifications, provide the fabric of social continuity within which alone traditions, including religious traditions, can take root and flourish. This is not, of course, to say that people should never be permitted to change; but it is to say that they should never be encouraged lightly to do so.

In such a perspective, what might survive of the traditionally universal and hence conflicting claims of those of the great religions that most typically find themselves struggling to work together in ecumenical partnership today? Essentially, that religion must inevitably, if it is to answer to our basic rootedness in the particularities of historical place and time, take on whatever the several particular forms that may be appropriate to the different social contexts which such a diverse history has produced. But this recognition must carry with it an acceptance of the sacrifice of any traditional claims to uniquely valid conceptualizations of religious truth, of uniquely true prophets or of uniquely appropriate symbolizations or myths. In short, a serious commitment to the reciprocity of equal mutual respect among ecumenical partners has to be understood as carrying with it a further commitment to the common development of a new and common ecumenical theology, a universal theology of the compatibility and equal validity of the different participating religious traditions in all their diverse particularities—a task and a challenge for the ecumenical theologians of tomorrow.

NOTES

Grateful thanks are due to the late Rabbi Hugo Gryn and to Sylvain Piron for their critical comments on an earlier version of this essay as well as for a number of valuable and stimulating suggestions. They bear, of course, no responsibility whatsoever for such flaws as may remain.

1. Johann Martin Chaldenius, *Introduction to the Correct Interpretation of Reasonable Discourses and Writings,* par. 173 (published in Leipzig in 1742); extracts from this *Introduction* are included in *The Hermeneutic Reader,* edited by Kurt Mueller-Vollmer (Blackwell, 1986), 59.

2. From an interview published in the *Times Magazine* for Saturday, December 23, 1995, p. 12.

3. Ibid., 11.

MIDWEST STUDIES IN PHILOSOPHY, XXI (1997)

"In the Beginning Was the Proposition,"
"In the Beginning Was the Choice,"
"In the Beginning Was the Dance"

D. Z. PHILLIPS

In modern and post-modern epistemology there are two pictures of our relations to reality which vie with each other for supremacy. According to the first picture, we make contact with reality by showing that we know that our fundamental beliefs concerning it are true. According to the second picture, it is we who determine what is real and unreal. In these pictures, we are seen either as autonomous knowers or as autonomous choosers of the world in which we live. In this essay, I want to show the unsatisfactoriness of these pictures, and to illustrate an alternative which illuminates the notion of our being in the world.

I

According to the first epistemological view, what are the fundamental beliefs concerning reality which, it is said, we must show to be true? They are expressed in the form of general existential propositions: 'Physical objects exist', 'Sensations exist', 'Values exist', and so on. It is tempting to think that they can be shown to be true or false in the way in which we show the truth or falsity of more specific existential claims. We ought to be able to settle whether or not physical objects exist in the way in which we settle whether there is a chair in the next room. In the latter case we might settle the matter by going to have a look. This constitutes one feature of our dealings with physical objects, dealings in which we can say whether there is or there is not a chair in the next room. But, now, we are asked whether these dealings themselves tell us anything about reality, as though there were some wider context in which we could settle whether 'Physical objects exist' is a true or false proposition. In the case of the chair, we checked whether it was in the next room in a familiar way. But how is the belief in the existence of physical objects to be checked? It may be said that what corresponds to the content of the room in the more specific case is the contents of reality, how things are, in the more general case. The question is whether there are things called physical objects. But this is confused. In investigating whether the chair existed we looked at the room. Now, in investigating whether physical objects exist we are supposed to look at 'things'. How are we supposed to do this? We can ask, "What kind of thing is a table?" "What kind of thing is a chair?" but, not, "What kind of thing is a thing?" We cannot teach anyone the use of 'thing' by saying "This is a thing." The 'big thing' against which so-called existential beliefs, such as 'Physical objects exist' are supposed to be checked is called Reality. 'Reality', so conceived, cannot fall under any description, because any description offered will itself be predicated of this 'thing' called Reality. We have indeed a something, we know not what.

Our difficulty comes from treating the language concerning physical objects, or the contexts in which we have dealings with physical objects, as themselves constituting existential claims about one ontological subject called Reality. In fact, when we say, "This is a physical object," "This is a sensation," or "This is a value," what we are doing is indicating into which conceptual context what is being talked about falls. Once we realize this, we are not led to speak of a Reality to which these contexts correspond. What we mean by making contact with reality is as humble as making contact with a chair by locating it or sitting on it. Contact with reality gets its sense from within these familiar contexts. Realizing this is often said to be one of the primary achievements of post-modernism.

Yet, this conclusion is often expressed in terms of the second epistemological view we mentioned. It is argued that since what constitutes the distinction between the real and the unreal is not determined by reference to some ultimate ontological subject, the distinction must be the product of our choice; we determine what we mean by the distinction between the unreal and the real. But this second view leads to difficulties of its own. What kind of choice is being referred to? Not the choices we make in the everyday contexts of our lives, since these contexts themselves are said to be the product of choice. We can say what considerations inform our everyday choices, but what is supposed to inform the choices which determine what we mean by reality; when are these choices supposed to occur?

The two epistemological answers we have considered inherit comparable difficulties. In the first answer, we found we could give no account of the relation between general existential beliefs, such as, 'Physical objects exist' and the Reality of which they are supposed to be true. In the second answer, we found we could give no account of the relation between the ways we distinguish between the real and the unreal, and our choices which are supposed to determine them. In both epistemological accounts, human beings are thought of as being over against the world. How or whether they entertain true beliefs about that world, or whether they exercise effective choices concerning it, are said to determine whether they are in contact with reality. But these notions of truth and choice are problematic.

According to the first epistemological account, contact with reality is via propositions. I shall argue that it is an intellectualist distortion. According to the second epistemological account, contact with reality is via choice. I shall argue that it is a voluntaristic, romantic distortion. The first view says: "In the beginning was the proposition." The second view says: "In the beginning was the choice." A third alternative is worthy of consideration. It says: "In the beginning was the dance."

But before this consideration begins, a general objection to my use of the term 'dance' has to be answered.[1] It may be said that I object to the use of the alternatives 'proposition' and 'choice', in the contexts in question, because the characterizations of what we do in these terms makes no sense. We can speak of making or considering propositions, making or considering choices, in all sorts of contexts, but these will not give us what we want. But, then, why cannot the intellectualist and the voluntarist counter this point by saying that they are using 'proposition' and 'choice' in a special sense, a sense required to counter the inadequacies of the other point of view? What is more, they might argue, am I not doing exactly the same thing. I, too, am using the word 'dance' in a special sense; a sense which requires me, at the very opening of the next section of the essay, to speak of our acquaintance with the external world as a *kind* of dance. I cannot appeal to a special use for my term, while denying them a special use for theirs.

These considerations stem from a more general difficulty. *Whatever* term I use for what I want to convey in the phrase, 'In the beginning was the ———' will already have an ordinary employment elsewhere. It is for reasons such as these that some have wondered whether propositions such as those we have mentioned, propositions which we rarely formulate outside philosophy, ought to be called 'propositions' at all, and whether 'choices', such as those we have mentioned, which seem different from choices we make in our everyday lives, should be called 'choices' at all. It might be said that my extended use of 'dance' is even stranger than the admittedly extended uses of 'proposition' and 'choice'. But that latter suggestion is what my essay is concerned to contest. Unlike the uses of the other two terms, I am able to specify the sets of reactions I have in mind which I hope to illuminate by the use of 'dance'. Furthermore, my claim is that it is reactions such as these, so fundamental in our practices, that are distorted by the intellectualist and voluntaristic points of view. This is the claim which I now try to establish.

II

It may seem, at the outset, that I am countering the intellectualist and voluntaristic theses, each of which is foundationalist, by offering a third thesis which offers foundations of its own. Instead of saying that our contact with reality is based on beliefs or choices, it may seem that Wittgenstein is saying that it is based on certain primitive reactions. Wittgenstein has been read as though he were propounding a genetic theory of language; language which makes possible an understanding of the world. Certain remarks of his seem to encourage this reading: "The origin and the primitive form of the language-game is a reaction; only from this can the more complicated forms grow. Language—I want to say—is a refinement; 'in the beginning was the deed'."[2]

Reacting to such comments, Elizabeth Wolgast says: "Here is the picture that is suggested by these remarks: In accounting for language as we have it, we should start with reactions and rudimentary activities that are at an animal level, so to speak. Later concepts and language come on the scene and embody features belonging to that level."[3] The whole of language, in all its complex forms, seems to depend, on this view, on prelinguistic animal reactions. After all, doesn't Wittgenstein say that by 'primitive' he means: "Presumably that this sort of behaviour is *prelinguistic,* that a language game is based *on it,* that it is the prototype of a way of thinking and not the result of thought."[4] Norman Malcolm argues that "not merely is much of the first language of a child grafted onto instinctive behaviour—but the whole of the developed, complex, employment of language by adult speakers embodies something resembling instinct."[5] Malcolm's paper emphasizes the genetic aspects of language: its emergence from instinctive reactions.

On the other hand, reading Wittgenstein in this way leads to tensions with other aspects of his work. Lars Hertzberg says that if Wittgenstein "is to be taken to say something substantive about the origins of language to the exclusion of certain other possible conceptions, it comes to seem a form of *a priori* theorizing, of the sort Wittgenstein himself was anxious to rule out of court."[6] Wolgast wonders what we know "about a connection like this? The answer has to be, nothing, for they go beyond what we can confirm by records about the development of languages. Indeed records necessarily involve an existing complicated language, and we cannot go outside of it to see what was there before. As an historical claim this one has great weaknesses."[7]

But should Wittgenstein be read in this way? Peter Winch has pointed out that if Wittgenstein is taken to be conducting a historical enquiry, "it would be amazingly off-hand."[8] Further, Wittgenstein "explicitly warns *against* supposing that a historical development is what is at issue":[9]

The basic form of our game must be one in which there is no such thing as doubt. What makes us sure of this? It can't surely be a matter of historical certainty.

'The basic form of the game can't include doubt.' What we are doing here above all is to imagine a basic form: a possibility, a *very important* possibility. (We often confuse what is an important possibility with historical reality).[10]

Winch, I believe, makes the essentially important point when he says: "It is perfectly true that we are speaking of reactions that people may have before they learn to talk; however, the language-games, a 'primitive form' of which we see in those reactions, provide the framework within which we identify in the first place the reactions of which we speak. Only thus are we able to make the distinctions between them which we need and which would be indiscernible, would indeed make no sense, if the wider context of the language-game were not presupposed."[11]

Similarly, Rush Rhees argues that when a language-game is called a further extension of "so many natural, instinctive kinds of behaviour towards other human beings,"[12] this primitive behaviour is *already* to be understood as within a language, "*as belonging to* the thinking and speaking with other people."[13] If this were not the case, it would make no sense to refer to the primitive thinking as a prototype of a way of thinking, or as a prototype at all. Rhees emphasizes that "what the more refined forms grow out of are still *Lebensformen* (forms of life)."[14] Even when Wittgenstein says: "I want to regard man here as an animal; as a primitive being to which one grants instinct but not ratiocination. As a creature in a primitive state,"[15] Rhees says "he is speaking of ein primitives Wesen . . . in einem primitiven Zustande (a primitive being . . . in a primitive state)—but in a situation in which he is living together with other 'primitive beings': beings which *understand* one another—understand one another's actions and reactions, if you like—in the sense in which *we* understand one another in what we say and do, or the sense in which we understand the language we speak. (If you say: "Understand the form of life in which we live" this comes to the same thing)."[16]

Within the form of life, it is extremely important that there is an agreement in reactions. As Rhees says, "when Wittgenstein tries to suggest that 'eine *Sprachverwirrung* ('linguistic confusion') would be like, he sometimes imagines a situation in which no two people would react in the same way to the question whether this is the same colour as that, or whether his whistle went on for a longer or a shorter time than the other man's, whether this man was pronouncing the same sound as the other man, etc, etc. . . . We couldn't talk to one another."[17]

Rhees insists, however, that there is an important difference between 'agreement in reactions' and in a form of life, and the agreement we may note in the reactions of animals. He points out that animals of many different species may lie down when tired, become restless when long without food, start to fight at a sudden noise, fix attention on a moving light in the dark, etc. Rhees concludes, however:

> But if most dogs (or—to eliminate the human influence—most foxes) 'agree' in the ways they react in such circumstances, this agreement does not belong to an understanding or a language between them.
>
> It may not interest my dog, whether my neighbour's dog does or does not react in the same way, e.g., whether he sneezes when exposed to a strong whiff of exhaust fumes or not. But if my 'instinctive reaction to something as the cause' is eine Wurzel des Ursache-Wirkung Sprachspiels (one root of the cause and effect language game), then it *is* important that I and other people agree in eine Lebensform (a form of life)—that the reaction was

an action, eine Handlung in einer Lebensform (within a form of life),—
that people who are with me may notice and ask questions and perhaps
take steps to do something about it.[18]

As Rhees points out, there is no *necessity* that primitive behavior is taken
up in a particular way in a form of life. Referring to an island primitive Rhees
says: "Suppose I went through the motions of putting food in my mouth and
chewing it: perhaps the island man would bring me food; (perhaps he would run
away, perhaps he would attack me . . .). If he did, he might not do so a second
time."[19] Yet, if others *do* react to the primitive reactions of the hungry person in
the ways with which we are familiar, it does not mean that the primitive reactions
emerged from reasoning or reflection.

The discussions we have referred to in this section of the essay are of central importance in reflecting on the two epistemological pictures of our contact
with reality we mentioned at the outset.

III

It has been said that perception, our very acquaintance with the external world,
is a kind of dance. Why should anyone say this?

Let us begin with the example of sensations. In the language game we play
with tastes, we call certain things bitter or sweet. We react in characteristic ways
in relation to them, and we take these reactions for granted when we talk of them.
According to the first epistemological account we have considered, our reactions
would follow if we first establish the truth of the proposition, 'Sweetness exists'
or 'Bitterness exists'. No doubt there are countless occasions on which the propositions 'The oranges are sweet' and 'The lemons are bitter' may be formed without reference to our characteristic reactions, and without their occurrence. But
this does not mean that our notions of sweetness or bitterness would be what
they are independent of our common reactions. In fact, we do not react because
we first establish the truth of the above propositions. Rather, the possibility of
the propositions depends on taking for granted the agreement in our reactions;
reactions which do not emerge from reasoning or reflection.

It is important to note that our reactions are common reactions. If our reactions were random, it is tempting to say that some would find lemons sweet,
while others would find them bitter, and yet others have no reactions at all. But
the supposition is confused. Without the common reactions, the common dance
of the body, there would be no conception of 'bitter' or 'sweet'. One might say
that the common dance is a condition of the thought of such epithets in our form
of life. There are no common conceptions without the common dance.

It should not be difficult to see how our conclusions concerning taste apply
equally to auditory and tactile sensations such as 'loud' and 'quiet', 'hot' and
'cold' respectively. The possibility of these distinctions, too, in our language game,
is rooted in the dance of the body, our common reactions to the sounds we

hear and the surfaces we touch. We jump at the explosion and remove our hands quickly from the hot surface. The dance of the body is involved in our visual experiences, for example, in the way we shield our eyes from bright lights. The same point can be made concerning colors. Some have said that after individuals have experienced colors in isolation, we *choose* to call *the* color of an object that color which the majority have seen. But this supposes a sense of a color, in the particular case, which *could not* be mistaken. But *which* sense? Without an agreement in reactions, we have no conception of one color as distinct from another. When we teach someone a color by means of samples and say, "And so on," the understanding of "and so on" is shown in the common reaction to the teaching we expect. These reactions are taken up in various ways in our form of life.

When we reflect on the dance of the body with respect to our sensations, we see how ill served we are by the two epistemological perspectives outlined at the beginning of the essay. We have seen what happens if we try to say, "In the beginning was the proposition." We should have to say that we first have a belief that lemons are bitter and, as a result, think it appropriate to react in the way we do to bitter fruit. A similar argument would have to be advanced for the reactions we think appropriate as the result of the truth of the propositional beliefs, 'The explosion is loud', 'The fire is hot', and 'The light is bright'. But, as we saw, the possibility of such beliefs depends on a conceptual agreement rooted in our common reactions. As we have seen, it is misleading to ask which came first, dance or thought. We are rescued from an intellectualized account of our contact with reality in our sensations by recognizing how the dance of the body, our common reactions, are involved in perception and, hence, in our contact with the world.

Such a recognition also rescues us from a voluntaristic, romantic conception of our involvement with the world. If we do not react to lemons in the way we do by first checking on the truth-value of the proposition 'Bitterness exists', or even 'Lemons are bitter', it does not follow that we determine what reality amounts to in such contexts. The common reactions are ours, but this does not mean that they are the products of our choice or decision. We do not decide that lemons are bitter, that explosions are loud, that the light is bright, that the fire is hot. There are, of course, plenty of occasions when we do have to make decisions concerning tastes, sounds, sights, and touches, but we do so against a background of an agreement in reactions which is not itself the product of choice or decision. In the beginning was the dance.

IV

It may be thought that the example of sensations makes it easier than most to say 'In the beginning was the dance'. Sensations are felt by us, so it is easy to invoke our necessary involvement in this aspect of our perception of the world. But what if we concentrated on some central feature of our naturalistic understanding of the world, such as causal relations? Could the same argument be advanced? There is little temptation to say, "We decide what is the cause of such-

and-such." The world will soon put such decisions in their place. We are answerable to what is the case. What we can say or do is determined by the truth or falsity of the proposition, 'X is caused by Y'.

In a multitude of contexts these remarks are unexceptionable. We experiment to find out what is the case. We find out by looking. In contexts such as these, those who say that Reality is a mental construct would be invited to jump out of a ten-story window to see what happens.

It has been said, however, that we choose the scientific, theoretical frameworks within which such investigations are carried on. It is true that there can be major conceptual shifts in science, but this cannot be reduced to a matter of choice. Some scientists felt unable to accept new directions in their subject and chose to stay where they were. But this does not mean that "where they were" or the new directions others took could be reduced to choice.

These points having been made, we still have to appreciate the role our reactions play in the formation of causal concepts in our language game; a role which shows the point of saying here, too, 'In the beginning was the dance'. Consider, to begin with, the example of a boy being hit down by another in a schoolyard. He does not have to be hit a number of times before concluding what is the cause of his fall. He does not reach his conclusion by inductive argument. He does not *reach* a conclusion at all. His reaction to the cause is immediate and unreflective: 'He's to blame!' He looks away from himself to the one who hit him. This reaction is not individualistic or idiosyncratic. It is one we all share. This brute fact is important if we want to recognize the difference between giving reasons for our conclusions in a specific causal investigation, and the claim that we must have reasons for having causal interests as such. The latter claim is confused, and an emphasis on our unreflective reactions to a cause in our form of life helps us to see why.

If someone touches us on the shoulder, we look away from ourselves. In this immediate, unreflective 'looking away' an elementary distinction is effected between oneself and what is other than oneself. We do not first ascertain the truth of the proposition 'Something touched me' and look away as a result. Rather, the possibility of a distinction between myself and what is other than myself is rooted in the primitive reaction. Of course, I may look away to find out exactly who it is that has touched me, but suppose someone asked me why I look away. I should be extremely puzzled. Like everyone else, I take the reaction for granted. Suppose this were not the case; that when touched on the shoulder we did not look away; showed no reactions at all. Then one major avenue of our sense of something independent of us would be closed. We do not react in this way as a result of determining the truth-value of the proposition 'There is something independent of me'. Rather, our sense of this independence is given in the reaction in the language game, the reaction to a cause. In the beginning was the dance.

These conclusions do not tempt us to say that we decide what is the cause of such-and-such, or that we choose to have causal interests. As in the case of sensations, here, too, we see the inadequacy of the two epistemological accounts we are offered. Our primitive causal reactions are neither the product of choice, nor the consequences of determining the truth-values of causal propositions which can be understood independently of them.

V

When we turn from a consideration of sensations and causal reactions to a consideration of values, it may seem that the second epistemological perspective comes into its own. We are not tempted to argue that the sense of the proposition 'Values exist' is independent of the responses of human beings. How could we establish that generosity, kindness, or loyalty exist without taking into account the generous, kind, or loyal deeds of human beings? Some have said that we cannot, because human values are prescriptive judgments concerning how we should act in the world. We determine our values, it is said; they are the product of our choices.

Consider, however, our reactions to the pains of others. In our form of life, we are interchanging constantly between giving natural expressions of our pains, and reacting in characteristic ways to those natural expressions by others. Our concept of pain has its life in this traffic of natural expressions and reactions. We do not first determine the truth of the proposition, 'This human being is in pain' and decide to react in a certain way as a result. Neither do we first determine the truth of the proposition, 'I am in pain' and decide to express it accordingly. Rather, propositions concerning pain, even when formed in the absence of these expressions and reactions, get their sense from them; primitive reactions which are taken for granted and are one aspect of the dance of the body in our form of life.

Once again, we have to reject the picture of human beings set over against the world. We act in the world. We express our condition and others are moved by it. When someone is hurt we move towards the injured one. Sometimes, we recoil from the injury. The relation between distress and our affective responses is not a contingent one. It could be said that pity is one form which the conviction that another is in distress may take. It is one of the affective responses which are constitutive of the possibility of perceiving that another is in distress; responses which are the product neither of choices nor of finding out the truth of antecedent propositions.

Choice is emphasized, sometimes, in an attempt to emphasize that to be serious, morally, one must make values one's own. But, then, one has the problem of accounting for this 'choice'. 'Making values our own' is shown in our relation to them; in our regard for them. Our values inform our choices, including those we have to make in moral dilemmas. (Cf. we can decide to attend the lecture, but not to be interested in it. Yet, we can make the arguments our own.)

The point we have made is no isolated observation with respect to pain, pity, and distress. It can be extended to our reactions to each other as human beings. These reactions are mixed: we love and hate, we admire and despise, we are generous and mean, we are courageous and afraid, and so on. There is a generality in these reactions, despite the variety they cover, or the complexities they may lead to in sophisticated situations. We do not first determine the truth of the proposition, 'There are human beings', and react in these characteristic ways as a result. Rather, our sense of the human is given in these reactions. Furthermore, these reactions are not the product of decision or choice. When actions fall outside this range of reactions, the agents are marked off as the strange ones. Their behavior may be marked by one of a number of terms we reserve for such occasions. It may be called unintelligible, strange, inhuman, demonic, or monstrous. But it is against the background of our familiar reactions to each other, the dance of the body, that these extremities are to be seen.

VI

Having looked at the examples of sensations, causal relations, values, and our sense of the human, we have seen that, with respect to concept-formation, compared with saying, 'In the beginning was the proposition', or 'In the beginning was the choice', there is considerably more merit in saying, 'In the beginning was the dance'. It may be doubted, however, whether similar considerations would throw light on concept-formation where religious sensibilities are concerned. This is because the epistemological considerations we have discussed may seem to be necessarily anthropocentric. Our primitive reactions are an agreement in *human* reactions, therefore, it is argued, they cannot constitute contact with anything other than human realities. The proposition, 'Spiritual realities exist' has no application; it can be accorded no truth-values. If, on the other hand, we try to make spiritual realities a product of our choice, by calling them a 'mental construct', this will simply be taken to mean that we create the gods; we create God in our own image.

I want to show that these conclusions are premature. Let us reflect again on the examples we have considered. We have noted that the agreement in reactions which play an essential role in our distinctions between tastes, sounds, colors, our reactions concerning causes and values, are brute facts about us. Things could have been otherwise. These reactions need not have been taken up in our form of life in the ways they are. It has been said that we know by a grace of nature. The roots of knowledge, the conditions of its possibility, are not in reflection or in choice, but in a grace of nature. The realization of this fact, the appreciation of the centrality of the role of our agreements in reactions and responses, can themselves become a source of wonder. Wonder at what is a 'sheer given' in this way.

I am not saying that this sense of wonder is religious, or that the grace of nature by which we know can be equated with a religious sense of grace. On the other hand, it should not be difficult to appreciate how the phenomena which occasion wonder can be related to reactions which are, in fact, moral and religious. For example, it is well known that many have reacted to nature in ways which make them want to talk of its majesty—a sweeping landscape or a towering mountain range. Confronted by such majesty, many of our squabbles seem petty by comparison. Confronted by such majesty, peace has often descended on human turbulence.

In the light of this moral example, let us look back at the conclusions I said were premature. The reactions to nature I have mentioned are certainly not universal, nevertheless, they are primitive relative to the context in which they occur. The reactions are not the consequence of determining the truth-value of the proposition 'Nature is majestic'. Rather, the sense of the majesty of nature is given in such reactions. Further, it clearly will not do to say that human beings decide to react in this way. They simply find that they can do so. And when this is so, though the reactions are human reactions, how could it be said that they constitute contact with nothing other than human realities? It would be insane to try to reduce the majesty of nature to any kind of human majesty. No human being could speak to fellow human beings in the way the majesty of nature does.

Religious reactions are related to, but go beyond the moral reaction we have just considered. The religious reactions go further than seeing that we know by a grace of nature. They find nature to be a means of grace. As in the moral case, the sheer given character of nature makes an enormous impression. But, now, its 'givenness' is reacted to as a gift; a gift which inspires gratitude. The majesty of nature comes as something unbidden and undeserved. With respect to it, a sense of creatureliness dawns. In short, nature is seen as a miracle. It has been said that a miracle is a gesture on the part of God. To see nature as such a gesture is to see it as a kind of dance. But to see it in this way is to be involved in a kind of dance with it oneself—the dance we call 'worship'.

We can contrast concept-formation facilitated by these reactions with the two epistemological theories I have found to be inadequate. In relation to the first epistemological theory, the reactions I have mentioned are said to be the consequences of determining the truth-value of the proposition 'God is the Creator of Nature' or 'Nature is a gift from God'. But the sense of a Creator and of nature as a gift is internally related to these reactions. The reactions are not based on the proposition, 'God is the Creator'. Believers do not praise God *because* he is the Creator. To speak of 'the Creator' is already to engage in praise. It may be said that religious teaching may take the form of saying, "Believe these doctrines" (accept these propositions). After all, we speak of religious instruction. This is true. I certainly do not want to deny the interaction between worship and doctrinal teaching. But religious instruction has its sense in the context of worship in which reactions such as those I have talked of are central. (Cf. musical instruction.) Cut off from the context of worship, doctrines would be lifeless. While many philosophers of religion attempt to argue from the world to the truth of the proposition 'God created the world', the religious reactions capture the sense of a miracle which comes undeserved and unbidden. So often, the philosophical movement is upward, from world to God, while religious movement is downward, from God to the world. Better: the world mediates grace. Alternatively, in relation to the second epistemological theory, it obviously will not do to say that believers decide to react in the ways they do. People simply find that they are able to do so. This possibility, it might be said, itself comes to them as a grace. That is why I spoke of believers as both seeing nature as a dance, and being involved in a dance with it. I called the dance 'worship'. Believers speak of worshipping God, but also of that very worship as the work of God in them. As in the case of the majesty of nature, it would be ludicrous to say that any human could give what God is said to give. The objection to reductionism is not its falsity, but its conceptual unintelligibility.

The notion of grace I have been talking about has analogies in primitive religion. Rain dances are but one example. Animism captures the inadequacies we have found in our first epistemological theory which proclaims, 'In the beginning was the proposition'. According to Animism, primitives peopled the world with spirits. They postulated their existence to explain phenomena they could not control, such as the coming of the rains. As a result of believing the hypothesis, 'Spirits cause the rains to come', they danced to initiate this causal relation. The problem with this analysis is that it intellectualizes notions of 'the spirit' and deadens the dance. Rain dances did not cause the coming of the rains. We do not find them during droughts when the rains are needed most, but when the rains are due anyway. The dances do not cause the rains to come, but celebrate their coming; they come as a kind of grace. Animism explains, it attributes the rains to the causal operations of spirits, and misses the spirit of the rain which does not explain anything. Animism turns praise into a proposition.

Others, seeing through the intellectualization of Animism, said that religion is not so much thought out, as danced out. But they could not see that the realities constituted by the possibilities of the dance were anything other than human realities. Yet seeing the coming of the rains as a gift, or celebrating at dawn rites of the coming of the day, cannot be thought of by analogy with one human being handing over a gift to another. The nearest analogy is in the way we speak of a gifted child, precisely because here, too, we regard the talents as a grace, as something 'given'. It would be as ludicrous to think of a human being giving such talents as it would be to think of a human being giving a day or making the rains come.

In relation to the religious reactions I have mentioned, in its development in a form of life, some have spoken of the beauty of the world and of the acknowledgment of it as a kind of love—a love of the beauty of the world. That is why acknowledging one's creation is, at the same time, an acknowledgment of one's redemption. I have been suggesting that there is epistemological profit in thinking of this religious acknowledgment, not primarily as assigning truth-values to propositions, but as an involvement in the dance of the spirit, a dance which constitutes the possibility of coming into contact with realities other than human realities. In Christianity, God's creation is not an initial, completed event, over and done with, but a sustaining grace at all times. I believe that in one Christian tradition the world is thought of as God's body. That being so, acknowledgment would be response to nature as the dance of creation, but this acknowledgment, too, is not a matter of assenting to propositions, but of involvement in worship, involvement in the dance. This sense is captured in the traditional hymn arranged by Sydney Carter:

> I danced in the morning
>> When the world was begun,
> And I danced in the moon
>> And the stars and the sun
>
> . . . . . .
>
> Dance, then, wherever you may be;
> I am the Lord of the Dance, said he,
> And I'll lead you all, wherever you may be,
> And I'll lead you all in the dance, said he.

In the hymn we are bidden to the dance. This 'bidding' may seem to conflict with what I have said about the primitive character of the religious response. If 'primitive' why the need for the bidding? Please remember that I have already insisted on the *mixed* character of our primitive reactions, our responses to each other. We not only move towards those in distress; we also recoil. One of the most primitive gestures in which we mark a difference between ourselves and what is independent of us is the reaching out to grasp. So in more sophisticated situations, any of these primitive reactions may be extended and developed in various ways in different relationships and situations. We reach out, not only to help, but also to possess. In these new contexts, some developments and extensions may occur in the lives of some people, but not others:

> I danced for the scribe
>> And the pharisee,
> But they would not dance
>> And they wouldn't follow me;
> I danced for the fishermen,
>> For James and John
> They came with me
>> And the dance went on.

It must also be noted that reactions to nature and to other human beings which may be called 'spiritual' may not be taken up religiously in a form of life. They may be taken up in a range of secular spiritual responses. In Christianity, the love of the beauty of the world is related to the love of the neighbor, where the latter, too, is received as an undeserved grace. Receiving the other, however, as revealed in the Cross, includes the recognition that this may not be accepted by the other. It may inspire hatred and persecution. When the body is involved in a dance of pain and suffering, it may seem grotesque to suggest that this could reveal anything divine. It may seem that someone is cursed who hangs from a tree. Yet, in the words, "Father forgive them, for they know not what they do," that dance is exalted, raised on high in the very grace it mediates in the context of the Passion:

> They buried my body
>> And they thought I'd gone;

But I am the dance
　　And I still go on;
They cut me down
　　And I leapt up high;
I am the life
That'll never, never die
I'll live in you
　　If you'll live in me:
I am the Lord
　　Of the dance, said he.

VII

This essay has deliberately confined itself on the whole to the topic of primitive reactions and some of their bearings on epistemological considerations. Nothing which has been said is meant to deny the need to go further in discussing more complex situations which call for reflection, development, criticism, and so on. Such a denial would be ludicrous; a denial of developments and extensions within our forms of life. Even in the case of the simplest sensations, we can talk of acquired tastes. Once we consider ways in which colors and sounds are taken up into art and music, we have to pay attention to the force of language in a culture. Theory and experiment are central in complex causal inquiries. Moral disagreements and moral dilemmas show the need for criticism and reflection. In religion, too, it makes sense to speak of a growth of understanding; for example, when naïve conceptions of God and worship are put aside.

How could any of this be denied? And yet, though I do not begin to argue the matter here, I contend that such developments and complexities will themselves be misunderstood if the various roles of primitive reactions are ignored. That is why, in the case of Christianity, it has been said that it is not a matter of doctrines, divorced from the life of the spirit. That life does not depend on the truth-values we assign to certain propositions. Rather, if propositions are formulated, they get their life from the religious responses.

Nothing said in the essay is meant to deny either important grammatical differences between the primitive responses we have discussed. 'Common reactions' do not amount to the same thing in all contexts. For example, if certain primitive reactions are missing in young children, say, reaching out successfully for an object, this is a sign that the child is seriously impaired. Think of the wide ramifications of such an inability. Again, in the case of colors, the color-blind are deficient by standards they themselves recognize. Moral and religious reactions, though primitive, are not universal. Those who do not share them may be called 'blind' by those who do. The accusation may or may not be shared by the accused. Someone may say he is blind to possibilities he wishes he could embrace. Others may call their accusers blind. Yet, these differences, important though they are, do not lead to the conclusions that assigning truth-values to proposition, or an appeal to fundamental choices displace the role of primitive reactions in the formation of our concepts.

VIII

A final postscript. I said at the outset that in many discussions of modern and post-modern epistemologies, we are offered a choice between saying that we can only make contact with reality if certain fundamental beliefs concerning it can be shown to be true, or saying that we choose what our distinctions between the real and the unreal come to. I said that these two pictures stand in the way of the reception of Wittgenstein's insights in our philosophical culture.

In the second section of the essay, I drew on recent discussions of Wittgenstein's notion of primitive reactions. It is obvious, however, that elsewhere in the essay I have drawn on Wittgenstein's remarks on "Cause and Effect: Intuitive Awareness," in his discussion of indeterminacy in the *Philosophical Investigations* and in *On Certainty,* and his discussion of rituals in his "Remarks on Frazer's *The Golden Bough.*" I am indebted to Simone Weil's *Lectures on Philosophy* for the striking suggestion that perception, our acquaintance with the world, is a kind of dance. In *Waiting for God* she speaks of love of the beauty of the world as an implicit form of the love of God.

It may seem puzzling that, on this occasion, I have not discussed the contemporary proponents of the other epistemological pictures, as I have done on numerous other occasions. I decided not to do so in order to bypass the likely baptismal reception such a discussion would have received in our philosophical culture—a baptism of signs. I would be expected to say whether my views are cognitive or non-cognitive, propositional or non-propositional, realist or non-realist, objective or attitudinal, rational or fideistic, and so on. I am not saying that discussions of such terms is always unprofitable, but, for once, I hoped to have a respite from such battle-cries by inviting a certain kind of consideration of a range of examples.

In the examples considered, there were cultural reasons for paying more attention to religion than to other topics. This is because those who trade in labelistic contrasts accuse those described as embracing non-cognitive, non-propositional, or attitudinal views, all derogatory labels, of seeking epistemological exceptions on behalf of religion. My reason for beginning with discussions of sensations and our reactions to a cause was to show that my epistemological conclusions were not meant to apply solely to religion. If the central role of our primitive reactions in concept-formation is enough to earn the epithet 'attitudinal', we had better be prepared to speak of our 'attitude' concerning sensations, colors, and causes, as well as our attitude to other human beings and to God. What is important is not to fight over such labels, but to pay attention to practice, to the place our concepts have in our lives.

I have suggested that such attention throw light on 'our being in the world'. I have said that we know by a grace of nature: that neither our primitive reactions nor our responses to them in language games and forms of life emerge from reasoning and reflection. I have shown how some respond religiously to this realization, in seeking nature as a means of grace. I have insisted, however, that there is no necessity in this response. Other responses appear in our forms of life. What can be said is that there is a confusion in those epistemological pictures which insist that either we know that our fundamental beliefs concerning reality are true, or we choose what we mean by 'the real' and 'the unreal'. These pictures, it seems to me, are involved in the omniscient knowers of the Enlightenment ideal, and in the omnipotent choosers of Existentialism, in relation to reality—pictures still dominant in our culture. Wittgenstein presents a very different account in which our being in the world is a grace of nature. How recognizing this develops in our forms of life is something philosophy can comment on, but not determine. In this essay all I have tried to show is that such comment needs to recognize the epistemological profit in saying, 'In the beginning was the dance'.[20]

NOTES

1. I am grateful to my colleague, R. W. Beardsmore, for pointing out the necessity of making this point.

2. Ludwig Wittgenstein, *Culture and Value,* p. 31e.

3. Elizabeth Wolgast, "Primitive Reactions," in *Philosophical Investigations* 17, no. 4 (October 1994): 589.

4. Ludwig Wittgenstein, *Zèttel,* §541.

5. Norman Malcolm, "Wittgenstein: The relation of language to instinctive behaviour," *Philosophical Investigations* 5 (Jan. 1982): 11–12.

6. Lars Hertzberg, "Primitive Reactions—Logic or Anthropology?" *Midwest Studies in Philosophy,* 17, *The Wittgenstein Legacy,* 26.

7. Wolgast, "Primitive Reactions," 591.

8. Peter Winch, "Discussion of Malcolm's Essay" in *Wittgenstein: A Religious Point of View?* by Norman Malcolm with a Response by Peter Winch (Ithaca, N.Y., 1994), 123.

9. Ibid.

10. Wittgenstein, "Cause and Effect: Intuitive Awareness," *Philosophia* 6, nos. 3–4, (September–December 1976): 411.

11. Winch, op. cit., p. 124.

12. Rush Rhees, "Language as Emerging from Instinctive Behaviour," edited by D. Z. Phillips, *Philosophical Investigations* (January 1996), 2.

13. Ibid.

14. Ibid., 5.

15. Wittgenstein, *On Certainty,* §475.

16. Rhees, op. cit., 3.

17. Ibid., 6.

18. Ibid.

19. Ibid., 7.

20. I am extremely grateful to participants in the discussion at the Philosophical Society, University of Wales, Swansea, in the Michaelmas Term 1994, especially R. W. Beardsmore and Timothy Tessin, which led me to revise an earlier version of my essay. Reflecting on the occasion also led me to edit Rush Rhees's paper which was originally a letter in response to Malcolm's paper.

God and the Philosophers

HILARY PUTNAM

When I reflected on this topic I thought that, drawing upon the particular philosophers and issues I have been studying in recent years, I might write about the different ways in which twentieth-century philosophers relate to religious belief. As a practicing Jew, I am also interested in the ways in which those issues have played themselves out in the Jewish tradition; but apart from a few remarks about Maimonides at the end of this essay, I shall leave that as a topic to be addressed on a future occasion. It would be problematic indeed to claim that the philosopher I shall discuss at greatest length here, Ludwig Wittgenstein, counts as a "Jewish philosopher."[1] At any rate, I now turn to the twentieth-century scene.

In the twentieth century, many—perhaps most—of the celebrated figures in philosophy have been non-believers if not militant atheists: Bertrand Russell, the Logical Positivists, John Dewey, John Austin on the "Anglo-Saxon" side, and Heidegger (for much of his life), Sartre, and Derrida on the "continental" side are examples of this. Here are two examples of this attitude:

(1) In *Of Grammatology* (13 ff) Jacques Derrida describes belief in God as simply a part of the past, and wonders out loud about why belief in the existence of *truth* refuses to disappear along with the belief in God. (I don't mean to suggest that Derrida himself disbelieves in the existence of truth; he finds himself unable to, and that is his problem, since he sees *that* belief as historically and metaphysically linked to the belief in God which no longer has any hold on him.)

(2) A few years ago, towards the end of an otherwise laudatory review of Taylor (1989), Bernard Williams accused the author of not seeing Nietzsche's "main importance," which lay, according to Williams, in "pressing all the way the thought that if our moral aspirations do not, cannot, mean everything they seem to mean, then they cannot come from where they seem to come from, and another kind of inquiry will be needed to understand their hold on us." And a little further down the page, Williams makes his meaning clear: "I think that Taylor, in

his search for sources of value, seems not to have taken seriously enough Nietzsche's thought that if there is, not only no God, but no metaphysical order of any kind, then this imposes quite new demands on our self-understanding. Though Taylor inhabits, unlike many philosophers, what is clearly and vigorously planet Earth and relishes its human history, his calculations still leave it being pulled out of orbit by an invisible Being."[2]

Having myself written about Williams's own metaphysical views (Putnam, 1990, ch. 11; 1992, ch. 5) and having discussed those views in classes more than once in recent years, I am familiar with the system of thought that lies in back of Bernard Williams's declaring the Death of God in the *New York Review of Books.* What the ordinary reader cannot know is that Williams believes in something that he calls an "absolute conception of the world." His declaration that there is "no metaphysical order of any kind" is not a rejection of the enterprise of metaphysics, not by any means. Williams has also explained (Williams, 1978) that his notion of "an absolute conception of the world," that is, a conception of the world as it is "independent of perspective," is not a blank check against some future metaphysics, because we already possess a kind of sketch or blueprint (even if it gets details wrong here and there) of this ultimate conception of the world in "present day physics." In short, by rejecting a "metaphysical order," all Williams means to reject is any metaphysics that *goes beyond materialism.* In Williams's view, we already *have* the final metaphysics: it is materialism. We *know* there is no God; that is simply a fact of science, or the only reasonable conclusion from the facts of science. And as for ethics, ethical truths, Williams (1985) tells us, are only true from the perspective of "some social world or other"; they can never be part of the absolute conception of the world.

If Williams thinks that such a mixture of materialism and cultural relativism was what Nietzsche was driving at, his is a remarkable misreading, but my concern today is not with Nietzsche, but with two ways of thinking about religious and ethical questions. One way, the way for which Bernard Williams has been an extremely clever and extremely sophisticated spokesman, holds that modern science has answered, or at least sketched a satisfactory answer to, *all* the problems with which metaphysics was traditionally concerned, and the answer simply leaves no room for religion (or absolute values of any kind, for that matter) except as a historically and culturally important kind of *escapism.* (Feurbach is another of Williams's heros; as Williams paraphrases him in the same review, he is absolutely indistinguishable from Williams's Nietzsche: "If there is no higher consciousness to aspire to, then this consciousness cannot mean what it seems to mean, and it demands another kind of account altogether; one that does not suggest that these aspirations might, as they present themselves, be satisfied.") Of course, if you find the claims of reductionist thinkers absurd—no matter whether the claim be that the very idea that our thoughts have determinate content is an illusion,[3] or if the claim be that the properties of reference and truth that make thought thought can be reduced to facts about matter and efficient causation;[4] if you think that the possibility of logical or mathematical knowledge can never make sense as long as one supposes that the only genuine facts there can be are facts about matter and efficient causation; if you find no sense in the idea that the *warrant* or *confirmation* of a belief can be just a matter of efficient causation—then this materialist backing behind Williams's declaration of the Death of God may seem just a bit naive.[5] Nietzsche himself did not speak as a philosopher who was drawing conclusions from "present day physics," but as a thinker whose sense of his own autonomy would not permit him to countenance a transcendent God. Nietzsche's defiant stance is as deep an existential commitment as Kierkegaard's religious stance; both thinkers would have regarded an appeal to "present day physics" as the worst form of bad faith—not just because it is "physics" that is appealed to, but even more because of the "present day."

WITTGENSTEIN

I believe that a very different attitude can be found in the writings of Ludwig Wittgenstein.[6] Today, unfortunately, many see those writings through accounts offered by philosophers with very different sensibilities—through the eyes of Saul Kripke (1982)[7] or Richard Rorty (1989), for example, and I will have to first caution you against those accounts. While Rorty and Kripke differ between themselves, both of them read Wittgenstein as thinking of language as the production of "marks and noises" (as Rorty puts it) according to practices which are determined by a community. Standards of truth and falsity, and of rightness and wrongness in language use generally, to the extent that there are any such things, are determined by communal agreement. And if communities conflict? There is no "fact" corresponding to the idea that one community is right and the other is wrong; they just play different language games.

You would never know from such readings that the real Wittgenstein felt contempt for reductionist claims. And while Wittgenstein famously said that very often it is best to think of the meaning of a word as its use in the language, he certainly did not think of using a word as following a habit in a behaviorist sense of "habit," or a program in the brain in the style of today's "AI" (Artificial Intelligence). Even if using words involves habits and programs in those senses (as a matter of empirical fact about the efficient causation of the "marks and noises" of which speech consists), the description of our abilities at either a behaviorist or a computer-scientific level makes their *normativity* completely invisible. When Wittgenstein speaks of our "natural history" in *Philosophical Investigations* (§25), he speaks of *commanding, questioning, recounting* as "parts" of it; he does not attempt to *reduce* commanding, questioning, recounting to non-normative notions as both Skinnerian psychologists and functionalists would. In particular, the idea that using a word is just producing a mark or noise in an observable situation according to some standard imposed by a community is certainly foreign to everything Wittgenstein thought.

According to a very different interpretation,[8] *the use of the words in a language game cannot be described without employing concepts which are internally related to the concepts used in the game.* This point has been made in connection with the language games of preliterate peoples, and also the case of religious utterances in our society, but I believe the same point applies to all language games. The philosopher who never tired of saying that in philosophy it is more important to discern differences than to find similarities did not suppose there was some single vocabulary in which our multifarious life with our language can be described.

Nor did Wittgenstein think that truth is determined by rules, or by the verdict of the community as a whole. For example, when he discusses learning to tell if another person is feigning a feeling they do not have[9] Wittgenstein stresses that here it is not a matter of following rules but of perceiving and appreciating the significance of "imponderable evidence," and he adds that not everyone can learn to do this. Nothing could be farther from the idea that what is right and wrong in a language game is merely a matter of what the community says.

Since we are going to talk about religion, it is important to note that on this interpretation someone who does not see the "point" of a language game, and who cannot imaginatively put himself in the position of an engaged player, cannot judge whether the "criteria" are applied *reasonably* or unreasonably in it. *Understanding a language game is sharing a form of life.* And forms of life cannot be described in a fixed positivistic metalanguage, whether they be scientific or religious or ethical or historical or political or literary-critical or whatever.

THE POINT OF THE DIGRESSION

I have let myself digress, but the digression had a point. For Williams, as I pointed out, talk of truth is to be understood in terms of an elaborate set of metaphysical distinctions (in spite of his repudiation of a "metaphysical order of any kind"). To give you the flavor, here are some of Williams's distinctions: truths, according to Williams, are to be classified as "absolute" or "perspectival." Only truths of finished physics are "absolute"; truths about secondary qualities (color, etc.) are "perspectival" (though not significantly culturally relative, it seems, reading Williams), ethical truths are both perspectival and culturally relative, and there are no such things as religious truths. (Religion was just a mistake.)

Wittgenstein's view is clearly very different. But what happens on the view I have attributed to Wittgenstein? Is religion simply immunized from criticism? Do we have to say "science is one language game and religion is another language game," and that is the whole story? As I read Wittgenstein, the answer is (not surprisingly) "yes and no." If "immunizing religion from criticism" means denying that a religious point of view is simply another scientific hypothesis, to be examined by the criteria of predictive efficacy, simplicity, and conservation of previous (scientific) belief, then "yes," Wittgenstein does deny that *that* is the way to look at any serious religious person's utterances. Indeed, in the first of his three "Lectures on Religious Belief" (Wittgenstein, 1966), Wittgenstein argues that if one *were* to believe that something will happen which matches the description of the Last Judgment *on the basis of scientific evidence alone,* one's belief would be something quite different from what the religious person believes. Wittgenstein says that even if the prediction were as certain as any scientific prediction could be, it would not lead him to change *his* life at all. On the other hand, he says, the man whose belief in a such a forecast was religious and not scientific "would fight for his life not to be dragged into the fire." "No induction. Terror. That is, as it were, part of the substance of the belief." And Wittgenstein goes on to say:

> If you ask me whether or not I believe in a Judgment Day in the sense in which religious people have belief in it, I wouldn't say, 'No, I don't believe there will be such a thing'. It would seem to me utterly crazy to say this.
>
> And then I give an explanation. I don't believe in— But then the religious person never believes in what I describe.
>
> I can't say. I can't contradict that person.
>
> In one sense I understand all he says. The English words. 'God', 'separate', etc. I understand. I could say, I don't believe in this. And that would be true. Meaning I haven't got these thoughts, or anything that hangs together with them. But not that I could contradict the thing.

Of course, it is not only the scientistic intellectual who confuses scientific and religious language games; the literalistic fundamentalist who deduces the age of the earth, or the falsity of the theory of evolution, or whatever, from his reading of his Scripture also confuses the spheres, and to the detriment of both. But this confusion is not a new one: the warning that when the Bible says the world was created in seven days, this is not to be taken as a literal description of cosmological fact is not a recent bit of "liberal theology," but something that goes back to the sages of the Talmud. The sages taught that the Bible is not a textbook of astronomy or history or geography. "The Torah speaks the language of human beings," they wrote.

By the same token, I may add, when a serious atheist thinker like Nietzsche or Rudolf Carnap *denies* the existence of God, what they are asserting is likewise not something to be established by empirical science. Just as the serious religious believer holds that the existence of God is *necessary,* and not a matter of empirical contingency at all, the serious atheist holds that the existence of God is, in a sense, *impossible,* or as Carnap would have said "cognitively meaningless." Of course, many atheists today would say that too; in fact, many atheists talk as if the existence of God were meaningless *and* empirically falsified by natural science! But that reveals the depths of their confusion.

Although the language games of science and of religion do not (that is to say, should not) contradict one another, it is important to notice that what Wittgenstein said does *not* have the tone of "it's true in his language game but not in mine." What Wittgenstein says instead is,

> If Mr. Lewy [Cassimir Lewy, one of the students present at these sessions] is religious, and says he believes in a Judgment Day, I won't even

know whether to say I understand him or not. I've read the same things as he's read. In a most important sense, I know what he means.

So Wittgenstein *both* "knows what he means" in the sense of being an educated person who has read the religious texts in question, and, indeed, pondered them deeply and with what he himself described as a religious sensibility, *and* (at that moment in his life) "won't even know whether to say he understands him or not." This is not at all saying that the religious language game is fine and dandy if you like that sort of thing; it is a statement of Wittgenstein's own deeply felt reaction to a particular religious tradition at a particular point in Wittgenstein's life. Wittgenstein speaks not from the point of view of something called "reason," but from the point of view of the philosopher who was capable of answering a question in the epistemology of mathematics by saying "This is where *my* spade is turned" (emphasis added).

To see what I am saying, contrast all three of the "existential" positions I have mentioned so far, the position of a believer like Kierkegaard, the position of Nietzsche (who *combats* religion in the name of an existential vision), and the position of Wittgenstein at the moment he wrote the above words (which I take to be a sort of respectful refusal), with the position of Bernard Williams that I cited at the beginning of this essay. Williams wants to say that *from the point of view of the Universe, there is no God.* But the physical universe does not have a "point of view." And, as I already remarked, Williams's is surely a misreading of Nietzsche; as many of my readers know, Nietzsche was forever denouncing philosophers for imagining that their all-too-human perspectives are "the point of view of the Universe." The question, what one's stance towards religious belief is to be, is only an easy question if one is able to be indifferent to the fact that many of one's friends, and certainly many of one's fellow human beings—including people one loves and respects—have a very different attitude than one's own, no matter what one's own attitude may be. To be sure, there are many who *are* indifferent to the views of all those who do not share their own attitude, but that indifference to one another's ideals is, as William James put it, "the trait in us most likely to make the angels weep." When people you love and respect differ from you over a matter both you and they regard as a matter of enormous importance, you have a profound responsibility, if you want to do justice both to who you are and to who they are. And there is no "Universe's point of view" on which to shrug off the responsibility. The question is an *ultimate* question, in that not only the answer but the means for answering it, the resources you bring to it, must be chosen by you.

CONFLICTS BETWEEN ETHICS AND RELIGION

To complicate matters, not only do religious literalists sometimes believe that their religions *can* pronounce on scientific matters, but there is an important kind of conflict—one that by no means involves only "fundamentalists" on the one side and "atheists" on the other—that can and does arise between the claims of religion and the claims of autonomous ethics. Religious people in our society may be able to grant that religion is not in the business of teaching us astronomy or biology or geology, but they cannot grant that religion is not concerned with *ethics,* for the major religious traditions in our society picture God as primarily concerned with our morality, our pursuit of justice and kindness and forgivingness. But our society is also one that honors the Enlightenment—the book by Taylor that Williams reviewed, *The Sources of the Self,* is among other things a moving defense of the central Enlightenment values by a leading philosopher who is also a Roman Catholic. And the Enlightenment stood, in part at least, for a morality based on the value of human moral autonomy.

Now, at an abstract level, there is no conflict between valuing justice and kindness and forgivingness and valuing autonomy, that is, valuing *thinking for oneself in moral matters.*[10] I was very moved a few years ago when a young Roman Catholic philosopher who had read my *The Many Faces of Realism* told me that he very much liked my defense of autonomy, and summed it up in his own words, saying that "you are saying that God didn't simply write a script, and give us the choice of accepting our roles in the play or turning them down; he offers us a chance to *help write the play."*

Unfortunately, however, not all religious people are as tolerant as this young philosopher or as Charles Taylor, nor are all religious people as impressed by the sacredness of autonomous moral personality. To make matters worse, there are elements of sexism and homophobia and episodes of genocide that are alleged to be divinely sanctioned in the Torah. The person who takes the question of the Last Judgment to be a scientific question and the person for whom scientific evidence would be irrelevant may, as Wittgenstein claimed, be talking past one another, but the person who offers arguments for discrimination against women or gays based upon the Torah or upon Jewish or Christian or Muslim tradition and the person who sees this as a violation of the equally scriptural injunction to "love your neighbor as yourself" are not simply talking past one another, but prescribing incompatible practical attitudes.

In one sense, what I have to say about this will show "where my spade is turned" (when ultimate questions are involved, I have already said that that is what one has to do), to use the Wittgensteinian phrase again, but in another sense, it seems to me, discussing these conflicts intelligently requires us to acknowledge a significant shortcoming in Wittgenstein's perspective.

Wittgenstein's great fear—not only in the "Lectures on Religious Belief," but in his *Remarks on Frazer's Golden Bough,* in *On Certainty,* and even in the posthumously published work on the philosophy of mathematics and the philosophy of psychology—is of a certain kind of scientism. When people criticize religious ways of life, or the ways of life of preliterate peoples, or the existential choices that we have been discussing from the point of view of what they call "reason," Wittgenstein (no doubt correctly) takes them to be identifying reason with the sort of technical-instrumental rationality with which he was familiar from his early training as an engineer. This sort of scientism was something that Wittgenstein regarded as the enemy of philosophy and the enemy of life. But

Wittgenstein significantly fails to see that one need not simply *hand over* the word "reason" to the scientistic among us. And this leaves him, apparently, with nothing to say about the sort of conflict I am talking about except (if I read him correctly) to hint (Wittgenstein, 1969, §609–610) that we should refrain from resorting to "all kinds of slogans" (*allerlei Schlagworten* [*Slogans*]). And this is simply not enough.

In the Pragmatist tradition there is, I think, a better answer. To be sure, it is not an answer that will convince the dogmatist; but that is not a reasonable objective for us to have anyhow. If it enables us to find our way a little further in a dark situation, that is surely all that can reasonably be demanded.

The Pragmatist answer is, I think, implicit in the writings of Peirce and explicit in James (especially in the essay in *The Will to Believe and Other Essays* titled "The Moral Philosopher and the Moral Life") and in the writings of John Dewey. That answer is highly nuanced, and I *hate* to state it so briefly, but I shall make an attempt to do so.

Let me begin by recalling Peirce's arguments for the scientific method itself: in the two famous articles in *Popular Science Monthly* in which Peirce launched the pragmatist movement,[11] he argued that we have *learned from experience* that the method of believing what the authorities say, the method of "tenacity" (sticking blindly to an opinion), and the method of "what is agreeable to reason" (allegedly apriori metaphysics) don't work.

Now, the idea of James and Dewey, stated in my own words, is that, although there is no algorithm for deciding what it is reasonable and what it is unreasonable to believe (and James, in particular, was aware of the importance of existential commitment, and quoted with approval Kierkegaard's remark that "we live forward but we understand backward"), nevertheless *we have learned something about how to conduct inquiry in general, and what applies to intelligently conducted inquiry in general applies to ethical and religious inquiry in particular.* What most distinguishes pragmatist writers on ethics and religion from all others is, in fact, just their reliance on this key principle.

I have, in effect, stated the thesis negatively—avoid dogmatic reliance on authority, blind tenacity, and apriorism—but it can also be stated positively. To do so, it is best to break it up into three principles, all familiar to readers of the great pragmatists:

(I) The Principle of Experiment. *Ideas must be tested in practice.* What saves this claim from becoming a narrow scientism is the generous pragmatist conception of testing. Not all tests can be performed in a laboratory, and even in physics (Dewey insisted in the *Logic*) tests performed in the laboratory of life are ultimately more important, even epistemologically, than tests performed in the laboratory.

(II) The Principle of Fallibilism. No human being and no body of human opinion is infallible. Applied to religion, what this means is that we must admit that religious inspiration (if we allow that there is such a thing) uses the whole personality of a time-bound and culture-bound human being, who expresses what she or he takes to be truth in a language full of both cultural assumptions and personal idiosyncrasies. The naive "dictation" model of revelation is rejected. We *have learned from experience* that claims to infallibility always conflict (even the claims to infallibility made by one single religious community always conflict with themselves), and lead to horrible consequences.

(III) The Principle of Communication. (This is implicit in the pragmatist understanding of fallibilism, but because of its importance I am stating it separately.) Truth by its very nature aspires to be public. Whatever your existential commitments may be, if you claim truth for them, you must be willing to discuss them. This principle is intimately connected with James's wonderful statement (James, 1983) of "the principle of live and let live": "be tolerant, *at least outwardly,* of everything that is not itself intolerant."[12]

Any "existential commitment," religious or secular, that rejects or flouts these principles flies in the face of what I, for one, am willing to call reason. Conversely, any serious commitment that accepts these principles and lives up to them is one that should have no conflicts with autonomous moral judgment.

THE ISSUE OF ELITISM

Wittgenstein's views owe a clear debt to Kierkegaard, who is present, both explicitly and implicitly, in many of the remarks in the selection from Wittgenstein's private notes posthumously published under the (English) title *Culture and Value.* Like Kierkegaard (and also like Maimonides), Wittgenstein is concerned to draw a line between *religion* and *superstition.* In the first of the "Lectures on Religious Belief," the example of "superstition" is a Father O'Hara who tried to offer "scientific proof" for the truths of religion. Wittgenstein's comment is:

> I would definitely call O'Hara unreasonable. I would say, if this is religious belief, then it's all superstition.
>
> But I would ridicule it not by saying it is based on insufficient evidence. I would say, here is a man who is cheating himself. You can say, this man is ridiculous because he believes, and bases it on weak reasons.

Kierkegaard can be even harsher in tone (Kierkegaard, 1968, p. 385):

> A superstitious belief which embraces an error keeps the possibility open that the truth may come to arouse it; but when the truth is there, and the superstitious mode of apprehending it transforms it into a lie, no awakening is possible.

(And Maimonides would have understood and agreed with this remark.)

To some these remarks sound extremely elitist, and indeed they *would be* elitist if what Wittgenstein and Kierkegaard were saying was that to be "religious" as opposed to "superstitious" you have to be an intellectual of some kind. Indeed, Maimonides has been accused of thinking exactly this. But this is not the thought at all. The thought is rather that a commitment may be of the wrong *kind* to be religious. (In *Culture and Value,* Wittgenstein remarks that religion is based on trust and superstition is based on fear.) A commitment which is merely the automatic acceptance of what others have said, or a way of propitiating fate, or a way of being "respectable," or an indulgence in infantile fantasy, is not worship of God.

Again, it has been said, sometimes by secular readers but sometimes by sophisticated theologians, that Wittgenstein and Kierkegaard and Maimonides are dismissing the religiosity of the "average believer" as mere superstition. Here, I think, we have another case of thinkers talking past one another, but in a different way from the way in which the believer and the atheist talk past one another. It could, of course, be the case (but I think this must be rather rare) that those who make this criticism are ascribing to Wittgenstein and Kierkegaard and Maimonides a doubt about the capacity of the "average believer" to undertake what *they* (that is, Wittgenstein and Kierkegaard and Maimonides) would regard as an authentic religious commitment; if that is the issue, I would reply that, on the contrary, it is the intellectual who offers the criticism who makes the assumption that an authentic relation to the divine is beyond the many. I doubt that any of these thinkers would find the notion of an "average" believer intelligible!

What is more often going on when such a criticism is voiced, especially when it is voiced by a theologian, is something very different. The theologian, whether he be "liberal" or not, whether he be contemporary or not, has often conceived of his task as one of *reinterpreting* the notion of God. The medieval Islamic theologians who suggested that God does not have knowledge of particulars, and the medieval Jewish and Christian theologians who explained God in terms of the neo-Aristotelian machinery of "essence," "substance," etc., were, for example, already engaging in the activity of finding a less "literal" and more "sophisticated" understanding of the notion of God. I suspect that the critic is assuming that Wittgenstein and Kierkegaard and Maimonides in his so-called "negative theology" are engaged in a similar enterprise. The "religion is *only* a language game" reading of Wittgenstein is, of course, one way of reading this activity into Wittgenstein's philosophy. Likewise, the reading of Maimonides' theory of attribution with respect to God as "negative theology" is often a way of assimilating him to Kant (God as the *Ding an sich*), in the fashion of Hermann Cohen, or reading him as a "noncognitivist" with respect to religious discourse (which seems to be what Leibowitz was doing). Like the atheist, such a theologian thinks of "literally" believing that God is personal, or "literally" believing that God loves individuals as a matter of "believing a proposition." If Wittgenstein or Kierkegaard suggest that what is involved is not a belief in a form of words but rather a form of life, they are not saying that *all* that is involved is a form of life; they are saying that *what it is to believe that God is personal and loves individuals depends on who one is all the way down and how one lives all the way down.* (They are also saying that the notion of "literally" describing God has no sense; which is *not* to say that we cannot talk about God.) Wittgenstein and Kierkegaard, as I read them (and on this point I think they are in agreement, although Kierkegaard differs importantly from Wittgenstein in standing within the religious life while Wittgenstein stands, as it were, always on the threshold), are rejecting, not endorsing, the game of philosophically reinterpreting the notion of God. Trying to assimilate God to one or another philosophical construct, whether the construct be Platonic, or Aristotelian, or Kantian, or Whiteheadian, or what have you, is like trying to improve the appearance of gold by covering it with tinsel. Yet that does not mean that the notion of "God" is self-explanatory; rather it means that how you understand the notion can only be shown by how you live. Metaphysics is, so to speak, too *superficial* to be of help here.

Someone may say, perhaps that is the view of these "existentialist" thinkers, but surely it was not the view of Maimonides. Ehud Ben-Or, in a recent and brilliant study of Maimonides' philosophy (Ben-Or, 1995), shows that when Maimonides tells us that we can only conceive of God by understanding his manifestations in the world, those manifestations are such that it requires *virtue,* in all its ethical and non-ethical senses, to perceive them and to see them as pointing to a supreme teleological source. And virtue, in the Aristotelian tradition to which Maimonides belonged, is not something that can be reduced to a theory or mastered by learning a theory.

This issue raises *the* one all-important point; for these thinkers, your religion is not just a matter of what you say and what you publicly do, but a matter of the whole spirit in which you live your life. If there is a conception of religious experience here, it is not the epiphany, or the traditional miracle. As Kierkegaard wrote, "uncertainty" is "the mark and form of faith" (1968, p. 453), and in our time seeing a conventional "miracle" happen with one's own eyes would be an unauthentic ground for religious belief, one that would create the illusion of being exempt from this "mark and form of faith." On the other hand, there is a sense in which the religious person strives to make all of his experience religious (so that the question "Have you ever had *a* religious experience" is a logical mistake). A paradoxical consequence of this view is that whatever words you believe and say, however "true," may not suffice to show that you are religious, or that you are worshipping God and not an idol. In this sense, claiming to be "religious" is an awesome responsibility.

NOTES

An earlier version of this essay was delivered as a Samuel Atlas Memorial Lecture at Hebrew Union College, New York, in May 1993.

1. See Yuval Lurie (1989) for a searching discussion of Wittgenstein's relation to his Jewishness.

2. All the quotations above are from p. 48 of Williams (1990).

3. This is the claim famously made by Quine (1960). Recently, though for different reasons, this "eliminationist" line has been defended by Paul and Patricia Churchland. Bernard Williams (1978) cautiously endorses the Quinian position.

4. Fodor (1990) vigorously defends this line.

5. I have discussed all of these difficulties with materialism in the books cited in the References.

6. This section is an all too brief synopsis of some of the points made with some care in chapters seven and eight of Putnam (1992).

7. I discuss Kripke's interpretation at length in "Was Wittgenstein *Really* an Antirealist

about Mathematics?" forthcoming in a volume to be edited by Peter Winch. Putnam (1996) contains an abbreviated form of the discussion.

8. Cf. my "The Dewey Lectures 1994: Sense, Nonsense, and the Senses," *Journal of Philosophy* 91, no. 9 (September, 1994), especially lecture 3; Putnam (1992), chapters 7 and 8; "Was Wittgenstein *Really* an Antirealist about Mathematics" (forthcoming); as well as Part IV of Putnam (1994). My interpretation is in large part inspired by the writings of Stanley Cavell and Cora Diamond. Peter Winch was, of course, long active in making just this point.

9. Cf. Wittgenstein (1953), II.xi, p. 227; I have rectified the translation:

> Is there such a thing as 'expert' judgment about the genuineness of expressions of feeling?—Even here there are those whose judgment is 'better' and those whose judgment is 'worse'.
>
> Correcter prognoses will generally issue from the judgments of those who understand people better (*des besseren Menschenkenners*).
>
> Can one learn this knowledge? Yes; some can. Not, however, by taking a course in it, but through '*experience*'.—Can another be one's teacher in this? Certainly. From time to time he gives him the right *tip*. This is what 'learning' and 'teaching' are like here.— What one acquires is not a technique; one learns correct judgments. There are also rules, but they do not form a system, and only experienced people can apply them right. Unlike calculating rules.

10. For a discussion of autonomy and its relation to the Jerusalem-based religions, see "Equality and Our Moral Image of the World" in Putnam (1987).

11. "How To Make Our Ideas Clear" and "The Fixation of Belief," reprinted in Peirce (1965).

12. Op. cit., p. 5. The entire concluding paragraph of the preface, from which this quotation is taken, is a paean to tolerance and an attack on "the pretension of our nation to inflict its own inner ideals and institutions *vi et armis* upon Orientals" (James was referring to the Philippines).

REFERENCES

Books

Ben-Or, E. 1995. *Worship of the Heart: A Study of Maimonides' Philosophy of Religion.* Albany, N.Y.

Derrida, J. 1976. *Of Grammatology.* Baltimore.

Fodor, J. 1990. *A Theory of Content.* Cambridge, Mass.

James, W. 1983. *The Works of William James: Talks to Teachers on Psychology,* edited by Fredson Bowers and Frederick Burkhardt. Cambridge, Mass.

Kierkegaard, S. 1968. *Concluding Unscientific Postscript.* Princeton, N.J.

Kripke, S. 1982. *Wittgenstein on Rules and Private Language.* Cambridge, Mass.

Peirce, C. S. 1965. *The Collected Papers of Charles Sanders Peirce,* vol. 5, *Pragmatism and Pragmaticism,* edited by Charles Hartshorne and Paul Weiss. Cambridge, Mass.

Putnam, H. 1981. *Reason, Truth, and History.* Cambridge.

Putnam, H. 1987. *The Many Faces of Realism.* LaSalle, Ill.

Putnam, H. 1988. *Representation and Reality.* Cambridge, Mass.

Putnam, H. 1990. *Realism with a Human Face.* Cambridge, Mass.

Putnam, H. 1992. *Renewing Philosophy.* Cambridge, Mass.

Putnam, H. 1994. *Words and Life.* Cambridge, Mass.

Quine, W. V. 1960. *Word and Object.* Cambridge, Mass.

Rorty, R. 1989. *Contingency, Irony, Solidarity.* Cambridge.

Taylor, C. 1989. *Sources of the Self.* Cambridge, Mass.

Williams, B. 1978. *Descartes: The Project of Pure Enquiry.* Hammondsworth, Middlesex.
Williams, B. 1985. *Ethics and the Limits of Philosophy.* Cambridge, Mass.
Wittgenstein, L. 1953. *Philosophical Investigations.* Oxford.
Wittgenstein, L. 1966. *Lectures and Conversations of Aesthetics, Psychology, and Religious Belief,* edited by Cyril Barrett. Berkeley.
Wittgenstein, L. 1969. *On Certainty.* Oxford.
Wittgenstein, L. 1983. *Remarks on Frazer's Golden Bough,* edited by Rush Rhees. Atlantic Highlands, N.J.

Articles

Lurie, Y. 1989. "Jews as a Metaphysical Species." *Philosophy* 64, no. 249 (July).
Putnam, H. 1990. "Objectivity and the Science/Ethics Distinctions." In his *Realism with a Human Face.*
Putnam, H. 1994. "The Dewey Lectures: Sense, Nonsense, and the Senses." *Journal of Philosophy* 91, no. 9 (Sept.).
Putnam, H. 1996. "On Wittgenstein's Philosophy of Mathematics." *Proceedings of the Aristotelian Society.*
Putnam, H. Forthcoming. "Was Wittgenstein *Really* an Antirealist about Mathematics?"
Williams, B. 1990. Review of Charles Taylor, *Sources of the Self,* in *New York Review of Books,* Nov. 8, pp. 44–48.

Circular Explanations, Cosmological Arguments, and Sufficient Reasons

WILLIAM ROWE

Within philosophy of religion, cosmological arguments are understood to be arguments from the existence of the world to the existence of God. Typically, such arguments proceed in two stages. The first step argues from the existence of the world to the existence of a first cause or necessary being that accounts for the existence of the world. The second step argues that such a first cause or necessary being has, or would very likely have, the properties associated with the idea of God. My concern here is only with the first stages in these arguments. For convenience, I will use the expression 'cosmological arguments' to refer to the first stages of these arguments.

Cosmological arguments may be divided into two broad types: those that depend on a premise denying an infinite regress of causes and those that do not depend on such a premise. Among the former are the first "three ways" presented by Aquinas, as well as an interesting argument, developed by Islamic thinkers, that the world cannot be infinitely old and, therefore, must have come into existence by the creative will of God. An important difference between the arguments represented by Aquinas's first "three ways" and the Islamic argument is that while both reject an infinite regress of causes, only the latter bases the objection on the alleged impossibility of an infinite *temporal* regress. Unlike Bonaventure who adopted the Islamic argument, Aquinas did not think that philosophy could show that the world had a temporal beginning. Instead, he rejected an infinite regress of essentially ordered causes (a *nontemporal* causal series), identifying God as the first cause in such a nontemporal series.

The major eighteenth-century proponents of cosmological arguments, Leibniz and Clarke, allowed an infinite regress of causes, arguing only that there must be a sufficient reason for the existence of such a series of causes. Thus, their arguments do not depend on rejecting an infinite regress of causes. Appealing to the principle of sufficient reason, Clarke and Leibniz insist only that such a series could not be self-explanatory and, therefore, would require an explanation in the causal activity of some being outside the series.

Although it is difficult to imagine that an absolutely infinite number of *temporally* discrete events have already occurred, philosophical objections to the idea have been found wanting.[1] And although Aquinas thought it obvious that a *nontemporal* causal series must terminate in a first member, itself uncaused, many philosophers in the modern period find the idea of a nontemporal causal series unclear, and, even supposing such a series, do not see why it must terminate in a first member. As a result, current interest has been drawn to those cosmological arguments—for example, the arguments advanced by Leibniz and Clarke—that allow the possibility of an infinite regress of causes, insisting only that such a series would require a sufficient reason for its existence. To see the role that the principle of sufficient reason plays in such arguments, it will be instructive to focus on the argument advanced by Samuel Clarke.[2]

If we think of a *dependent being* as a being whose sufficient reason for existence lies in the causal activity of other beings, and think of a *self-existent being* as a being whose sufficient reason for existence lies within its own nature, Clarke's cosmological argument (the first stage) can be put as follows.

> Every being (that exists or ever did exist) is either a dependent being or a self-existent being.
> Not every being can be a dependent being.
> Therefore, there exists a self-existent being.

What the first premise implies is that no existing being can lack a sufficient reason for its existence. That is, for each being that exists there is a sufficient reason (explanation) of its existence. Moreover, that reason will lie either within the causal activity of the being(s) that produced it or in the thing's own nature, in which case it will be a necessary being, a being whose nonexistence is impossible. But why should we think this first premise is true? And even if it is true, why should we think that not every being can be a dependent being, as the second premise states? To see why Clarke and Leibniz think these premises are true, we must look at the principle of sufficient reason.

The principle of sufficient reason (PSR) is a principle concerning facts, including facts consisting in the existence of individual beings. Thus the fact that John exists is a fact for which the PSR requires that there be a sufficient reason, some fact that fully explains the fact that John exists. But PSR also requires an explanation for facts about individual beings, for example, the fact that John is happy. In addition, PSR requires an explanation for general facts such as the fact that someone is happy, the fact that there are elephants, or the fact that there are dependent beings. Leibniz expresses PSR as the principle "that no fact can be real or existent, no statement true, unless there be a sufficient reason why it is so and not otherwise."[3] And Clarke, under pressure from Leibniz, states: "Undoubtedly nothing is, without a sufficient reason why it is, rather than not; and why it is thus, rather than otherwise."[4]

If we understand a contingent fact to be a fact that possibly might not have been a fact at all, it is clear that Leibniz held that every contingent fact has a sufficient reason or explanation. And so long as we restrict ourselves to contingent facts concerning the existence of things, it is clear that Clarke held that all such facts must have a sufficient reason.[5] If either view should be correct, it does seem that Clarke's second premise must be true. For if every being were dependent it does seem that there would be a contingent fact without any explanation—the fact that there are dependent beings. But if PSR is true, the fact that there are dependent beings must have a sufficient reason, a full explanation.[6] So, given Clarke's convictions about PSR, it is understandable why he should hold that not every being can be a dependent being. For if every being that exists or ever did exist is a dependent being, what could possibly be the sufficient reason for the fact that there are dependent beings? It won't do to point to some particular dependent being and observe that it produced other dependent beings.[7] The question why there are any dependent beings cannot be answered by appealing to the causal activity of some particular dependent being any more than the question why there are any human beings can be answered by appealing to Adam and Eve and their causal activity in producing other human beings. Nor will it do to observe that there always have been dependent beings engaged in causing other dependent beings. The question why there are any dependent beings cannot be answered by noting that there always have been dependent beings, any more than the question why there are any elephants can be answered simply by observing that there always have been elephants. To note that there always have been elephants may explain how long elephants have been in existence, but it won't explain why there are elephants at all.

Should we conclude that Clarke's cosmological argument is sound? No. For all we have seen is that his argument is sound *if* PSR is true.[8] But what of PSR itself? Is it true? In its unrestricted form PSR holds that every fact has an explanation; in its restricted form it holds that every contingent fact has an explanation. Even if we take PSR in its restricted form, there are serious objections to it. Let's turn to a consideration of three objections to PSR in its restricted form. Of course, these objections, if sound, also refute PSR in its unrestricted form.

I will assume in what follows that any fact or true proposition that constitutes a sufficient reason for another fact or true proposition is an explanation of that fact (true proposition) that *entails* the fact (true proposition) it explains. If an explanation of a fact only makes that fact probable, then it does not count as a sufficient reason for that fact; it is at best a partial reason for that fact. I believe this assumption is one way of stating a condition that is shared by Leibniz and Clarke. Moreover, it expresses a condition that recent discussions of PSR take as given.

One objection to PSR is that it cannot avoid the dark night of Spinozism, a night in which all facts appear to be necessary. This difficulty was particularly acute for Leibniz. He explained God's creation of this world by this world's being the best and God's choosing to create the best. But what accounts for God's choosing to create the best, rather than some inferior world or none at all? God chooses the best because of his absolute perfection—being absolutely perfect he naturally chooses to create the best. The difficulty is that God's being perfect is, for Leibniz, a necessary fact. It seems, then, that God's choice to create the best must also be necessary and, consequently, the existence of this world is necessary. If we avoid this conclusion by saying that God's being perfect is not the sufficient reason of his choice to create the best, we run into an infinite regress of explanations of his choice to create the best. For suppose we say that it is God's perfection in conjunction with his choice to exercise his goodness that constitutes the sufficient reason for his choice to create the best. What then of his choice to exercise his goodness? A similar problem would arise in providing a sufficient reason for it. And we seem to be off to the races, each reason determining a choice only by virtue of a prior choice to act in accordance with that reason.

A second and more serious objection to the restricted form of PSR is that it appears to be impossible for every contingent fact to have an explanation. Consider the huge conjunctive fact whose conjuncts are all the other contingent facts that there are. This huge conjunctive fact must itself be a contingent fact, otherwise its conjuncts would not be contingent. Now what can be the sufficient reason for this huge conjunctive fact? It cannot be some necessary fact. For the sufficient reason for a fact is another fact that entails it; and whatever is entailed by a necessary fact is itself necessary. The huge conjunctive fact cannot be its own sufficient reason since only a necessary fact could be self-explanatory. So, the sufficient reason for the huge conjunctive fact would have to be one of the contingent facts that is a conjunct of it. But then that conjunct would have to be a sufficient reason for itself, since whatever is a sufficient reason for a conjunctive fact must be a sufficient reason for each of its conjuncts. It follows, then, that the huge conjunctive fact cannot have an explanation. It thus appears that PSR is false.[9]

In the above argument it is important not to confuse the huge conjunctive fact constituted by every other contingent fact with the general fact that there are contingent facts. The latter fact—that there are contingent facts—is not itself a contingent fact. It is a necessary fact. For every possible world contains some contingent fact or other. Consider the contingent fact that there are elephants. That there are elephants is a fact in the actual world. But if some possible world in which there are no elephants were to be actual, it would be a fact that there are no elephants. So, no matter what possible world is actual, either that there are elephants will be a fact or that there are no elephants will be a fact. Thus, that there are contingent facts is itself a necessary fact. But the huge conjunctive fact described above is itself a contingent fact. Had some other possible world been actual, the huge conjunctive fact described above would not have been a fact.

Finally, there is an objection I presented some years ago to the effect that there is a certain nonconjunctive, contingent, general fact that cannot possibly have a sufficient reason in the sense of another fact that entails and explains it.[10] The objection involves the idea of a positive contingent state of affairs.

> X is a positive contingent state of affairs if and only if from the fact that X obtains it follows that at least one contingent being exists.[11]

I pointed out that *there being elephants* is a positive contingent state of affairs. For, from the fact that it obtains, it follows that at least one contingent being exists. *There being no unicorns,* however, is not a positive contingent state of affairs. I then drew attention to the following state of affairs:

> t: There being positive contingent states of affairs.

I argued that it is impossible for there to be a sufficient reason for the fact that t obtains. That it is impossible follows from two considerations. First, any sufficient reason (full explanation) for the fact that t obtains would itself be a positive contingent state of affairs. For from the fact that t obtains it follows that at least one contingent being exists. Therefore, since any sufficient reason for t would entail t, and therefore entail whatever is entailed by t, any sufficient reason for t would entail that at least one contingent being exists, and thus would itself be a positive contingent state of affairs.

Our first consideration establishes that any sufficient reason for t must itself be a positive contingent state of affairs. Now we come to the second consideration. Any sufficient reason for the fact that t (there being positive contingent states of affairs) must constitute a full explanation for why there are positive contingent states of affairs. But surely, nothing that itself is a positive contingent state of affairs can be an explanation for why there are positive contingent states of affairs. For such a proposed explanation is simply circular. I then illustrated this reasoning by an example.

> suppose we try to explain why there are positive contingent states of affairs by citing the fact, let us suppose, that God willed that positive contingent states of affairs be actual—just as, for example, we might explain why there are men by citing the (supposed) fact that God willed that men should exist. The fact, then, consisting of God's willing that positive contingent states of affairs be actual is what explains why there are positive contingent states of affairs. But now let us consider the fact of God's willing that positive contingent states of affairs be actual. If that fact does explain why there are positive contingent states of affairs it must entail that some positive contingent states of affairs are actual. And if this is so, then the fact that God willed that there be positive contingent states of affairs entails that at least one contingent being exists. We then ask whether the fact in question is contingent or necessary. It cannot be necessary, for then it would be necessary that at least one contingent being exists—and, as we have seen, it seems to be a contingent matter that contingent beings exists. What follows, then, is that the fact consisting of God's willing that positive contingent states of affairs be actual is *itself* a positive contingent state of affairs; for it is contingent and, from the fact that it obtains, it follows that at least one contingent being exists. But clearly, the fact that *accounts* for why there are

positive contingent states of affairs *cannot* itself be a positive contingent state of affairs.[12]

In a review of *The Cosmological Argument,* Robert Adams questioned this argument.[13] Noting my contention that any explanation of t (in the sense of a sufficient reason for t) would be circular, Adams, in effect, denies that this is true. His argument seems to be this. Suppose that what is offered as the sufficient reason for t is, unlike God's willing that positive contingent states of affairs be actual, a *conjunction* of two factors, neither of which is itself a positive contingent state of affairs. Let one of these factors be

    a. God's having a prima facie desire to bring about the existence of another being. (Here we understand God as a necessary being and also understand that any being he brings into existence will be a contingent being.)

God's prima facie desires to create, as in what theologians call his "antecedent will" (as in "God wills all men to be saved"), as opposed to his "all things considered will," does not logically necessitate its realization. For he may have good reason not to act on such a desire. Let the second factor be something like

    b. God's having no good reason not to bring into existence another being.

Let us agree that although neither (a) nor (b) entails t, the conjunction of (a) and (b) does entail t. Adams's point is that since neither (a) nor (b) is a positive contingent state of affairs, and since they obtain independently of each other, they may "jointly provide a noncircular explanation of t."

My response to this objection is that the conjunctive fact that (a) and (b) cannot explain the fact that there are positive contingent states of affairs because the conjunctive fact in question is itself a positive contingent state of affairs. Such an "explanation" would be circular. Of course, Adams admits that the conjunctive fact is itself a positive contingent state of affairs.

> It does seem that this conjunction must be a positive contingent state of affairs if it is contingent. But in determining whether it would be circular to explain something by a conjunction, one must consider the conjuncts separately, if they are independent.[14]

We thus seem to be in a stalemate. I insist that no explanation for t can itself be a positive contingent state of affairs, and Adams allows that in some circumstances an explanation for t can itself be a positive contingent state of affairs. But we do seem to agree that an explanation cannot be circular. So, there is room here for further discussion. For I hold that his conjunctive explanation is circular, whereas he denies this. And what this suggests is that I need to say something more about what it is for a proposed explanation to be circular. Before turning to that task, however, it will be helpful to consider one other serious objection to my argument against PSR.

In "Explanatory Rationalism and Contingent Truths" Quentin Smith argues against my objection to PSR.[15] Since much of his discussion proceeds in terms of propositions, rather than states of affairs, it will be convenient here to follow him and discuss positive contingent truths rather than actual positive contingent states of affairs. As Smith notes: "His [Rowe's] 'states of affairs' are identical or isomorphic to our propositions and the following equivalence obtains: 'states of affairs either obtain or do not obtain and exist even if they do not obtain' is logically equivalent to 'propositions either are true or false and exist even if they are false'."[16] Suppose, then, we introduce the notion of 'a positive contingent truth' as follows:

1. P is a positive contingent truth iff P is contingently true and entails that some contingent concrete object exists.

Thus, the proposition that *there are elephants* is a positive contingent truth, but neither the proposition that *there are no unicorns* nor the proposition that *there are 18-foot-tall basketball players* is a positive contingent truth. Consider now the proposition:

2. There are positive contingent truths

(2) is contingent, true, and entails that some contingent concrete object exists. So P *itself* is a positive contingent truth. Could there be a sufficient reason for the truth of (2)? As Smith notes, in *The Cosmological Argument* I argued (using the language of states of affairs) that there could not be. As we've seen, my argument comes down to this. Any true proposition that gives a sufficient reason for (2) would have to entail (2) and constitute an explanation of why there are any positive contingent truths. But any true proposition that entails (2) would itself be a positive contingent truth and therefore could not provide an explanation of why there are positive contingent truths at all. It seemed to me clear that no positive contingent truth could itself explain why there are any positive contingent truths. Adapting my remarks to the language of propositions (rather than states of affairs), I said that

3. God (effectively) wills that there be positive contingents truths

could not explain why there are positive contingent truths at all, since it itself is a positive contingent truth. The purported explanation would be viciously circular in that it employs a positive contingent truth to supposedly explain why there are any positive contingent truths.

Why does Smith hold that I am mistaken in believing that there can be no sufficient reason for (2), the truth that *there are positive contingent truths?* Switching from propositions to states of affairs, he explains as follows.

All that needs to be explained is that there obtain positive contingent states of affairs, which is logically equivalent to the state of affairs *that there are contingent concrete objects.* Now this state of affairs does appear to have an explanation, namely, by the state of affairs

  (s) God wills that there are contingent concrete objects.[17]

Before quoting the sentence that immediately follows this passage, let me say that I agree entirely with the point Smith makes here. Moving back to the idiom of propositions, we note that the proposition

  2. There are positive contingent truths

is logically equivalent to

  3. There are contingent concrete objects.

Moreover, on the supposition that it is true that God wills that there are contingent concrete objects, it seems to me entirely correct to cite the proposition

  4. God wills that there are contingent concrete objects

as a sufficient reason for the truth of 3. For 4 entails 3 and provides an explanation of the truth of 3. Of course, there would be a circularity in the explanation if God were himself a contingent concrete object. But both Smith and I are allowing here (for purposes of discussion) that God is a necessary being. So, the portion of his argument quoted above strikes me as altogether correct. But he continues the quotation as follows.

  (s) is a sufficient reason for t (there obtain positive contingent states of affairs), since necessarily, if s obtains, t obtains, (ii) s relevantly entails t and (iii) s explains t. Thus, it seems that Rowe is mistaken in believing that there can be no sufficient reason for t.[18]

In the idiom of propositions, what Smith says here is that proposition (4) (God wills that there are contingent concrete objects) is a sufficient reason for the truth of (2) (There are positive contingent truths). Why does Smith think (4) is a sufficient reason for (2), and, therefore, an explanation of (2)? So far as I can determine, no answer to this question is given in "Explanatory Rationalism and Contingent Truths."

  I agree with Smith on two points. First, I agree that (4) can be an explanation of (3). Second, I agree that (3) is logically equivalent to (2). Is it supposed to follow from this that (4) can be an explanation of (2)? By my lights (4) cannot be an explanation of (2) because such an explanation would be circular, using a positive contingent truth to try to account for why there are positive contingent truths. For (4), no less than (2), is itself a positive contingent truth.

  In further discussion of this matter,[19] Smith supported his position by defending the Principle of Explanatory Equivalence, according to which if *p* explains *q*, and *r* is "relevantly equivalent" to *q*, *p* also explains *r*. He appealed to this principle in order to argue that since, as I agree, (4) can explain (3), and (2) is equivalent to (3), it follows that (4) can explain (2). The Principle of Explanatory Equivalence, then, fills the gap in the argument he presented in "Explanatory Rationalism and Contingent Truths." And I must concede that if this principle is correct, Smith has succeeded in showing that

4. God wills that there are contingent concrete objects

can be an explanation of

2. There are positive contingent truths.

And this will be so even though (4) is itself a positive contingent truth.

In response to Smith I could take the position that although he has shown that (4) can be an explanation of (2), he hasn't shown that it is a good or even adequate explanation of (2) because he hasn't shown that such an explanation escapes the charge of being viciously circular. For Smith will still have to admit that the explanation in question appeals to a positive contingent truth, (4), in order to explain why there are any positive contingent truths, (2). But such a response on my part might strike some as little more than sophistry. So, let's agree that being noncircular is a condition of being an explanation. Thus, if Smith has shown that (4) can be an explanation of (2), he has shown that an appeal to (4) as an explanation of (2) can be noncircular, and this despite the fact that we are appealing to a positive contingent truth in order to explain why there are any positive contingent truths. On this approach to the problem, my only possible response to Smith is to question his Principle of Explanatory Equivalence.

In defending his principle, Smith carefully distinguishes *strict equivalence* from *relevance equivalence.* To use his example, the proposition

An isosceles triangle has three angles

is strictly equivalent to

All red things are red

since any possible world in which the one is true is a world in which the other is true. If the Principle of Explanatory Equivalence were stated in terms of strict equivalence it would clearly fall prey to obvious counterexamples. For an explanation of why an isosceles triangle has three angles need not be an explanation of why all red things are red. For two propositions to be *relevantly equivalent,* each must relevantly imply the other. And one proposition relevantly implies another if and only if it "strictly implies it by virtue of its meaning."[20] Smith then argues, correctly (by my lights), that proposition

2. There are positive contingent truths

is *relevantly equivalent* to

3. There are contingent concrete objects.

He then concludes that since the proposition

4. God wills that there are contingent concrete objects

explains (3), it also explains (4).

The difficulty with this argument is that the Principle of Explanatory Equivalence is false. And it is not just false when equivalence is understood as *strict equivalence,* it is also false when equivalence is understood as *relevance equivalence.* Consider, for example, propositions

5. John is angry at t

and

6. John exists at t and John is angry at t.[21]

These two propositions are *relevantly equivalent* in Smith's sense. But an explanation of the former need not be an explanation of the latter. It is one thing to explain why John is angry at t and another thing to explain why he exists at t.

It would be nice to be able to claim victory here. But all I've shown, at best, is that a particular argument to establish that (4) can explain (2) is unsuccessful. I haven't shown what I've claimed to be true: that any proposed explanation of (2) cannot be successful since it would be viciously circular. Is there anything more to be said here? Or must we simply end with differing intuitions on the matter of whether (2) can have an explanation? Perhaps that is where we will end. But I can at least say a bit more about two types of circularity that I believe may defeat a proposed explanation of some fact or true proposition.

The two types of circularity that may defeat a proposed explanation can be expressed in two general theses:

I. If you are going to explain why there are *any* objects of a certain kind (where it is a contingent matter that there are objects of that kind), you cannot do so by citing a fact of the form 'X caused there to be Ys', where X is an object of the kind in question. For to do so is circular.

To illustrate this thesis consider the following. Suppose I ask why there are any elephants. In response you say that Dumbo, an elephant, was rather prolific and gave birth to some elephants. Your response is circular. To explain why there are entities of a certain kind you appeal to the causal activity of an entity of that very kind. A noncircular explanation would be illustrated by the claim that God willed that there should be elephants and proceeded to create some.

II. If you are going to explain why there are *any* truths of a certain kind (where it is a contingent matter that there are truths of that kind), you cannot do so by citing a truth that is itself a truth of that very kind. For to do so is circular.

To illustrate this thesis let's use a concrete example: 'a truth about Abraham'; where it is understood that p is a truth about Abraham if and only if p is true and p entails the proposition that Abraham exists.[22] (This is not how we would normally understand the expression 'a truth about Abraham', but we are giving it a technical sense here for purposes of clarifying this second kind of circular explanation.) Clearly, the true proposition that Abraham exists is itself a truth about Abraham, for it entails itself. If I ask why there are any truths about Abraham (truths that entail that Abraham exists), it is not enlightening to respond by saying it is because it is true that Abraham exists. For the proposition that Abraham exists is itself of the very kind about which we are inquiring as to why there are any truths at all of that kind. Such an explanation is circular.

We don't know who Abraham's mother was. But let us name her *Elizabeth*. For present purposes, let us agree that the true proposition that Elizabeth begat Abraham *explains* the fact that Abraham exists. Now the proposition

7. Abraham exists

entails the proposition that there are truths about Abraham. Moreover, (7) is entailed by the true proposition that there are truths about Abraham. So, (7) is logically equivalent to

8. There are truths about Abraham.

Now we have agreed that

9. Elizabeth begat Abraham

explains (7). Should we say that (9) also explains (8), that is, that (9) also explains why there are truths about Abraham. By my lights we should not. For we would be using a truth about Abraham to explain why there are any truths about Abraham.

I wish I could produce some decisive argument in support of the conclusion just reached. However, I don't know of any such argument. I simply find myself thinking that such a proposed explanation is circular. It is a case of trying to explain why there are any Xs by appealing to something (in this case a proposition) that is itself an X.

Where does all this leave us? I can see how one rightly wants to count (9) as an explanation of (7). (9) can satisfy that role, even though it cannot satisfy that role without itself having the property of being a truth about Abraham. I can see too an initial inclination to say that (9) explains (8). But I think this inclination is naturally explained by another inclination: the inclination to construe truths about Abraham as truths of the following sort: (10) Abraham lived for many years; (11) Abraham had a wife; (12) Abraham was prevented by an angel from killing Isaac, etc. These are the sorts of propositions that we naturally think of when we think of truths *about* Abraham. Along this line, we naturally think of (9) as a truth about Elizabeth. And, of course, if we think of 'truths about X' in this way, we will be inclined to say that (9) does explain why there are any truths about Abraham. For it explains why Abraham exists. And the proposition 'Abraham exists' is a truth about Abraham. So, we might reason, since (9) is not what we initially take to be a truth *about* Abraham, and since (9) does explain the fact that Abraham exists, (9) can explain why there are truths about Abraham. What could be clearer than that? But we must keep before our minds what we here mean by 'a truth about Abraham'. And what we mean is such that (9) itself is a truth about Abraham.

Another temptation to think that (9) explains why there are any truths about Abraham is this: (9) does explain a very fundamental truth about Abraham—the truth that Abraham exists. We might also reasonably argue that (9) plays an important role in explaining why there are *many* truths about Abraham. But we can, I think, have an explanation of why there are *many* truths about Abraham without thereby having an explanation of why there are *any* truths about Abraham. Consider the following proposition:

12. God effectively willed that many logically independent propositions that entail that Abraham exists should be true.

Suppose we agree that there are many truths about Abraham just in case many logically independent propositions that entail that Abraham *exists* are true. If so, then we can perhaps agree that (12) explains why there are many truths about Abraham. But if a proposition explains why there are *many* truths about *X,* doesn't it seem that it also must explain why there are *any* truths about *X?* But again, by my lights, it is not clear that the answer is yes. For (12) is itself, if true, a truth about Abraham. Consider the analogy with thesis I. Let us say that Dumbo's prolific activity explains why there are many elephants. Nevertheless, although Dumbo's prolific activity in generating many elephants may explain why there are *many* elephants, it cannot explain why there are *any* elephants at all. For Dumbo himself is an elephant.

All I am doing here is trying to explain why I believe that the truth that Elizabeth begat Abraham fails to explain why there are any truths about Abraham. It does explain why Abraham exists. And, therefore, it seems right to say that it explains something that is necessary for there to be *any* truths about Abraham. But none of this implies that the truth that Elizabeth begat Abraham explains why there are *any* truths about Abraham. In fact, so long as we hold that an explanation cannot be circular, and that a truth about Abraham is any truth that entails that Abraham exists, the only conclusion we can reach, I think, is that there cannot be an explanation (in the strong sense required by PSR) of why there are any truths about Abraham. The same reasoning leads to the conclusion that there cannot be an explanation (in the strong sense required by PSR) of why there are any positive contingent truths.

We've looked at three serious objections to PSR. Since PSR plays a crucial role in the most interesting and appealing cosmological arguments advanced by Leibniz and Clarke, must we conclude that these arguments are without hope? No. For the premises of these cosmological arguments may find sufficient support in weaker principles of explanation than PSR, principles that are not subject to objections of the sort that appear to be decisive against PSR.

In *The Cosmological Argument* I suggested one such principle which I will now formulate as follows:

A: For every kind of being such that beings of that kind can be caused to exist or can cause the existence of other beings, there must be a sufficient reason for the existence of each being of that kind and for the general fact that there exist beings of that kind.

This principle is at least as initially plausible as PSR. What distinguishes it from PSR is that it does not require that every fact, or even every contingent fact, has an explanation. Also, it does not imply that every positive contingent state of affairs has an explanation. But since it is a fact that there are dependent beings, Principle A requires that there be a sufficient reason (full explanation) for the fact that there are dependent beings. So Principle A, rather than the much stronger PSR, is all we need in order to justify the second premise of Clarke's cosmological argument: Not every being can be a dependent being. For as we've seen, if every being were dependent any proposed explanation of why there are dependent beings would be viciously circular. Thus, if every being (that can be caused or can cause other things to exist) were dependent, there would be a kind of being (dependent) such that the fact that there are beings of that kind would have no explanation. Also, so long as the first premise of Clarke's argument is restricted to beings that either can be caused or can cause the existence of other beings, Principle A will justify the first premise: Every being is either a dependent being or a self-existent being. I might add that Principle A, unlike PSR, does not raise problems for free acts of will. While there may be a determining cause of an individual being free (in the incompatibilist's sense) to will or not will, there can be no determining cause of the agent's freely causing one volition rather than another. It was this issue that made Clarke hesitant to fully endorse Leibniz's statement of the Principle of Sufficient Reason. Principle A does not conflict with the existence of free acts of will. God's freely choosing to create Adam may constitute a determining cause of the existence of Adam. And this may be true even though there is no determining cause of God's freely choosing to create Adam.

NOTES

1. See, for example, Quentin Smith, "Infinity and the Past," *Philosophy of Science* 54 (1987): 63–75.

2. His argument is presented in Samuel Clarke, *A Discourse Concerning the Being and Attributes of God,* 9th ed. (London, 1738), reprinted in *British Philosophers and Theologians of the 17th and 18th Centuries* (New York, 1978).

3. Gottfried Leibniz, *Monadology* (1714) in *Leibniz Selections,* ed. Philip P. Wiener (New York, 1951), paragraph 32.

4. Samuel Clarke, and Gottfried Leibniz, *The Leibniz-Clarke Correspondence* (1717), ed. H. G. Alexander (Manchester, 1956), third reply.

5. Clarke held that in the case of two choices, where nothing recommends one over the other—for example, choosing either of two pawns to put on a particular square—that there is no sufficient reason for the will contingently making the *particular* choice that it makes. See Clarke's third reply, *The Leibniz-Clarke Correspondence.* Clarke's reservations concerning the application of PSR to all contingent facts are, I believe, of some importance, particularly in light of the decisive objections to PSR. I will return to this point later.

6. A full explanation of some fact, as opposed to a partial explanation, is an explanation

that logically implies the fact it explains. See Richard Swinburne, *The Existence of God* (Oxford, 1979), chapter 2.

7. For a critical discussion of this view of mine, see Richard Gale, *On the Nature and Existence of God* (Cambridge, 1991), 265–71.

8. Actually, we can't be absolutely certain that Clarke's argument is sound if PSR is true. For PSR is insufficient to justify the second premise of Clarke's argument: Not every being can be a dependent being. PSR requires that there be a sufficient reason for the existence of dependent beings. Since no dependent being exists necessarily, and since no dependent being could explain why there are dependent beings, Clarke thinks the only *possible explanation* left is the causal activity of a self-existent being. But he overlooks the idea that although no dependent being necessarily exists, it might, nevertheless, be *necessary* that some dependent being exists. We know that although no horse in a given race necessarily will be the winner, it is, nevertheless, necessary that some horse in the race will be the winner. Can we be sure that, although no dependent being necessarily exists, it isn't, nevertheless, necessary that some dependent beings exist? For my part, I am quite willing to agree that it is a contingent fact that dependent beings exist. It seems clear to me that there is a possible world in which no dependent being exists. But I know of no proof that this is so. In any case, I will here proceed on the assumption that it is a contingent fact that dependent beings exist.

9. Versions of this objection have been developed by Bennett, Ross, and Van Inwagen. See Jonathan Bennett, *A Study of Spinoza's Ethics* (Indianapolis, 1984), 115; James F. Ross, *Philosophical Theology* (Indianapolis, 1969), 298–302; Peter Van Inwagen, *An Essay on Free Will* (Oxford, 1983), 202–204.

10. See *The Cosmological Argument* (Princeton, 1975), 145–48.

11. Ibid., 103.

12. Ibid., 106.

13. See *The Philosophical Review* (July 1978): 445–50.

14. Ibid., 447.

15. Quentin Smith, "Explanatory Rationalism and Contingent Truths," *Religious Studies* 31 (1995): 237–42. A similar paper was the occasion of a colloquium at the APA Central Division meeting in Chicago, April 1995. I served as commentator.

16. Ibid., 239.

17. Ibid., 240.

18. Ibid.

19. At a colloquium of the APA Central Division meeting in Chicago, April 1995.

20. Comments by Quentin Smith at a colloquium of the APA Central Division in Chicago, April 1995.

21. I am indebted to David Widerker for this example. My own counterexamples were more complicated and, therefore, less clear than this example.

22. The example was introduced by Bill Hasker during discussion at the colloquium referred to above. I'm indebted to Hasker for helpful correspondence on some of the issues discussed in this essay.

MIDWEST STUDIES IN PHILOSOPHY, XXI (1997)

Hierarchical Theories of Freedom
and the Hardening of Hearts

DAVID SHATZ

In certain biblical passages, God seems to take away a person's free will. Sometimes God makes the person will wicked acts, an occurrence known as the
hardening of hearts; sometimes, He makes the person will good acts, an occurrence known as sanctification.[1] The most famous example of heart-hardening
occurs during Exodus's depiction of the sixth, eighth, and ninth of the ten
plagues which God inflicted upon Egypt: "The Lord hardened the heart of Pharaoh, and [so] he did not let the people [of Israel] go."[2] Other examples of hardening in the Hebrew Bible involve the Moabite king Sihon and the Canaanite
army, who are "hardened" to be hostile to Israel;[3] in the New Testament, Paul
declares that "God hardens whom He will" (Romans 9:18). As for God making
a person will the good, Deuteronomy 30:6 promises that God will "circumcise
the hearts of you and your descendants," i.e., remove your inclination for evil,
and the Hebrew prayerbook includes a plea to "compel our evil inclination to be
subjugated to You."

Theologians and biblical exegetes have long grappled with difficulties that
these concepts pose to conventional theistic assessments of the importance of
free will and also to the goodness and justice of God.[4] Analytic philosophers,
by contrast, have devoted almost no attention to such problems. One exception
is an elegant and ingenious article by Eleonore Stump.[5] Stump proposes that
we understand hardening of the hearts and sanctification in terms of the "hierarchical" account of free will associated with Harry Frankfurt, and she seeks to
show that hardened and sanctified agents can have free will on this sort of account.[6]

In what follows I want to take up two *prima facie* difficulties with this solution—one exegetical, the other philosophical—and to explore ways of respond-

ing to them. The difficulties will pave the way to either (1) rejecting Stump's solution, (2) modifying it while keeping the hierarchical framework, or (3) modifying it by switching to a non-hierarchical account that achieves a similar overall result. Which path a reader takes will depend on his or her intuitions and, rather than attempt a knockdown defense of my own intuitions (a task that may be impossible), I will be content to articulate the problems, lay out options for dealing with them, and reveal my own preferences. I shall focus here on understanding hardening of the hearts, deferring analysis of sanctification until later in the essay.

We should enter this discussion with an appreciation of how deeply the hardening of hearts cuts against conventional theistic assertions. Typically, theistic philosophers of religion are forced to assign a high value to free will as a means of combatting challenges to theistic belief, notably the problem of evil and the hiddenness of God.[7] Theists declare that God cares a good deal about free will; so much so, that He allows evils of various kinds—suffering, wrongdoing, atheism—in order to secure and preserve it. But even if we accept the judgment that free will is more valuable than the removal of suffering or faithlessness, religious texts do not always appraise matters this way. On the contrary, theistic traditions sometimes license coercion to ensure a recalcitrant agent's conformity to orthodox belief and practice, casting doubt on the proposition that the value of free will outweighs the disvalue of bad behavior.[8] Again, the biblical God tries to secure obedience to His commands by promising rewards for compliance and dire punishments for disobedience. Arguably, compliance in the face of threatened punishment is *unfree* compliance.

It is in the light of such challenges to the theodicist's evaluations of free will that hardening of the hearts takes on its full significance. If free will is such a great good according to theists, why would a good God deprive a person of it? Theodicists portray God as allowing certain evils to *secure* free will; but by hardening hearts, God is allowing certain evils, indeed actively producing them, precisely by *taking away* free will. If Pharaoh would have released the Israelites, then Pharaoh would have been a better person, and also the Israelites and Egyptians would have suffered no longer. The problem with Pharaoh being deprived of free will is not just that he has been deprived of a good. It is that this particular deprivation also generated further evils, evils which theodicies imply should not exist where the good of free will is not being assured.

The problem of free will deprivation will be my focus, but it is not the *only* one that hardening of the hearts creates. At least three other difficulties arise:

- The responsibility problem: If God causes Pharaoh to will an evil act, namely, keeping the Israelites enslaved, why should Pharaoh be held responsible for this act?[9]
- The theodicy problem: If God causes Pharaoh to will an evil act, namely, keeping the Israelites enslaved, has God not (a) caused an evil act, (b) made a person morally worse, and (c) caused further suffering to the Israelites

and Egyptians? (We have seen that the problem of evil is linked to the problem of free will deprivation.)

- The repentance problem: If God wants sinners to repent, as both Judaism and Christianity preach, why would he prevent any individual from changing his ways for the better?

I will comment briefly on the responsibility and theodicy problems later.

THE HIERARCHICAL SOLUTION

The hierarchical solution seeks to show that an agent who has been "sanctified" or whose heart has been hardened is not thereby *deprived* of free will; on the contrary, the agent is thereby *given* free will. Frankfurt's basic view is that a person has freedom of the will only if her first-order "volitions"—those of her first-order desires that are "effective," that move her to action—are in accord with or approved by her second-order desires, and only if those second-order desires are not opposed by conflicting ones. Now consider Pharaoh. Pharaoh's *second*-order desire is to have a first-level volition to keep the Israelites in captivity, and he has no opposing second-order desire. Most of the time, Pharaoh manages to keep his second- and first-level volitions aligned with each other. In the face of certain plagues, however, he is tempted to let the Israelites go; this temptation is the result of a "nonmoral accident" that "causes the control to weaken" (419). Consequently, when, on these occasions, God causes Pharaoh's heart to harden, causes Pharaoh to resist temptation, He is not *depriving* Pharaoh of his free will. Quite the contrary, He is enabling Pharaoh to have free will, since Pharaoh's first-order effective desire to keep the Israelites enslaved now reflects his (unopposed) second-order motivational stance.[10] God gives hardened and sanctified agents the will they want to have; and on a hierarchical analysis, having the will you want to have is having free will.

Stump introduces a number of modifications into Frankfurt's account. Most importantly, she replaces Frankfurt's emphasis on second-level desire with an emphasis on "intellect." For the will to be free, first-order desires must be reflective of intellectual judgments and reasoning about what is morally or prudentially approvable; second-level desires are significant only insofar as they reflect these judgments. Stump also sharpens Frankfurt's distinction between desires and "volitions," where volitions are "effective desires."[11] But these modifications do not affect her basic thesis about both hardening of hearts and sanctification: "In each case, God responds to an agent's desires by giving that agent the first-order volition [= effective desire] he wants" (420). The difference between speaking of second-level desires and speaking of judgment lies in how to define what the agent really "wants."[12] For ease of exposition, I will generally stick to the language of second- and first-order desires in what follows, with the understanding that second-order desires are significant only because they reflect intellectual judgments.[13]

HIERARCHICAL THEORIES
AND FREE WILL THEODICIES

A first reaction to the hierarchical solution may be that it transports the theist from the frying pan to the fire. Even if it helps the theist solve the problem of hardening, it does so, one may reason, at the tremendous cost of nullifying free will theodicies.[14] The hierarchical account of free will is generally presented as eliminating the requirement that a free agent have open to him alternative possibilities. Now the free will theodicies we spoke of earlier presuppose a conception of free will as demanding alternative possibilities. As John Martin Fischer (who rejects the notion that acting freely requires alternative possibilities) points out,

> [On the free will defense] one claims that a perfect God must have created the best of all possible worlds, which in turn must contain human beings who act freely. If the proponent of the problem of evil as casting doubt on the existence of God responds that God could have created agents who always freely do the right thing, the typical response is to deny that this is possible. . . . God could not possibly *cause* agents to freely do the right thing (causation being incompatible with acting freely), and absent causation God could not *ensure* that agents always do the right thing. . . . Now it might be that the proponent of the free will defense thinks that acting freely requires freedom to do otherwise. . . . But I have severed this connection [in an earlier argument]. And, given the separation of acting freely from freedom to do otherwise, I do not see why God could not have set things up so that human beings always choose the right thing.[15]

Now if accepting a hierarchical conception involves abandoning the requirement of alternative possibilities, as some writers imply, then accepting a hierarchical conception sends the theist in search of another theodicy. And ironically, if the free will theodicy is abandoned, that removes one motivation for theists to be troubled by the free will deprivation problem in the first place and to find a way of showing that Pharaoh really has free will.[16]

The correct reply to this concern is that, if a theist wants both a free will theodicy and a hierarchical account, he can have them. For the hierarchical account can be incompatibilist in character, and need not be built along the compatibilist lines implied by Frankfurt. This incompatibilist version can be developed in two ways. A hierarchical account can include a requirement that there be alternative possibilities at either the first level or the second level or both, and can embrace the view that determinism rules out alternative possibilities, thereby generating incompatibilism. Alternatively, the account can reject the alternative possibilities requirement but insist that determinism deprives an agent of freedom because it violates a separate principle that an agent's choices must be up to him.[17] No matter which motivation for incompatibilism is chosen, the free will theodicy may coexist with a hierarchical conception.[18] For the free will theodicist needs only to argue that God cannot create persons who always freely do the right, because for God to do so, He would have to determine their wills, and that, for some reason, such determination rules out the persons' acting freely. Thus the hierarchical solution need not be rejected by theists out of considerations regarding its impact on theodicy.

AN EXEGETICAL DIFFICULTY

Considerations of theodicy aside, the hierarchical solution is problematic from an exegetical standpoint. Hierarchical views of free will impose a requirement for freedom of the will beyond mere *accord* between levels of desire; and it is not plausible to hold that Pharaoh satisfies this requirement.

The crucial condition is contained in the following passage of Stump's article:

> To express Frankfurt's concept of freedom using this revised understanding of second-order desires and volitions, we should say that an individual has freedom of the will just in case he has second-order desires, his first-order volitions are not discordant with his second-order desires, and he has the first-order volitions he has *because of his second-order volitions.* (401; emphasis mine. Volitions are effective desires.)

Stump glosses the italicized "because" clause (henceforth BC) as follows: "His second-order volitions have directly or indirectly produced his first-order volitions, and if his second-order volitions had been different, he would have had different first-order volitions" (397).

The necessity for a "because" clause is easily supported. Imagine that Lex, a nefarious scientist, spends his day randomly implanting first-level volitions in people's brains. One of his targets is a drug addict who has been struggling against his addiction. The addict has a second-level desire not to have a first-level volition to shoot up. It just so happens that Lex, in his random pressing of buttons, winds up implanting this particular first-level volition in the addict. Thanks to this coincidence, the addict now enjoys accord between his first- and second-level desires. But intuitively this should not be enough to ensure that the addict has free will vis-à-vis taking the drugs. The first-level desire is not arising *because of* the second-level one.[19]

Does Pharaoh satisfy the "because" clause (BC)? If God hardened Pharaoh's heart *because* He wanted Pharaoh to have freedom of the will, Pharaoh would satisfy BC.[20] On the most plausible reading of the biblical story, however, this was not God's purpose. God's *stated* purpose in hardening Pharaoh's heart and continuing the plagues was to "multiply my wonders in the land of Egypt" (Exodus 12:9). Thus God tells Moses:

> I will harden the heart of Pharaoh, and will multiply my signs and wonders in the land of Egypt. (Exodus 7:3)

And more pointedly

> . . . for I have hardened his and his servants' hearts, *in order that* I place these signs of mine in their midst, and *in order that* you recount to your children and your descendants what I have wrought upon Egypt and the signs I placed there—so you shall know that I am the Lord. (Exodus 10:1; italics obviously mine)

Commentators suggest that the ten plagues divide into various categories which jointly—but only jointly—make God's full power manifest to both the Egyptians and the Israelites.[21] What God is telling Moses, therefore, is that He must make *all* of His power manifest to both Pharaoh and the Israelites before He will allow Pharaoh to "let my people go." The plagues must run their full course. This account nicely explains why God did not harden Pharaoh's heart yet again after the tenth plague, even though his release of the Israelites then would seem to go against his second-order desire. The reason is that, by this time, God has shown His wonders.[22] The hierarchical theorist will have trouble explaining why God stops after the tenth.[23]

The texts I cited suggest that there is *no* "because" connection between Pharaoh's having the second-level desire to want to keep the Israelites enslaved and his having the first-level desire to keep them enslaved. God's purposes seem to require that Pharaoh keep the Israelites enslaved no matter what Pharaoh's second-order desires (or intellectual judgments) are. That is, even were Pharaoh to have a second-order desire to have a first-order volition to *release* the Israelites (and the correlated intellectual judgment), God would not have allowed him to have this first-order volition. And in that case, the hierarchical solution will not go through, since Pharaoh does not satisfy BC.

A point of clarification. Even if BC does not hold in the biblical account, as I am suggesting, the hierarchical solution can be framed more modestly. Specifically, suppose it is granted that, due to the failure of BC to obtain, Pharaoh's willing to keep the Israelites enslaved was not a "free willing." Still, the hierarchical theorist will point out, had Pharaoh willed to release the Israelites due to the pressure of the plagues, this would not have exhibited free will either, since Pharaoh's second-level desire was to not will to release them. The hardening did not "deprive" Pharaoh of free will, because even were it not for the hardening he would not have manifested freedom of the will by *releasing* the Israelites, this due to the dissonance between his first- and second-level motivations. This defense against the charge of free will "deprivation" can survive even if the reason for the hardening is that God needs to manifest His power rather than that God is trying to preserve Pharaoh's free will. Thus the failure of BC to hold in the biblical story would signal only that the hierarchical theory fails to establish the bold claim that Pharaoh has free will, not that the theorist fails to provide any response at all to the problem of free will deprivation. I presume, though, that proponents of the hierarchical solution will want the stronger claim that Pharaoh's will is free when he keeps the Israelites enslaved, and it is this, I believe, that the biblical text fails to support, insofar as it casts doubt on BC.

DEVIANT CAUSAL CHAINS

The preceding argument against the "bold" claim rests, I think, on a plausible understanding of the biblical narrative. A hierarchical theorist might respond, however, that, although preserving Pharaoh's free will is not God's *motive* for the hardening, it is a *necessary condition* of God's multiplying His wonders. In other words, the following counterfactual will be said to be true:

> (C) If Pharaoh were to want to will to release the Israelites, then God would not have multiplied His wonders.

I do not think (C) fits well with the biblical text; I regard (C) as implausible from a purely textual standpoint. Do we have the sense that, even though God's main purpose in the hardening is to display His wonders (a fact stated three times), He would abandon that purpose just because Pharaoh "really" wanted to release the Israelites? Still, while the hierarchical theorist's position is not exegetically cogent, it is logically possible. (Something akin to Duhem's thesis holds for exegesis: rare is the objection to an interpretation that permits its target no logical space to repel the attack.) Moreover, people's "interpretive intuitions" will differ widely. And finally, in the interests of advancing discussion of the *philosophical* issues, I am willing to set aside the purely exegetical difficulty posed by the Bible's statement of God's purposes.[24]

So let us assume, then, that were Pharaoh to have different second-order desires, in particular, a desire to want to release the Israelites, God would *not* have produced (or strengthened) in him the first-order volition to keep the Israelites enslaved. However, even if BC is thus satisfied, we must recall that, when an account utilizes a "because" condition, i.e., "*A* happens because of *B*," not just any causal connection between *A* and *B* will typically serve to satisfy the condition. Some causal chains from *A* to *B* will be of the "right" or "appropriate" kind, but others will be "deviant," i.e., not of the "right" or "appropriate" kind. Now suppose the *way* in which Pharaoh reaches accord between his second-order volitions and his first-order volitions, while not violating BC outright, is *not* the right kind of causal chain. Then, when he keeps the Israelites in captivity, Pharaoh does *not* have free will—even on a hierarchical account.

How is the accord between Pharaoh's first- and second-level volitions produced? It is produced not by the second-order volitions "acting on" the first-level ones—ruling over them, as it were—but rather by God's producing a first-order volition by manipulating Pharaoh's motivational system. This He does not by giving Pharaoh some brand-new desire, but by strengthening the king's first-order desire to keep the Israelites enslaved and/or weakening a competing first-order desire to release them, when He sees Pharaoh having certain second-order desires which are not effectively "ruling."[25] The intervention of God in Pharaoh's first-level desires, His providing assistance, threatens to produce a "deviance" of the sort that will undermine Stump's effort to grant Pharaoh free will.[26]

Is the chain truly deviant? In approaching this question, it is useful to note how Frankfurt motivates his hierarchical theory. As Stump explains:

> The common conception of freedom as the ability to do what one wants to do, Frankfurt says, is best thought of as applying to freedom of action. Freedom of will can then be construed analogously as the ability to will what one wants to will, or the ability to have the sort of will one wants.[27]

The hierarchical theorist's account of freedom of the will is structured so as to be isomorphic to the familiar account of freedom of action. If so, however, then if a chain is deviant in the case of free action, the analogous chain is likely to be deviant in the case of freedom of the will.

Bearing this in mind, consider the following example. Suppose I have a first-order desire to lift a satchel, but for some reason I temporarily can't move my hand. A friend "reads" my first-order desire and moves my hand with his, so that my hand lifts the satchel. Assume there to be a tight causal connection between my having the first-order desire to raise the satchel and the satchel being lifted: if I were to want the satchel to remain in place, my friend wouldn't lift the satchel, nor would anyone else. Here, there is a causal connection between my first-order desire and a certain event, the satchel's rising. But I do not lift the satchel at all—my friend does—and a fortiori I do not lift it freely.

Pharaoh's first-order desire to keep the Israelites enslaved is something Pharaoh (at the second tier of his motivational structure) wants to be effective. And there is a causal connection between his having the second-order desire and his having this particular first-order one, since God provides the necessary accord. Yet Pharaoh's second-level desire seems not to produce the conforming first-order volition in the "right way." Arguably, the chain here is deviant for the same reason it is deviant in the case of "free/unfree action," i.e., in the case of the satchel. An external agent produces the result.

What I am claiming is that, no matter how otherwise tight a connection obtains between my willing to bring about a certain outcome and that outcome occurring, the intervention of an outside agent who brings about that result interferes with freedom of action. In the cases described it interferes in an especially sharp way, because it takes away the result's status as an *action,* as something I *did.* However, someone might object that, if there really is an invariable chain of causation leading from my first-order desires to events that fulfill those desires, then I "act" even if some necessary intermediate part of the sequence leading from desire to result involves other agents. After all, there are intermediate events in *every* act sequence. Also, people often use fancy technological devices to bring about the fulfillment of their (first-level) desires.[28] Why should a particular class of intermediate events, to wit, those events that involve the activity of other agents, be thought to interfere with action?

The theological doctrine of occasionalism provides us with an interesting contrast to this argument. Occasionalists claim that, when people appear to move their limbs, they in truth do not. Rather, when God sees certain desires present in people's minds, *God* moves their limbs. The occasionalist's intuition is that even if God were to always implement our first-order desires, we do not do anything. Occasionalists do not reason that if God is an intermediate part of *every* chain, human beings *do* move their limbs! The fact that another agent steps in takes away the act's status as something I did. And that same intuition colors our reaction to the satchel example. Furthermore, suppose the occasionalist's intuition is wrong here (intuitions admittedly are fuzzy on this point). At best this implies that when another agent *invariably* (or nearly invariably) implements S's desires, we attribute certain actions to S. It does not follow that when a second agent intervenes *episodically*—as God does with Pharaoh—we credit S with the action. Furthermore (more on this later) there may be a difference between intermediate steps that are invited and intermediate steps that occur without the agent's solicitation.

A further, and indeed very important, objection to the argument I sketched is that an external agent's interference does not necessarily result in the denial that the person whose conduct is interfered with performs a (free) act. Mark Ravizza raised the following point in correspondence:

> I agree that . . . a certain type of intervention by an external agent interferes with freedom. But does all intervention need to take such a dramatic form [as in the case of the satchel]? What if the intervention is simply in the form of *assisting* someone, or strengthening him so that he is able to do what he wants to do? For example, imagine that instead of lifting the package for me, my friend simply used some magic ray so that my muscles would become stronger just as I lifted the satchel? Why should this increase in power undermine my freedom of action? Does it matter that I didn't know or ask the friend to intervene? Analogously, what if we construed hardening of the heart in this weaker sense of (not directly bringing about the volition) but merely strengthening the agent's will so that *she* is able to will what she wants? For example, what if God simply strengthens Pharaoh's weakening first-order volition (but does not produce it), thereby enabling Pharaoh to will what he wants? In this case, the first-level willing would still be something Pharaoh "does," but he is able to do it because his will has been strengthened by God.[29]

My first observation about this argument is that the muscles analogy is not exact. The analogue to an outsider's strengthening someone's muscles is not God's strengthening Pharaoh's *first*-level desire to keep the Israelites enslaved. It is, rather, His strengthening *the connection between* Pharaoh's second-level desire and his first-level desire, that which leads from will (in this case, second-level will) to result (in this case, first-level will). Muscles are what enable me to implement my will to lift the satchel; "volitional muscles" are what enable my second-level desire to control my first-level ones and result in a volition I want to have. It is hard to think of what would serve as the analogue to physical muscles here.

It may seem that this disanalogy does not affect Ravizza's main point—

that an agent can get credit for an action, for producing a certain result, despite the fact that another agent has intervened (assisted) in the production of that result. But to the extent the analogy falls short of being exact, we should feel unsure that Pharaoh has free will. Moreover, to the extent that Pharaoh is not using his volitional muscles as the "lifter" is using physical muscles, Pharaoh's behavior falls that much shorter of being considered something he does. This ushers in a second problem with the muscles analogy.

This second problem can be set out as follows. In the "muscles" example, once the external agent has acted on S, strengthening S's muscles, there is still something left for S to do—namely, lift the package. In the hierarchical theorist's hardening example, however, once desire D1 is made stronger than desire D2,[30] D1 will prove effective in action, and there is nothing further for the agent S to will: S already has the will that S wants to have.[31] But if the hardened agent has nothing else to do once the desires' intensity levels have been set by the hardener, then the muscles case is not analogous to the hierarchical case. After all, we would not say that S strengthened his own muscles, but only that, his muscles having been strengthened by someone else, S lifted the package. That last step is missing from the Pharaoh example—as I put it earlier, Pharaoh is not using volitional muscles.

The hierarchical theorist will respond that it is not true that the hardened agent does nothing vis-à-vis his will after God hardens it. The agent still has to make one of the desires effective in action. But, one may ask, hasn't the agent been trying to do that all along? Hasn't the agent been exerting force—unsuccessfully—on his first-level desires? When God, say, reduces the strength of those of Pharaoh's desires that tend toward releasing the Israelites or strengthens Pharaoh's first-order desires to keep them enslaved, is not Pharaoh's second-order desire to have those other desires be effective in action precisely what it was before?[32]

To sum up, we have seen that, on plausible intuitions, the hierarchical theorist cannot use the muscles example to protect against the claim that BC is satisfied in a deviant fashion.

HARDENING VS. SANCTIFICATION

My preceding argument leaves some room for hierarchical theorists to maneuver. For instance, if God makes Pharaoh's two desires equal in strength, then perhaps Pharaoh now has "something to do"; alternatively, suppose Pharaoh has given up trying to control his will and now, after the hardening, has to muster the power of his second-order desires anew. Here again the king has "something to do." By resorting to these scenarios, hierarchical theorists are conceding the need to present a more exact, limiting description of the circumstances under which their solution can be applied to Pharaoh's case. I have some suspicions about these strategies. But even if they were to rebut my contention that Pharaoh's willing to keep the Israelites enslaved is not a deed he deserves credit for, another difficulty can be raised.

We can distinguish two different charges of deviance. One charge, already explored, is that Pharaoh cannot be given credit for making his desire to keep the Israelites enslaved effective in action—this is not something *he* did, but rather something that God did. The other charge is softer. It is that even if Pharaoh did something, he did not have free will when he did it. Let me look now at this softer charge. I will argue that, even if the stronger charge does not stick, the second, softer charge does—again, on some plausible intuitions.

Hierarchical theories seek to capture an important intuition about free will: that one who has free will has *control,* more precisely *self-control.*[33] An agent whose first-order volitions are discordant with his second-order desires lacks control; and so does an agent whose first-order volitions accord with his second-level desires but do not arise "because" of them. The critical question is: does Pharaoh have *control* over his first-order volitions? The answer, I suggest, is no.

Suppose Sheila finds that, despite her (unopposed) second-order desire to have a first-level volition to fire her incompetent friend Rachel, her first-order volition is to keep Rachel employed. Joe realizes Rachel's situation and puts a drug in Sheila's coffee. The drug strengthens Sheila's weak first-level desire to fire Rachel (or weakens her inhibitions against doing so), thus producing in Sheila a first-level volition to fire Rachel. Even if Joe acts as he does out of a desire to secure conformity between Sheila's first-level volitions and second-level desires, so that the "because" relation holds, it seems to me that, not only did Sheila not have control over her first-order volitions before Joe acted, but she does not manifest control even once the drug takes effect. Suppose Rachel sued Sheila for firing her. Surely Sheila could protest, "it wasn't my fault; Joe is the culprit. It's true I was quite happy with the result, i.e., Rachel's losing her job, but I did not bring that about." Sheila, in Frankfurt's terms, acted freely (she did what she wanted), but did not have freedom of the will. She lacks control; and so does Pharaoh at those moments in which his second-order desires could not produce conforming first-order volitions without God's help.[34]

Let me make explicit what *is* required for control in my opinion. Suppose person S produces a first-order volition V in Y that Y wants to have. What conditions must Y satisfy if Y is to exercise control over V? In our earlier example of Sheila, the following conditions obtained:

(a) Joe wants to give Sheila whatever first-order volitions she wants to have (if he wants Rachel fired no matter what Sheila wants or wants to want, and has the ability to secure this result, even a hierarchical theorist would deny Sheila lacks control, as she violates BC); (b) Joe is not oblivious of what Sheila's desires are; (c) Joe has the ability to implant the first-order volition if he wants to implant it.

However, if Sheila is to exercise control over her first-order volition, she must satisfy at least two further necessary conditions, (d)-(e):

(d) Sheila is aware of Joe and his abilities; (e) Sheila asks Joe to intervene or otherwise consciously tries to influence him to do so.

To exercise control in a particular case is to utilize a technique.[35]

In the Pharaoh case, analogues to (a)-(c) would seem to hold, and per-haps—though this is unclear—an analogue to (d) holds as well (Pharaoh is aware of God and His abilities). Certainly, though, an analogue to (e) does not hold. And so Pharaoh lacks control when his heart is hardened. (Pharaoh might even *resent* having his desires manipulated.)[36]

Herein lies a difference between hardening of the hearts and sanctification. Delineating a case of sanctification, Stump writes: "Suppose that Patricius also recognizes that this is his state [viz., he can't get his first-order volitions to line up with his second-order desires] and prays to God for help" (416). So far, so good: since the creation of the good first-order volition results from the prayer, an act Patricius decides to perform—has control over—Patricius's control is en-hanced. But prayer is part of the process that *leads to* sanctification.[37] It has no true analogue in hardening of the heart: there, prayer to God is absent. So, if prayer or some other attempt at eliciting another's intervention is necessary for control, as Stump implies in discussing sanctification, then Pharaoh lacks control.

Stump describes the one whose heart is hardened (Goebbels in this exam-ple) as exhorting *himself,* "be hard, my heart, be hard." Later she adds: "Suppose that God were to respond to Goebbels' exhortation to himself to be hard as if it were the atheist's analogue to prayer" (416). But the analogy, I suggest, is flawed. In sanctification the agent *asks God* to intervene. In hardening of the heart, the *self*-exhortation, "be hard, my heart, be hard," is just an attempt to shape the first-order desire on one's own. Saying that the exhortation takes place adds nothing to the description of the case: we knew already that the agent couldn't get the first-order desire he wanted. Hence in sanctification, where the agent prays, the agent is more in control than in hardening of the heart—unless, perversely, the hardened agent has prayed to God or, less perversely, to another agent, to make his heart hard. Stump's reference to Goebbels' "quasi-prayer" (418) obscures this point.

My insistence on the agent's having a technique for "activating" God's in-tervention is reinforced by another consideration, this one pertaining to theodicy. The hierarchical theorist's approach to hardening of the hearts and sanctification allows for some willings to be free even though an external party interferes *somewhat* in the agent's motivational makeup. So, in particular, God could cause certain agents—those whose unopposed second-level desire is to make their good first-order desires effective in volition, but who lack control—to do the good, without removing their free will. He could, in other words, sanctify them. If so, however, the hierarchical theorist will have trouble adopting a free will theodicy. For if God can sanctify even agents who do not ask for assistance and in that way *give* them free will, why do we discover agents who perform evil acts that are contrary to their uncontested second-level desires? Couldn't God sanctify any such agent without depriving that agent of free will? But in point of fact, there are many agents in the real world who perform evil acts contrary to uncontested second-level desires (and indeed are *un*free on the hierarchical the-ory!).[38] If so, the existence of moral evil cannot be defended just on the grounds that God must preserve free will. Now, the hierarchical theorist can mitigate this problem to *some* extent by saying, as I did, that sanctified agents have free will only if they take the initiative in petitioning God to make them will the good. We may assume that not many such agents fail to will the good. But if agents who are assisted by God have free will only if they petition God, as hierarchical theorists must claim if the free will theodicy is to be preserved, what will hierarchical theorists say about *hardened* agents? Why do they have free will, given that they do not influence God to intervene?

Thus, considerations about the free will theodicy support my view that an agent whose motivational structure is interfered with by others has free will only if the agent deliberately influences the intervener to step in. To resist the foregoing argument, the hierarchical theorist must either repudiate the free will theodicy, supplement it with some other explanation of how moral evil occurs, or despair of applying the hierarchical theory to the case of hardening (on the grounds that an agent whose will is interfered with by other agents has free will only if the agent has a technique for bringing about the other agents' intervention).

In sum, even if we allow that, sometimes, as in the case of sanctification, person Y may be said to have control over her first-order volition V even though person S's intervention is needed to produce V (the first-level volition Y wants) in Y, Pharaoh does not intuitively satisfy the conditions under which such a description would be accurate. The king does not try to get God to intervene. But if Pharaoh lacks control over his first-level volitions, the BC ("because" condition), now made properly precise, is violated; hence Pharaoh does not have freedom of the will.

CONTROL AND INTERVENERS

Advocates of a hierarchical solution may charge that I have driven too hard a bargain. They are not likely to concede that Pharaoh lacks control. How, though, can they vindicate this perspective? One argument proceeds as follows. When God reduces the strength of Pharaoh's first-order desire to release the Israelites or strengthens his first-level desire to keep them enslaved, He is creating a new *context of choice* for the king. Pharaoh did lack control before God intervened, hierarchical theorists may concede. However once God has altered the intensity of Pharaoh's desires, Pharaoh has free will in the new context provided that, given the *present* intensities of his first-level desires, his second-level desire *now* determines which first-level desire will be effective in action.

To explain more fully: suppose that at time t, S has a first-level desire D1 of intensity i, a conflicting first-level desire D2 of intensity i', and a second-level desire to have D1 be effective in action. Call this the *original choice context*. Because i is a weak level of intensity and i' is fairly strong, S does not succeed in making D1 effective. Then imagine that something causes D1 to grow stronger—a change in weather, say. In the new context, in which D1 is strengthened—call this the *changed choice context—S* acts on D1 because he wants to and would not act on D1 if he were to want not to. So BC is satisfied in the altered situation, but not the original one. The claims that the hierarchical theorist puts before us are, first, that S clearly has control in the changed context, and, second, that it doesn't matter, for purposes of determining whether S has free will, whether some other agent alters the intensity of S's desires because He wants S to have free will, or instead some impersonal atmospheric change creates the new context. What matters is only that BC is satisfied in the altered situation, and that given present levels of intensity, S wills in accordance with his second-level desires (without anyone's further manipulation of the intensity levels). For this reason, Sheila has control and so does Pharaoh—in their *changed* choice contexts.

This analysis necessitates a revised understanding of the "because" clause. Earlier we stated that BC is satisfied in the Pharaoh situation because God would give Pharaoh whatever will Pharaoh wants to have. According to the present argument, it is really irrelevant whether BC is satisfied in the original choice context. Thus, if a change in weather—rather than an act of Joe's—alters the intensity of Sheila's desires, BC is not satisfied in the original context; but according to what we have been told by my hypothetical theorist, that does not matter. Similarly if Joe was just fiddling around with drugs and would have put the drug in Sheila's coffee no matter what Sheila's desires were, we may still say that Sheila has control in the changed context because BC is satisfied *there*. It should also be noted that, on the present interpretation, the power of the drug could not be so great that Sheila's second-order desires are irrelevant; it cannot be that if Sheila now wanted not to will to fire Rachel, she would fire her anyway.[39]

Emphasizing that BC must hold in the changed context strikes me as a reasonable way of explaining how an agent whose desires have been interfered with nonetheless might be said to exercise control. While I would not make too much over the fact this is a revised account, such a change in the theory should not sneak in without notice. The hierarchical theorist now holds that so long as BC operates in the changed context, the manipulated agent has free will in that context.[40] But this means that whether God is trying to help Pharaoh realize his second-level desires is irrelevant; what matters is that God in fact does produce an alignment between the king's first- and second-order desires.

How does the new analysis fare? An objection appears almost immediately. Earlier I said that once the intensity levels of the hardened agent's desires are altered to suit the hardener's purposes, the hardened agent has nothing to do. If so, then in the changed context the agent's second-level desires are not causing the first-level volitions. They are causally inert at this juncture.

More fundamentally, though, a case can be made that satisfying BC in the changed choice context does not suffice for free will if free will requires control. I propose three examples to justify my resistance.

First, suppose that Jalens has to downsize his company. On Monday he feels a first-level desire to fire an employee and a second-level desire to act on this desire. He fires an employee. On Tuesday, Jalens feels a first-level desire to fire an employee and an uncontested second-level desire to act on this desire, but the first-level desire is too weak (relative to conflicting first-level desires) to produce a volition. God then strengthens Jalens's desire and Jalens fires an employee. On Wednesday, Monday's situation repeats itself and Jalens fires an employee (without divine assistance). On Thursday, Tuesday's repeats itself and Jalens fires an employee (with divine assistance). According to the hierarchical theorist, there is no difference from day to day in terms of whether Jalens exercises control. Yet intuitively there is a difference in this regard between Monday and Wednesday on one hand and Tuesday and Thursday on the other. Jalens displayed self-control on Monday and Wednesday, but not on Tuesday and Thursday.

Second, suppose Jalens feels a desire to strangle his business partner. He wishes he could bring himself to do it, but he can't. Someone then strengthens that weak desire (without Jalens's solicitation) and Jalens strangles his partner. Is Jalens responsible for this killing? No doubt upon learning the whole story Jalens would say, "I wanted to kill him, but I couldn't bring myself to do it, so I'm not responsible. The brainwasher is." He would have a good case, I think. But if Jalens's responsibility for killing his partner is diminished because of the brainwasher's intervention, it seems odd to regard that as an act that is brought about by his free will. Or that he had control over.

Third, suppose that Jalens has a first-level desire to burn down his company's building and collect the insurance, and a second-level desire for that weak desire to be effective in action. Suppose that the initial desire to start the fire is very weak relative to conflicting first-level desires, but Jalens wants to have such a desire and wants it to be effective. Each day the devil slightly strengthens Jalens's desire to burn down the company, until finally Jalens, after many days, carries through. Did Jalens display control? I think not: his second-level desires did not exercise control over his first-level desires, even though he satisfied BC in the last of the choice contexts in which he found himself.

To see how these kinds of worries apply to the case of Pharaoh, imagine Pharaoh in dialogue with God:

> *God:* You kept those people enslaved, and for that you will pay.
> *Pharaoh:* But I wanted to release them. I couldn't stand those plagues any more. *You* are the one who kept them enslaved. If you hadn't interfered in my will, they'd be free.
> *God:* But I did what I did because I wanted you to do what you really wanted to do. In other words, I did what I did so you could have free will.
> *Pharaoh:* What kind of reason is that to hold me responsible? Suppose someone wants to will to commit a crime but is scared to do it because he's deterred by the long arm of the law. So he lives in a law-abiding fashion, contrary to his second-level desire. Someone comes along and makes this guy less fearful of the law by manipulating the strength of his desires. Then the guy commits a crime. Are you going to hold him responsible?

I suggest Pharaoh is right.

Now the hierarchical theorist could admit that when an intervener hardens hearts, the hardened agent's responsibility is *diminished,* but still insist that this agent's responsibility is not *eradicated.* That may be right, but surely even acknowledging diminished responsibility—and with it, one supposes, diminished freedom—is an important change in the hierarchical theory's approach to Pharaoh, and its rationale should be spelled out.[41] Furthermore, the more reprehensible the act, the more troubled we are by the idea that the manipulated agent is responsible *at all.*[42]

Even to concede a diminution of responsibility exacerbates another problem about hardening of the hearts—the one I labelled the theodicy problem. That problem, recall, is this: How can a good God make a person morally worse? And how can He *actively* produce further suffering? Now, if a sanctified agent is made morally better, and sanctification and hardening are said by the hierarchical theorist to be analogous, it seems to follow that a hardened agent is made morally worse. How can this be, if God is perfectly good? Aware of this problem, Stump first labors to vitiate the inference from sanctification to hardening by saying that the hardened agent is not morally worse, for, *inter alia,* he follows his "erring conscience," and an "erring conscience" binds (416–20).[43] But even if an erring conscience binds, and what the hardened agent wills is not subjectively evil, is it not *objectively* evil? In response, Stump goes on to explain why God might prefer to prevent subjective worsening even if this involves producing objective worsening. Despite her efforts, at the end of the day I cannot avoid believing that the hardened agent is made morally worse without adequate justification. In particular, if the hierarchical theorist thinks that the hardened agent's responsibility for his will and his deeds are diminished, then someone—and who else but God?—bears responsibility for the *remaining part* of those evils (which we certainly would view as evil if the agent did them on his own). This problem strikes me as worse than the general problem of evil, for God is not merely *allowing* evil but is, rather, *producing* it by collaborating with Pharaoh's evil desires.[44]

A NON-HIERARCHICAL VARIANT

While Frankfurt's view of free will has enormous explanatory power and may serve to explain sanctification, I have shown why, on my intuitions, it does not extricate theologians from the problems posed by the hardening of hearts. God's intervention reduces Pharaoh's responsibility, indicates he lacks control, and may even take away the status of Pharaoh's deed as something he did.[45]

Intuitions will differ over my examples. However, it seems to me that a strategy very similar to the hierarchical theorist's solution—but not itself hierarchical—can moot much of the controversy over intuitions. The solution I have in mind is advanced by the sixteenth-century Jewish philosopher Joseph Albo.[46] Albo's basic idea is that God reduced the intensity of certain elements in Pharaoh's motivational makeup—specifically his fear of the plagues—and in that way restored him to a situation in which he had two alternative possibilities between which he would have to choose. Pharaoh then, on his own, chose to keep the Israelites enslaved.[47]

One difference between Albo's proposal and the hierarchical strategy is that on Albo's proposal God's intervention is not influencing Pharaoh to imple-

ment a particular first-order desire, namely the first-order desire to keep the Israelites enslaved that he wanted, at the second level, to be effective in action.
Rather God simply wanted to place the king in a situation of real choice, with
no particular outcome in mind.[48] Another difference is that, on Albo's reading,
after the hardening Pharaoh is definitely more active in producing the result to
keep the Israelites enslaved than he is in the hierarchical theorist's picture. As
the hierarchical theorist presents matters, Pharaoh's decision flows automatically
from the configuration of desires that God has set up (albeit God sets up these
desires in response to Pharaoh's second-order will). I recognize that whether
these differences make Pharaoh any more responsible (and God any less responsible) than in the hierarchical theorist's construction is once again a matter of
intuition; after all, God still has played *some* role in enticing Pharaoh to evil. But
to the extent Albo's view creates greater distance between God and the hardened
agent's volitions and deeds, it seems to yield at least somewhat more palatable
results than the hierarchical theory, and has a better chance of preserving Pharaoh's free will and moral responsibility. A full examination of the position cannot
be undertaken here, and surely such an examination would have to take into account the general merits of introducing a hierarchical theory on top of a theory
that requires merely alternative possibilities and an "actual choice." Maybe there
are good reasons for such a move. But insofar as the problem of hardening is
concerned, I am suggesting that it is in a theist's interests to avoid a hierarchical
strategy.

I have not sought to prove the correctness of the intuitions that move me
to depart from the hierarchical solution and ultimately to suggest that its basic
idea—that Pharaoh has free will—be developed, if at all, along non-hierarchical
lines. But clearly the hierarchical theory has more work to do before declaring
that it has solved the rich but neglected conundrum of hardening of the hearts.[49]

NOTES

1. This is the term used in Christian theology.

2. See Exodus 9:12, 10:20, 11:10; also 7:3, 10:1, 12:9. God also says He will cause Pharoah
not to listen when Moses will *warn* the king of the impending death of the Egyptians' firstborn
(Ex. 11:9). During the tenth plague, Pharoah finally gives in. But after the plagues are finished
and Pharaoh releases the Jews, his heart is hardened again and he decides to give pursuit (14:4,
8, 17, and arguably 14: 5, 18).

3. God induces Sihon to refuse passage to Moses and his people, in order to deliver Sihon
to the Israelites (Deut. 2:30), and He hardens the hearts of the Canaanites so that they wage
battle with Joshua's army (Joshua 11:20). In 1 Kings 18:37, the prophet Elijah insinuates that
God has led the hearts of the sinning Israelites astray.

4. Classic discussions include: Thomas Aquinas, *Summa Theologica* Ia–IIae, q. 79; Moses
Maimonides, *Commentary to the Mishnah,* introduction to the commentary on the tractate
Avot (the introduction is popularly called "Eight Chapters"), chapter 8, as well as his *Mishneh
Torah* (his legal code), *Book of Knowledge: Laws of Repentance,* chapter 6. (An English ver-
sion of the former is available in *Ethical Writings of Maimonides,* edited by Raymond L. Weiss
and Charles Butterworth [New York, 1975], 89–94; *Book of Knowledge* is translated by Moses

Hyamson [Jerusalem, 1962]); Joseph Albo, *The Book of Roots,* I V:25 (translated by Isaac Huzik [Philadelphia, 1929]). For detailed analysis of Aquinas's discussion, see Norman Kretzmann, "God among the Causes of Moral Evil: Hardening of Hearts and Spiritual Blinding," *Philosophical Topics* 16, no. 2 (Fall 1988): 189–214.

5. Eleonore Stump, "Sanctification, Hardening of the Heart, and Frankfurt's Concept of Free Will," *Journal of Philosophy* 85, no. 8 (August 1988): 395–420, repr. in *Perspectives on Moral Responsibility,* edited by John Martin Fischer and Mark Ravizza (Ithaca, N.Y., 1993). See also Kretzmann, "God Among the Causes of Evil"; William Alston, "The Indwelling of the Holy Spirit," in *Philosophy and the Christian Faith,* edited by Thomas V. Morris (Notre Dame, Ind., 1988), 121–50.

6. For our purposes it suffices to use Frankfurt's original essay, "Freedom of the Will and the Concept of a Person," *Journal of Philosophy* 68, no. 1 (January 14, 1971): 5–20, repr. in *Moral Responsibility,* edited by John Martin Fischer (Ithaca, N.Y., 1986). Page references are to the original. Frankfurt refines his approach significantly in subsequent essays, many of which are included in his *The Importance of What We Care About* (New York, 1988). Cf. Gary Watson, "Free Agency," *Journal of Philosophy* 72 (1975): 205–20, repr. in Fischer as well. I have offered a critique of hierarchical theories in my "Free Will and the Structure of Motivation," in *Midwest Studies in Philosophy,* vol. 10, edited by Peter A. French, Theodore E. Uehling, Jr., Howard K. Wettstein (University of Minnesota Press, 1985), 451–82, and of Watson's approach in "Compatibilism, Values, and 'Could Have Done Otherwise'," *Philosophical Topics* 14 (1988): 151–200.

7. Thus we hear that suffering and wrongdoing are justified by the "greater good" of free will and responsible moral choices. The problem of divine hiddenness is why a good God did not provide sufficient, incontrovertible evidence for His existence. The usual explanation is that, were God to reveal himself fully and evidently, people would no longer believe in him *freely* but would rather be *coerced* into believing. For a defense of this sort, see Michael Murray, "Coercion and the Hiddenness of God," *American Philosophical Quarterly* 30 (1993): 27–38. For criticisms of theistic responses to the problem of hiddenness, see Robert McKim, "The Hiddenness of God," *Religious Studies* 26 (1990): 141–61, and J. L. Schellenberg, *Divine Hiddenness and Human Reason* (Ithaca, N.Y., 1993). (Bertrand Russell reputedly was once asked what he would say if in the next world God were to ask him to justify his atheistic ways. I would ask Him, Russell is said to have replied, "O God, why did you make the evidence for your existence so insufficient?")

8. For an interesting rejection by a theist of the assertion that the value of free will outweighs the disvalue of evil, see Robert M. Adams, "Theodicy and Divine Intervention," in *The God Who Acts,* edited by Thomas F. Tracy (University Park, Penn., 1994), 31–40.

9. Actually, the biblical narrative does not force us to think that Pharaoh was held responsible for the hardened act of keeping the Israelites enslaved. True, God punishes Pharaoh and his people. But the eventual fate of the Egyptians—the death of their firstborn sons and, later, their warriors drowned at sea—suggests that it is the original crime of drowning male Hebrew children (Exodus 1) that meets with retribution, and not necessarily any obstinacy shown by them or their king in the face of the plagues. We need not assume that God held Pharaoh culpable for *any* of his resistance to the plagues; and even if God did so, there is no evidence that He held Pharaoh responsible for his hardened acts in particular.

On the other hand, if Pharaoh was not held responsible for his hardened acts, that suggests he was not free either, and then we are back to the problem of free will deprivation. So if our concern is with free will deprivation, it will be philosophically more attractive to posit that Pharaoh *is* responsible for his hardened acts (something not ruled out by the text), and then to try solving the free will deprivation and responsibility problems in one swoop.

10. There is a huge assumption here, namely, that Pharaoh has no conflicting second-order desire to have his first-order desire to release the Israelites be effective. It seems to me that Pharaoh is likely to have such a desire, since he wants to spare his people further destruction and humiliation, and releasing the Israelites is thus the rational thing to do. Does he not have *some* desire to will that which is rational and in his interests? Stump views the pressure of the plagues, as I note, as a "non-moral accident," but I differ with this effort to minimize its im-

portance vis-à-vis Pharaoh's second-level motivations. Nonetheless I will be pressing a different set of problems here. Cf. n. 23.

11. See especially 400–401. Because I do not lay out her theory fully, my usage of the term "second-level desires" will differ from Stump's, but not, I think, in a way that affects the argument.

12. Stump's solution resembles a point made by the Babylonian Talmud: "In the way a person wants to go, we lead him" (*Makkot* 10b). However, the Talmud does not explicitly pass judgment on whether the resulting act is free. See also Babylonian Talmud, *Sabbath* 104a. Note Psalms 81:11–12: "But my people would not listen to me; Israel would not submit to me. So I gave them over to their stubborn hearts to follow their own devices."

13. Watson, "Free Agency." Note Stump's criticisms of Watson in "Sanctification," 402, n. 11.

14. To be precise, it nullifies free will theodicies of moral evil but not "soulmaking" theodicies of physical evil. The latter explain evil as necessary for the development of such virtues as courage, faith, sympathy, and benevolence. So far as I can see soulmaking theodicies do not depend on the principle of alternative possibilities.

15. Fischer, *The Metaphysics of Free Will* (Oxford, 1994), 182–83. In the quoted sentences, Fischer is not supposing a hierarchical concept of free will but instead his own conception of freedom as a certain kind of responsiveness to reasons.

16. Of course, they may value free will on other grounds, in which case the problem is reinstated.

17. On these different motivations for incompatibilism, see Robert Kane, *The Significance of Free Will* (New York, 1996). But cf. Fischer, *The Metaphysics of Free Will,* 148–54: he denies that determinism can threaten freedom even if we do not endorse an alternative possibilities requirement.

18. This paragraph owes something to a point made to me by Eleonore Stump, though she may not agree with my formulation. See also Stump, "Sanctification," 398, n. 6. Elsewhere (namely, the essays I cited in n. 6), I have argued that despite the perception of many hierarchical theorists that they are rehabilitating compatibilism, their theories actually fit incompatibilist intuitions better than they do compatibilist ones.

19. I thank Robert Nozick for suggesting this example. Whether Lex's manipulation interferes with freedom even when Lex is trying to produce an accord between his subject's first- and second-level desires (so that BC ostensibly is satisfied) is a question I will address later.

20. We would also need to assume that God endorses the hierarchical account of free will. Hierarchical theorists will cheerfully make that assumption!

21. See, e.g., the commentary of the Jewish exegete Isaac Abarbanel. For a digest of various approaches to dividing the plagues in a way that establishes the need for all of them to occur, see Yehudah Nachshoni, *Studies in the Weekly Parashah: Exodus,* translated by Raphael Blumberg (New York, 1988), 376–82.

22. A variant of this approach is that only the first nine plagues were intended as displays of divine power. The display is over by the time the tenth plague arrives. The tenth is punitive rather than probative.

23. The hierarchical theorist might say the explanation is simple: after the tenth, Pharaoh acknowledges the wrongness of his deeds. So he is undergoing a change in his second-level desires. If there was such a change and he now has conflicting second-level desires, releasing the Israelites would not be an unfree willing on his part. The problem is, why does God harden his heart after that as well (14:8)? We would have to posit that he completely lost that second-level desire (10:20, 12:9)! Note that Pharaoh spoke contritely at Exodus 9:27 and 10:16–17, only to be hardened twice more (10:20, 12:9).

The statement in 9:27 is significant in its own right. As David Widerker pointed out to me, the verse implies that Pharaoh had *conflicting* second-order desires. Now Stump states that if the hardened agent has dissenting second-order desires, God is not enhancing his free will by the hardening (397; 401; 418, n. 20). How then can we explain why God hardens Pharaoh's heart yet again (Exodus 10:20)?

24. It is nonetheless worth looking at some ways of upholding (C). First of all, one might try to defend (C) by inferring it from a different counterfactual, (C′):

(C′) If (i) Pharaoh were to want to will to release the Israelites after the sixth plague, and (ii) he were to do so because he recognized God's greatness, and (iii) the Israelites by that time were to recognize the full greatness of God, then God would have let Pharaoh release the Israelites.

But apart from the possible implausibility of assuming that conditions (ii) and (iii) could be satisfied without the full array of plagues, (C′) does not entail (C). For it may be that the nearest possible worlds in which Pharaoh wants to will to release the Israelites are worlds in which he wants to will to release them because he cares about the devastation to his country, not worlds in which he wants to release them because He appreciates God's greatness. And in such worlds, God would have to continue the plagues. For in such worlds neither the Egyptians nor the Israelites adequately recognize God's greatness. And so the hierarchical theorist's strategy of inferring (C) from (C′) fails.

Another proposal for defending the hierarchical strategy would assert:

(C″) Had Pharaoh wanted to will the Israelites' release, God would have found some other way to multiply His wonders in Egypt.

I would claim that the proliferation of wonders could not have continued without the Israelites' remaining as slaves. This is in part because the Israelites too needed to know God, and in part because in some plagues God needed to highlight that the Israelites were not subject to the plague. Still, the hierarchical theorist might say, God could give Pharaoh a first-order volition to release the Israelites even if God wants the Israelites to remain in Egypt for other purposes. For suppose Pharaoh were to have such a volition and were to issue an order to release the slaves. God could still see to it that the order is given but that it is not communicated to or not implemented by the Egyptian people. In those circumstances, God would be responding to Pharaoh's second-order desire to have a first-order volition to release the Israelites by giving Pharaoh the first-order volition he wants; yet the Israelites could remain in Egypt as slaves and the plagues could multiply in accordance with God's purpose. So long as God wants both to preserve Pharaoh's free will and to multiply His wonders, He can achieve both ends, and BC would be satisfied.

I concede that God's having a purpose of ensuring Pharaoh's freedom of the will can in this way be shown *logically consistent* with His having the additional purpose of "multiplying my wonders in Egypt." But the above attempt to show that Pharaoh might satisfy BC even given the aim of "multiplying my signs" is contrived and ad hoc. Nothing in the biblical text gives the slightest support to the view that preserving Pharaoh's free will had anything to do with the hardening. Why would the Bible omit such a critical detail?

Someone could also argue that God needed to multiply His wonders only because Pharaoh was a strong king. He needed to show His wonders because Pharaoh was so defiant of him and so spiteful toward the Israelites. In this sense, C is true. But if Pharaoh were to release them after six plagues, wouldn't God *already* have shown His supremacy over him?

In general, I think we should distinguish interpretations that are logically possible from interpretations that are plausible. Furthermore, even if one of these rationales were to go through, the hierarchical theorist's solution confronts another exegetical obstacle: it may not be general enough to handle other biblical cases of heart-hardening.

25. God could accomplish this in turn by manipulating Pharaoh's belief system.

26. The need for modifying the "because" clause in hierarchical theories so as to block cases of intervening agents was first pointed out by Peter Van Inwagen. See the example Keith Lehrer credits to van Inwagen in "Preferences, Conditionals, and Freedom," in *Time and Cause,* ed. van Inwagen (Dordrecht, 1980), 187–201, 193, n. 3. Some of the problems I will raise about the intervention of other agents can profitably be explored through the classic discussion of "voluntary interventions" in H. L. A. Hart and A. M. Honore, *Causation in the Law,* 2nd ed. (New York, 1985).

27. Stump, "Sanctification," 396. See Frankfurt, "Freedom of the Will," 15. Frankfurt is clearly using the classical compatibilist account of free action. However, Stump stressed to me (in correspondence) that her account is not intended to be compatibilist. (See also n. 17 above.) It should be noted that some of my later objections to her account draw on intuitions that incompatibilists are more likely to accept than compatibilists. In that sense the move to incompatibilism may be at least moderately counterproductive to the hierarchical solution.

28. This last point was made to me by Eleonore Stump.

29. Eleonore Stump argued for a similar distinction in her comments on the original version of this essay.

30. Or for that matter D2 is made weaker than D1.

31. I am supposing here that in a hierarchical theory, a second-order desire (or intellectual judgment) can never make the weaker of two desires be effective; the stronger desire is the one that is effective. This assumption can be questioned, since perhaps the point of the hierarchical theory is that sometimes a second-level desire can make the *weaker* of two desires first-level effective. I find hierarchical theorists' stance on this issue unclear, but I follow a natural reading.

32. Perhaps Ravizza's example can be remodelled. Suppose I am straining and straining to lift the satchel, and in the midst of my strenuous effort my friend turns on the rays. That same amount of effort that previously produced nothing now results in a raised package. Analogously, it will be said, Pharaoh was straining and straining to make his first-level desire to keep the Israelites enslaved effective in action, and God then "turned on the rays," i.e., changed the intensity level of his desires. Just as the straining lifter is said to lift the satchel, Pharaoh may be said to make his first-level desire to keep the Jews enslaved effective in action.

The biblical text does not convey this picture of a Pharaoh arduously "lifting" his first-level desires; we have evidence at most for a picture of someone who has made a sober, rational decision to release the Israelites due to the pressure, who has excellent reasons to release them, and then is abruptly halted. (David Widerker pointed this out.) But suppose we accept the picture of Pharaoh as "straining and straining." Go back to the satchel example where the lifter is "straining and straining." Is it really so clear that he lifts the satchel when he contributes no more effort than he did originally?

33. Stump refers to "control" at various points in "Sanctification." See 416, lines 6,11; 419, line 11. For further analysis of "control," see Fischer, *The Metaphysics of Free Will,* esp. chaps. 7–8. (He argues that "control" has two senses, one which requires alternative possibilities, another which does not.)

34. That Pharaoh shows self-control on earlier and later occasions when faced with similar incentives does nothing to show that, when God hardens his heart this time, Pharaoh controls his first-level volition. All that Pharaoh's earlier (and later) self-initiated hardenings show is that he does not suffer from some lasting disability of the will with respect to his treatment of the Israelites. They tell us about the *agent,* Pharaoh, not about a particular willing on his part. To see this point, suppose that, during the sixth plague, Pharaoh, despite a contrary second-level desire, had issued an order to release the Israelites, but for some reason they remained in Egypt as slaves anyway (e.g., his servants didn't hear the order). Thereafter, Pharaoh changes his mind, and from then on the plot continues as in the Bible. Surely Pharaoh's previous and still-to-come successes in resisting temptation would not be relevant to whether he had control *then,* during the sixth plague. They do not deserve to be considered relevant either when God hardens his heart. A person can have self-control with regard to forming a particular first-level volition, even if she does not exercise control with regard to that volition-type on every occasion.

35. A similar view of control is proffered by Daniel Dennett in *Elbow Room: The Varieties of Free Will Worth Wanting* (Cambridge, Mass., 1984), ch. 3.

36. Stump maintains that it would not be appropriate for God to let Pharaoh release the Jews *just because* of the pressures exerted by the plagues: "There is something morally dubious about a villain such as Goebbels falling into some creditable action simply through fatigue" (418). And she says that, thanks to God's hardening, "a second-order will bent on such evil

may maintain its control over these first-order desires when fatigue or some other nonmoral accident might have caused the control to weaken" (419). Her implication is that all God is doing is nullifying the effects of an incentive or influence which from a moral point of view is extraneous. It seems to me, though, that whatever moral advantages are purchased by God's letting Goebbels or Pharaoh indulge their tendencies for evil can be purchased without claiming that when God hardens their hearts they have free will. If God hardens their hearts, that paves the way for their having free will on *other, later* occasions; one needn't assume that the "hardened" acts themselves reflect free will.

37. On 412-14, Stump acknowledges that the sanctified agent must at least want God to produce good first-level desires. But prayer seems necessary too, at least assuming that God will not respond without prayer.

38. Cf. Stump, "Sanctification," 412. There are many even if a further requirement is imposed that the person be basically good.

39. I suppose there could be a view that looked only at the original context. This view would require that BC be satisfied in the original context, not that it be satisfied in the changed context. But I do not think this has any plausibility.

40. This same point can be made using Ravizza's example of the person who lifts a satchel only because an intervener strengthens his muscles. The hierarchical theorist held that the lifter in that case gets credit for lifting the satchel. Notice, however, that S is given credit for lifting the satchel even though there is no interesting causal relationship between S and the intervener. Suppose the intervener accidentally turned on the muscle-strengthening rays: do we have any more trouble saying that S lifted the package than when the intervener is trying to help? No—the content of S's second-level will seems to be causally irrelevant in these cases. If so, then by analogy, the intuition that Pharaoh wills freely to keep the Israelites enslaved should hold regardless of whether the intervener (God) would have done something different if S had a different second-level desire. But this suggests that the hierarchical theorist has gone too far in requiring that were Pharaoh to have a second-order desire to desire to release the Israelites, then God would not have influenced him to desire to keep them enslaved. Rather it suffices if Pharaoh satisfies BC in the changed case. I suggested, however, that Pharaoh does not do anything in the changed context.

41. Here is a possible rationale. Earlier I mentioned that a theistic hierarchical theorist will want to put some constraints on actions produced by interveners, in order to hold on to the free will theodicy. Thus the notion that interveners undermine responsibility is not inconsistent with other things that a theistic hierarchical theorist will want to say.

42. If the responsibility of someone who is caught by a police entrapment is unclear because the police have contributed to crime by enticing him, how much more so should we be worried about an agent whose desires have been manipulated as in the hardening example. Cf. Gerald Dworkin's remarks about entrapment: "Suppose I form the intent to steal something, but cannot overcome a residual fear of being apprehended, and it is only your encouragement that enables me to carry out the original intent." Of this case Dworkin says that "the question of whether crime has been manufactured is often hard to settle." Conflicting intuitions in this context, I suggest, resemble conflicting intuitions about my cases. See Dworkin, "The Serpent Beguiled Me and I Did Eat: Entrapment and the Creation of Crime," in *The Theory and Practice of Autonomy* (New York, 1988), 141. I thank Lawrence Davis for suggesting I think about entrapment in this connection.

43. She uses this point to render the analogy between sanctification and hardening more precise.

44. But cf. Stump's reply on 419-20, which I think implies that the distinction between allowing evil and producing evil is not valid here. I thank David Widerker for suggesting I bring the problem of moral worsening into play at this juncture.

45. I want to note another problem. The hierarchical theorist claimed that Pharaoh's releasing the Israelites under pressure of the plagues would have not reflected free will because Pharaoh's second-level desire was to keep the Israelites enslaved. To the extent that this explanation seems plausible, it gains that plausibility from what in truth is a weakness in hierarchical

theories. Hierarchical theories are problematic because they do not permit a distinction between compulsion and akrasia; both cases end up being labelled as unfree, for in both akrasia and compulsion an agent acts contrary to her better judgment and her second-level desire. (See my "Compatibilism, Values, and 'Could Have Done Otherwise'.") Had Pharaoh released the Israelites, this would have been an akratic act, but one he did with free will, albeit he would lack free will according to the hierarchical theorist's conditions. Cf. Gary Watson, "Skepticism about Weakness of the Will," *Philosophical Review* 86 (1977): 316–39. One could of course say that Pharaoh releasing the Israelites would be unfree because it would be *coerced,* or performed under *duress,* but I presume that a hierarchical theorist would need to explain the freedom-depriving character of coercion and duress in terms of levels of motivation.

46. Albo, *The Book of Roots* IV:25. A bilingual edition of this Hebrew work was published by Isaac Huzik (Philadelphia, 1929). See also the commentary of Ovadyah Seforno to Exodus 7:3.

47. Albo also explains that had Pharaoh released the Israelites under pressure of the plagues, his act would not have been free insofar as it was coerced (actually, he stresses that it would not have been a true repentance, rather than that it would have been free).

48. This claim runs into a problem we noted earlier: doesn't the text suggest that the plagues must run their full course? I agree that this is a problem, but remember that Albo is no worse off than the hierarchical theorist on this score.

49. An ancestor of this essay was read at the Eastern Division meetings of the American Philosophical Association. I profited significantly from Eleonore Stump's incisive comments at the A.P.A. session and also from subsequent correspondence with her and with Mark Ravizza. I am also deeply grateful to David Widerker for long hours of conversation, during which he offered generous and thorough comments on an earlier draft. His suggestions helped greatly to shape the final version.

Against Middle Knowledge

PETER VAN INWAGEN

As a result of my teen-age conversion to the Catholic Church . . . I read a work called *Natural Theology* by a nineteenth-century Jesuit . . . and found it all convincing except for two things. One was the doctrine of *scientia media,* according to which God knew what anybody would have done if, e.g., he hadn't died when he did. . . . I found I could not believe this doctrine: it appeared to me that there was not, quite generally, any such thing as what would have happened if what did happen had not happened, and that in particular there was no such thing, generally speaking, as what someone would have done if . . . and certainly that there was no such thing as how someone would have spent his life if he had not died a child. I did not know at the time that the matter was one of dispute between the Jesuits and the Dominicans, who took rather my own line about it. So when I was being instructed a couple of years later by a Dominican at Oxford . . . and he asked me if I had any difficulties, I told him that I couldn't see how that stuff could be true. He was obviously amused and told me that I certainly didn't have to believe it, though I only learned the historical fact I have mentioned rather later.

> —G. E. M. Anscombe, *Metaphysics and the Philosophy of Mind* (Introduction)

According to the sixteenth-century Spanish Jesuit Luis de Molina, God's knowledge—the *content* of His knowledge, the things that He knows—may be divided into three parts.[1] There is, first, His *natural* knowledge: the set of true propositions knowledge of whose truth belongs to His *nature*. This is just exactly the set of all metaphysically necessary truths, for knowing that p is an essential property of God if and only if p is a metaphysically necessary truth. There is, secondly, His *free* knowledge: those propositions that are true but are such that it is or once was within His power so to arrange (or so once to have arranged) matters that they be false—that there are exactly 80,966 hairs on Tom's head, for example, or that there is a physical universe. There is, thirdly and finally, God's *scientia media* or middle knowledge, which comprises those metaphysically contingent truths such that it is *not* (and never has been) within God's power so to arrange or so to have arranged matters that they be false. Many philosophers and theologians would insist that this third class of propositions is empty. Molina, however, insisted that it contains propositions of the type nowadays called "true counterfactuals of freedom."

I shall assume that there is such a thing as middle knowledge only if there are true counterfactuals of freedom—or, as I shall sometimes say, only if there are such things as "middle facts."[2] A counterfactual of freedom is a "would" conditional that says of a certain agent that that agent would freely have performed a certain act in certain circumstances that do not in fact obtain. For example:

> If Curley had been offered a bribe of $20,000 at noon last Friday to permit the destruction of Old North Church, he would freely have accepted it

is a counterfactual of freedom, provided that Curley was not in fact offered a bribe of the kind specified at noon last Friday. And if this proposition is *true,* it is a middle fact. (If, that is, facts are true propositions. Those who wish to distinguish between facts and true propositions may substitute whatever phrase they think is appropriate for 'is'.)

My purpose in this essay is to argue that there is no middle knowledge because there are no middle facts. (If there are no middle facts, then, obviously, the proposition that God does not have middle knowledge does not entail that God is not omniscient. If something is not there to be known, then even an omniscient being will not know it. If all counterfactuals of freedom are false—or lack truth-values—then an omniscient being will know *that,* but knowing of each counterfactual of freedom that it is false or truth-valueless does not constitute middle knowledge.)

I will argue that all counterfactuals of freedom are false.[3] My argument proceeds from two premises that I believe to be true but will not defend. The first is that David Lewis's semantics for counterfactual conditionals is the correct semantics for counterfactual conditionals.[4] The second is incompatibilism, the thesis that free will is incompatible with determinism. Anyone who rejects either of these premises may regard my argument as having a conditional conclusion: *If* Lewis's semantics is correct and *if* free will is incompatible with determinism, then all counterfactuals of freedom are false. (As regards the second of these premises, it should be pointed out that the defenders of middle knowledge have always assumed that free will is incompatible with determinism—or that, as they sometimes put it, "a libertarian account of free will is correct."[5] It would, I suppose, be a part of what most people who use the term mean by 'middle knowledge' that the existence of middle knowledge entails that free will is incompatible with determinism. I much prefer to say that if free will and determinism are compatible—and if determinism is true and if people do sometimes act freely—

then there will, of necessity, be true counterfactuals of freedom and an omniscient being would, of necessity, have middle knowledge.[6])

Here, briefly, is Lewis's semantics for counterfactual conditionals (I use his well-known symbol for the counterfactual-conditional connective):

> $p \:\Box\!\!\rightarrow\: q$ is true if and only if either p is impossible or some world in which p and q are both true is closer to actuality than any world in which p is true and q is false.[7]

(The second disjunct of the definiens is sometimes informally stated like this: q is true in all the closest p-worlds.) In the sequel, I shall ignore the first disjunct of the definiens; I shall always assume that the antecedent of whatever counterfactual we may be considering is possible. The above counterfactual of freedom is then true in just the following case:

> Some world in which *Curley was offered a bribe of $20,000 at noon last Friday to permit the destruction of Old North Church* and *Curley freely accepted the bribe* are both true is closer to actuality than any world in which *Curley was offered a bribe of $20,000 at noon last Friday to permit the destruction of Old North Church* is true and *Curley freely accepted the bribe* is false.

Is there a world having this property? In attempting to answer this question, we must remind ourselves what incompatibilism actually implies about free actions. We must remind ourselves what the proposition that a certain action is free actually implies if free will is incompatible with determinism. Let us examine the case of the thief and the poor-box that I discussed in *An Essay on Free Will:*

> [A hardened thief] is in the act of lifting the lid of the poor-box in a little country church. He sneers and curses when he sees what a pathetically small sum it contains. Still, business is business: he reaches for the money. Suddenly there flashes before his mind's eye a picture of the face of his dying mother and he remembers the promise he made to her by her deathbed always to be honest and upright. This is not the first occasion on which he has had such a vision while performing some mean act of theft, but he has always disregarded it. This time, however, he does *not* disregard it. Instead, he thinks the matter over carefully and decides not to take the money. Acting on this decision, he leaves the church empty-handed. (Van Inwagen, pp. 127–28)

We assume that this was a free act and that free will is incompatible with determinism. What does this imply? It implies that if God had caused the world to revert to exactly the state in which it was just before the thief made the decision not to steal the money (and had then allowed the world to "go forward again"), the thief might well have stolen the money "this time." If, moreover, there were a large number of occasions on which God caused the world to revert to exactly the state it was in just before the thief made the decision not to steal the money, a suitably placed observer of all these "replayings" would find that sometimes the thief stole the money and sometimes he did not.[8] In other words, if t is the moment at which the thief made his decision, there are physically possible worlds (worlds in which the laws of nature are the actual laws) of two kinds: Worlds whose histories are identical with the history of the actual world up to t in which the thief stole the money (no doubt there are infinitely many such worlds if there are any at all); and worlds whose histories are identical with the history of the actual world up to t in which the thief did not steal the money (the actual world, at least, is such a world, and no doubt there are infinitely many others). If there are no worlds of the former kind, the thief's act (leaving the church empty-handed) was determined by the past and the laws of nature, and—if free will is incompatible with determinism—that act was therefore not free.

Now suppose that at the moment the thief was about to decide whether to steal the money, he was alarmed by some noise and fled the church without making a decision. What (free) decision *would* he have made if the noise had not occurred (and if nothing else had prevented his making the decision)? In the actual world—proper name 'α'—the thief freely decided not to steal the money; our question concerns some very close world w in which a sudden noise frightened him and sent him running. We want to know whether the counterfactual conditional *If things had been at t exactly as they were in α at t, the thief would have freely decided not to steal the money* is true or false in the world w—or we might ask the same question about *If things had been at t exactly as they were in α at t, the thief would have freely decided to steal the money.* (These two propositions are contraries: in any given world, either one is true and one false, or they're both false.) Does the thief freely decide not to steal [freely decide to steal] the money "in all the worlds closest to w" in which things were at t exactly as they were in α at t? If he freely decides not to steal in every member of this class of worlds, then the former proposition is true in w; if he freely decides to steal in every member of this class of worlds, the latter proposition is true in w; if he freely decides not to steal in some of them and freely decides to steal in others, then both propositions are false in w.[9]

It would seem that α is one of the worlds in this class—one of the worlds closest to w in which things were just as they were in α at t. (We could certainly so choose w that α is one of the worlds closest to w in which things were just as they were in α at t. Let us suppose that we have done so.) It follows that *If things had been at t exactly as they were in α at t, the thief would have freely decided to steal the money* is false in w. But what about its contrary, the proposition that he would have freely decided not to steal the money? Could that proposition be true in w? That proposition will be true in w only if *every* world whose history is identical with the history of α up to t and in which the thief freely decides *to* steal the money is more distant from w than α is.

Let β be such a world—a world whose history is identical with the history of α up to t and in which the thief freely decides to steal the money. Let us recapitulate what we know about ways in which the three worlds are related to one another: their histories are identical up to the moment at which the thief is distracted from his deliberations by the noise; thereafter, α and β diverge from w. A brief moment later, at t, the thief freely decides (in α) not to steal the money, and freely decides (in β) to steal the money and α and β accordingly diverge.

Does it follow from these things we have stipulated that α is closer to w than β is? Well, what are the relevant considerations? If α is closer to w than β is, this must be due to what goes on in the two worlds after t. How should one go about making judgments about the "distances" between these worlds and evaluating these judgments?

There are various ways to think about this sort of question. Suppose we follow David Lewis and think about the "distances" between worlds in terms of their overall similarities and differences. Suppose we identify our question with the question whether α is more similar to w than β is. It is hard to discern any factor that could be relevant to answering this question other than the "ranges of particular fact" that hold in the three worlds. The laws of nature are the same in all three worlds, these laws are indeterministic, and the case of the thief as we have imagined it implies that no miracle (no "large" miracle, no "small" miracle, no miracle in either the usual sense of the word or in Lewis's special technical sense) is involved in the divergence of α and β.[10]

Is there anything about the way things go in β from which we are obliged to infer that β is more unlike w than the actual world is? It would not seem so, if only because we have not said very much about β. In fact, β is not really a particular world at all but an "arbitrarily chosen object."[11] We have picked out β by means of an indefinite description: 'a world that is identical with α up to t, and in which the thief freely decides to steal'. There no doubt exists a vast infinity of worlds that satisfy this description and nevertheless differ radically from one another. And what it seems most reasonable to believe about this vast infinity of worlds is this: some of them are less like w than α is, some of them are more like w than α is, and some of them are neither more nor less like w than α is. All the worlds that satisfy our indefinite description are, after all, indeterministic, and anything that is consistent with their common indeterministic laws and their common state at the moment of their collective divergence from the actual world will happen in one or another of them given sufficient time—including "reconverging" with w.[12]

We are not obliged to look at the concept of distance between possible worlds as Lewis does—in terms of overall similarity among worlds. I myself prefer to think of the "p-worlds that are closest to w" as those worlds in which p is true that could be "obtained" from w by making the smallest possible "changes" in w. (I assume that we are able to distinguish between a change and its consequences, and between the magnitude of a change and the magnitude of its consequences.) A moment's reflection will show that the class of p-worlds that can be obtained from w by the smallest possible changes in w and the class of p-worlds that are most similar to w need not be the same—for some of the worlds in the former class might, throughout the entire future, diverge radically from w, and thus not belong to the latter. (The minimal changes in w that secure the truth of p might be miracles, replacements of the "entire past" of w by other "entire pasts," or indeterministic "swerves" of some of the inhabitants of w. Or some of them might be of one of these types and some of the other two. However we understand the idea of a "change," some worlds produced by the smallest changes in w that are sufficient to secure the truth of p will not be among the worlds that are—over all—most similar to w.)

Suppose, then, that we look at distance among possible worlds as a function of "size of change." Does it follow from any of the stipulations we have made about β and w that β is farther from w than the actual world is? It would not seem so. A certain event—the noise that frightens the thief—occurs in w but not in α and β, and thereafter the latter two worlds (still "coinciding") diverge from w; a bit later, at t, the thief makes one decision in α and another in β, and those two worlds diverge. To change w into α, therefore, what is required is the noise plus the undetermined course of the thief's deliberations taking one "fork in the road"; to change w into β, what is required is the noise plus the undetermined course of the thief's deliberations taking the other fork. The noise, so to speak, cancels out. Can the fact that the undetermined course of the thief's deliberations went one way in the actual world and the other in β have the consequence that the actual world could be got from w by a smaller change than any that would suffice to produce β? Remember that if, on a vast number of occasions, God miraculously caused the universe to revert to the precise state it was in just before t, and then allowed things to proceed without further miracles, on some of these occasions the thief would refrain from stealing the money and on some of them he would steal the money. Given that this is the case, it is very hard indeed to see why anyone would say that a larger change in w is required to produce the state of affairs *the thief decides to steal* than is required to produce the state of affairs *the thief decides not to steal*.

It would therefore seem that whether we understand "q is true in all the p-worlds closest to w" as

q is true in all the p-worlds that are, over all, the most similar to w

or as

q is true in all the worlds that can be got from w by the smallest changes that suffice for the truth of p,

it is not the case that the thief freely decides to refrain from stealing in all the worlds closest to w in which his deliberations about whether to steal are uninterrupted by the noise. On either interpretation, therefore, the counterfactual conditional

If the thief's deliberations about whether to steal had not been interrupted by the noise, he would freely have decided not to steal

is false in w. (We have already seen that 'If the thief's deliberations about whether to steal had not been interrupted by the noise, he would freely have decided to steal' is false in w.) But the arguments that have led us to this conclusion in no way depend on the particulars of the case we have imagined. If these arguments are sound, then there are no middle facts (no true counterfactuals of freedom) and hence no middle knowledge.

We should note that this conclusion depends on no features of free acts other than the fact that they are undetermined (a consequence of incompatibilism). Arguments that differ from the above in no important way show that there are no facts about what the outcome of any non-actual course of events would have been if its outcome would have been undetermined. Consider, for example, a contraption that has the following design. It is a little box on the outer surface of which there are a button and two lights, a red light and a green light. If someone presses the button, one or the other (never both) of the lights will light. And suppose that it is genuinely undetermined which light will light on any particular occasion on which the button is pressed. (Perhaps the outcome of pressing the button depends on individual quantum events.) Suppose that no one pressed the button at noon. If someone *had,* which of the lights would have lit? If our arguments concerning the thief are correct, similar arguments will show that we can say only that one or the other would have lit; we cannot say that the green light would have lit, because it is false that the green light would have lit; we cannot say that the red light would have lit, because it is false that the red light would have lit. (Of course it is also false that the green light would *not* have lit, and false that the red light would *not* have lit.) God, being omniscient, knows all these things, knows that it is true that one light or the other would have lit, and knows that all the other propositions I have mentioned are false. But He does not know which light would have lit because no such thing is there to be known.

God might, however, know—He would if it were true—that if the button had been pressed at noon, the green light would *probably* have lit. And such a thing could easily be true. (Suppose that there is a magical, truly indeterministic coin—a fair coin such that if it is tossed it is truly undetermined whether it will fall "heads" or "tails." God cannot know whether, if you had tossed the magical coin once at noon—you didn't—it would have fallen "tails," for, again, no such thing is there to be known. Nor does He know that if you had tossed it five times at noon, it would have fallen "tails" at least once, for in some of the closest worlds in which you tossed it five times at noon, it fell "heads" every time. But He can and does know that if you had tossed it five times at noon, it would *probably* have fallen "tails" at least once. He knows this because it is true. It is true because, in *most* of the closest worlds in which you tossed the coin five times at noon, it fell tails at least once (in 96.875 percent of them, to be exact).[13] Depending on the details of the design of the red-green device, the probability of the red light's lighting if the button is pressed may be 0.5 or 0.25 or 0.3333 . . . or any other number between 0 and 1. And whatever the probability of the red light's lighting may be (conditional on the button's being pressed), God will know what it is, for this thing, this probability, *is* there to be known.

No matter how probable it may be—short of certainty—that the red light would light if the button were pressed, God does not know whether that light would have lit if the button had been pressed on some occasion when it was not pressed.[14] Even if the probability of "red" is 0.9999999, it will still be true that if the button had been pressed, the red light *might* not have lit, and this proposition is equivalent to the denial of the proposition that, if the button had been pressed, the red light would have lit. As Lewis has pointed out (1973, p. 2), the "would" and "might" conditional connectives are interdefinable:

$$p \mathbin{\square\!\!\rightarrow} q =_{df} \sim(p \mathbin{\lozenge\!\!\rightarrow} \sim q)$$
$$p \mathbin{\lozenge\!\!\rightarrow} q =_{df} \sim(p \mathbin{\square\!\!\rightarrow} \sim q).$$

The second of these schemata suggests another sort of argument for the nonexistence of true counterfactuals of freedom, a very simple argument indeed. Let us suppose that if Curley had been offered a certain bribe (which a building contractor in Chelsea was seriously considering offering him, but, in the end, did not), he would freely have accepted it. I will argue that if free will is incompatible with determinism, then the falsity of this counterfactual of freedom follows from its truth. Assume

  (1) Free will is incompatible with determinism

and

  (2) Curley was offered the bribe $\mathbin{\square\!\!\rightarrow}$ Curley freely accepted the bribe.

Premise (2) entails

  (3) Curley was offered the bribe $\mathbin{\square\!\!\rightarrow}$ Curley was able not to accept the bribe.

Premise (1) and proposition (3) together entail

  (4) Curley was offered the bribe $\mathbin{\lozenge\!\!\rightarrow}$ ~ Curley accepted the bribe.

By the second $\square\!\!\rightarrow$/$\lozenge\!\!\rightarrow$ schema above, proposition (4) entails

  (5) ~ (Curley was offered the bribe $\mathbin{\square\!\!\rightarrow}$ Curley accepted the bribe),

and (5) entails

  ~ (Curley was offered the bribe $\mathbin{\square\!\!\rightarrow}$ Curley freely accepted the bribe),

which is the denial of (2), the counterfactual of freedom with which we started. It is obvious that a parallel argument could be constructed with respect to any counterfactual of freedom.

I wish finally to consider two minor but interesting points about counterfactuals of freedom.

1. Alvin Plantinga has presented a very pretty little argument for the conclusion that there are true counterfactuals of freedom (Plantinga, p. 177). Suppose (he argues) that Curley was offered a bribe of $20,000 and accepted it. Then, surely, it is evident that if he had been offered a bribe of $35,000 on the same occasion to secure the same service, he would have taken it? But then there is at least one true counterfactual of freedom.

One might wonder, however, how we know that Curley would have *freely* accepted the larger bribe. For all anyone but God knows, Curley was able to refuse the smaller bribe but would have been unable to refuse the larger. Well, let us simply *assume* that it is true that he would have been able to refuse the larger bribe. But then—given incompatibilism—we know that if he had been offered the larger bribe, he might have refused it. And how could we know, how could even God know, that what might have happened would not have happened? We certainly could *not* know this (for it would not be true) if 'it might have happened' is logically equivalent to 'it is false that it would not have happened', as it is on Lewis's semantics. (At *t,* I am asked to toss the magical coin once; I immediately do so, and it lands "heads." Do I know that if, at *t,* I had been asked to toss it twice and had immediately done so, it would have landed "heads" at least once? I do not, for that is not true.)

2. If my arguments are correct, they show not only that there are no true counterfactuals of freedom, but that there *could* not be any (for my premises, if they are true at all, are necessary truths). Does it follow that counterfactuals of freedom are necessary falsehoods? That they are is not a formal consequence of my conclusion, since *being a counterfactual of freedom* is an accidental property of those propositions that have it, and it might be that some counterfactuals of freedom are only contingently false because they are true in some worlds in which they are not counterfactuals of freedom. Counterfactuals of freedom are only accidentally counterfactuals of freedom because they are not counterfactuals of freedom (as I have defined the term) in worlds in which their antecedents are true. Proposition (2) above, for example, is not a counterfactual of freedom in those worlds in which Curley was offered the bribe. Might (2) be true in some of these worlds? It not only might be true in some of these worlds but *is* true in some of them on one version of Lewis's semantics, the version that incorporates the assumption of "unweakened centering"—that is, the assumption that no other world is as close to any world as that world is to itself.[15] (And that assumption derives a certain degree of plausibility from the normal associations of words like 'closer' and 'distance'. In their normal, nonmetaphorical sense, these words apply to places, and no other place is as close to any place as that place is to itself. If we think of closeness among worlds as Lewis does, as a function of similarity, the unweakened centering assumption can seem undeniable: if w_1 and w_2 are distinct worlds, then things must go differently in them—and in that case, how could w_2 be as similar to w_1 as w_1 is?[16] Perhaps, however, the assumption can seem less obvious if we think of the distance from w_1 to w_2 as being given by the size of the change in w_1 that would be required to "turn it into" w_2; if w_1 is indeterministic, then it may be that, in one sense, *no change at all* is needed to turn it into a world with which it coincides up to some point in time and in which the same indeterministic laws hold.) On the version of Lewis's semantics that incorporates unweakened centering, '$p \;\square\!\!\rightarrow q$' is a logical consequence of '$p \;\&\; q$', and (2) will therefore be true in any world in which Curley is offered the bribe and takes it. If, however, we reject the unweakened centering assumption—if we accept "weakened centering," if we allow the formal possibility of other worlds that are as close to a world as that world is to itself—there is no formal or logical reason to suppose that there is any counterfactual of freedom that is only contin-

gently false. If, moreover, it is indeed possible for some world to be as close to some other world as the latter is to itself, there would seem to be no reason to doubt the following thesis: For every world *w*, and for every "would" conditional of freedom *p* whose antecedent and consequent are both true in *w*, there is (assuming incompatibilism) a world as close to *w* as *w* is to itself in which the antecedent of *p* is true and its consequent is false. And if that is the case, then every "would" conditional of freedom is a necessary falsehood.

NOTES

1. The brief account of Molina's concept of middle knowledge that is contained in this paragraph is based on Flint (1988). Flint's article may be consulted for citations of Molina and for an overview of the literature on middle knowledge and related topics. Many useful references can also be found in Adams (1977). (I may say that I find little to disagree with in Adams's classic essay, and that there is perhaps little in the present essay that cannot be found, at least in embryo, in Adams. This essay is a rather more technical version of what I have been saying in undergraduate lectures in courses on the philosophy of religion for many years. It is my hope that the reader who finds the general outline of the arguments presented here "old news" will at least find some of the details interesting.)

2. My business in this essay is with counterfactuals of freedom. I will not address the question whether, if there are true counterfactuals of freedom, at least some of them would have to be items of God's middle knowledge in Molina's sense. Nor will I address the question whether my assumption that there is middle knowledge only if there are true counterfactuals of freedom is in fact correct. It should be noted, however, that if God does indeed have middle knowledge of some truths, it cannot be that all of them are true counterfactuals of freedom. It should also be noted that, if true counterfactuals of freedom are possible, it would seem to be possible for at least some true counterfactuals of freedom to belong to God's free knowledge. As to the first point: If a true counterfactual of freedom belongs to God's middle knowledge, then so does any contingent truth that it entails; for example, the material conditional with the same antecedent and consequent. (And if true counterfactuals of freedom are items of God's middle knowledge, then no doubt so are certain "true counterfactuals of indetermination"—such as the counterfactual about the "red-green device" that will be considered later in the body of the essay—that are not themselves counterfactuals of freedom.) As to the latter point: Suppose that in all the closest possible worlds in which Adam is placed in a certain determinate set of circumstances, he freely disobeys God. Then it is true that if he were placed in that set of circumstances, he would freely disobey God. But, consistently with this, we can go on to suppose that there is a world that it is within God's power to actualize in which Adam is not placed in those circumstances and in which it is false that if he were placed in those circumstances he would freely disobey God.

3. My argument for this conclusion will depend on the assumption that every proposition is either true or false. Without this assumption, my argument would show only that no counterfactual of freedom is true. But this conclusion is sufficient to establish the further conclusion that there is no middle knowledge. My argument for the nonexistence of middle knowledge does not therefore depend on my assumption that every proposition is true or false.

4. My official term for the type of conditional of which Lewis's semantics treats is '"would" conditional'. Officially, I apply the term 'counterfactual conditional' only to "would" conditionals with false antecedents. But I shall not usually speak officially. When I am speaking generally about "would" conditionals I shall mostly follow established usage and call them 'counterfactual conditionals' or 'counterfactuals'. But I shall in every case apply the special term 'counterfactual of freedom' to a conditional only if it has a false antecedent.

5. Or, worse, that in the phrase 'counterfactual of freedom', the word 'freedom' is to be understood "in its libertarian sense." I keep telling people not to use the word 'libertarian', but no one listens. There are no "libertarian accounts of freedom," or, more exactly, all incompatibilist accounts of freedom that anyone has actually offered are entirely unsatisfactory. And the word 'freedom' does not have a "libertarian sense," because the compatibilist and the incompatibilist use the word in the same sense.

6. It does not, however, follow that for any given pair of contrary counterfactuals of freedom, one of them will be true. If the mechanisms underlying human deliberation were, although fully deterministic, sufficiently "chaotic"—if small, indeed humanly imperceptible, variations in the conditions under which these mechanisms operated could change the outcome of a deliberation—it might be that both members of many such pairs of contraries were false. Let us suppose that we are compatibilists and determinists. Still, if we believe that the mechanisms that underlie human deliberation are chaotic, we must admit that there are many worlds in which the proposition *Curley was offered a bribe of $20,000 at noon last Friday to permit the destruction of Old North Church* is true. And if we believe that human deliberation is a "chaotic" process, we must admit that, for all we know, there are two such worlds, both of them among the closest worlds in which Curley was offered the bribe, in one of which he freely accepted the bribe and in the other of which he freely refused the bribe. Then it is false that if Curley had been offered a bribe of $20,000 at noon last Friday to permit the destruction of Old North Church, he would freely have accepted it—and false that he would freely have refused it. And we should generalize this concession: for all we know, both members of many such pairs of contraries are false, owing to the extreme sensitivity of the outcome of human deliberation to imperceptible variations in the conditions under which that deliberation is carried out.

7. Lewis (1973).

8. Or, to be pedantic, the probability that this is what the observer would see would approach 1 as the number of replayings increased without limit.

9. Here is another way they could both be false in *w:* suppose that for every world in which the common antecedent of the two counterfactuals is true and he steals, there is a world closer to *w* in which the antecedent is true and he does not steal; and that for every world in which the common antecedent of the two counterfactuals is true and he does not steal, there is a world closer to *w* in which the antecedent is true and he steals.

10. This paragraph contains some allusions to the discussion in Lewis (1979) of the factors that are relevant to judgments of overall similarity among worlds. The reader can follow the argument of the present essay without understanding the allusions.

11. As is *w*, which is specified as follows: a world that coincides with α up to some point after the thief has begun his deliberations, in which a noise frightens him away before he can reach a decision, and which is such that α is among the worlds closest to it in which the thief completes his deliberations.

12. And even if we neglect the fact that these worlds are indeterministic, we should note that there are lots of ways in which the event by which β diverges from α—the thief's deciding to steal—might happen. (The thief might take a shorter or longer time to decide to steal; he might decide to put the money in his left pocket or his right pocket.) If, therefore, the physical world is at all "chaotic" then the worlds in which the thief decides to steal might differ radically from one another, some being more like *w* than α is. (Cf. n 6.)

13. No doubt there are infinitely many possible worlds. If there are infinitely many worlds, no doubt there are infinitely many worlds in which the coin is tossed five times and falls "tails" at least once and also infinitely many worlds (an infinity of the same cardinality) in which the coin is tossed five times and falls "heads" every time. What we are supposing is that many infinite sets of worlds have a "size," a measure, that is not determined by their cardinality. Sets of possible worlds are thus analogous to sets of points on a plane, many of which have sizes or measures that are not determined by their cardinalities: one set of points may occupy two square feet, and another set of the same cardinality (the power of the continuum) may occupy one square foot—or a square light-year or square micron. In my view, it is impossible to make

sense of probabilities without making this assumption. When I say that the coin falls "tails" at least once in 96.875 percent of the worlds in which it is tossed five times, I mean that the ratio of the measure of the set of worlds in which the coin falls "tails" at least once out of the five times it is tossed to the measure of the whole set of worlds in which it is tossed five times is 96.875.

14.   A set of points may easily have the same area as one of its proper subsets. No doubt the same thing may hold, *mutatis mutandis,* for sets of worlds and their measures. There is, therefore, at least a formal possibility that $p \;\square\!\!\rightarrow q$ might be false even if the probability of q, given p, is 1. I shall not explore the implications of this formal possibility for the problem of God's middle knowledge.

15.   See Lewis (1973), pp. 14–15, 26–31.

16.   But see Lewis (1973), p. 29.

REFERENCES

Adams, Robert Merrihew. 1977. "Middle Knowledge and the Problem of Evil." *American Philosophical Quarterly* 14: 109–17.

Flint, Thomas P. 1988. "Two Accounts of Providence." In Morris.

Lewis, David. 1973. *Counterfactuals.* Cambridge, Mass.

———. 1979. "Counterfactual Dependence and Time's Arrow." *Noûs* 13: 455–76.

Morris, Thomas V., ed. 1988. *Divine and Human Action: Essays in the Metaphysics of Theism.* Notre Dame, Ind.

Plantinga, Alvin. 1974. *The Nature of Necessity.* Oxford.

Van Inwagen, Peter. 1983. *An Essay on Free Will.* Oxford.

Mencius on Courage

BRYAN W. VAN NORDEN

M*encius* 2A2 is one of the most interesting passages in this classic Confucian text.[1] It is, therefore, not surprising that it has occasioned an extensive secondary literature in English. David S. Nivison, Jeffrey Riegel, Kwong-loi Shun, and Lee Yearley have all written important essays on this passage.[2] Most of the scholarly literature so far has focused on Mencius's intriguing critique of the rival philosopher Gaozi, in "verses" 9 through 16.[3] Despite the emphasis of previous scholarship on verses 9 through 16, the passage opens with a tantalizing discussion of *yong,* normally translated "courage," in verses 1 through 8. In this essay, I shall discuss Mencius's conception of courage, using the opening of 2A2 as my focus. I hope to render the passage less cryptic and show that Mencius, in fact, has a nuanced and philosophically defensible account of courage.

Before I turn to the text of 2A2, I want to situate my discussion by providing a brief overview of some Western and early Confucian views about courage. To begin with Western philosophical discussions of courage is *not* to assume that Western approaches are the paradigm against which all non-Western philosophy must be measured.[4] However, since I (and many of my readers) have been deeply influenced by Western concepts, it will be helpful to begin by clarifying our own understanding of courage. We shall see that courage is a disputed notion even if we limit our discussion to the West. Then, turning to the *Analects,* we will see that many of the issues regarding courage that are raised in the Western tradition are also dealt with in the early Confucian tradition.[5]

People generally agree that courage is a good quality to have. In other words, courage is generally agreed to be a virtue rather than a vice. Furthermore, courage is somehow connected with fear, because courage seems to involve doing things that most people would regard as fearful. Beyond this, though, there are many substantive points of disagreement. I'll mention a few areas of dispute. (1) When we think of courage, we often think immediately of courageous *behavior.* It might seem, at first, that courage consists in *doing* things like rescuing children from burning buildings, or charging against the enemy in battle. However, a little reflection suggests that no *behavior* or even *kinds* of behavior by themselves are courageous or cowardly. To use a well-worn example from Plato, running away from the enemy seems paradigmatic of cowardice. However, the Spartans pioneered the tactic of strategically retreating to draw the enemy forward, and then turning suddenly and counterattacking. Although it involves running away from the enemy (at least at first), the Spartans' tactic is courageous, not cowardly.[6] To pick a more up-to-date example, in the movie *The Guns of Navarone* there is a scene in which a partisan grovels and begs for mercy from his Nazi captor. Groveling and begging for mercy is stereotypically cowardly. However this partisan does so only to make his captor let down his guard long enough so that he can grab his weapon and shoot him. Thus, the partisan's action was, in fact, courageous. So it seems that courage is not determined by *what* actions we perform, but, in some sense, by *how* we perform those actions.[7]

(2) Does acting courageously require acting *in spite of fear?* Or is the courageous person the one who is *not afraid?* The philosopher Philippa Foot nicely summed up the dilemma:

> we both are and are not inclined to think that the harder a man finds it to act virtuously the more virtue he shows if he does act well. . . . Who shows most courage, the one who wants to run away but does not, or the one who does not even want to run away?[8]

To provide some specific examples, there seems to be, on the one hand, something admirable in Sydney Carton's equanimity on the scaffold as he selflessly sacrifices himself for the one he loves in Dickens' *A Tale of Two Cities.* On the other hand, there seems something almost inhuman and absurd about someone who is completely indifferent to his or her own death or injury. One is reminded of Mel Gibson's character in *Lethal Weapon,* who seems not so much courageous as insane, because his character really is not afraid of dying.

(3) How is courage related to other virtues? I said earlier that courage is a good quality to have. But consider a Mafia hitman. It *may* be a compliment to say that he is a courageous murderer—carrying out his "contract" in the face of risks that most of us would find quite fearsome. But the hitman's "courage" makes him better at doing bad things. If there are to be hitmen in the world, we would prefer them all to be cowardly. Some would say that this shows that courage is sometimes a bad thing for a person to have. However, others would say that the quality the hitman possesses is not "courage" at all. Rather, it is a *semblance* of courage, such as rashness, a semblance being a quality that is not a true virtue, but superficially resembles one.[9] Courage, on this second view, requires the presence of other virtues, such as practical wisdom and benevolence, while rashness is a semblance of courage sometimes found in those who lack other virtues.

In summary: first, it seems that courage is *not* just a matter of certain kinds of *behavior.* Second, there is disagreement about whether courage requires genuine fearlessness or instead requires acting in spite of fear. Third, there is disagreement about whether courage requires the presence of other virtues, such as practical wisdom.

I. COURAGE IN THE *ANALECTS*

What did Confucians in ancient China think about issues like these? The *Analects* of Confucius gives a sense for some of the views regarding courage that were prevalent in early China. The *Analects* is, of course, a composite text. It was composed by many hands over many years.[10] Some parts of it probably represent things Confucius actually said, while other attributions in it are apocryphal. On this much, almost all scholars agree. Disagreement arises when we attempt to determine which parts of the *Analects* are authentic and which are not. However, for the purposes of this essay, it doesn't make much difference which portions of the *Analects* are authentic. My point in citing it is only to establish some of the views regarding courage that were "in the air," as it were, in ancient China. Whether Confucius himself actually held any of these views is, for my purposes in this essay, moot.

One of the key figures connected with courage in the text of the *Analects* is Confucius's disciple Zilu. In *Analects* 5:7, Confucius remarks, "The Way is not put into practice. If I were to get on a boat and float out to sea, I suppose [Zilu] would accompany me?" Zilu heard this and was pleased, apparently thinking that Confucius was complimenting his loyalty. However, Confucius went on to remark, "[Zilu] is more fond of courage than I."

That Zilu was obsessed with courage is suggested by another passage, *Analects* 17:21, in which he asks Confucius, "Is a noble supremely courageous?" Confucius once again tries to temper Zilu's regard for courage, saying, "Nobles regard righteousness as supreme. If nobles have courage but are without righteousness, then they will be chaotic. If petty people have courage but are without righteousness, then they will be thieves."

One might wonder, based on these passages, whether Confucius and other early Confucians thought of *yong* as a virtue at all. (Indeed, perhaps we should be translating *yong* as "rashness" rather than "courage"!) However, other passages in the *Analects* suggest a positive role for courage in a virtuous life. Indeed, both *Analects* 9:29 and 14:28 present what appears to be a list of three cardinal virtues, of which courage is one: "Those who are wise are not confused; those who are humane are not anxious; those who are courageous are not afraid." Similarly, in Chapter 20 of the *Zhongyong,* a work usually known in English as *The Doctrine of the Mean,* it says, "Wisdom, humaneness and courage—these three are the universal virtues (*de*) of the world." It seems clear, then, that at least some early Confucians regarded *yong* or courage as a virtue.

Other passages in the *Analects* provide more detail about the relationship between courage and other virtues. Thus, from *Analects* 14:4 we learn that, "Those who are humane must be courageous; [but] those who are courageous need not be humane." In other words, those who are fully virtuous will be courageous, but courage is possible in the absence of genuine virtue. As Alasdair

MacIntyre has noted, this suggests that early Confucians did not accept what is known in the West as the doctrine of the "unity of the virtues."[11] Finally, important for our later discussion of *Mencius* 2A2 is *Analects* 2:24, which advises us, "To see what is right and not act is to fail to be courageous."[12] This passage links courage and "what is right" in a manner reminiscent of what Mencius will later do in *Mencius* 2A2. We see, then, that there was general interest and concern among early Confucians about courage and its relationship to other virtues. It is not surprising that Mencius, too, should address this issue.

II. *MENCIUS 2A2*

A. Verses 1 to 3

Let us turn now to *Mencius* 2A2. The text begins with Mencius being presented with a hypothetical question by his disciple Gongsun Chou.[13] If Mencius were to be made prime minister of Qi, Gongsun Chou suggests, it would not be surprising if the lord of Qi were to become a king or at least ruler of the feudal lords.[14] If this were to happen to you, Mencius, would it "perturb your heart"? Mencius replies that it would not. His heart, he explains, has "not been perturbed" since he was forty. The expression "perturb one's heart" occurs in only two passages in the *Mencius*, here in 2A2 and in 6B15. The phrase is not defined in either passage, but both contexts suggest that for something to perturb one's heart is for it to disturb or frighten one.[15] Thus, to have an "unperturbed heart" is to fail to be disturbed or frightened.[16]

Gongsun Chou next suggests that, in having achieved an "unperturbed heart," Mencius has surpassed someone named "Meng Ben." Mencius responds that what he has achieved is not all that difficult. After all, says Mencius, "Gaozi had an unperturbed heart before I did." We know little about Meng Ben. The Han Dynasty commentator Zhao Qi reports simply that he was "a courageous knight." The Qing Dynasty commentator Jiao Xun has culled a few more references to him in some early texts. Typical is the statement that "Meng Ben, when travelling by water did not avoid serpents, and when travelling by land did not avoid rhinoceroses and tigers." I think it tells us something interesting about Gongsun Chou that he should pick such a person as an example of someone who is "unperturbed." (Compare a contemporary American whose idea of a courageous person is "Rambo.")

We know more about Gaozi. He was a rival philosopher whom Mencius criticizes later in 2A2, and with whom Mencius debated in Book 6A. As I noted earlier, there is already an extensive body of literature discussing Gaozi. Consequently, I will limit myself here to suggesting that my interpretation of the opening of 2A2 is consistent with Mencius's comments about Gaozi elsewhere in the text.[17]

Gongsun Chou next asks, "Is there a Way to have an unperturbed heart?" Mencius says that there is and then refers to four people, three of whom explicitly "cultivated courage." This is the first time the term *yong*, courage, is mentioned in the discussion. However, I have suggested that to have an unperturbed heart is to not be disturbed or frightened, so being courageous can be seen as, at least, one way in which one can have an unperturbed heart.

B. Translation of Verses 4 to 8

What are we supposed to learn about courage from the paradigms provided by the four individuals to whom Mencius refers? Let's start answering this question by reading what Mencius says about them in verses 4 through 8:

(iv) As for Bogong You's cultivation of courage, his body would not shrink, his eyes would not blink. He regarded the least slight from someone like being beaten in the market place. [Insults] he would not accept from a coarsely clad fellow he also would not accept from a lord of ten thousand chariots. He looked upon running [a sword] through a lord of ten thousand chariots like running through a common fellow. He did not revere the various lords. If an insult came his way he had to return it.

(v) As for Meng Shishe's cultivation of courage, he said,

I look upon defeat the same as victory. To advance only after sizing up one's enemy, to ponder [whether one will achieve] victory and only then join [battle], this is to be in awe of the opposing armies. How can I be certain of victory? I can only be without fear.

(vi) Meng Shishe resembled Master Zeng. Bogong You resembled Zixia. Now, as for the courage of the two, I do not really know which was better. Nonetheless, Meng Shishe preserved something important (*yue*).

(vii) Formerly, Master Zeng speaking to Zixiang said, "Are you fond of courage? I once heard about great courage from the Master:[18]

If I examine myself and am not upright (*su*) although [I am opposed by] a coarsely clad fellow, I would be afraid.[19] If I examine myself and am upright, although [I am opposed by] thousands and tens of thousands, I shall go forward."[20]

(viii) Meng Shishe's preservation of his *qi* was still not as good as Master Zeng's preservation of what is important (*yue*).

So we need to know about four individuals: Bogong You, Meng Shishe, Master Zeng, and Zixia. We know almost nothing about Bogong You and Meng Shishe outside of what this passage tells us. Fortunately, we do have additional information about Master Zeng and Zixia. Both were disciples of Confucius, and the *Analects* sketches a pretty clear picture of each.

C. Zixia and Master Zeng

Zixia was apparently very acute intellectually. In *Analects* 3:8 Confucius compliments Zixia on his interpretation of one of the classic odes. In addition, Zixia is identified as being outstanding in "culture and learning" in *Analects* 11:3. That Zixia placed great emphasis upon learning is also suggested by some of the quotations attributed to him, several of which discuss learning (19:5,6,7). Apparently, Confucius's other disciples also regarded Zixia as especially smart. For example, in *Analects* 12:22, Fan Chi receives a teaching from Confucius and is unsure about its meaning. Consequently, he seeks out Zixia to explain it to him.

But Zixia also had certain characteristic weaknesses. Confucius found it necessary to admonish Zixia, "Be a noble scholar (*ru*), not a petty scholar" (6:13). In addition, when Zixia came to occupy a government office, Confucius thought it wise to offer him the following advice: "Do not see petty profits. . . . If you see petty profits, the great tasks will not be accomplished" (13:17). Once again, other disciples apparently agreed with Confucius's judgment: in 19:12, fellow Confucian Ziyou carps,

> The disciples and younger followers of Zixia are acceptable when it comes to sweeping and cleaning, responding and replying, coming forward and withdrawing. But these are only details (*mo*). As for what is basic (*ben*), they lack it. What is one to do with them?

Master Zeng was, in many ways, the very opposite of Zixia. Whereas Zixia was smart, Master Zeng is bluntly characterized in *Analects* 11:18 as "stupid" (*lu*). Furthermore, the quotations attributed to Master Zeng in the *Analects,* while often quite moving, do not, in general, suggest an acute mind.[21] What the *Analects* does suggest about Master Zeng is that he had an intense personal commitment to being a good person. It was, after all, Master Zeng who famously said, "I daily examine myself on three counts"—loyalty, faithfulness, and practice (1:4). Perhaps especially relevant to the contrast between Master Zeng and Zixia is *Analects* 8:4, where Master Zeng says,

> There are three things that a noble, in following the Way, places above all the rest: from every attitude, every gesture that one employs one must remove all trace of violence or arrogance; every look that one composes in one's face must betoken good faith; from every word that one utters, from every intonation, one must remove all trace of coarseness or impropriety. As to the ordering of ritual vessels and the like, there are those whose business it is to attend to such matters.[22]

We may safely assume, I think, that the phrase "those whose business it is to attend" to "the ordering of ritual vessels and the like" is meant as a put-down of people like Zixia.

How would Mencius have thought about these characterizations? Although it is common to speak of "Confucianism" as if it were a monolithic movement, there were in fact different, competing Confucian sects soon after the death of Confucius. Master Zeng and Zixia each founded a sect. Now, Zhao Qi, the Han Dynasty commentator, says that Mencius was a student of Confucius's grandson, Zisi, while the Han historian Sima Qian claims that Mencius studied, not under Zisi himself, but under the *disciples* of Zisi. Whichever account is correct, the important point here is that Zisi is reputed to have studied under Master Zeng. So Mencius is, as it were, in the spiritual line of descent from Master Zeng. So we can expect Mencius to favor Master Zeng over Zixia.

In fact, another passage in the *Mencius* confirms that our philosopher favored Master Zeng over Zixia. *Mencius* 3A4, verse 13, provides the following story. After the death of Confucius, three of his disciples—including Zixia—thinking that someone named You Ruo "was similar to" Confucius, wanted to serve him, in the way that they had served Confucius, and tried to force Master Zeng to join them. However, Master Zeng refused, suggesting that no one could compare to Confucius. This anecdote is perfectly in line with the characterization of Zixia as superficial.

Master Zeng is, in fact, quoted a number of times in the *Mencius.* Several of these citations stress the fact that Master Zeng excelled at filial piety (3A2, 4A20, 7B36). Typical of these passages is 7B36, which says that, after his father died, there was a certain sort of date that Master Zeng could never again bring himself to eat—because it had been his father's favorite. As we shall see, at least one interpreter sees Master Zeng's filial piety as being important to understanding 2A2.

D. Bogong You and Meng Shishe

Now, what does *Mencius* 2A2 indicate about the other two individuals mentioned in the passage, Bogong You and Meng Shishe? There is one important similarity between the two: both fail to distinguish or discriminate aspects of the situations they are in. Of Bogong You, the text says, "He regarded [*si*] the least slight from someone *like* being beaten in the market place. . . . He looked upon [*shi*] running [a sword] through a lord of ten thousand chariots *like* running through a common fellow." Similarly, Meng Shishe says, "I look upon defeat *the same as* victory." (In contrast, we shall see that Master Zeng's courage involves being much more discriminating about one's situation.)

The text also suggests that there are important differences between Bogong You and Meng Shishe. Note that the description of Bogong You is largely (although not exclusively) a description of Bogong You's actions. This is not to deny that Bogong You's courage involves "looking at" or "perceiving" the world in a distinctive (albeit undiscriminating) way. However, it seems clear that, for Bogong You, a major component of courage is *behaving* in certain ways.

In contrast, for Meng Shishe courage consists in being "without fear," regardless of the likelihood of victory or defeat.[23] Notice that we have no corresponding description of Bogong You's emotional state. (Indeed, for all we know, Bogong You acts as he does because he is terrified of being humiliated or defeated.) Notice also that the text gives us a third-person description of Bogong You and a first-person description of Meng Shishe. This stylistic factor reflects, I think, Meng Shishe's emphasis upon the first-person, emotional aspect of courage, and Bogong You's emphasis upon the third-person, behavioral aspect of courage. In summary, there is an important respect in which the courage of Meng

Shishe is similar to that of Bogong You: neither emphasizes discrimination or judgment about the situations they are in. However, Meng Shishe's courage is distinct in that it specifically requires the absence of fear.

E. Verse 6: How Is Meng Shishe Like Master Zeng and Bogong You Like Zixia?

Given what we have learned about Zixia, Master Zeng, Bogong You, and Meng Shishe, we can make sense of Mencius's next comment, in verse 6: "Meng Shishe resembled Master Zeng. Bogong You resembled Zixia. Now, as for the courage of the two, I do not really know which was better. Nonetheless, Meng Shishe preserved something important (yue)." Zixia was accused of emphasizing insignificant and petty matters of detail—things like "sweeping and cleaning"—over the real substance of virtue. Similarly, Mencius is suggesting, Bogong You attends to superficial manifestations of courage in behavior.

How, then, is Meng Shishe similar to Master Zeng? In his commentary on this text, Zhao Qi offers the following suggestion:

> Mencius regards Master Zeng as outstanding in filial piety. Filial piety is the basis of all [other] activities. Although Zixia knew many things, this is still not as great as Master Zeng's filial piety. Hence, [Mencius] compares [Meng Shi-] She to Master Zeng, and [Bogong] You to Zixia. Since [Meng] Shishe's aim was not to be afraid, he aimed at what is important. (Commentary on 2A2.6)[24]

Thus, this commentary suggests that Master Zeng and Meng Shishe are similar in that each emphasizes something that is of central importance—filial piety and being fearless, respectively—whereas Zixia and Bogong You emphasize things that are peripheral, and less important—things like "sweeping and cleaning" and stereotypically courageous actions, respectively. This interpretive hypothesis seems very plausible because it provides a comprehensible explanation of what Mencius is saying, and also fits in with what we understand about Master Zeng and Zixia from other texts. (This is the most we can ask of any interpretation.) So Mencius is making two parallel points: first, the kinds of virtues that Master Zeng had, especially filial piety, are a more important part of being a good person than the ritual and intellectual activities that Zixia emphasized; similarly, being fearless is a more important part of being courageous than is just acting in stereotypically courageous ways.

This is surely *part* of the message that Mencius wants to convey, but I believe there is more. I have suggested that Meng Shishe was more concerned with what we might describe as the emotional aspect of courage, whereas Bogong You emphasized the behavioral manifestations of courage. This too, I submit, has an analogue in the differences between Master Zeng and Zixia, for, as we saw, Master Zeng showed a strong, personal, emotional commitment to the Confucian Way, whereas Zixia emphasized the behavioral manifestations of Confucianism. Perhaps this is what the Song Dynasty philosopher Zhu Xi is hinting at when he remarks, in his commentary on this passage, that "Master Zeng reflected and 'sought it within himself'."[25]

Finally, is it relevant to the comparison that Zixia was intelligent and learned? At first, I thought not. However, the Qing Dynasty commentator Jiao Xun has an interesting observation on this point:

> Bogong You in all affairs sought to defeat others. Hence, he is similar to Zixia, who knew many things. Meng Shishe did not ask whether he was necessarily able to defeat others or not. He simply concentrated upon maintaining his own fearlessness. Hence, he is similar to Master Zeng, who grasped what is great in the Way. (Commentary on 2A2.6)

In other words, this commentary suggests that Zixia's desire for learning was a manifestation of his desire to be better than others, rather than a commitment to virtue for its own sake. And in his passion for victory over others, he is like Bogong You. Again, this interpretation seems plausible because it makes sense of what Mencius is saying and fits in with what we know about the individuals involved.

In summary, there are at least three respects in which Master Zeng and Meng Shishe may be contrasted with Zixia and Bogong You. (1) The former emphasize what is centrally important, while the latter emphasize what is peripheral and less important. (2) The former emphasize certain emotional states, while the latter emphasize behavior. (3) The former emphasize achieving their own excellence, while the latter emphasize being better than others.

F. Verses 7 to 8: Master Zeng on Courage

In verse 7, Mencius tells us about Master Zeng's own views on courage, once again giving a first-person account:

> Formerly, Master Zeng speaking to [his disciple] Zixiang said, "Are you fond of courage? I once heard about great courage from the Master:
>
>> If I examine myself and am not upright, although [I am opposed by] a coarsely clad fellow, I would be afraid. If I examine myself and am upright, although [I am opposed by] thousands and tens of thousands, I shall go forward."

Here, Master Zeng explicitly links courage with being a good person,[26] and uses the rhetorical device of paradox to make his point. The expression "a coarsely clad fellow" suggests someone who is poor and lacking in social status. Mencius's literati audience would find nothing fearsome about such a person. In contrast, most people *would* find fearsome being opposed by "thousands and tens of thousands." In contrast, "the Master" says that, if, upon self-examination, he finds that he is in the wrong, then even if the person opposing him is not fearsome, he *would* be afraid. In other words, he is suggesting that one ought to be afraid of doing what is not "upright."[27] Furthermore, if self-examination reveals that he is doing what is right, then the Master would continue to pursue the correct course of action, regardless of how powerful his opponents are.

Mencius invidiously compares this sort of courage to that of Meng Shishe in verse 8, saying, "Meng Shishe's preservation of his *qi* was still not as good as Master Zeng's preservation of what is important (*yue*)." Explaining this line requires saying a little bit about what *qi* is. This is really a topic unto itself, and here I can sketch only some of the uses of this concept. *Qi* can refer to mist generally (clouds, fog, etc.) and breath. More esoterically, *qi* was thought of as a kind of fluid, found in both the atmosphere and the human body, responsible for the intensity of one's emotions. For example, in the *Zuo zhuan,* we find the comment, "The people have likes, dislikes, delight, anger, sorrow and joy. These are generated by the six *qi.*"[28] Consequently, in saying that Meng Shishe preserved his *qi,* Mencius is saying that he controlled his emotions. Specifically, he controlled the emotion of fear.

In contrast, Master Zeng preserves something more "important" than fearlessness alone. Specifically, Master Zeng preserves, and acts on, his sense of "uprightness." Some confusion might be occasioned here by the fact that Meng Shishe is himself described, earlier in 2A2, as having "preserved something important." The point is presumably that fearlessness and uprightness are both important parts of courage. Consequently, in being fearless, Meng Shishe preserved "something important" in comparison with Bogong You. However, Mencius holds that uprightness is a more important aspect of courage than fearlessness alone. Consequently, in being upright, Master Zeng recognized a more important aspect of courage than did Meng Shishe. In other words, Mencius's point is that what is really important in courage is not simply being without fear regardless of the circumstances; rather, the highest courage involves responding to one's situation in a virtuous manner.

So *Mencius* 2A2, verses 4 through 8, present us with a hierarchy of kinds of courage. The lowest sort of courage is that of Bogong You, who simply acts in stereotypically courageous ways. Meng Shishe recognizes a more important aspect of courage: fearlessness. But Master Zeng has grasped the most important aspect of courage: being virtuous.

2A2 continues with Gongsun Chou asking Mencius to explain the difference between his own "unperturbed heart" and that of the rival philosopher, Gaozi. I think Gongsun Chou had a very good reason for being curious about this. Gaozi was *like* Mencius, but unlike Bogong You or Meng Shishe, in being concerned with righteousness. However, as we learn from both book 6A of the *Mencius* and 2A2 itself, Gaozi had very different views from Mencius about the proper way to *cultivate* righteousness.[29]

III. THE FULLY COURAGEOUS AND FEAR

There are obvious connections between Mencius's views on courage and the other Confucian views we found in the *Analects.* In both the *Mencius* and the *Analects* (14:4), the fully virtuous will be courageous, but as the examples of Bogong You and Meng Shishe demonstrate, the courageous need not be fully virtuous. In addition, recall that the *Analects* claims that "To see what is right and not act is to fail to be courageous" (2:24). This is reminiscent of the connection Mencius sees between being courageous and being "upright."[30] On one issue, however, it is not obvious whether Mencius is continuing or departing from the *Analects*' view of courage. The *Analects* twice says, "those who are courageous are not afraid." Now, recall the saying attributed to "the Master" in verse 7 of 2A2:

(a) If I examine myself and am not upright, although [I am opposed by] a coarsely clad fellow, I would be afraid. (b) If I examine myself and am upright, although [I am opposed by] thousands and tens of thousands, I shall go forward.

There are at least two ways to interpret the significance of the first sentence in this quotation, which I have labeled (a) for convenience of reference. (1) It may mean that true courage requires being afraid if one finds that one is in the wrong. (2) However, it may be that (a) does not describe "great courage"; rather, only the second sentence, (b), describes "great courage."[31] In other words, on the interpretation being considered, being afraid when one recognizes that one is not upright is *not* part of "great courage"; rather, "great courage" consists only in "going forward" when one recognizes that one is upright. Which reading is correct? In favor of the first reading is the fact that (a) is immediately preceded by Master Zeng introducing the topic of "great courage." Having just introduced the topic of "great courage," it is somewhat misleading for Master Zeng to immediately quote something that does not illustrate this virtue. However, there are several reasons for believing that (b) alone describes "great courage." First, as we have seen, the view that the courageous are fearless was common among at least some other early Confucians. Second, Meng Shishe, who is fearless, is described earlier in 2A2 as preserving "something important."

It also seems to be the view of several recent Western interpreters of Mencius that a morally perfected person will feel no fear. Thus, Donald Munro suggests that one of the goals of the Confucian process of self-cultivation is "tranquility," and says (specifically discussing 2A2), "When one has successfully carried through this process, external objects will be unable to move the bodily [qi], causing it, in turn, to move the mind; instead, the mind will be in control of the external objects and will stay on the straight path."[32] Similarly, Lee Yearley has argued that "Mencius's depiction of perfect courage seems to describe a state in which the truly courageous person has no fear of the objectionable results, of the loss of real goods."[33]

Although Mencius holds that the fully courageous are completely fearless, he also seems to hold that a fully courageous person has a vivid awareness of the goods that one may have to sacrifice if one is to do what courage requires. For example, in both 3B1 and 5B7, Mencius approvingly quotes what appears to be a saying: "Purposeful scholars do not forget that they may end up in a ditch or gutter. Courageous scholars do not forget that they may lose their heads." In addition, Mencius holds that the courageous value their lives, even when they are willing to sacrifice them. Thus, in 6A10, he says,

> Life is something I want, and righteousness is also something I want. If I cannot succeed in getting them together, I shall forsake life and choose righteousness. Life is something that I want, [but] there are things that I want more than life. Hence, I will not do just anything to obtain it.

Indeed, Mencius is critical of those who would carelessly give up their lives, as is shown by 4B23, where he remarks, "If it is permissible to die, [but also] permissible not to die, to die is an abuse of courage."

So, Mencius holds that fully courageous individuals are fearless. But Mencius also holds that the fully courageous act with awareness of the goods they are sacrificing, and are not indifferent to their own well-being. This suggests a philosophical problem, though. Is it even coherent to suggest that I anticipate sacrificing some great good, yet am not afraid? Admittedly, some anticipated sacrifices need not occasion fear. I anticipate that I must forgo buying new speakers for my sound system, because it is more important to buy new tires for our car, and we cannot afford both. This irritates me, but does not frighten me.[34] However, new speakers are merely something I *want,* not something I *need.* Does it really make sense to say that I anticipate sacrificing something necessary for my well-being, such as my own life, yet am not afraid?

Perhaps we can rescue Mencius from this difficulty by distinguishing between *being afraid* and *feeling afraid.* It does seem to me, at least, that it is possible for one to greatly value one's own life, and regret its loss, without actually *feeling* fear. I think James Wallace, in his discussion of courage, makes an important point in this regard:

> In thinking of fear, there is a tendency to think exclusively of the set of physiological occurrences and feelings that accompany panic and terror.... Such physical changes and the feelings that accompany them, however, are but one aspect or facet of fear, which is a far more complex and complicated phenomenon.... Being afraid of something can be thought of as a syndrome of symptoms: in a particular case, certain symptoms may be particularly pronounced while other symptoms may be slight or even missing altogether.[35]

If this is correct, then I may be afraid to die even if I do not actually have the subjective feeling of fear. And perhaps it is only the subjective feeling of fear that, according to Mencius, the fully courageous lack. It is worth noting, though, that this is a very speculative suggestion, as the text of the *Mencius* does not directly address this issue. We do not yet know enough about Mencius's psychological and physiological views to judge this issue with any degree of confidence.

The statement that the Mencian sage is "unperturbed" must be qualified in another way as well. In one of the most famous passages in the *Mencius* (2A6), our philosopher says,

The reason why I say that humans all have hearts that will not bear [the suffering of] others is this. Suppose someone suddenly saw a child about to fall into a well: everyone [in such a situation] would have *a feeling of alarm* [*chu ti*] *and compassion.*

Mencius must think that sages, like ordinary people, have hearts that will not bear the suffering of others. Indeed, Mencius's view is that sages have *heightened* concern for others. And a feeling of "alarm" is a sort of perturbation; it even seems properly described as a sort of fear. So even sages can be "perturbed." More direct evidence that sages can, in some sense, be perturbed comes from 5A1, which states that the sage Shun "cried out and wept to the autumn sky" because his parents did not love him. Shun's sadness would seem to be a kind of perturbation. How can Mencius reconcile his suggestion that the fully courageous are unperturbed with the admission that even sages can be alarmed or greatly saddened?

I submit that the examples Mencius uses suggest that there are at least two ways in which the fear or perturbation of the sage differs from that of those who are not courageous. First, the *objects* of the fear of sages differ from the objects of noncourageous fear.[36] Master Zeng, it seems, is not "perturbed" by the possibility that *he* will be harmed, even if acting righteously requires putting his life at risk. However, anyone who saw a child about to fall into a well would be alarmed *for the sake of the child.* Likewise, 5A1 specifically says that Shun had available to him sex, wealth, and prestige, so Shun did *not* weep to the autumn sky because he lacked these things. Instead, Shun was perturbed because his parents did not love him. And this is a perfectly virtuous concern. So Mencius's examples suggest that the *objects* of the perturbations of the fully courageous differ from the objects of the perturbations of the unvirtuous.

A second difference, I submit, is that sages manifest "motivational harmony" even when perturbed.[37] For example, *I* am not fully virtuous myself. If *I* recognize that doing the right thing requires endangering my own well-being, *I* will feel fear, because my strong desire for my own well-being will conflict with my desire to do what is right. *I* feel fear because my motivations are in conflict. We might say that I am "of two minds." In contrast, even when a Mencian sage is perturbed or afraid, the sage still possesses "motivational harmony." Specifically, a sage who has a feeling of alarm because a child is about to fall into a well is not of two minds and is not pulled in two directions about what to do. The only thing the sage wants to do is to save the child. Likewise, Shun does not weep because he finds his motivations pulling him in two directions. He wants only that his parents should love him.

Consequently, careful examination of what Mencius says about courage and perturbation suggests the following conclusions. Those who are fully virtuous lack a particular sort of fear. Specifically, although the fully virtuous value their own well-being, they do not feel fear when righteousness requires them to sacrifice their lives. In addition, the fully courageous may be frightened by the prospect of the suffering of others, and may be saddened by the absence of things

like familial love. However, even when perturbed in these ways, the fully courageous continue to manifest motivational harmony.

IV. A PARTIAL DEFENSE OF MENCIUS

I have tried to argue that, when we come to understand the intellectual, historical,
and literary background against which he spoke, we can see that Mencius is presenting a detailed and nuanced typology of courage in the opening of 2A2. In
addition, we have seen that he takes stands on many of the philosophical issues
regarding courage that I noted at the opening of this essay. However, those familiar with Western discussions of courage might perceive a weakness in Mencius's account. Specifically, in 2A2, Mencius makes clear *that* he prefers the courage of Master Zeng to that of either Meng Shishe or Bogong You, and he makes
clear *what* is distinctive about the courage of each, but he does not explain *why*
the courage of Master Zeng is superior to the other two kinds. This might lead
us to conclude either that Mencius is not a philosopher, or that, if Mencius is a
philosopher, he is not a very good one. I think either of these conclusions would
be precipitate.

One point we should keep in mind is that Gongsun Chou is one of Mencius's disciples, and he is asking for *clarification* of the nature of courage. Gongsun Chou did not ask for a *justification* of the claim that Master Zeng's courage
is superior. Consequently, it is not surprising that Mencius does not provide such
a justification in this passage. Furthermore, it is often the case that Mencius's
arguments on a given topic are spread out over a number of different passages.
What I want to do next is to survey some of what Mencius says about courage in
other passages, and argue that he *does* provide some justification for his hierarchy
in 2A2. Mencius's general line of argument is this: those who possess the lesser
forms of courage will be led to perform actions that frustrate the achievement
of goals and concerns they can be expected to have.

A. Passing Comments on Courage: Mencius 4B30 and 7B1

A passing remark in 4B30 is illuminating. In a catalogue of things that are unfilial,
Mencius includes "being fond of courage and conflict so as to endanger one's parents." One can easily see how the mindless bravado of a Bogong You, or the undiscriminating fearlessness of a Meng Shishe, could lead one to acquire enemies
who would be threats to one's parents. And it is not only children who might
endanger family members with their rashness. In 7B1, Mencius laments, "Un-
benevolent was King Hui of Liang!" He goes on to relate that King Hui fought
a war for the sake of territory and suffered a great defeat. The king decided to
launch another campaign and sent his own son to lead it. The son died in battle.
Mencius remarks, King Hui *"was afraid that he would be unable to be victorious.
Hence, he urged the son whom he loved to his death."*[38] Unlike Master Zeng,
King Hui valued the wrong thing, territory, and was afraid of the wrong thing,
failure to be victorious. And because of this he acted against his love of his son.

B. Mencius *1B3*

Next to 2A2, the most extensive discussion of courage in the *Mencius* may be found in 1B3, which is a dialogue between Mencius and King Xuan of the state of Qi. This is one of a number of recorded conversations between Mencius and King Xuan. From a long conversation in an earlier passage, 1A7, we learn that Xuan wishes to expand his rule beyond the borders of the state of Qi, and become ruler of all of the Middle Kingdom. Mencius warns him that, given the military resources of the state of Qi, the consequences of trying to conquer all of the Middle Kingdom would be disastrous. In a justly famous simile, Mencius tells King Xuan, "To seek what you want by the means that you employ is like climbing a tree in search of a fish."[39] Instead, Mencius advises, Xuan should concentrate on making his own subjects healthy and happy, which would not only be benevolent but would also have the good practical consequence of solidifying his own rule. Note that, in order for Xuan to act on this advice, he must *not* be like Meng Shishe. Mencius is advising Xuan that he *should* "advance only after sizing up the enemy, . . . ponder [whether he will achieve] victory and only then join [battle], . . . [and] be in awe of the opposing armies."

1B3 itself opens with Mencius lecturing King Xuan on proper relations between states of unequal power. The king responds, "Great are your words! But I have a weakness. I am fond of courage." Mencius replies,

> I beg your Majesty not to be fond of petty courage. If one brandishes a sword and looks fierce, saying, "How dare he stand up to me?!" this is the courage of a common fellow, and is just a matter of opposing a single person. Let your Majesty make it into something greater.

Mencius then discusses the courage of the ancient sage kings Wen and Wu, each of whom "brought peace to the people of the world in a single burst of anger." In other words, the sage kings used military force *only* when it *benefited* the common people by bringing *peace* to them. Given the context of Mencius's previous discussions with King Xuan, the significance is clear. The courage of a "common fellow" is useful only in "opposing a single person." The bravado of a "common fellow" is useless, or even dangerous, for a ruler to have, since a ruler's sphere of activity is not a one-on-one confrontation but large-scale interstate politics and warfare. To try to rule with this sort of mindless bravado can only lead to disaster. Instead, Mencius urges King Xuan to rule in the virtuous manner of the sage kings. The relevance to 2A2 is, I hope, clear. The courage of the "common fellow" corresponds to the courage of Bogong You, while that of the sage kings corresponds to the courage of Master Zeng. Consequently, 1B3 can be seen as providing argument that courage growing out of virtue, like that of Master Zeng, is superior to mindless bravado.

I have been arguing that Mencius *does* have reasons, which he supplies in other contexts, for holding that the sort of courage he ascribes to Master Zeng in 2A2 is superior to the sort he ascribes to Bogong You or Meng Shishe. But as a philosopher I am also interested in whether his reasons are *good* reasons. As I noted earlier, Mencius's basic argument is that those who possess the lesser forms of courage will be led to perform actions that frustrate the achievement of goals and concerns they can be expected to have. Most of us do, I think, have the sorts of goals and concerns that Mencius identifies. Almost all of us care for some other people—family members and friends. It does seem likely that the mindless bravado of a Bogong You would cause us to act in ways that would damage the interests of those about whom we care. Admittedly, very few of us are, like King Xuan of Qi, rulers of powerful states. However, very many of us *are* in situations similar to King Xuan in important respects. Specifically, any of us who are committed to complicated projects that involve the cooperation of others will, like King Xuan, find the courage of a Bogong You counterproductive. The success of complicated projects involving the cooperation of others—including such diverse things as running a business enterprise, engaging in academic administration, playing on a sports team—requires that we often avoid conflict and respond to obstacles and threats in a more nuanced way than would a Bogong You. So if we have any of these sorts of commitments, there will be good reason to prefer the courage of a Master Zeng.

C. Two Deeper Objections

There are two deeper objections to Mencius's position on courage that I want to at least mention. (I will confess in advance, though, that I plan to only *sketch* what responses to these deeper objections would look like.) First, what if one lacks *any* of the commitments that Mencius has been assuming we have? What if one cares neither about the well-being of any other humans nor about the success of any complicated cooperative projects? Second, we might accuse Mencius of being guilty of offering us a "false trichotomy." Perhaps the courage of Master Zeng *is* demonstrably preferable to the courage of either Bogong You or Meng Shishe. But surely there are other kinds of courage that are combined with more prudent and nuanced responses to one's situation, yet are not as explicitly moralized as is Master Zeng's courage. To return to an earlier example, what about the courage of a prudent hitman? Such a person would, ex hypothesi, not be virtuous, since he would be neither benevolent nor just, so he would not have the courage of Master Zeng. But a prudent hitman would not have to be as mindless or undiscerning in responding to his situation as are Bogong You or Meng Shishe. He could wisely choose which "contracts" to accept, and prudently choose the right moment to make his "hit." Mencius would prefer Master Zeng's courage to that of the hitman, but does he have any justification for this preference?

I have raised these two questions together because I think the form of Mencius's answer to each would be very similar. Virtues are dispositions that contribute to living a flourishing or choiceworthy life. Thus, in order to show that a disposition is a virtue, one must explain how that disposition contributes to living a flourishing or choiceworthy life. On the other hand, if a disposition detracts from living a flourishing or choiceworthy life, it is a vice. Consequently, in order to answer the first of the objections, Mencius would have to show that one who lacked commitments to other people and to complicated cooperative projects could not lead a flourishing or choiceworthy life. Similarly, in answer to the second objection, Mencius would have to show that a prudent hitman could not lead a flourishing or choiceworthy life. Can Mencius succeed in showing either of these things? Here I must beg off. In order to show either of these things, I would have to construct a Mencian justification for a certain sort of virtuous life. In other words, Mencius's response to either of these objections would have to be a special case of his answer to the general question, "Why be a good person?" And that is a bigger question than I can tackle in a brief essay.

V. CONCLUSION

I have tried to achieve several things in this essay. I have attempted to explicate and provide a partial defense of Mencius's conception of courage, using verses 1 through 8 of *Mencius* 2A2 as the focus of my inquiry. Although this passage seems, at first, extremely obscure, I tried to show that it is perfectly coherent once we understand the intellectual background that Mencius and his interlocutors assumed. Furthermore, I argued that, in other portions of the text, Mencius presents arguments for his evaluation of the different types of courage discussed in 2A2. Finally, I have provided a partial defense of Mencius's evaluation.

One of the things distinctive of great philosophers is that careful, critical reading of their works both requires and stimulates one's own philosophical reflection and engagement. To read the *Republic* carefully, for example, is not to passively absorb Plato's philosophy; it is to do philosophy *with* Plato. It is my hope that this essay at least suggests that, as I. A. Richards long ago argued, Mencius is a philosopher in a league with Plato.[40] To read carefully Mencius's views on courage is to be challenged to think deeply about courage itself.

NOTES

1. Versions of this essay were presented at the University of Michigan, Vassar College, and the Neo-Confucian Seminar of Columbia University. I learned much from the comments on each occasion, and from the comments of an anonymous referee. All translations in this essay are my own, unless otherwise noted. I shall identify portions of *Mencius* 2A2 using the so-called "verses" in James Legge's translation, *The Works of Mencius* (New York, 1970; o.p. 1895). I have also consulted the following translations and commentaries: D. C. Lau, *Mencius* (New York, 1970), Uchino Kumaichiro, *Moshi*, vol. 4 of *Shinshaku Kambun Taikei* (Tokyo, 1962), Zhao Qi, *Mengzi zhu,* Sun Shi, *Mengzi zhushu,* Zhu Xi, *Mengzi jizhu,* Jiao Xun, *Mengzi zhengyi.*

2. David S. Nivison, "Philosophical Voluntarism in Fourth Century China," originally written in 1973 and reprinted in Nivison, *The Ways of Confucianism: Investigations in Chinese Philosophy* (La Salle, Ill., 1996), Jeffrey Riegel, "Reflections on an Unmoved Mind: An Analysis of *Mencius* 2A2," in *Journal of the American Academy of Religion Thematic Issue S,* edited by Henry Rosemont a supplement to 47: 3 (September 1980): 433–57, Kwong-Ioi Shun, "Mencius and the Mind-Inherence of Morality: Mencius' Rejection of Kao Tzu's Maxim in *Meng Tzu* 2A:2," *Journal of Chinese Philosophy* 18 (December 1991): 371–86, Lee H. Yearley, *Mencius*

and Aquinas: Theories of Virtue and Conceptions of Courage (Albany, N.Y., 1990), especially 151–53.

3. In the works previously cited, Nivison and Shun do not discuss verses 1–8. Yearley devotes only two paragraphs to this section of 2A2 in all of his book (pp. 151–52). Riegel has an interesting discussion of the verses on pp. 437–39 (although I differ from him on many points). Probably the best previous discussion is in Shun's dissertation, "Virtue, Mind and Morality: A Study in Mencian Ethics," Department of Philosophy, Stanford University, 1986 (UMI Order No. 8700818), 41–57.

4. For my own views on the relationship between Western and Chinese philosophy, see "What Should Western Philosophy Learn from Chinese Philosophy?" in *Chinese Language, Thought and Culture: Nivison and His Critics,* edited by Philip J. Ivanhoe (La Salle, Ill., 1996).

5. My comparison suggests an important methodological issue: How do I know that *yong* is properly translated as "courage"? The only way to show this is to see whether the hypothesis that *yong* is properly interpreted as "courage" results in translations of sentences from classical Chinese that make sense. The fact that interpreting *yong* as "courage" does result in sensible translations of sentences from the *Analects* and the *Mencius* provides evidence that my interpretive hypothesis is correct. If someone claims that *yong* is not properly interpreted as "courage," the burden of proof is on her to show how some alternative interpretation of *yong* makes better sense of the translated passages.

6. Plato, *Laches and Charmides,* translated by Rosamond Kent Sprague (Indianapolis, 1992), p. 32 (191A-C).

7. If we think of an action as a combination of behavior, intention, emotion, etc., then courage at least *involves* performing certain actions. My point is that courage requires more than certain kinds of external behavior.

8. Philippa Foot, *Virtues and Vices* (Berkeley, 1978), 10.

9. On the notion of semblances of virtues, see Yearley, *Mencius and Aquinas,* p. 17ff. Foot's (rather complex) view on this issue is that "courage is not operating as a virtue when the murderer turns his courage, which is a virtue, to bad ends" (Foot, *Virtues and Vices,* 16).

10. The two best published English-language summaries of the textual issues regarding the *Analects* are Robert Eno, *The Confucian Creation of Heaven* (Albany, 1990), 80–81, and 239–41, nn. 2–4, and Steven Van Zoeren, *Poetry and Personality* (Stanford, Calif., 1991), 17–28. There is also an outstanding forthcoming textual study of the *Analects* by E. Bruce Brooks and A. Taeko Brooks, *The Original Analects: Sayings of Confucius and His Successors* (New York, 1997). Citations of the *Analects* in this essay follow the sectioning in the Harvard-Yenching Institute concordance.

11. Alasdair MacIntyre, "Incommensurability, Truth, and the Conversation between Confucians and Aristotelians about the Virtues," in *Culture and Modernity,* edited by Eliot Deutsch (Honolulu, 1991), 106.

12. Similar is this comment from the *Zuo zhuan,* Duke Ai, 16th year: "Adhering to benevolence is what I call being trustworthy, and practicing righteousness is what I call being courageous. . . . Just doing what one has sworn to do is not trustworthiness, and dying when the time comes is not courage" (translation modified from Burton Watson, *The Tso Chuan* [New York, 1989], 203).

13. Riegel suggests that Gongsun Chou, far from being a disciple, is actually criticizing Mencius in 2A2 and other passages ("Reflections on an Unmoved Mind," p. 450, n. 4). However, Zhao Qi identifies Gongsun Chou as one of Mencius's disciples in his commentary to 2A1, and Gongsun Chou identifies himself as Mencius's disciple in 2A1.7. Moreover, both the content of his questions ("I venture to ask wherein you excel, Master?") and the form (he allows Mencius to answer at great length) are inconsistent with hostile cross-examination.

14. Mencius was, at some point, some sort of minister in Qi (see 2B6). Riegel thinks that Mencius had already been prime minister by the time of this conversation, and that Gongsun Chou is needling Mencius about his failure to reform the ruler of Qi. He interprets *ba wang bu yi yi* as meaning that there was no difference between acting as a true king and acting as a hegemon during the time Mencius was in office ("Reflections on an Unmoved Mind," p. 436,

and p. 451, n. 6). David S. Nivison has observed (in conversation) that Mencius's standard manner of saying that A is not different from B is not A B *bu yi* but is rather A *yu* B *wu yi yi ye* (1A4) or A *wu yi yi yu* B (6A4). In addition, the use of *yi* to mean "to regard as surprising" is attested in other passages in the *Mencius* (e.g., 5B9). Legge, Uchino, and Lau also read the opening of 2A2 as I do.

15. In Lau's translation, the relevant portion of 6B15 reads, "That is why Heaven, when it is about to place a great burden on a man, always first tests his resolution, exhausts his frame and makes him suffer starvation and hardship, frustrates his efforts so as *to shake him from his mental lassitude,* toughen his nature and make good his deficiencies." The emphasized phrase is Lau's translation of the phrase I render "to perturb one's heart."

16. A more literal translation of the Chinese (*bu*) *dong xin* would be "to (not) move one's heart." However, in English, saying that someone's "heart is unmoved" suggests callousness, and that is not what Mencius has in mind here, so I have followed Legge in using the word "unperturbed."

17. Briefly, Mencius and Gaozi are similar in that both think courage should grow out of a commitment to "righteousness." However, Gaozi regards righteousness as "external." This means, at least, that Gaozi does not think we have innate dispositions toward righteousness. Mencius, of course, claims that we do have such dispositions, and that righteousness is "internal."

18. By "the Master" he means Confucius. What follows may be intended as a direct quotation from Confucius, but it may also be Master Zeng paraphrasing the Master's teaching.

19. In Chinese, this sentence is *zi fan er bu su, sui hekuanbo, wu bu zhui yan,* which would most naturally be translated as, "If I examine myself and am not upright, although [I am opposed by] a coarsely clad fellow, I would not be in fear." This does not make any sense in context, however. There have been five proposals for interpreting this sentence, the first four of which give basically the same sense: (1) The second *bu* is an interpolation. (2) The second *bu* is equivalent to *qi bu.* (This reading is suggested by Yan Ruoqu, cited in Jiao Xun, and followed by Legge.) (3) The second *bu* is a mistake for *bi.* (This is D. C. Lau's suggestion in "Some Notes on the *Mencius,*" *Asia Major,* n.s., 15:1 [1969], 71.) (4) The final *yan* is an interrogative particle, making the sentence a rhetorical question. (Uchino reads this way.) (5) The *zhui* is transitive, giving the sense, " . . . I will not make him afraid." The problem with this last reading is that it is not clear what not making someone else afraid has to do with courage. (I am indebted to Scott Cook for making clear the need to address this issue.)

20. *Su* (read *suo* in modern Mandarin), which I have translated as "upright," is a rare character. Jeffrey Riegel, following one reading of an occurrence of *su* in the *Shi jing* (Mao 237), interprets it as "bound tight" ("Reflections on an Unmoved Mind," p. 438, and p. 452, n. 18). However, Zhao Qi glosses *su* both as "upright" (*zhi*) and as "righteous" (*yi*). Furthermore, Zhu Xi, in his commentary, provides two examples from the *Li ji* in which *su* is contrasted with *heng,* "transverse." In addition, a passage in the *Hanfeizi* (which Riegel cites, loc. cit.) parallels 2A2.7 except that *su* is replaced with "upright." Finally, I think that even in the *Shi jing* passage that Riegel cites *su* can be read as "to make upright."

21. The only apparent exception to this generalization is *Analects* 4:15, in which Master Zeng is presented as unravelling a cryptic dictum of Confucius. However, I follow many scholars (e.g., Brooks and Brooks, *Original Analects*) in regarding the incident reported in this passage as a fabrication, the motive of which was precisely to combat the image of Master Zeng as a dullard.

22. This translation is modifed from Arthur Waley, *The Analects of Confucius* (New York, 1989; o.p. 1938), 133.

23. I take it that Meng Shishe does *not* think one ought to "advance only after sizing up one's enemy, to ponder victory and only then join [battle]." To do so would make one's courage dependent upon being "certain of victory." In contrast with this, Meng Shishe does not care what the odds of victory are, he does not care whether he is certain of victory. Regardless of the situation, he is "without fear."

24. Let me explain my use of the commentarial tradition. I do not quote traditional com-

mentaries because I assume that they are always right. (They could not be, since they often disagree with one another.) However, I think there are a variety of good reasons to use commentaries. First, the authors of traditional commentaries are often linguistically closer than we are to the texts we are interpreting. Zhao Qi's Chinese is closer to Mencius's than is that of any contemporary human. Likwise, even though he is separated from Mencius by more than a millennium of linguistic and cultural evolution, Zhu Xi was immersed in classical Chinese from an early age in a way that no one will ever be again. Second, the classical commentators are our colleagues. Just as I can learn something from an interpretive hypothesis or argument offered by one of my contemporary colleagues, so can I learn from ancient or medieval colleagues. In fact, as will be evident, I think many of the interpretive hypotheses offered by classical commentators are the "best explanations" of the meaning of 2A2.

25. Paraphrasing *Analects* 15:21.

26. Does Master Zeng link courage to being a good person, or merely to following one's own sense of what is right? (In other words, is courage a matter of virtue, or simply a matter of "authenticity"?) For Mencius, the two are not separable. He thinks that our innate sense of righteousness will (if we nurture it) guide us to do what is really right. Mencius would have understood Master Zeng along the same lines.

27. In discussion, Luis Gomez has suggested that the Master's fear might be due to the social disgrace consequent upon being defeated by a social inferior. There are several problems with this reading. (1) If the cause of the fear were the social disgrace of being defeated by an inferior, then there would be no reason for "the Master" to raise the issue of whether, upon self-examination, one is upright. (2) I am aware of no texts in which any early Confucians express (or even mention) the fear of being defeated by a social inferior. Indeed, (3) early Confucians do not disdain those who have low social status. Sage King Shun, for example, began life as a farmer (6B15), and Confucius condemns those who are ashamed of "poor clothes and poor food" (4:9).

28. Duke Zhao, Year 25, summer. This and many other early references to *qi* are helpfully collected in the appendix to A. C. Graham, *Yin-Yang and the Nature of Correlative Thinking* (Singapore, 1986), 70–92. *Qi* is also referred to later in 2A2 (verses 9 to 15), and in 6A8 and 7A36.

29. As I noted at the beginning of this essay, Mencius's critique of Gaozi has been extensively discussed in previous literature. Consequently, the remainder of this essay will focus on other interpretive and philosophic issues raised by verses 1 through 8.

30. Admittedly, the ethical terms here are different: "upright" in Mencius is *su,* while "right" in the *Analects* is *yi.* However, in his commentary, Zhao Qi glosses *su* as *yi.* So both the *Analects* and *Mencius* see a relationship between at least the highest kind of courage and virtue.

31. This interpretation was suggested by Stephen Darwall and Jennifer Church in separate discussions.

32. Donald J. Munro, *The Concept of Man in Early China* (Stanford, Calif. 1969), 153.

33. Yearley, *Mencius and Aquinas,* 156. For more discussion, see ibid., 150–68, and Shun, "Virtue, Mind and Morality," 41–57.

34. If it irritates me, it perturbs me. Is Mencius committed to saying that *this* shows a lack of courage on my part?

35. James D. Wallace, *Virtues & Vices* (Ithaca, N.Y., 1978), 71–72.

36. Yearley also makes this observation (*Mencius and Aquinas,* 156).

37. I borrow the phrase "motivational harmony" from Shun, "Virtue, Mind and Morality," 41–57.

38. Emphasis mine. On King Hui's son, see 1A5.1.

39. *Mencius* 1A7.16.

40. I. A. Richards, *Mencius on the Mind: Experiments in Multiple Definition* (London, 1932), 28.

MIDWEST STUDIES IN PHILOSOPHY, XXI (1997)

Awe and the Religious Life:
A Naturalistic Perspective

HOWARD WETTSTEIN

I. ANALYTIC PHILOSOPHY
AND THE STUDY OF RELIGION

That philosophy provides scrutiny of fundamentals is its great virtue, one that brought many of us to its study. Virtues and vices—theoretical no less than personal—are often intimately linked. In the theoretical domain, the linkage is evident in philosophical studies of religion, at least in those carried out in the analytic tradition. Concern with what seems fundamental—the existence of God—often has been all-absorbing and, would argue, distracting.

There are intellectual arenas in which we get along quite well in the absence of settled doctrines about the fundamentals, the philosophy of mathematics, for example. While questions about the existence and status of mathematical entities like numbers and sets is of great interest, no one would suggest that work in the philosophy of mathematics awaits a satisfactory treatment of these basic questions. Imagine the folly of the even stronger thesis that work in mathematics itself awaits such philosophical underpinning. However, with regard to the philosophy of religion and even to religion itself, we commonly assume that we need to attend to the fundamental questions first.

The difference is of course explained by our complete confidence in mathematical practice. We are surely more confident about mathematics itself than about any philosophical account of its nature. In the case of mathematics, the institution and its practices, we might say, are primary, the interpretation a much more dubious business.[1] Whereas with respect to religion, the institution awaits the sort of justification in which philosophers trade, or so we usually assume.

Were we confident of the power of religious practice, confident about the virtues of the life that religion facilitates, we might well be willing to treat religion as we do mathematics. It would be natural, that is, to see the institution as primary, and the justification or interpretation as of great interest, but a delicate business. Such is the view I will defend in this essay. Having great confidence in the power of religious practice and the virtues of the religious life, I will freely employ terminology central to that practice and life. The reader should bear in mind the analogy with mathematics.

Concerning my own outlook on those fundamental questions, a topic to which I return at the end of this essay, I am with those who reject belief in the supernatural. While the deniers are thus correct, they are correct on a technicality, as it were. They almost universally miss the point.

There is at the core of our religious institutions something of the first importance. This is not to endorse as true some sectarian theological doctrine or, even worse, some general non-sectarian one. What I have in mind is in the spirit of one who thinks that, say, Aristotle's ethics hits upon features of the human condition that are fundamental, easily overlooked, and crucial to at least one way to pursue human flourishing. The analogy is perhaps especially suggestive, since, as I see it, the western religions (and perhaps the phenomenon is more widespread) encourage a distinctive take on human flourishing, one that is tragically unappreciated in secular, including philosophical, culture. The analogy is also suggestive since I don't presume to have views about what is essential or indispensable to flourishing; only about one way that flourishing has been and might still be successfully pursued.

A distinctive understanding of human flourishing ought to be of great interest to philosophy. Moreover, if it is in the domain of our subject to explore fundamental ideas and institutions—as we were led to believe as undergraduates—it is indeed strange that the power and character of religious institutions have been so radically underexplored. These institutions show no sign of going away, notwithstanding the views of secular messianists who see such development just around the next corner. The persistence alone might suggest to the open-minded that there is something of interest here, that religious life seems to touch something deep in us.

This is not to say that recent philosophy has ignored religion. The past few decades have seen a resurgence of interest among analytic philosophers. Often, however, such studies have been advanced in defense of theistic belief and have not spoken to the wider philosophical community concerning the power and character of religious ideas. Nor has any distinctive approach to human flourishing been emphasized or made available. Spirituality has not been a central concern; indeed the term has been virtually abandoned to the philosophically vulgar. Needless to say, I am speaking here of the dominant trend; there are notable exceptions.

Religion in all its generality—even western religion—is big game. Here I explore the only religious tradition I have studied, my own, Judaism. Perhaps what I say will be to some extent applicable elsewhere. This is not to suggest that it is less than controversial at home.

I have spoken of something important and right about our religious traditions, specifically about my own, something to do with an approach to human flourishing. But to say more, to say what it is that is distinctive and important is very difficult. In part, this is because such a tradition is a collection of ideas, themes, practices that touch many bases. Any attempt to say what it is "all about" is going to fail. Indeed, that such an attempt is bound to fail is reinforced by the perspective I have emphasized: We should see the institution and its practices as primary, the interpretation secondary.

Accordingly, and only partly joking, my project here is "What is it all about?" In this failing effort I take my cue from a common practice in Jewish thought: the Hebrew expression *k'neged kulam* is used to describe a principle, idea, or practice as "the most basic or fundamental."[2] In some contexts we are told that the study of the Torah is *k'neged kulam;* in others, it's the keeping of the Sabbath, or the loving of one's neighbor. . . . Such rhetorical excess is part of my heritage.

II. WHAT'S IT ALL ABOUT?

A. J. Heschel, in his discussion of awe and faith in *God in Search of Man,* suggests that we have overemphasized the doxastic in our thinking about religion. We have given pride of place to religious belief; we think of a deeply religious person as a "true believer." Heschel would have us emphasize something more attitudinal, something more like a posture, a manner of carrying oneself, a way of facing life, the universe, God. (If God is hard for you, stick to the first two for now: a way of facing life and the universe. God will show up later in any case.)

At the heart of the religious orientation is a distinctive and natural human responsiveness.

Awe rather than faith is the cardinal attitude of the religious Jew.[3] (p. 77)

In Judaism, *yirat hashem,* the awe of God, or *yirat shamayim,* the awe of heaven, is almost equivalent to the word "religion." In Biblical language the religious man is not called "believer," as he is for example in Islam (*mu'min*) but *yare hashem* (one who stands in awe of God). (p. 77)

In Woody Allen's movie, *Crimes and Misdemeanors,* someone says of a deeply religious person that his religious sensibility is a beautiful thing, "like having an ear for music." As with music, the most primitive form of awe-responsiveness is something that almost everyone possesses. The most advanced and heightened forms may require a certain aptitude and are the products of sustained attention, training, and nurture.

To say that we have undervalued awe and given pride of place to belief, or religious faith is not to dismiss these latter concepts. While religious belief is not treated in the present essay, faith is focal. Awe, you might say, is most fundamental, it is *k'neged kulam,* but it finds its completion in faith. We need to begin with awe, to provide it with sustained attention and nurture, to heighten our awe-re-sponsiveness, if we are to attain faith.[4]

III. AWE

If we are to explore the idea that awe is at the core of the religious attitude, perhaps we should start by thinking about quite simple and ordinary cases of awe, experiences that are not religiously charged and that are available to all from time to time. Can we discern elements of the religious in such ordinary happenings?

Here are some ordinary examples.

1. Cases of awe at natural grandeur: the feelings of an astronaut standing on the moon, even me or you powerfully moved by the night sky at the top of a mountain, or a relevantly similar ocean experience.
2. Awe at human grandeur. There are examples that seem available to everyone, given a certain openness and sensitivity: awe at the power of people to find inner resources in horrible circumstances, awe at human goodness and caring. Other examples require artistic and/or intellectual sophistication: powerful responses to great art of all varieties, or to great achievements in science, mathematics, philosophy.
3. Awe at the birth of one's children. Perhaps this is a compound of, or intermediate between 1 and 2.
4. Even more sophisticated, more rare, are other sorts of combinations of 1 and 2. For example, one at the top of the mountain, awestruck not only by the overwhelming beauty and majesty of nature, but also by the fact that humans, constructed of the stuff of the mountain, can take such a thing in, and indeed that they can feel awe at it.

Of course, reactions to such events may vary from person to person. And even if we can agree that a sense of awe is neither idiosyncratic nor unusual in such circumstances, it may still be that what I feel at such times is not, and almost certainly not quite, what you do. Nevertheless, the sort of feelings and thoughts often engendered seem to me to have something importantly religious about them, as I will explain.

I begin with a curious duality that seems characteristic[5] of such experiences, a duality of special interest to religion. The two aspects to be distinguished appear in all sorts of admixtures, with one or the other getting the focus.[6]

In the face of great power, or majesty, or beauty, one characteristically feels a sense of humility. The more intense experiences may engender not only humility, but a sense of being overwhelmed. Often one feels a sense of distance between here and there, between oneself and the object of awe.[7]

Experiences of the overwhelming can sometimes diminish the agent, as in the case of almost shrunken-looking children of very powerful parents. Remarkably, awe experiences are not like this. One does not feel crushed or diminished, rather elevated, even exhilarated. At the top of the mountain one feels a sense of great privilege; one stands tall, breathes deeply. The cabalistic concept of "tzimtzum" provides a beautiful image: creation involves God's pulling back and making room, as it were, for the world. Here, with respect to awe, it's as if God pulls back so as not to completely overwhelm. He pulls back, as it were, out of respect, to make room for the awestruck person.

When I say that that awe is *k'neged kulam,* this is in no small measure a matter of the central place played by the duality—humbled yet elevated, affirmed in one's dignity. This duality brings to mind a related, albeit distinct, duality that seems very close to the bone of the religious orientation encouraged by so much of Jewish religious life.

1. A sense of the fragility, fleetingness, finitude, and severe limitations of human life.
2. A sense of the great significance of human life.[8]

A crucial piece of the big project,[9] you might say, is achieving a conception of human life and an approach to human flourishing—not just a conception of flourishing but a way of implementing it—that provide a central role for 1 and 2 and achieve balance between them. There is a Hasidic adage that a person should carry two pieces of paper in his pocket, one that says "I am but dust and ashes," and the other that says "The world was created for me."[10]

Elliot Dorff, in *Knowing God,*[11] suggests that the idea of God is a powerful instrument for touching both bases. First, the idea suggests a contrast between us and God, and thus emphasizes human limitation, finitude, et al. At the same time, we reflect God's image. Such reflection cannot be a one-way street; reflection is reflexive. We and God must have important similarities. There is perhaps no more powerful imagery than that of people as God's reflections for underscoring human significance and dignity.

We have been exploring ordinary awe experiences for their religious content. And we have hit upon the duality, humbled but elevated, a powerful religious idea. But there is more. Awe experiences, perhaps as a consequence of the duality, characteristically engender a generosity of spirit, a lack of pettiness, increased ability to forgive and to contain anger and disappointment. To feel and behave in these ways is to feel and behave as, according to the tradition, God does. You might say that in the grip of awe, *imitatio Dei* becomes easy and natural, at least for the moment. One also typically feels a powerful sense of gratitude.

Turning from the affective/behavioral to the cognitive, awe experiences engender a godlike perspective, the ability to (almost) see things under the aspect of eternity, as Spinoza put it.

A friend who has no contact with institutional religion was recalling early experiences at an Episcopal retreat. He and his father were closer than ever at this retreat, even though the retreat involved remaining silent—they never spoke. Every morning they would be awakened at some ungodly hour to some "hocus-pocus." My friend says, though, that the memory remains very warm. His sense of the real content of all the hocus-pocus, the point of the practices, was "to organize one's life around one's better instincts." This seems to me an interesting comment about the religious life, about which there will be more later. In the present context, it's striking that those better instincts come to the fore at moments of awe.

There is at least one additional aspect to the religious content of ordinary awe experiences, one of great moment. For many people, and not only those who consider themselves religious, there is something *holy* about objects of awe experiences—childbirth, a great symphony, the Grand Canyon. There is, moreover, a feeling of horror associated with the thought of destroying such objects, events, and so on. To do so—even to allow such a thing—would be sacrilege.

Although it seems natural to invoke concepts like *holiness* and *sacrilege* in contexts like these, it's difficult to know how much to make of this. Perhaps such concepts make essential reference to the religious, and so the use of them by secularists is always derivative—in scare quotes, as it were. Maybe so. Still it seems significant that the terms seem apt.

I want to linger a moment with the concept of *holiness,* one that seems to me as difficult as it is crucial to Judeo-Christian, as opposed to (philosophical) Greek, thinking about human flourishing. Even from a traditional religious perspective, the concept is very difficult to explicate.[12] What emerges, though, indeed strikingly from our survey of ordinary awe experiences, is that awe may furnish us with an entry point into this difficult topic. For as the examples suggest, where there is awe, there is holiness. It's as if awe were a faculty for discerning the holy. This seems an important topic for further exploration.

The experiences explored so far may not be felt or identified as religious by the agent; they do not pertain specifically or explicitly to God. However, they are, as I see it, the originals, the primitive cases of religious responsiveness. This is not to say that they are the paradigm cases; paradigm cases identify themselves as religiously significant.

IV. AWE, FEAR, MYSTERY

A bit more about awe, specifically its relation to fear and mystery, before we turn to its relation to faith. The Hebrew word that Heschel translates as "awe" is *yirah.* In biblical Hebrew, the word sometimes means "awe," sometimes "fear," and sometimes has the quality of both awe and fear. In contexts in which *yirah* is seen as a great virtue, awe needs at least a good deal of the emphasis. Despite some of the standard translations, it's far from clear why simply being frightened of God is supposed to be of great ethical value, or why such fright is so admirable as to be considered "the beginning of wisdom," as we are told that *yirah* is in Psalms. That awe of heaven is a great virtue, or that it's the beginning of wisdom, is quite another matter. There is a passage in the Jewish morning liturgy to the effect that a person should always stand in *yirah* of heaven in private as well as in public. The suggestion is a powerful one, but much of its power seems lost if "fear" gets all the emphasis.

Awe and fear have an important connection, one that is perhaps underscored by the occurrence of a single Hebrew word, *yirah*, that incorporates both aspects. Many awe experiences, insofar as they involve powerful natural or spiritual forces, involve an element of fear. Indeed, the aspect of fearfulness grows with the intensity of the experience. Think here of the extremes: being present when worlds collide, as it were, or, as in the Bible, meeting God face to face, where a misstep can be fatal. Even when we consider relatively tame examples, like the awe of heaven with which one is to approach life quite generally, a bit of fear may not be far off. The more intensely one feels such awe, the more one feels himself to be in God's presence, the closer one is to at least a tinge of fright.

To allow myself some rank speculation, it seems plausible to suppose that awe, as something separable from fear, shows up relatively late on the human scene. One imagines primitive religiosity to involve a greater admixture of fear in awe experiences. As Heschel sees it, quite plausibly, by the time of the Hebrew Bible awe takes center stage.

Another idea whose connections to awe are well worth exploring is that of mystery. "In awe and amazement the prophets stand before the mystery of the universe," writes Heschel. Nor is it just the prophets. We often feel awe at things that seem beyond our comprehension, childbirth for example, or the birth of ideas or art.

But how essential to awe is a lack of comprehension? To suppose that it is essential is to suppose that sufficient understanding precludes awe. This does not seem correct. On the contrary, one's appreciation of grandeur might well be enhanced by greater understanding. In my more midrashic moments, I like to think of God as in awe of His creation. Moreover, the heavens declare the glory of God, and not only to creatures who don't understand. The angels, perhaps lacking in the freedom to make bad choices, but possessed of perfect understanding, nevertheless stand in awe of the Creator. (Admittedly, my intuitions about angels are corrigible. . . .)

Nevertheless, it would be a mistake to dismiss the connection with mystery. For one thing, the connection is widely felt, and this should give us pause. Let's come at this from a different direction.

Heschel, in discussing concepts like awe and wonder, sometimes speaks of what he calls "radical amazement." A rich source of examples of the sort of thing Heschel has in mind is Annie Dillard's *Pilgrim at Tinker Creek*,[13] a book that opens a window on Dillard's distinctively heightened sensitivity and provides many masterful descriptions of awe at nature. Dillard's examples are particularly interesting since they are not restricted to aspects of nature that are friendly to us and our projects. One sort of recurrent example involves constellations of the exquisite and the horrendous. After one such description, of waves of sharks in a feeding frenzy, rising from churning waters, she writes, "The sight held awesome wonders: power and beauty, grace tangled in a rapture with violence." She concludes, "We don't know what's going on here."

Dillard encourages us to wonder about what we are to make of such a world. How, one wants to know, are such things—fill in your own examples of constellations of the exquisite and the dreadful—possible? This sort of question—or the state of mind that issues in the question—does not essentially pertain to constellations of beauty and horror. Heschel mentions another sort of example, a person struck by the wondrousness of existence who asks why there is anything at all, why there is something rather than nothing. There are of course many sorts of examples in which one is awestruck, amazed, and cannot make sense of what one has experienced.

Two things seem striking about such questions in such contexts. First, it is very difficult to know what to make of them, what exactly they ask. Second and related, a perfectly rational, sensible, sensitive person, faced with such a question, may not feel the force of the question. She may not know what the questioner is talking about. And the questioner may well be hard pressed to explain. Next time you are overwhelmed with the wondrousness of existence, ask your colleague who occupies the next office in the philosophy department why there is something rather than nothing.

Of course, if your colleague shares your sense of awe, or if you can instantaneously generate it, she will understand the question, at least in the sense that she understands the urge to ask it. She will share the feeling that "we don't know what's going on here." So whether or not one feels the force of the question seems to depend upon whether one shares a sense of awe. But the question's content remains dark.

The trouble with such questions is that it's difficult to characterize the gap in one's understanding that prompts them. What is it exactly that we don't understand, and what would count as an answer? One's puzzlement, for example, is not for a lack of empirical information. Even empirical omniscience would not bridge this sort of cognitive gulf. Perhaps, then, what one is missing, what one seeks, is some other sort of information, news from another realm. If one knew enough about the spiritual realm, perhaps, one would then understand how it is all possible. One would then know what's going on here. I want to suggest, on the contrary, that our discomfort is of another sort, that the mystery associated with awe does not concern a lack of information.

It seems significant that we are as apt to ask what these things mean—existence, the constellation of exquisite beauty and ugly, wanton destructiveness, childbirth, and so on—as we are to ask how they are possible. Nor do we distinguish these questions very sharply in such contexts. I want to suggest that such questions do two things. First, they themselves are a kind of expression of wonderment—they give voice to the awe. Second, they reflect the powerful sense that the subject is beyond one's comprehension, but not in the sense that one lacks information that would bring the matter into clear view. The problem is rather that one is dazed, confused; one cannot come to terms with the thing, wrap one's mind around it.

An idea of Wittgenstein's about philosophical quandaries may be suggestive here.[14] "I don't know my way about," is for Wittgenstein a kind of general form of philosophical question. Of course, this is not how we put our philosophical queries. Instead we may ask how various things are possible, empirical experience, for example. But the discomfort, thought Wittgenstein, is not for a lack of information. It's that we are lost, in over our heads.

There are of course differences between philosophical worries, as Wittgenstein saw them, and our awe-inspired sense of not knowing what's going on. Indeed, Wittgenstein's idea was that with respect to philosophical questions, we might well come to learn our way about; we might work our way out of the confusion. (But not by providing the usual sorts of solutions. A deeper understanding of the relevant domain, Wittgenstein supposed, would render the original puzzle irrelevant.) With wonderment, however, the phenomenon of being in over our heads is, unlike that of being in the grip of a distorting philosophical conception (and also unlike that of lacking information), not remediable. We don't (or shouldn't) even want a remedy.

The cognitive dissonance signaled by "How is it possible?" the sense that we are in over our heads, is easy to confuse with, or attribute to, ignorance of information. In other contexts, after all, wonderment prompts a perfectly appropriate request for information. Woody Allen's *Sleeper* concerns a kind of modern-day Rip Van Winkle who awakens after several decades to the wonders of modern gadgetry including, notably, an *orgasmitron*. "How do these things work?" is both natural and appropriate. Such amazement is the mother of science, and it takes considerable sophistication to know when there is an explanation to be had, and when, on the contrary, one need rest with the amazement. The sophistication in question is a kind of philosophical discernment available to the public. Which is not to say that it is readily available even to the philosophically trained. It is a kind of practical wisdom, where the practice is an intellectual one.

Mystery, then, is closely related to awe, where mystery is understood in terms of wonderment and the sense that we are in over our heads. I'm not sure whether to think of mystery as a necessary condition for awe, so much as a concomitant. But it's an important idea in the neighborhood.

V. FROM AWE TO FAITH:
FROM THE PRIMITIVE TO THE PARADIGM

Awe is relatively rare in our lives, and strikingly transitory. This would appear to make it a strange choice for what is *k'neged kulam*. One would naturally assume that what undergirds the religious outlook would need to have broad and sustained impact on our lives.

It is here that the concept of the *y're shamayim,* one who stands in awe of heaven, comes to the fore. What is distinctive about the *y're shamayim* is not merely a distinctive object of awe, an explicitly religious object. Also distinctive—and my focus for the present—is the steadiness that the *y're shamayim* has achieved. Awe, while not a constant companion, has become characteristic of everyday experience. It is not only a question of frequency. The *y're shamayim* lives in the presence of awe; awe is a kind of background condition against which he carries on.

Nor is it only awe that has become characteristic and habitual. With awe come the godlike tendencies to feeling and behavior, the perspective *sub specie aeternitatis,* the gratitude. Moreover, since awe engenders a sense of the holy, to characteristically feel awe is to be confronted by the holy in all sorts of unlikely places. The *y're shamayim* lives quite a different life than those of us for whom awe is both rare and transitory.

This is pretty astounding. It's very difficult even to imagine such a person. How might one go about configuring such a life? One can, so to speak, put oneself in the path of awe. But a single-minded quest seems futile, self-defeating, in a word, quixotic.

Perhaps what makes the whole thing so hard to imagine is that we are thinking about a kind of quick transition, a quick fix. What could I do to turn my life into that sort of life? Instead, perhaps we should think about something much more slow and painstaking, something more like character development.

Seeing *yirat shamayim* as the product of character development helps, but the whole business is still pretty astounding. It remains difficult to imagine how we would affect such character development. It is here that religious practice makes an invaluable contribution.

I can perhaps best explain what I see as the role of religious practice by contrasting religion with philosophy, or at least with what I take to be an important aspect of what we do in philosophy. As I'm envisioning the philosophical project, one confronts questions that are beyond the pale of normal good sense, questions with respect to which it's very difficult to bring good sense to bear. So far perhaps this is uncontroversial. More controversial is the idea that a philosopher need do no more, and can do no more, than bring good sense to bear. The long-term project is one of seeking increasingly natural ways to think about the hard questions. Philosophers tend to think that there must be much more to it, that there may be many natural ways to pursue such questions, and that what is needed is some principled way to decide between the proposed answers. Sometimes perhaps there are a number of such natural approaches. But we tend to lose sight of just how very difficult it is to find thoroughly natural ways to think about philosophical things.

Religion, by contrast, is not in the business of bringing plain sense to bear on a distinctive question or range of questions. I don't mean, of course, that there is no common sense exhibited in the tradition; there is, and in many ways. But there is so much else. One need not point to especially strange seeming practices—for example, the prohibition concerning wearing garments of certain mixed fabrics—or arcane theological doctrines. Even more typical and reasonable seeming religious practices—traditional Jewish Sabbath observance, for example—are not what common sense would have naturally suggested.

To say that religion is less a matter of good sense than is philosophy is not to denigrate it. One cannot get from A to B, from where we are to *yirat shamayim,* by simply thinking hard on the matter—not that this is a bad idea. What religion seeks to achieve requires something more. It requires more in the way of equipment than individuals have been granted. What is required, you might say, is

God's help. It comes in the form of inherited practices of some thousands of years standing, practices that conduce to *yirat shamayim*. How exactly they do so is as interesting a matter as it is difficult. Nor should we assume that only *these* practices could do so. Still, such a gift of tradition is striking, itself awe-inspiring.

This gift is dramatized in the fiction of Chaim Grade, a twentieth-century Yiddish poet, novelist, and author of short stories.[15] Despite Grade's own misgivings about traditional religion, his heroes are often people who have achieved such character transformation as a product of deep and sustained engagement with the religious tradition.

In the next section I will turn to how the religious tradition might pull off such magic, but for the moment I want to focus on this idea of developed religious character. I propose—and there are such suggestions in Heschel—that we see *faith* as involving, although not wholly exhausted by, the sort of character transformation, the sort of generalization of awe, that we have been discussing. Heschel writes,

There is no faith at first sight.

Faith does not come into being out of nothing, inadvertently, unprepared, an unearned surprise. Faith is preceded by awe.

Faith, to paraphrase Wittgenstein's remarks on understanding, is not the sort of thing that occurs in a flash. This is not to say—to continue the parallel with Wittgenstein—that a datable occurrence cannot be the felt onset of faith, or of an increase or intensification of faith. To deny that faith can occur in a flash is rather to emphasize the antecedents, the long and difficult business of character development. Nor can faith be achieved by a single person, and occur only once in the person's life—I'm getting carried away with the Wittgenstein analogy. The necessary character development is the product of socialization and training; it's a product of engagement with religious practice.

Clearly this is not to think of faith as an unearned gift of grace, unless one means by this phrase to underscore the sense that no amount of hard work can furnish a guarantee of the hoped-for result. Nor is it to see faith as what gets religious practice and the religious life off the ground, as it were. Faith is rather a virtue that is the outcome of engagement with such practice and such a life.

Alasdair MacIntyre, in a lecture at the University of Notre Dame, characterized an ancient Greek outlook on institutional arrangements and their characteristic virtues. A young person joins the community of mathematicians, or philosophers, or poets, and grows, develops specific virtues, by his participation in the practices of the community. The idea is that associated with different institutions may be different virtues, characteristic capabilities that are particularly emphasized, particularly relevant to the practices. In just such a respect, I see *yirat shamayim*, awe of heaven, and the faith in which *yirat shamayim* plays so large a role, as characteristic virtues of Judaism.[16]

VI. *YIRAT SHAMAYIM* AND RELIGIOUS PRACTICE

To attain the heightened responsiveness of the *y're shamayim* is of course quite a feat. Indeed, the more one thinks about what is involved, the more enormous the task appears. What is called for is a substantial change of orientation, including a deepening of wonder, of appreciation, and of one's character. Effecting such change is intrinsically difficult, and external factors often make it more so. The frailties and limitations of one's fellows often inhibit their support for such development. And the distractions, discouragements, frustrations, and sufferings of the human situation only increase the difficulty.

How then is such character development and sustenance possible? What are the tools by which the tradition facilitates *yirat shamayim?* The tradition employs a multiplicity of such tools. The sampling of *yirah*-inducing practices delineated below may, of course, have other consequences for the religious community and the religious life. Indeed, the finding of meanings and purposes in such traditional practices needs to respect what I emphasized above, the primacy of practice, and the delicacy of interpretation. Interpreting the practices is in some ways like interpreting poetry. New and different meanings emerge—certainly against the background of continuities—sometimes from day to day, and certainly from generation to generation.

1. Study

The practice sometimes said to be the most fundamental, another *k'neged kulam,* is study of the tradition. Indeed, "study" is not adequate, for this word fails to convey the intensity of intellectual engagement. Jewish liturgy says of the words and teachings of the Torah, "For they are our lives and the length of our days, and with them we are engaged [or on them we meditate] day and night." For millennia, in fact as well as in fiction—Grade's protagonists, for example—Jewish heroes often have been saintly figures who are giants of scholarship. Jewish tradition awards a central place to what one might call the culture of learning, a rich and fascinating topic that can only be touched upon here.

It is significant that traditional rabbinic education makes little room for theology. One's time is given largely to Talmudic study, the theoretical physics, as it were, of the tradition, and to the study of the later codifications of the law. The Talmud is itself multifaceted, but rabbinic education emphasizes the theoretical study of the legal code, a code that encompasses Jewish life quite generally, from civil law to religious practice. The rabbi is an expert then, not in theology, but in the practices—both their details and their legal-theoretic analysis—that constitute the life of the community.

This description of rabbinic education may elevate learning in a kind of consequentialist way. Study alone makes one an expert on the character of the practices. Indeed, the practices come to life when one has struggled with their details and meanings. But study is revered not only for its results. Such intense encounter with God's word, as understood and developed by the tradition, is seen as among the highest forms—if not *the* highest form—of religious engagement. The Jew prays that his or her eyes may be illuminated—'luminous' is perhaps an even better translation—with Torah. Spinoza, in the context of his own conception, spoke of the intellectual love of God, an idea that is deeply rooted in Jewish tradition.

The tradition distinguishes *yirat Ha'shem,* awe of God, from *ahavat Ha'shem,* love of God, the other crucial component of the religious attitude. That we speak of learning as the intellectual love of God indicates that learning, while it serves the development and sustenance of *yirah,* has other salutary effects. Clearly, though, participation in such a culture of learning is instrumental in the transition to *yirat shamayim.*[17]

2. Blessings

Traditional practice includes ritualized blessings that one makes on all sorts of occasions, on eating and drinking, on smelling fragrant spices, herbs, plants, on seeing lightning, shooting stars, vast deserts, high mountains, a sunrise, the ocean, on seeing trees blossoming for the first time of the year, on seeing natural objects (including creatures, even people) of striking beauty, on meeting a religious scholar, on meeting a secular scholar, on seeing a head of state, on hearing good news, on hearing bad news.

As a younger person, such blessings seemed to me burdensome. Indeed, who could remember all the relevant occasions, not to speak of the relevant formulas? Heschel suggests that the practice of saying such blessings is training in awe. One develops the habit, before so much as sipping water, to reflect and appreciate. In addition to the blessings' training function—practicing *yirat shamayim*—blessings also function as reminders. Ordinary living is distracting, and such reminders assist us in maintaining focus. Finally, the blessings serve as expressions of awe and of gratitude for all of us, from the novice to the *y're shamayim.*

In addition to occasion-related blessings, there are blessings specific to the performance of other mandated practices: before study, for example, or before donning a prayer shawl, or hearing the shofar, the ram's horn. Crucial in the formula of such blessings is reference to God's having sanctified us by means of the practices, the commandments. Such blessings encourage focus, indeed a reverential focus, on the activity one is about to undertake. They also invite reflection on the specific practice as one in a system of such practices.

3. Prayer

Robert M. Adams, in his essay "Symbolic Value,"[18] reflects on the course of an ordinary day. Adams points out that our days are filled with activities that are rather disconnected with the deep values that give meaning and shape to our lives. We academics, for example, go to department meetings, committee meetings, grade papers; we spend significant time on the upkeep of our homes, autos, and so on. Even with respect to activities closely related to what gives meaning, we are all too human, our motives are mixed, our successes only partial. Prayer, says Adams, offers a wonderful opportunity to spend daily time focused upon our deepest values, to think about them, praising those who exemplify them, expressing heartfelt desire for a genuine and lasting improvement in the human condition. Declaring oneself to be for the good, as Adams puts it, is psychologically reinforcing and spiritually centering.

My initial reaction to reading Adams's piece was a powerful sense of an important void in our culture. This is not to say that what is lacking is necessarily something religious, that religion is the answer for everyone. But finding time, making a place, for some such activity seemed of immense importance, and, by and large, we don't do any such thing. Prayer may be only one answer, but it is at least that. For one who has made *yirat shamayim* one's project, prayer is indispensable, in part just for Adams's reasons.

Traditional Jewish prayer is a thrice-daily activity. If what is at stake is the development of pervasive awe with its affective, perspectival, and behavioral concomitants, then timing is of the essence. Too much prayer would be counterproductive; too little would miss opportunities. Three times a day may seem excessive, but it grows on one, particularly in connection with the great difficulty in keeping one's eye on the ball in the face of ordinary experience. It's as if an omniscient being brought His attention to bear on the question of how often such *yirah*-seeking but distractible creatures would need a period of reflection and reminder.[19]

Traditional Jewish prayer is not only thrice daily, it is fixed prayer. The central portions of the three services are either identical or very closely related. Such repetition and fixity raises a question, perhaps *the* question, about ritual. It is certainly not clear that it was fixed prayer of which Adams wrote, nor is fixed prayer the only or obvious answer to the felt need that Adams articulated. Indeed it is sometimes suggested, and tempting to suppose, that so to regularize expressions of awe, gratitude, and the rest is to constrict them, ultimately to demean them. And whatever one thinks of the ritualized blessings discussed above, at least the blessings are appropriate to one's current experience.

We should remember, however, the magnitude and ambition of the project of facilitating *yirat shamayim*. While fixed prayer can and does degenerate into mechanical, unthinking, unfeeling performance, it offers great opportunities. Some of the usual translations notwithstanding, Jewish liturgy is a compilation of passages of literary magnificence. That such literature, Psalms, for example, has survived the ages is a tribute to its expressive power, its ability to articulate and illuminate religious experience. To engage regularly with such literature— not merely to read the words but to declare them, to wrestle with them—is to occupy oneself with the project. Encounter with literature of such power, first thing in the morning for example, encourages the regularization of attitudes to which the literature so ably gives voice. Indeed, ritualization turns out to be a great virtue: we need not wait until the appropriate experiences present themselves.

Ritualized prayer has another distinct advantage over spontaneous prayer. Spontaneous expressions, for example, of awe—and who would deny that these have a place?—are limited by the expressive capacities of the agent. How many among us are up to the challenge of summoning words adequate to powerful experiences and their concomitant thoughts and emotions?

Ritualized prayer does indeed present challenges of its own. The challenge is presented not by the repetition but rather by the difficulty, the sheer hard work, involved in summoning up the thoughts and feelings appropriate to such literary magnificence. The founder of Hasidism, the Ba'al Shem Tov, is reputed to have said that it would be easier to deliver two advanced Talmudic lectures than to offer a single *amidah,* a fixed prayer of a few pages.

4. Rhythms

As we saw in the discussion of thrice-daily prayer, a refined sense of rhythm and timing are important to the project. The tradition shows great sensitivity not only to the rhythms of the day but also to that of the week and the year.

The idea of *Shabbat,* the Sabbath, is crucial to the tradition's sense of rhythm and timing. The story of the seven days of creation has it that God, who could have been portrayed as considerably more remote, as more exclusively contemplative for example, seems quite involved with the project, giving serious attention to detail. He does not make a move, as it were, until He has pronounced the prior work to be good. What emerges is a conception of six days of creative engagement with the world, then a period of withdrawal, rest, celebration of the creative achievement, and spiritual renewal. It's as if one is being told to find something important to do with the six days, something one will want to celebrate. Further, one should make time to celebrate, and to renew, to "re-soul," as the unusual biblical word, *va'yinafash,*[20] may suggest.

Shabbat is a day of involvement with family and immediate community, but it is also a day in which one has, we are told, an additional soul, a day of enhanced spiritual capacity. The withdrawal provides time to reflect, and the spirit of the day encourages reflection on the wonder of creation itself, and on the wonders provided by one's family, one's work, one's community. *Shabbat* is instrumental in the development and sustenance of *yirat shamayim.*

Turning to annual rhythm, the month of *Elul* (in the fall) is devoted to communal and individual reflection on the past year, on where we have been, on how we have done, on where we are going. The period culminates in the ten "days of awe," the last day of which is *Yom Kippur,* the Day of Atonement, a day of fasting, prayer, and profound reflection. A ritual of great power throughout *Elul* is the blowing of the *shofar,* the ram's horn. The sound is searing, eerie, almost other-worldly. It conveys as no words could the call to self-examination, a call from on high.

VII. GOD

Yirat shamayim involves, we have seen, a distinctive object of awe as well as a distinctive steadiness. I have been focused on the latter. It is time to remark on the distinctive object of awe, God.

To pick up a theme from the beginning of this essay, as in the philosophy of mathematics with the numbers, I want to discuss God in a rather naïve way, without concern for what I called the fundamental questions of metaphysics and epistemology. If the concept has great utility in our practice, then surely it is doing important work, even if it is difficult to say what that work is. Of course, if one is convinced that the only possible work for the concept violates naturalism, then naturalistic scruples may encourage the rejection of the whole package, no matter how attractive it may be otherwise. I will return to this matter below. But first I want naïvely to pursue God's role in all of this.

Although my previous discussion of the practices has not emphasized the role of God, God is central to each of them. Indeed, that this is so has much to do with the effectiveness of the practices in conducing to awe as a steady state. Prayer, for example, at least in the context of traditional Judaism, is prayer *to God,* not simply an expression of values. Traditional Jewish prayer becomes more powerful, more effective in facilitating generalized awe, if one experiences prayer as a thrice-daily audience with God. Similar remarks apply to the blessings— grateful acknowledgments not only of God, but to God.

Another domain of practice, one that is not the focus of this essay but that surely deserves mention, is that of ethics. That persons reflect God's image and that it is of the utmost importance to become more perfect reflections are ideas at the core of the Jewish ethical attitude and practice. Such ideas have all sorts of implications for our project. Here is an example: Prosaic-seeming encounters with, or reflections on, these divine facsimiles—including ourselves—become occasions for awe, albeit sometimes tinged with irony. Not only are we more apt to be awestruck by others, we are more likely to treat them with reverence.

I said above that the *y're shamayim* lives in the presence of awe, that awe constitutes a kind of background condition for his ordinary experience. I could have said that he lives in the presence of God, and that God's presence constitutes the background condition. It is of course not merely God but a certain attitude or stance towards God that is essential and that informs the life of the *y're shamayim.*[21] For those of us in process—and of course no one has completed the process—feeling God's presence *in this way,* at least from time to time, is enormously effective in moving us towards something more like a steady state.

Earlier, in section III, I provided some examples of "ordinary awe," conceived as primitive cases of the religious. Jewish tradition moves us from the primitive cases to *yirat shamayim* by means of a system of practices. We have now seen that God is very much implicated in the practices; indeed God is key to the way that Judaism seeks to effect the transformation. It is crucial for the project, as conceived, that there be an object of worship, an instantiation of human excellences; a fount of creativity who loves and gives freely and generously of that love, one who loves justice, honesty, and integrity, and who is at the same time big on forgiveness. Such a conception affords not only an object of worship but also a model for us. And not only a model but a partner in our projects, both local and global projects like that of bringing justice to the world.[22]

VIII. NATURALISM

Although "fundamental" questions like that of God's existence are not the focus here, I will conclude with a comment on the matter. I wish to challenge the view, accepted by theists and atheists alike, that the sort of religious life I've described, with God at its heart, involves commitment to the supernatural and thus the denial of naturalism. To dispute what seems so obvious is a tall order, and I will return to the question in future work.

Let's begin by considering a traditional theist who is, for want of a better word, non-fundamentalist in her interpretation of certain parts of scripture, for example the story of the garden of Eden, or of Noah and the ark, or of the six days of creation. Let's focus on creation. With regard to the six days, perhaps she reinterprets talk of "days"; biblical "days" are extended periods, maybe eons. Another possibility, one in which I am particularly interested, is that she grants the words their ordinary meanings—"day," as she reads the creation narrative, refers to a twenty-four hour period as it always does—but she understands the story to be something like a parable or an allegory. (The reader should ignore many of the suggestions of the term "fundamentalism." I want this expression only for its suggestion that biblical passages are to be read as factual descriptions. "Literalism" will not do here, or would be confusing, in light of the fact that our "non-fundamentalist" understands the biblical words in their plain, everyday senses; she does not reinterpret the words, attributing to them new meanings.)

The biblical rendering of creation, on her view, is not a factually correct account of origins. That is not its aim, so to speak. The story as it stands—without reinterpreting the words to make the sentences come out true—has profound resonance for us. It is suggestive of deep insights about the human condition and about human flourishing. This is not to say that it actually states, discursively articulates, such insights. As noted, she offers no new account of the meanings of the words.

To think of the biblical creation story in this way is not to diminish its religious centrality. The notion of Sabbath, as creative retreat from creative engagement with the world, as spiritual renewal, will be unaffected. Indeed, such a person, no less than one who reads the passage as an actual description of creation, may participate wholeheartedly in Sabbath observance. She will be able to recite, with sincerity and enthusiasm, the traditional Sabbath liturgy that includes many references to God's working six days and resting on the seventh.

One might have supposed that she would have great trouble with such liturgy, or that she ought to have great trouble with it. After all she doesn't believe what it says, for example that God created the heaven and the earth in six days. Perhaps this *is* puzzling; certainly it deserves extended treatment not possible here. But such a religious outlook and practice is quite common, and it would be rash to simply rule it irrational, intellectually and spiritually out of order.

To dismiss her as religiously out of order, moreover, would be to miss the religious power of her treatment of the biblical narrative. She, not unlike one who reads the narrative as an actual account of creation, dwells in the potent imagery—God's presence hovering over the awesome formlessness; six days filled with creative activity; the separations of light and darkness, heaven and earth, land and sea; the creation of man and woman, reflections of divinity; the renewal of spirit on the seventh day. For her, of course, the story is not factually correct. But this is, to her mind, almost not worthy of mention; it is both obvious and completely beside the point, beside the religious point. The powerful religious resonances and intimations of the story are available to her, as they are to the fundamentalist, as a consequence of dwelling so wholeheartedly in the drama of creation.

Such a traditional theist exhibits a tendency towards the sort of naturalism of interest to me. This is of course not to say that her outlook is thoroughly naturalistic—she quite straightforwardly believes in a supernatural God. Let's turn to another biblical passage to help underscore the naturalness of the naturalistic impulse.

In traditional Jewish morning liturgy, before one dons a prayer shawl, a *tallit,* one recites a portion of Psalm 104 (which I translate/interpret freely to capture something of its spirit):

> My spirit bows in praise of God.
> *Adonai,*[23] nurturing and compassionate, *Elohim,*[23] powerful and
> just, in creating such a universe you have grown very great.
> Your clothing reveals inner majesty and outer splendor.
> Wrapped in pure light, you stretch out the heavens like a curtain.

This passage is very different than the creation narrative. My feeling is that it is best seen as poetry, as indicated by my arrangement of the sentences. This contrasts with the opening chapters of Genesis, which I see as a narrative description of creation, even if that description is formulated in poetic language. If I am correct about the poetic character of the Psalm—or even if not—a fundamentalist reading is not very tempting—except perhaps to a fundamentalist mystic.[24] Here a naturalistically spirited approach seems natural, usual. Again, the lack of belief in the factual adequacy of the depiction poses no threat to the religious power of the passage. One is nourished to the extent that one can inhabit the imagery of God's wearing a *tallit* of pure light and savor the sense of inner majesty and outer splendor.

Such depictions, I said above, are like parables or allegories. But neither "parable" nor "allegory" seems completely apt. What we need is a word that conveys the profound resonance and suggestiveness of a depiction or image, and implies (without being heavy-handed about it) factual incorrectness, all of this without misleading suggestions.[25] Perhaps the least objectionable expression is "myth," but this is not an altogether happy choice in light of its own associations. Until a more natural expression suggests itself, I will say that our non-fundamentalist theist sees the creation story as mythological, and that we (almost) all see Psalm 104 that way.

If we are to use the notion of myth in this way, it is important that we resist its deflationary overtones. Because of its deflationary ring—as if its meaning were exhausted by something like "a primitive, false belief"—we are apt to reserve the category of the mythological for traditions other than our own. I mean to suggest a much more positive estimation of the mythological, and to encourage the application of the concept to our own traditions.

I turn now to the matter of a thoroughly naturalistic approach. My idea is that a thoroughgoing naturalist might approach the creation narrative, for example, in very much the same way as the non-fundamentalist supernaturalist described above. The difference—at the level of theory it is enormous of course—is that the naturalist extends to God the sort of approach our supernaturalist applied to the six days of creation.

Like his theistic colleagues, the thoroughgoing religious naturalist dwells in the potent imagery of creation, and this makes available to him what it makes available to the theist, the same religious resonances, the same suggestiveness about the human condition and human flourishing. The drama of creation, like masterful fiction, is no less powerful, no less suggestive, for its factual untruth. Not that the creation myth is, for the naturalist, mere fiction. This story, like others that figure centrally in the tradition, is not just a story. It is our own story, our own mythology; our own both in the sense that our people figure centrally in this story (or in its continuation), and in the sense of a kind of non-exclusive ownership or possession. These stories play a crucial role in the continuity of the community over time: We have learned these stories from our parents and grandparents, and we teach them to our children. The constellation of such stories provides, or plays an enormous role in providing our moral horizons, our place and our point in the world. The term "mythology" starts to take on an honorific aura.

The non-fundamentalist theist felt no temptation to rid her vocabulary of expressions like "the six days of creation," and so it is for my religious naturalist with expressions like "God," "divine providence," "messiah," and the rest. Not only does the traditional vocabulary figure centrally in his thinking, he insists on the traditional understandings of these words. In this way, my religious naturalism is very different than what we might call religious reductionism.

The religious reductionist wants to understand "God" as a name or description of something natural, perhaps a tendency or capacity of people or of the universe, perhaps a force for good in the world, or the sum total of such forces. An intriguing suggestion is the idea that "God" represents or encapsulates those aspects of nature that evoke or inspire awe and/or love. While I can't argue for this here, I believe that to provide a naturalistic reduction of the concept of God is to lose something, indeed a great deal, of what is important in the concept. My naturalism does not then employ any sort of reinterpretation strategy. It is the traditional terminology, as traditionally understood, that figures in the religious experience of my naturalist.[26]

Let's turn to prayer, often seen as a sticking point for religious naturalism. My naturalist's experience of the traditional liturgy, like that of other religious practitioners, is multi-dimensional. The naturalist, like others who are serious about prayer, may engage the traditional liturgy in search of the imagery's applications to, or suggestions about, the human condition. Nothing naturalistically unacceptable so far. But there is another level, one that certainly seems to threaten naturalism.

In prayer, one engages God. One speaks to God, praises God, expresses awe and love towards God, asks things of God, even confronts God. That's the problem. We need here remember how we sought to resolve the parallel problem— of course not the same problem—for the case of the non-fundamentalist supernaturalist. Given the latter's disbelief in the six days of creation, we asked, how can she utter "the six days of creation" and really mean them in the sense required for real prayer? My idea, here as there, is that one engages wholeheartedly with a mythology, the factual incorrectness of which is quite beside the point.

The idea of engaging with, dwelling in, a mythology certainly stands in need of further exploration and elaboration. One source of assistance is the study of related notions in other arenas. To fully engage theatrical experience, for example, to be genuinely moved by it, the audience member needs to put aside his knowledge that it is "only a play"; he needs to go with it, to feel for the characters, to share in their joys and sorrows. He needs, that is, to "suspend disbelief," to engage with the as-it-were mythology, to put aside what we might call his meta-beliefs about the performed speech and behavior. Drama seems like a fertile field for exploring the matter of serious, focused engagement with the non-factual.[27]

Drama seems implicated in the religious life in any case, even for the fundamentalist. Playing in the background of the Jewish religious life there is a drama, a poignant one, with elements of triumph and tragic defeat, and with no small measure of irony, even comedy if one is in the right mood. Some elements of the drama are the creation narrative, and the biblical histories of the world, of the patriarchal families, of the Jewish people. Indeed the drama includes post-biblical, even modern, Jewish history. It includes projections about the future course of things, and may also include more mystical elements, the heavenly host, for example. Prominent in the drama is God, who himself plays, as it were, many roles, creator, parent, monarch, lover, judge, to name some of them. In light of his many roles, God stands in a special and quite complicated relation to human beings and specifically to the Jewish people.

Such theater quietly informs countless aspects of the religious Jew's everyday life. There are times when it assumes the foreground, as in prayer, when focused and serious. For many practitioners—perhaps most—the drama contains some fictional elements. That the existence of God is a non-fictional component is supremely important to the traditional theist. For my religious naturalist, many more key players and themes in the drama are fictional. In thus viewing the theist and naturalist as on a continuum, I do not mean to diminish or make light of the differences—my religious naturalism owes its possibility to their theoretical enormity. Drama thus provides a new arena for the study of religious engagement, and its substantial role in the religious life provides another vantage point on that life, and on religious naturalism.

In this essay, I have explored what I see as traditional Judaism's distinctive take on human flourishing. What is involved is not only a conception of the good life, but a system of practices that implements the conception. The fundamental notion I've explored is *yirat shamayim;* the ideal practitioner is the *y're shamayim,* whose stance is one of generalized humility and elevation with all the affective, behavioral, and cognitive concomitants. Such a life is not only a good life, but more to the point, it is also a life of holiness. The *y're shamayim,* living as he does in the presence of awe, sees holiness in all sorts of unlikely places. Being so in touch with the holy, he is himself touched by it. But the *y're shamayim* is holy in quite another sense. The character development he exhibits, the determination, the focus, the sustained hard work, indeed the success, is one of nature's most precious and awe-inspiring products.[28]

NOTES

1. I owe this way of putting the matter to Larry Wright.
2. See glossary of Hebrew expressions at the end of the essay.
3. All three quotations are from A. J. Heschel, *God in Search of Man* (New York, 1955). All subsequent quotations from Heschel are from this book.
4. Here I interpret Heschel, see Chapter 15, "Faith."
5. I am exploring aspects that are characteristic of awe. Neither conceptual analysis nor essential features are at issue here, only what is so usually or for the most part.
6 Heschel's style is diffuse and it is difficult for me to know how much of what I say about the duality is to be found in Heschel. Surely both humility and elevation are discussed there.
7. Humility needs considerably more attention than afforded here. To say that a person is characteristically humbled by awe experiences is not to suggest that she is "taken down a peg," although that may be true of some of the cases. My idea is that no adverse judgment about oneself need be a part of this sense generated by being in the presence of greatness. As Stephen Mitchell says, in his wonderful "Introduction" to his translation of *The Book of Job* (New York, 1987), "self-abasement is just inverted egoism. Anyone who acts with genuine humility will be as far from humiliation as from arrogance."
8. I see this new duality as distinct from the humbled-elevated duality because I don't see a focus on the agent's limitations as essential to humility. See note 7, above.
9. I am conscious of using such expressions as "the big project," that might suggest that I take there to be some single project that is the Jewish one. Nothing like this is intended. My aim is to provide one take on the life encouraged by the practices.
10. I have often thought that the really difficult trick is to get both on the same piece of paper. Maurice Friedman suggested to me that it would be better to leave them on separate sheets, maybe even in different pockets. The imagery of a single piece of paper suggests finding a way to make these consistent in some sense, perhaps finding an inclusive principle. What one needs is rather a kind of practical skill, the ability to negotiate experience so that at the

appropriate moments one pays heed to the appropriate idea. There are other dualities for which this seems so, for which the drive for an inclusive principle seems the wrong idea. Consider the universalistic and particularistic tendencies in Jewish religious thought. An undue emphasis on either of these either loses the religious richness (overemphasizing the universalistic) or threatens all manner of ugliness (overemphasizing the particularistic). The matter seems related, as Friedman suggested, to the Aristotelian golden mean idea.

11. Elliot N. Dorff mentions the Hasidic adage given in the last paragraph (see *Knowing God* [Northvale, N.J., and London, 1992]).

12. I once posed the question to one who had lived the religious life and had thought about such things for many years. We know something, I was told, of how to attain holiness; much less about what exactly one has attained.

13. Reprinted in *The Annie Dillard Reader* (New York, 1995). The quotations are from p. 287.

14. I owe to Larry Wright the connection with Wittgenstein.

15. See, for example, Grade's *Rabbis and Wives* (New York, 1982).

16. *Faith,* as I'm using this notion, is quite different than *belief.* (As noted, religious belief is not treated in this essay. This is not to say that the notion is unimportant or anything of the like.) Faith is not a matter of assent to, or conviction about, propositions. Interestingly, the Hebrew word usually translated as faith, *emunah,* has quite a different feel from *belief. Emunah* conveys commitment, trust, a steadiness in affirmation, perhaps even something like a sense of living in the presence of God.

Buber, in "Two Foci of the Jewish Soul" (an address given in 1930 and collected in his *Israel and the World*) writes

> "Faith," should not be taken in the sense given to it in the "Epistle to the Hebrews," as faith that God exists. That has never been doubted by Jacob's soul. In proclaiming its faith, its *emunah,* the soul only proclaimed that it put its trust in the everlasting God, *that he would be present* [Buber's italics] to the soul, as had been the experience of the patriarchs. . . .

17. One should not conclude that *yirat shamayim* is the sole property of the intellectually elite. There is much in traditional practice that conduces to developed religious character even in the absence of the theoretical physics of the tradition, in the absence of the highest or deepest level of Talmudic learning. Indeed there are all sorts of levels of study. The threat of elitism in traditions that so emphasize learning needs further discussion.

18. This volume.

19. Actually the thrice-daily structure is understood by the tradition to be a rabbinic innovation, as opposed to a God-given injunction.

20. Exodus 31:17.

21. While *yirah* is not the only component in the relevant attitude, it is an essential component. As Heschel remarks, "Forfeit your sense of awe . . . your ability to revere, and the universe becomes a market place for you" (p. 78). In the spirit of Heschel's remark, we might add that without awe, even with theistic beliefs galore, one still lives within the confines of a marketplace, albeit one with an unusually wide range of commodities.

22. I leave for another occasion discussion of a very important theme, that in the Hebrew Bible and much of rabbinic tradition, God seems to have limitations, perhaps even a dark side. He loves, and so needs that which he loves, he is sometimes wrathful, sometimes regrets things he has done or created (including us), perhaps plays favorites (as among the children of the patriarchs, for example), subjects his creatures to various tests (including that of Abraham being commanded to offer up Isaac), and so on. Far from seeing such things as bespeaking an incompletely developed conception of God, I see them as aspects of the richness and spiritual sensitivity of the tradition.

23. See Glossary at the end of this essay for an explanation of these two names of God.

24. One can be quite seriously mystical, I think, without being fundamentalist, without supposing that the mystical imagery correctly depicts the (or some) world.

25. "Parable," for example, suggests a simple story illustrating a religious lesson. It's not clear that we are here dealing with such a simple story or any straightforward lesson.

26. Reductionism is one of the two well-known paths of naturalism. Eliminativism is the other. In contemporary discussions of naturalism it often is assumed that a naturalistic approach to a naturalistically troublesome domain must either eliminate the troublesome entities or reduce them to something naturalistically acceptable. My naturalist's relation to the eliminativist is complicated. On one hand, contrary to the reductionist, both take the troublesome discourse at face value. Both agree that the troublesome discourse is not needed for the ultimate description of nature. But my naturalist and the eliminativist seem to disagree on the consequences for the utility of religious discourse. Perhaps this is not clear, since the eliminativist might allow that the non-referring terms, "God" for example, might figure in poetry and other forms of discourse that are not his concern. Such terms do not, however, figure in the scientific description of nature. Still, my emphasis on the religious life is far from the spirit of eliminativism as we know it.

27. The language of "engagement with a mythology" may be misleading in another way. (Other than, that is, the misleading associations of "mythology.") It might suggest, contrary to fact, that the naturalist experiences prayer, for example, *as* engagement with mythology, that he keeps before his mind the non-factual character of the narrative. As with theatrical experience, the moments of intense involvement are not typically moments that one is focused on the non-factual character of the drama. One "goes with" the drama and is not thinking about its fictional character. Indeed, if at a tragic moment in a play when one (an audience member) is feeling great sorrow, one is interrupted with the reminder that it's only a play, one will likely be very impatient. The fictional character of the play goes without saying, and is beside the point. This is true for the non-fundamentalist theist above, and for the thoroughgoing naturalist.

28. This essay appears here as an exception to the editors' practice of not publishing their own work in *Midwest Studies*. It appears at the suggestion of my 1995 Pacific Division APA commentators, Philip Quinn and Eleonore Stump, who were invited to publish in this volume and preferred to publish versions of their APA comments.

Talks which eventuated in this essay were given at the University of California, Riverside, Stanford University, Pomona College, the University of California, Irvine, and San Diego State University. I am very grateful to discussants at these sessions. I am especially grateful to my commentators, Philip Quinn and Eleonore Stump, and to Andrew Eshleman, Joel Gereboff, Ernie LePore, Andy Reath, Amelie Rorty, and Georgia Warnke for helpful comments on earlier drafts and related pieces. Finally I am grateful to the Shalom Hartman Institute of Jerusalem for much stimulation on these and related questions.

GLOSSARY OF HEBREW EXPRESSIONS

Adonai our Lord. It is traditional to pronounce the biblical Tetragrammaton name of God as if it were the word *Adonai*. *Adonai* thus comes to be seen as a name of God rather than describing God as a lord, which is closer to the literal meaning of *Adonai*. This name of God is often associated in the rabbinic literature with the attributes of mercy and nurture

ahavat Ha'shem love of God

Elohim Another name of God, often associated in the rabbinic literature with the attributes of power and justice *k'neged kulam* "the most basic or fundamental," as applied to a practice, idea, or principle

Shabbat The Sabbath

shofar Ram's horn, blown during the month of *Elul*

tallit A prayer shawl

yirah Awe, also fear, often awe with an admixture of fear

yirat Ha'shem Awe of God

yirat shamayim Awe of heaven

y're Ha'shem One who stands in awe of God

y're shamayim One who stands in awe of heaven

Awe and Atheism

ELEONORE STUMP

If one were to approach Howard Wettstein's "Awe and the Religious Life: A Naturalistic Perspective" in the way in which historical biblical scholars approach Genesis, one might well conclude that it had two strands and was the product of two quite different schools of thought. The first strand—'the J strand', as it might be called—is marked by sympathy towards and recommendation of many of the practices and beliefs of traditional Judaism. The second strand—'the P strand', we might call it—contains features commonly associated with professional philosophers, most notably rejection of the supernatural and a commitment to metaphysical naturalism. This is the strand reflected, for example, in the lines that naturalism is right and that atheists are correct in their views. Each of these strands is worth reflecting on in its own right; but, as in scholarly reconstructions of biblical texts, the really interesting thing is the fact that the differing strands have been woven together into this one document. In what follows, I will leave the P strand largely to one side, because it isn't possible to discuss naturalism and the large issues it raises in passing. (Furthermore, given the opprobium the P strand heaps on professional philosophical debates over the conflict between atheism and theism, I wouldn't want to say anything about the P strand's naturalism here even if I could think of a way to do so concisely.) Instead, I will focus on the J strand taken individually and then comment on the interweaving of these two strands into one document, which I'll call 'D'.

The J strand describes and praises religious awe, the sort of faith it gives rise to, and the practices that sustain and develop that faith. Much of what is in the J strand seems to me creative, insightful, and interesting.

According to the J strand, religious life often begins with or is strongly stimulated by a sense of awe. Awe is the affective reaction people sometimes have in the presence of something that strikes them as overwhelmingly great. This stimulus to awe can come from the realm of nature—the ocean, the starry sky— or it can result from the effects of human activity, from some product of human creativity, such as an achievement in science or a work of art. In either case, according to the J strand, the experience of greatness puts people in touch with something that is holy.

Furthermore, contact with the holy, however fleeting it may be, prompts a twofold reaction in a person. She will see herself as frail and fleeting, but she will also see her own dignity and value. Such an experience is humbling for the person who has it, on the view of the J strand, but it also affirms her. In consequence of this experience, her character will improve. She will, for example, become slower to anger and quicker to forgive. She will be filled with gratitude and grow in generosity. This transformation in her character constitutes or results in faith.

Faith is different from belief or assent to propositions. It is awe generalized and made habitual, according to the J strand. An emphasis on faith of this sort keeps religious persons from being too cognitivist in their religion and focuses their attention on affect. For the J strand, religious rituals, especially prayers and regular study of the Talmud, reinforce, train, and develop such faith. Part of the effect of rituals comes in the way they punctuate human life with a certain rhythm of reflection about matters of fundamental importance; another part of their effect stems from their focus on law, because in this way they contribute to organizing the relationship of the community and of the individual to God.

Finally, according to the J strand, the distinctive object of awe is God, and God is central to Jewish practices and rituals. "Prayer . . . is prayer *to God*. . . . [B]lessings [are] grateful acknowledgments not only of God, but to God" (p. 272).

Three things in the J strand seem to me to call for some comment.

First, although the J strand's point about the force of ritual and its rhythmic character seems right, it is nonetheless perplexing. For many people, the predictability and regularity of ritual are not only potent, as the J strand suggests, but also clearly comforting. In fact, the prescriptions of ritual are felt to be so valuable that those whose rejection of religion has deprived them of religious ritual often try to invent secular rituals, associated with families or holidays, to reintroduce the same effects. And yet ritual constricts human behavior. Ritual prayers, for example, are contrasted with spontaneous prayers just in this regard, that in ritual prayers the one praying determines neither the occasion for the prayer nor its content. Similarly, ritual mourning compels a mourner to restrict behavior and express grief in set and circumscribed ways. People, however, generally value being in control. They want to choose for themselves what to do and when to do it. Why, then, should people, who typically prefer being in control of their behavior, find ritual with all its constriction valuable and even comforting? There is something puzzling here which is worth further examination.

Second, the J strand emphasizes awe as a stimulus to religious faith, and the J strand focuses on faith as affective. There is something importantly right about the J strand's views here, but they also raise serious philosophical questions.

Consider, for example, awe as a force leading to religious faith. It is noteworthy that, as far as anecdotal evidence can determine, very few adult converts turn to religion in consequence of finding a persuasive argument for God's existence. Instead, they often turn to religion because something in their experience gives them some glimpse of what they take to be awesome goodness, which they come to associate with the holiness of God. Following that initial sight of goodness with determination not to lose it is what leads them into religious faith.

This process is movingly described in Philip Hallie's account of his discovery of Le Chambon, the French village that gave unstintingly in its attempts to rescue Jews during the German occupation of France.[1] Hallie, who was not a religious believer, was led to Le Chambon by his research on torture. He describes his initial discovery of the villagers' rescue efforts this way:

> I came across a short article about a little village in the mountains of southern France. . . . I was reading the pages with an attempt at objectivity . . . trying to sort out the forms and elements of cruelty and of resistance to it. . . . About halfway down the third page of the account of this village, I was annoyed by a strange sensation on my cheeks. . . . I reached up to my cheek to wipe away a bit of dust, and I felt tears upon my fingertips. Not one or two drops; my whole cheek was wet. (p. 3)

Those tears, Hallie says, were "an expression of moral praise" (p. 4); and that seems right. As Hallie describes it, he was overwhelmed by the greatness and goodness of what the villagers had done, and he was determined to learn more about that amazing period in their history. At the end of his increasingly personal investigation of Le Chambon, Hallie described himself this way:

> For me [the] awareness [of goodness] is my awareness of God. I live with the same sentence in my mind that many of the victims of the concentration camps uttered as they walked to their deaths: *Shema Israel, Adonoi Elohenu, Adonoi Echod.*

For Hallie the sense of awe raised in him by his initial acquaintance with the heroism of the villagers of Le Chambon led him, in the end, to a deeply rooted commitment to God, in just the way the J strand supposes awe might do.

But this phenomenon raises questions of moral psychology and epistemology. *Why* should awe work in this way? And is awe an epistemologically legitimate road to faith? These are important questions which are not addressed in the J strand. It is perhaps worth noting that some medieval accounts of faith, such as that of Aquinas, have a certain resemblance to the J strand's view of awe in this regard. For Aquinas, the road to faith in God begins with a glimpse of God's goodness and a great hunger for it. But Aquinas's account of the way in which a hunger for such overwhelming goodness leads to faith is embedded in a broader philosophical and theological context which has the resources for explaining why such a road to faith is appropriate and epistemically justified.[2]

Finally, the faith praised by the J strand is supposed to be affective rather than cognitive, and there is some suggestion[3] that the J strand's faith is to be distinguished in this respect from Christian faith, which, the J strand implies, is or essentially includes assent to certain propositions. But this characterization of faith is problematic as regards both religious traditions.

Christian faith, the kind of faith that puts a believer into a religiously desirable state, is traditionally thought to have an affective as well as a cognitive component. Aquinas, for example, distinguished between formed and unformed faith.[4] Unformed faith is the kind the devils have when they believe in God and tremble. The religiously desirable sort of faith, formed faith, consists in states of will as well as intellect; it requires a disposition to love God and to seek goodness. Without those states of will, Aquinas held, faith is lifeless and religiously inefficacious. And the same view is echoed in different terminology by Protestants, including the early Reformers.[5] So, contrary to the position of the J strand, Christian faith is like faith in Judaism in being committed to the central importance of an affective component.

On the other hand, it is clear that Judaism, too, takes a cognitive component to be an important element in faith. It's hard to see how study of the Talmud, for example, could be crucial for faith, as the J strand says it is, unless that were so. More importantly, emotion itself seems to have a cognitive component, so that to have an affective attitude towards something is to have a cognitive attitude of some sort towards it as well.[6]

So, there is an intellective and an affective component to faith, for both Judaism and Christianity, and the J strand is wrong to take faith as largely cognitive in Christianity and fundamentally affective in Judaism.

What is especially remarkable about this essay, however, is not any feature of the J strand or the P strand taken separately but rather the combination of them both into one document D.

Although the J strand claims that God is central to Jewish ritual and the distinctive object of awe, D maintains that God does not exist. D's position is, of course, complicated. On the one hand, atheists are right; but, on the other hand, they are right only, as D says, on a technicality. As regards religion, D holds, atheists are mistaken. Even if God does not exist, religion "encourage[s] a distinctive take on human flourishing, one that is tragically unappreciated in secular, including philosophical, culture" (p. 258); there is "something important and right about our religious traditions" (p. 259). Even an atheist can avail himself of the benefits of religion by treating talk about God and the supernatural as parables or myths giving some deep insights into the human condition.

To add to the complication, taking the supernatural in this way isn't a matter of eliminating all references to the supernatural or reducing supernatural terms to naturalistic ones. It is rather more like going to a play, where one engages wholeheartedly with the world of the play, entering into that world and leaving one's own world behind.

To explain and support its position, D gives an analogy. It describes a nonfundamentalist theist NF who doesn't believe certain elements of the story of creation in Genesis, such as that God did in twenty-four-hour periods what Genesis claims God did in a day, but who nonetheless is unwilling to treat the reference to days in the text in a reductionist or eliminativist manner. Such a person differs in belief from a fundamentalist reader of the text, but may be just as deeply moved by it. It is hard to explain, according to D, why such a person should be so moved, but it's clear that she can be. In just the same way, a naturalist N can refuse to accept elements of the Genesis story as literally true, but can nonetheless read the story without engaging in reduction or eliminativism and can be just as deeply moved by it, just as filled with awe, as any theistic reader.

But, contrary to the suggestion of D, there is nothing very perplexing about why NF should be moved by the reading of the Genesis story: she takes *most* of what it says, or at least a very great deal of it, as literally true. Although she dissents from some details of the story, the bulk of it strikes her as factually correct. She thinks it is literally true that there is a God, for example, and that he created the world in general, and human beings in particular; she believes that human beings are in some sense reflections of God and that God created them good; and so on. So it is not surprising that the story would be moving for NF, even if she doesn't accept all its elements as literally true.

But could the story, as D claims, have just the same power to move N and to stimulate awe in him? N takes virtually all of the story to be false. In consequence of his naturalism, for example, N thinks that it is literally false that there is a God, that God created anything, that God created human beings, that human beings were made by God in his image as a reflection of him, and so on. In what sense could the Genesis story resonate for N or cause him to react affectively in the way NF does?

Consider, by way of comparison, Homer's description of Apollo shooting plague-causing arrows at the helpless Greek army because Agamemnon has dishonored Apollo's priest. The passage is poetically powerful; it catches one's attention and remains in one's memory. But it's hard to imagine its stimulating religious awe in us or giving us a sense of the holy. And that's precisely because we think that there is no supernatural being such as Apollo, that no deity causes diseases by shooting arrows into people, and that there are perfectly good naturalistic explanations of diseases which have nothing to do with Apollo's seeking revenge for being dishonored. Just because we have such naturalistic views, though the literary beauty of the passage may strike us, it hardly moves us to religious awe. And this remains the case even though this story is part of a poem that has played "a crucial role in the continuity of the community over time" (p. 275),[7] and even if Homer has been part of one's childhood education or passed on to one's own children. The sort of affective reaction which a believing pagan might have is closed off to us because of our naturalism as regards Apollo.

Furthermore, it is hard to see how *all* the supernatural elements in the Genesis story could be understood as compatible with naturalism without engaging in eliminativist or reductionist strategies regarding religious discourse. In any literal understanding of the story, an eliminativist would recast the discourse to get rid of the references to non-existent entities (although, as D points out, an eliminativist might be willing to let some supernatural discourse remain for purposes of poetry or conventional modes of expression). For his part, a reductionist would be willing to accept the supernatural terminology, but he would do so because he would suppose he could reduce the troublesome expressions to something natural, in such a way as to avoid commitment to the non-natural. If it were neither eliminativist or reductionist, how would a completely *atheistic* interpretation of this same biblical story go?

For example, if there is no God, there is also no divine creation. Won't an atheistic interpretation of the biblical account of the origin of the world then have either to eliminate talk of divine creation or to translate it into something compatible with atheism? Such an interpretation may well give us deep truths about the human condition, as D maintains, but it will also be an eliminativist or reductionist interpretation. To put the same point the other way around, if the interpretation didn't eliminate or reduce supernatural terms, in what sense would it be an interpretation compatible with naturalism?

So while D is right in its claim that naturalistic interpretations of religious stories and doctrines are possible, it is hard to see how D could be right in its claim that such interpretations can be had without the elimination or reduction of references to the supernatural.

It is true, as D points out, that there are cases in which we enter whole-heartedly into another world, as when we are immersed in a play or caught up in a novel, without giving up our awareness that we are entertaining fiction. It isn't clear to me that one does enter wholeheartedly into the world of religion if one espouses atheism, any more than one can enter wholeheartedly into the world of marriage if one insists on permanently living alone. Nonetheless, the phenomenon regarding fiction that D wants to call attention to is clear enough. Could this be the right analogy to explain how it is possible to have atheistic reactions of awe to religious texts?

But what is it exactly that happens when we are moved by something we take to be fiction? Sometimes we say that in entering the world of fiction, as in the theater, we are suspending disbelief. This can't, however, be the right way to interpret an atheistic reaction of awe to religious texts. For an atheist to enter the world of religion by suspending disbelief is for him to become, with a part of his mind or for a certain part of time, a believer, a person who recognizes and accepts the God presupposed in the J strand. Suspending disbelief in this way, then, is not a means of reconciling the J strand and the P strand. It is rather a matter of wavering between them.

Kenneth Walton has argued that affective reactions to fiction should be understood in terms of simulation theory.[8] A person P responding affectively to fiction simulates the emotion of a person F in the fiction or of someone who is taking as reality what P believes to be fiction. This strikes me as an intriguing account of an otherwise perplexing phenomenon. If atheistic responses to religion are like reactive attitudes to fiction, as D suggests, perhaps Walton's account could be applied (mutatis mutandis) to this phenomenon.

There is, however, one drawback to applying Walton's account to the affective attitudes D hopes to account for. According to Walton, if P responds, for example, to some horror movie by engaging in a simulation of the fear of a character F in the movie, P doesn't have the affect of fear itself as a result of the simulation; rather, she has only the imagined analogue of fear. P may well have some real affect (such as tension or nervousness) as a result of imagining herself to be in the state of F, who (in the movie) does believe in the monster's existence and his own urgent danger from the monster; but she doesn't have real fear since she believes that the fear-inducing monster of the horror movie doesn't really exist. If we apply Walton's account to the case at issue for D, then though the atheist will have some affect or other as a result of imagining himself into the state of a religious believer, he won't have real awe, just because he doesn't believe that God exists.

In addition to these problems, it is hard to see how we can have what the J strand values and recommends on the P strand's metaphysics.

For example, according to D, awe is an affective reaction to perceived greatness in nature or in human accomplishment, and it puts the person feeling awe in touch with the holy. But why suppose that for a convinced atheist, perceived greatness, divorced from a belief in God, has any connection to holiness? For the convinced atheist, the secular analogue to awe, prompted by a perception of greatness, might be more a matter of being struck into amazement by a demonstration of natural or human beauty or power. As he records in his diaries, Goebbels seems to have had an affective reaction of awe of this sort in reviewing newsreel footage showing German destruction of Poland. But this reaction certainly didn't put him in touch with anything holy. If the person experiencing awe does not believe in God and if the perceived greatness doesn't move him by giving him what he takes to be some sense of the divine, is there any natural connection between the perception of greatness and an experience of holiness?

Furthermore, why suppose that the secular analogue to religious awe has anything necessarily affirming about it? Why should an atheist looking at the vast starry sky feel affirmed? Might she not just feel lonely, sad, or anxious? There was a period not so long ago, after all, in which atheism combined with overawed reflection on the cosmos was widely supposed to induce existential angst in thoughtful people, not an affirmation of the dignity of human beings. Even in the face of magnificent human creativity, human affect alone, divorced from some belief in a God supposed to be loving and providential, isn't necessarily affirming. It sometimes consists just in envy or depression instead. Salieri, for example, was powerfully moved by Mozart's musical genius, but Salieri doesn't seem to have felt affirmed by it.

In the same vein, why suppose that the secular analogue to religious awe will necessarily produce character transformations that are for the better, that lead in the direction of positive character transformation or saintliness? Jiang Ching had a great awe of her husband Mao, as did most Chinese, who tended to feel about Mao the way their forebears felt about the emperor. But the transformation wrought in Jiang by her affective reaction of awe was all for the worse, not for the better. It bred in her nothing more than a determined wish to match

Mao in power and influence, and the Cultural Revolution fomented in large part by her determination was one of the greatest social injustices in Chinese history. Perhaps for some people the moving sight of human greatness gives rise to affective reactions of the sort that transform character in positive ways. But, without a connection to religious belief in a loving and perfectly good creator of human beings, perhaps for some people the overwhelming sight of human greatness produces just envy, anxiety, and an unsavory determination to get their share of the available goods.

The problem is that if the sight of human or natural greatness isn't taken as a window on the holiness of God, it has no necessary tie to goodness of any sort. Consequently, affective reactions to it, however powerful, need not be either affirming or conducive to positive character transformations. They may, instead, lead to anything from sadness and withdrawal to malice and violence.

Finally, the practices recommended by the J strand are also hard to support on the metaphysics of the P strand. Consider, for example, only prayer and study of the Talmud.

Prayer is speech addressed to God, in which God is thanked, praised, or petitioned. How are we to construe these activities on the part of a person who is wholeheartedly convinced that there is no God? How are we to understand a person who believes, while he is praying, that the God to whom he is addressing petitions doesn't exist, hear prayers, or grant petitions, who thinks that the deity he is praising isn't there and hasn't done anything worthy of praise? It is possible, of course, to say prayers as a way, for example, to think about the abiding values of one's life or to put oneself in touch with one's own tradition. But then one would be engaged just in internal reflection, and it would be as much a stretch of language to consider such isolated reflection to be prayer as it would be to regard inner communion as a conversation with one's spouse.

As for study of the Talmud, if there is no God, then there is no divine law either. But then why study Talmud with such intensity? Why labor so to bring out all the law's sense and implications? D suggests that study of a common law code is beneficial because it brings a community together. But this claim alone wouldn't explain the devotion to a law code or to the Talmud in particular. There are many ways for a community to be brought together besides communal reflection on a law code. And if a community does want a law code to be its focus, then why pick the Talmud to focus on if it isn't a law code privileged by being promulgated by God? There are lots of law codes in the world, after all; and there are even some, such as Roman law, which are rich and powerful and important in Jewish history.

The practices that the J strand recommends are clearly predicated on a belief in the existence of God, and it is therefore much harder to understand or defend them on the P strand's metaphysics.

For all these reasons, even if there were no problems in the J and the P strands taken individually, the two strands are very difficult to weave together, and the fabric composed of them is likely to fray.[9]

NOTES

1. Philip Hallie, *Lest Innocent Blood Be Shed,* (Philadelphia, 1979). References to this work will be given with page numbers in the text.

2. See my "Aquinas on Faith and Goodness," in *Being and Goodness,* edited by Scott MacDonald (Ithaca, N.Y., 1991), 179–207.

3. See footnote 16, for example.

4. See *ST* II–II q.4 a.2–3 and q.5 a.2.

5. So, for example, Calvin says, "faith cannot possibly be disjoined from pious affection" (*The Institutes of the Christian Religion,* translated by Henry Beveridge [Grand Rapids, Mich., 1970], Book III, chapter ii, section 8).

6. For this position and some of the puzzles associated with it, see, for example, Amelie Rorty, "Explaining Emotions," in *Explaining Emotions,* edited by Amelie Rorty (Berkeley and Los Angeles, 1980), 103–26.

7. Since, as doesn't need saying, Homer has been immeasurably influential in Western tradition.

8. In a recent paper, "Spelunking, Simulation, and Slime: On Being Moved by Fiction," given at the University of Missouri, St. Louis. There is by now a large literature on simulation theory; for one of the classic early papers on simulation, see Robert Gordon, "Folk Psychology as Simulation," *Mind and Language* 1 (1986): 158–71; reprinted in *Folk Psychology: The Theory of Mind Debate,* edited by M. Davies and T. Stone (Oxford: 1995), 60–73.

9. I am grateful to Howard Wettstein and Philip Quinn for interesting discussion of the topics of this essay, and I am indebted to Norman Kretzmann for helpful comments and questions on an earlier draft.

MIDWEST STUDIES IN PHILOSOPHY, XXI (1997)

Religious Awe, Aesthetic Awe

PHILIP L. QUINN

Howard Wettstein begins his insightful and stimulating essay in this volume by remarking on analytic philosophy's neglect of the practical dimensions of religious life. I think the point is well taken, though perhaps the neglect is not as complete as his remarks might lead one to believe. I myself address the practical side of religious life fairly often in my teaching. But when I do, I must confess, what I ask my students to read is not work by leading analytic philosophers of religion such as Alvin Plantinga or Richard Swinburne. Instead I discuss with them such books as Rudolf Otto's *The Idea of the Holy*, Martin Buber's *I and Thou*, and Paul Tillich's *The Dynamics of Faith*. Books like these, however, lack characteristics analytic philosophers prize; they are not notable for clarity of expression or rigorous argumentation. Wettstein's work is notable for such intellectual virtues. Therefore I applaud his bold attempt to put the practical aspects of religion on the agenda of analytic philosophy.

Wettstein makes it abundantly clear that study of religious emotions raises a large number of philosophical questions, some familiar and others not. He tries to provide a map of a territory that has, to a considerable extent, been left unexplored by recent analytic philosophy. I do not think it would be helpful for me to devote these comments to criticism of the details of his map. So I shall instead sketch an alternative map of the same territory. Comparison of my map with his should serve to highlight some philosophical issues that call for further discussion.[1] I shall focus on two topics. The first is awe, and the second is the move from awe to faith.

I. AWE, RELIGIOUS AND NONRELIGIOUS

I subscribe to the view that the emotions are cognitive. A recent survey article opens with the claim that "cognitivism now dominates the philosophical study of emotions."[2] So my view appears to be the received view. Of course cognitive accounts of the emotions come in several flavors. Some theorists think emotions are beliefs, albeit beliefs marked by a special intensity or vivacity. Others regard emotions as compounds, containing both purely affective parts and cognitive parts, intimately related. Yet others identify emotions proper with pure affect but hold that it is causally dependent on belief. In the present context, I see no need to express a preference for a particular cognitive account of the emotions. So I shall proceed from the general assumption that emotions are in some way belief-dependent. Interestingly, textual evidence suggests that Abraham Joshua Heschel, whose work Wettstein makes use of, would endorse my assumption in the case of awe. Heschel says that awe "is more than an emotion; it is a way of understanding."[3] And he goes on to say that "awe is an intuition for the creaturely dignity of all things and their preciousness to God; a realization that things not only are what they are but also stand, however remotely, for something absolute."[4] For Heschel, awe is not merely an affective state; it contains or is tightly linked to something cognitive.

Cognitivism can explain what is going on in the following anecdote about awe. John Ruskin was traveling from England to Italy. During the journey through Switzerland, his coach was delayed one day by a snow storm. It arrived long after dark at the inn at which he planned to spend the night. Exhausted, Ruskin went immediately to his room. While he was waiting for sleep to come, the clouds broke, and the full moon shone forth. Through the window of his room, Ruskin saw what he took to be a snowy Alp glistening in the moonlight, distant and grand.[5] He was struck with awe. Unfortunately, closer inspection revealed that what he was looking at was really the sloping, snow-covered roof of a cow shed, only a hundred meters away from the inn. The awe abruptly disappeared.[6] It could not, if the story is to be believed, survive his loss of the belief that it was a vast Alp he was seeing.

Was Ruskin's awe religious? We cognitivists find it natural to classify emotions into kinds in accord with the kinds of beliefs on which they depend. An emotion is religious only if it depends upon belief that is religious. Of course it is notoriously difficult to draw a bright line of demarcation between religious and nonreligious beliefs. Is the belief system of Theravada Buddhism religious despite the fact that, in its purer forms, it does not include any belief in supernatural beings? Is Marxism a religious belief system because it contains eschatological and soteriological beliefs that are functionally equivalent to the beliefs on these subjects found in Judaism and Christianity? Such questions provoke lively debate in religious studies and anthropology, and nothing I have to say is likely to conclude that debate. The best I can do is to resort to the pragmatic expedient of proposing a characterization of religious belief that I hope will be useful in the present discussion. As I see it, religious beliefs are about a dimension of reality that transcends the world revealed to us by ordinary experience, common sense, and uncontroversial science and that offers the promise of salvation or liberation from the deepest ills to which human beings are liable.

With religious belief thus understood, I think it is clear that seeing a snowy Alp by moonlight can evoke religious awe. A theist's awe, for example, might depend on the belief that the Alp's sparkling grandeur reveals or makes manifest God's glory. But it also seems clear that Ruskin's awe need not have been religious, for his response could have been much like what it was even in the absence of any religious belief. I would say the same thing about the awe Kant professed to feel upon contemplating the starry heavens above and the moral law within and about Wettstein's examples of natural grandeur, human artifacts, and human heroism. One can respond to such things with religious awe, but one's response to them can involve awe without being dependent on religious belief as I have characterized it.

I am not for a moment tempted to deny that there can be genuine awe in the absence of religious belief. But how is awe of this kind to be understood? I suggest that we make use of the traditional aesthetic category of sublimity. The distinction between the sublime and the beautiful plays an important role in Kant's *Critique of Judgment,* and it also features prominently in the aesthetic writings of Edmund Burke. It is interesting that Heschel associates awe with the sublime. He says that awe "is the sense of wonder and humility inspired by the sublime or felt in the presence of mystery."[7] The sublime is grand, vast, and overpowering. One can respond in awe to what one takes to be grand, vast, and overpowering without also believing it to be an expression of the transcendent or a source of salvation.

Of course the sublime is not a category that does much work in recent philosophy of art. I suspect this is partly because contemporary artists seldom aim at expressing the sublime or evoking awe. It is too easy to aim at such lofty goals and wind up producing the most dreadful kitsch. I also conjecture that an explanation of this feature of contemporary art is to be sought in the neighborhood of Max Weber's claim that the inhabitants of modern technological societies live in disenchanted life-worlds. It would not be at all surprising if there were new limits on what artists could aspire to achieve after disenchantment. Nevertheless, it remains possible for some of us to be struck with awe by natural grandeur and older works of art. I think I have responded with awe to seeing the Grand Canyon and to hearing the final movement of Beethoven's Ninth Symphony. I cannot help thinking that these things are genuinely sublime. But though I treasure my memories of such experiences, I regard them as aesthetic rather than religious. I do not think of them as revealing to me a transcendent dimension of reality with salvific potential.

My distinction between religious awe and aesthetic awe has Kantian roots. Since Rudolf Otto's *The Idea of the Holy* has a neo-Kantian philosophical background, it is not surprising that it contains a similar distinction. According to Otto, holiness involves moral goodness. He claims that "in this sense Kant calls the will which remains unwaveringly obedient to the moral law from the motive of duty a 'holy' will."[8] When moral goodness is, so to speak, subtracted out from holiness, what remains is numinousness. Two parts of Otto's analysis of the numinous are the *mysterium tremendum.* The *tremendum* has within it the elements of awfulness, majesty, and urgency; it evokes awe. The *mysterium* involves the wholly other; it makes reference to the transcendent. As Otto sees it, there are analogies between the consciousness of the sublime and the consciousness of the numinous, but he wants to distinguish sharply between them. He says that we resort to the more familiar feeling-content of the sublime to fill out the negative concept of transcendence, explaining God's transcendence by God's sublimity. And then he goes on to say:

> As a figurative analogical description this is perfectly allowable, but it would be an error if we meant it literally and in earnest. Religious feelings are not the same as aesthetic feelings, and "the sublime" is as definitely an aesthetic term as "the beautiful," however widely different may be the facts denoted by the words.[9]

For my part, I doubt that there is a sharp distinction to be drawn between aesthetic and religious feelings because I doubt that there is a sharp distinction to be drawn between nonreligious and religious beliefs. In some cases, it may be difficult, if not impossible, to tell whether awe is aesthetic or religious, and indeed, in some cases, there may be no fact of the matter. After all, among readers who have found Spinoza's vision awe-inspiring, some have come away thinking of him as a God-intoxicated man while others have strongly suspected him of atheism. But I think Wettstein's suggestion that the object of awe need not be thought of as mysterious is more plausible in the clear cases of aesthetic awe than in the clear cases of religious awe. In addition, I believe aesthetic awe is more likely than religious awe to be susceptible to being understood naturalistically without arousing suspicions of illegitimate reductionism.

On my map of the terrain, then, there are at least two kinds of awe, religious and aesthetic, though the boundary between them is not a sharp line of demarcation. This suggests that there is more than one way to move from awe to faith. I next turn to exploring this suggestion.

II. FROM RELIGIOUS AWE TO RELIGIOUS FAITH, FROM AESTHETIC AWE TO SECULAR FAITHS

I also subscribe to a cognitivist view of faith. I take it to be the received view that faith is belief-dependent. Theists cannot have faith in God unless they believe that God exists. Or, at least, to mention in passing some complications discussed in detail by Swinburne, theists cannot have faith unless they believe that the existence of God is more probable than not or, at least, is more probable than any alternative that is a live option.[10] But belief by itself is not sufficient for faith. According to Christian scripture, the devils believe (indeed, they know) that God exists but lack faith in God. What must be added to belief to get faith? Leaving room, as it does, for both conative and affective components, Heschel's suggestion that faith is attachment is attractive. He says that "faith is an act of the whole person, of mind, will, and heart."[11] Wettstein quotes a passage in which Buber urges that faith involves putting one's trust in the everlasting God. Following Josiah Royce, I think faith involves the kind of loyalty that enables one to remain attached to the object of one's faith when assailed by strong temptations to deny it. And there are, no doubt, other ways to flesh out a conception of faith.

It is not hard to see how the transition from religious awe to religious faith might go. One is struck with awe in an encounter with what one takes to be a transcendent source of salvation or liberation, and one subsequently works to develop character traits, qualities of will and heart, that will attach one to what one believes to be a transcendent source of salvation or liberation. At this point traditional Christians may differ from others in insisting that the most one can do under one's own steam toward achieving such attachment is to make oneself receptive to a gift of faith if it is offered. But they will welcome Wettstein's eloquent description of the ways in which such development occurs by means of immersion in the life of a community, living inside its narratives and participating in its rituals.

It is not clear to me how the transition from aesthetic awe to the sort faith associated with it is supposed to go. In particular, as a cognitivist about faith, I want to know more about the beliefs upon which such faith depends. Wettstein speaks of awe as involving a sense of the great significance of human life despite its fragility and limitations. Perhaps there is a kind of secular faith that involves no more than the belief that human life has great significance despite its fragility and limitations. R. M. Hare has advocated a secular faith that depends on the belief that morality's ends will not ultimately be frustrated by the course of history.[12] Annette Baier has discussed a secular faith "in the human community and its evolving procedures—in the prospects for many-handed cognitive ambitions and moral hopes."[13] She describes a moral faith that depends on belief that one can establish the possibility of a Kantian kingdom of ends by living so as to qualify for membership in it. Obviously not much thought would be required to extend this short list of possible secular faiths. I wonder which, if any, of them Wettstein finds attractive. I also wonder whether any of them can be sustained apart from belief in a transcendent source of salvation or liberation.

It seems clear to me that secular faith of some sort can be very valuable, particularly to those for whom religious faith in a transcendent source of salvation is not available. So if aesthetic awe can motivate or prompt a transition to a secular faith or can sustain such a faith once acquired, it will have instrumental value in addition to whatever intrinsic value it may possess. What is more, it may have such instrumental value even if it cannot prompt a transition to a secular faith since it may motivate or sustain hope, which requires less by way of belief than faith. Roughly put, faith depends on the belief that the existence of its object is probable while hope only requires the belief that the existence of its object is not impossible. Hence aesthetic awe would remain valuable and worth cultivating even if it were to prompt and support only what Richard Rorty characterizes as the hope that we ourselves, rather than a power not ourselves, will do unimaginably vast good.[14]

Let me conclude on a skeptical note. Wettstein considers it desirable to live in the presence of awe, to have awe constitute a kind of background condition of ordinary life. If it is a question of aesthetic experiences of the sublime, I doubt that we have the capacity to make much progress toward such goals. If one listens very often to the last movement of Beethoven's Ninth Symphony, it tends to become boring. Park rangers who work there tend to come to see the Grand Canyon as mundane and ordinary. Such, I think, is the sad condition of what Augustine aptly describes as the restless human heart. But if it is a question of religious experiences of a transcendent source of salvation, perhaps we may hope to make ourselves receptive to steady and regular gifts of grace, to what Christians call the indwelling of the Holy Spirit.

NOTES

1. Alternatively, Wettstein and I could be understood to be disagreeing about taxonomy rather than cartography. Viewed in these terms, he is a lumper and I am a splitter. He supposes that the ordinary examples of awe at natural and human grandeur are primitive cases of religious responsiveness. I think many of them are aesthetic and not religious.

2. John Deigh, "Cognitivism in the Theory of Emotions," *Ethics* 104 (July 1994): 824.

3. Abraham Joshua Heschel, *God in Search of Man* (New York, 1955), 74.

4. Ibid., 75.

5. After hearing an oral presentation of an earlier version of this material, William P. Alston informed me that his only objection to what I had said was that an alp is a meadow rather than a mountain. But though the *OED* tells us that the term 'alp' is "applied in Switzerland to the green pastureland on the mountain side," its primary definition of the term is "a single peak." And my office dictionary, which is the College Edition of *Webster's New World*, says that an alp is "a high mountain, especially in Switzerland." For present purposes, I stipulate that an Alp is a mountain in the Alps.

6. The person who told me this story more than two decades ago assured me that it is to be found in Ruskin's writings. I have never tried to locate it. But I think it ought to be true even if it is not true.

7. Heschel, *God in Search of Man*, 77.

8. Rudolf Otto, *The Idea of the Holy*, translated by John W. Harvey (New York, 1958), 5.

9. Ibid., 41.

10. Cf. Richard Swinburne, *Faith and Reason* (Oxford, 1981).

11. Heschel, *God in Search of Man*, 54.

12. R. M. Hare, "The Simple Believer," reprinted in his *Essays on Religion and Education* (Oxford, 1992).

13. Annette Baier, "Secular Faith," reprinted in her *Postures of the Mind* (Minneapolis, 1985), 293.

14. Richard Rorty, "Religious Faith, Intellectual Responsibility, and Romance" (forthcoming).

MIDWEST STUDIES IN PHILOSOPHY, XXI (1997)

Perfect Goodness and Divine Motivation Theory

LINDA ZAGZEBSKI

PROLOGUE

Lately I have been exploring the possibilities for an ethical theory I call motivation-based virtue theory. Like all forms of pure virtue ethics this theory makes the concept of a good human trait, a virtue, logically prior to the concept of a right act. What is radical about it is that a component of virtue, a motivation, is *the* most basic evaluative concept in the theory. All other evaluative concepts in ethics are defined in terms of the evaluations of motives. Virtues are defined in terms of good motives in that a good motive is the primary constituent of a virtue; good states of affairs are defined in terms of the ends of good motives; and right acts are defined in terms of the behavior of virtuous persons. What I mean by a motive is an emotion that initiates, sustains, and directs action towards an end. So motivation-based virtue theory makes emotions the primary bearers of moral properties. They are not good or bad because of their relationship to other kinds of things that are good or bad, such as acts or the states of affairs that are their intentional objects.

I have a number of reasons for investigating this type of theory. First of all, I am attracted to the category of virtue theory, but I believe that many alternative structures for such theories have not been sufficiently explored. I suspect that part of the reason for the general lack of attentiveness to theoretical structure among contemporary virtue ethicists is that many of these philosophers find the conceptual mapping that constitutes the heart of theory-building distasteful, and they prefer to concentrate instead on morality in its particulars. I am certainly not opposed to these projects and find them frequently illuminating, but my aim in the general research program of which this essay is a part is to work on the purely theoretical side of virtue ethics. I am interested in working out the conceptual connections among the concepts of most interest to ethics—right act, good state of affairs, good qualities of persons—and I am investigating the possibilities for doing this by making personal emotional states (motives) the fundamental possessor of moral properties. I also believe that the metaphysics of morals is neglected in contemporary ethics, and so another reason I have for exploring the potential for making certain states of persons fundamental in ethics is that this move makes it easier to attach a theological foundation to ethical theory.

In this essay I will lay out a theological groundwork for a motivation-based virtue theory by making the emotional states of one person in particular the ultimate foundation of ethical concepts, and that person is God. What I will propose in what follows is that the ultimate ground of all value is God's motivations, where a motivation is understood as a motive-disposition. I believe this move has advantages both in theology and in ethics. It suggests a natural way to solve four traditional puzzles involving the attribute of perfect goodness and it permits a unified account of value, both divine and human. The extension of motivation-based virtue theory introduced here is structurally parallel to Divine Command theory (DC), but without the disadvantages of that theory. I call the theory Divine Motivation Theory (DM).

I. GOD'S MOTIVES AND GOD'S WILL

All ethical theories have the problem of justifying their foundations, although most do not give the question sufficient attention. Since persons are ontologically more fundamental than acts, it is reasonable to think that the moral properties of persons are more fundamental than the moral properties of acts, so virtues are more fundamental than right acts. The relative primacy of persons and states of affairs is a different matter. In a theistic ontology God is more basic than states of affairs outside of God, and so it is reasonable within such a framework to explore ways of making God's moral properties more basic than any other moral properties in the universe. In the theory I call motivation-based virtue theory, motivational states are basic. But the question of what makes certain human motives good is as serious for this theory as the question of what makes a certain form of life one of *eudaimonia* in a *eudaimonia*-based virtue theory such as Aristotle's. Let me first give what I think is the best naturalistic answer to this question before turning to my real answer, the topic of this essay.

What makes a human motive a good one? The answer that I think may be most promising is inspired by Plato's *Republic*. A good soul is a harmonious soul, and good motives are those emotions that are in harmony with each other within the soul. So good motives are emotions that integrate; bad motives do not integrate. This approach makes integrity in the sense of wholeness and unity of self the key moral concept. It would be very interesting to see if and how such a form of virtue ethics could be worked out, but that is not what I want to do here. Instead, I want to give my real answer to the question of what makes a motive a good one: a theological answer. I propose that a good *human* motivation is one that expresses, within the limits of finite human nature, divine motivations. Divine motivations are good in the deepest sense of good. This means that if, as my motivation-based virtue theory maintains, the other evaluative concepts that apply to human acts, traits, and states of affairs rest on the goodness of human motives, and if, as I am proposing here, the goodness of human motives rests on similarity to the divine motives, it follows that all of moral value ultimately rests on the goodness of divine motives, and all evaluative concepts in ethics are ultimately derived from the concept of a divine motive.

The Christian tradition does not ascribe very many motives to God, but it does ascribe a few, particularly motives directed towards human persons, and while God has no motives that are appropriately directed to superiors, he does, I believe, have motives that are appropriately directed towards equals. This is probably one of the lessons of the doctrine of the Trinity. The biblical motives directed to humans include anger, indignation, regret, tenderness, pity, love, forgiveness, and mercy—all of which are most naturally understood to be emotions.[1]

There are, however, some problems in claiming that God has motives that must be addressed before we proceed. It was usually maintained in traditional Christian theology that God is impassible, which is to say, he does not have emotions, yet as I have defined a motive, it is an emotion. In this century the idea of divine impassibility has been increasingly under attack, although the traditional Thomistic grounds for the doctrine have often been overlooked. These reasons are well worth examining, although I will do so only briefly.[2] As I understand Aquinas, he had two main reasons for thinking God has no emotions. First, a very long tradition lasting well into the modern era understood an emotion as a state in which a person is acted *upon,* i.e., is passive, which is why these states were commonly called "passions," and yet God is never passive with respect to any of his properties.[3] This impassivity was thought to follow from divine perfection and immutability. One important metaphysical reason for denying emotion to God, then, is that God is perfect and emotion was thought to detract from divine perfection. Second, God has no body, and since Aquinas followed Aristotle in thinking that emotions were body-dependent, it seemed to follow that God could not have emotions.

The objection that emotions are passive is inapplicable to the position I am defending since what I mean by a motive is not an essentially passive state. In fact, on my account there is no requirement that an emotion have any degree of passivity at all. It may arise solely from the nature of the agent, and in the case of God I would propose that that is exactly how an emotion arises. A divine emotion is a state that arises from the divine nature and is expressive of it. Some divine emotions are not only expressive of that nature but are aimed at producing something—creating a world and all its wonders, in the first instance. Such expressive and creative states need not detract from perfection in any way.

But, it may be argued, do not emotions detract from perfection through their incompatibility with immutability? Even if emotion is not essentially passive, doesn't it involve change? Again, I think the answer is "not necessarily." If God is temporal, then God is not immutable anyway, in which case the point that emotion requires mutability is not an objection. But even if God is timeless and immutable, I see no reason why he cannot have emotions in the sense I have described. Human emotions are very much tied to our temporality. Our emotions come and go because of the vividness of immediate experience and the tendency of our memories to fade. But these aspects of our nature are due to our finitude, and the emotions of an eternal God would not be limited in that way. I see nothing conceptually impossible about the existence of eternal and immutable emotions in a perfect deity. The way in which God's motives act as causes of events in time is a problem to be solved in any theory that links a timeless God with a temporal world, but I do not see that the idea that God has emotions adds any further problems to that view.

The other main Thomistic objection to the idea that God has emotions is that emotions are body-dependent, and yet God has no body. Aquinas maintained that an emotion, or *passio animalis,* exists in the sensitive appetite, and the sensitive appetite needs corporeal organs for its operation. The experience of emotion involves physical changes, most especially, he thought, in the heart and blood. In contrast to the sensitive powers, intellectual powers, including the intellective appetite, do not need corporeal organs for their operation. I will not here debate the question of whether emotions are body-dependent, or whether, as Descartes thought, they are not. Most accounts of human emotion connect them in one way or another with events in the body, but the issue for the question of God's nature, of course, is whether there is a conceptual connection between emotion and corporeality. On the traditional Christian view of a personal God, it is almost always maintained that God has intellectual states; it is rarely maintained that God has sensory states; emotional states are in between. As far as I know, no contemporary thinker construes an emotion simply as a raw *feel,* although I am not opposed to the position that a necessary component of an emotion is that it has a "feel" to it. But even if this is the case, the sense of "feel" need not be associated with the body by a relation of necessity.

Let us approach the question from a different direction. Are there reasons for thinking that God has motives? It certainly would be odd to deny it since it is hard to see how any person can act, even a divine person, without a motive. I have already mentioned that there is biblical evidence for divine motives and emotions, and some of these texts led Aquinas to the conclusion that God *does* have states that in humans are emotions. He simply denies that in the case of God they are emotions. The texts that concerned Aquinas are the following:

> "I regret having made them." (Gen. 6a:7)
> "Yahweh is tenderness and pity, slow to anger and rich in faithful love." (Ps. 103:8)
> "Yahweh's anger blazed out at his people." (Ps. 106:40)
> "God is love." (1 Jn. 4:16)

Since Thomas was unwilling to deny that God can experience pity, tenderness, love, and forgiveness, his only recourse, given his metaphysical reasons for denying that God has emotions, was to deny that these states as experienced by

God are emotions. The chief emotion of God for humans is love, and Aquinas thought of a way, compatible with his general philosophical psychology, to attribute love to God without attributing an emotion to God, and that is to locate some forms of love in the will or the intellective appetite. "Love is the first movement of the will and of every appetitive power" (ST I 20, 1 corpus). According to Aquinas, even in humans love is not limited to the sensitive appetite; love in the form of charity exists in the will. So while God does not have sensitive appetite, God does have intellective appetite and will. It is, therefore, not only permitted to say that God loves, it is required. In Aquinas's words:

> Loving, enjoying, and having pleasure are emotions when they signify activities of the sensitive appetite; not so, however, when they signify activities of the intellective appetite. It is in this last sense that they are attributed to God. (ST I 20, 1, ad 1)

This move still rules out most human emotions from the divine psyche, however. Aquinas maintains that God cannot experience emotions such as hate, sadness, fear, courage, and anger because their objects are evil.[4] And God cannot experience desire or hope because such states require that their objects are not yet present. All these states are unbefitting to God.

I agree that certain emotions appropriate in humans are inappropriate in God, and so a full account of the normativity of human motives that locates their goodness in similarity with the divine motives would need to explain how the goodness of the human motive of, say, hope or desire is grounded in something divine-like. Clearly, perfect states take on a very different form when projected onto the psyches of finite creatures. What is perfect love in God becomes desire for the good in humans. What is a perfect rest in goodness becomes hope in humans. What is an eternally perfect power over evil in God becomes courage in facing evil in humans, and so on. I am not confident yet that it is possible to understand God's perfect states and our imperfect ones in a way that is similar enough to permit the former to serve the function of grounding moral theory, but my purpose is to encourage exploration of such an idea as far as it can go. Thomas's psychology includes an idea that would go a long way towards permitting an account of human psychology based on similarity to the divine psychology if it could be made to work, and that is the idea that love is the root emotion. According to Aquinas:

> All other motions of appetite and will presuppose love; it is like their very root. No one desires an object or rejoices in it unless it be a good that is loved. Nor is there any hatred except for what is contrary to a thing loved, and the same applies to grief and the rest: they all come back to love as to their primordial source. (ST I 20, 1 c)

The idea that all emotions are related to love is worth exploring, not only for the purposes of charting human emotions in terms of similarity to divine emotions, but also for the purposes of understanding the unity of human consciousness. I hope that others will be tempted to work on this approach also.

Let me turn now to my own view of divine agency according to which God has no will. I doubt that humans have wills either, but to argue that would take us farther afield than we need to go for the theory I am proposing. Actually, it is not strictly necessary to accept my claim that God has no will in order to accept the theory that value is founded on divine motivation rather than on the divine will, but the theory is more strongly motivated if there is no divine will. In the case of human agency, the idea of a will was invented because it was thought that such psychic states as desires, emotions, motives, and beliefs are not sufficient to explain how a human person makes a choice. The idea was that if a choice is causally explained by some combination of these states, then the choice could not be free, and if it is noncausally explained by these states, the causal mechanism of free choice still has to be located in something other than these states.[5] That something was taken to be the faculty of the will. Now regardless of the merits of this view of human agency, the problems with which are many, there is very little to recommend it in the case of divine agency. Why would God be determined, and hence unfree, if his acts were fully explained by his motives, together with his beliefs, even if his beliefs and motives were sufficient to determine what he chooses? It is not as if God is faced with the human problem that, ultimately, beliefs and motives are, or might be, determined by events and persons outside of ourselves. There is nothing outside of God at all that is logically or temporally or causally prior to himself. To say that the divine motives determine what God will do, given any circumstance, is not to say that God is unfree. We will turn to the question of divine freedom momentarily, but the point here is just that there is no *particular* need for a concept of divine will to create a free space within which God can act. God's motives are as much his own as his alleged will can possibly be. There is no question of God's motives being put upon him or involuntarily suffered, or the like. If God acts because of his motives, he is no less free and no less perfect and no less himself than if he acts because of his will. There is no need for a will to act as an intercessor between the past and future, and there is no advantage to a will that acts independently of other parts of the divine nature. Nor does God need a faculty of pure pushiness that is untainted by the influence of emotion or desire and able to supersede it, since God's emotions and desires are not something he needs to rise above. God does not have a will, whether or not we humans have wills. God's motives, on the other hand, are an intrinsic and important part of God's nature.

II. PERFECT GOODNESS AND ITS PUZZLES

The lofty metaphysical view of the deity associated with St. Anselm and gradually developed throughout the high era of Christian theology in the Middle Ages understood God as the personification of the ancient Greek concept of perfect goodness. Let us turn now to an examination of that concept since I am proposing that perfect goodness is the fundamental evaluative concept, and that the motives of a perfectly good being ground all other evaluative concepts.

The concept of perfect goodness had roots in the philosophies of both Plato and Aristotle, and Aquinas synthesized elements from both traditions along with the work of Augustine, Boethius, and Anselm. Like Aristotle, Aquinas identified the good of a thing with its complete being and its end as the achievement of its complete being. The will is naturally directed towards the good of the willer. Aquinas combined this Aristotelian notion of the good as end with Platonic elements. Like Plato, Aquinas believed that creatures are good by participation in divine perfect goodness; the created universe is an outpouring of the goodness of God. I have already said that the picture of the will adopted by Aquinas and, to varying degrees, by most medieval philosophers, is problematic. But the Platonic part of the picture, as just described, is perfectly acceptable and even central to the theology of value I wish to promote. The world is good *because* God is good. Persons are good because God is good. Motives are good because God's motives are good. And because God is not only good, but *perfectly* good, his perfect goodness is the standard for all other concepts deriving from the concept of good.

But the idea of a perfectly good God leads to problems when combined with some of the other divine attributes traditionally considered important in the Christian God. In particular, I want to mention four problems that have been discussed in the recent literature, some of which have a long and important history.

First, there is the problem of the alleged incompatibility of perfect goodness and omnipotence. A perfectly good being was traditionally understood to be one whose will is so fixed in goodness that he is actually incapable of willing anything other than good, a property sometimes called 'impeccability'. An omnipotent being is one who has maximal power, and while there are many different accounts of what maximal power entails, it has often been understood to involve the power to do anything possible. But since sinning or doing evil is a possible thing to do, if a perfectly good being lacks the power to do evil, such a being lacks the power to do something possible and, hence, is not omnipotent. This puzzle has been articulated in the contemporary literature by Nelson Pike, but it was known to Aquinas.

The reasoning behind the alleged incompatibility of perfect goodness and omnipotence leads to a second difficulty. Under the assumption that a perfectly good being is incapable of doing wrong or willing anything but good, the will of such a being does not appear to be free in any morally significant sense. On a common interpretation of the conditions for moral praise and blame in the human case, persons are morally praised because they choose the good when they could have chosen evil, and they are morally blamed because they choose evil when they could have chosen good. Of course, the understanding of the conditions of moral praise and blame as entailing the ability to do otherwise is a modern idea, and the idea that the ability to do otherwise is morally meaningless unless it includes the ability to choose something with the contrary evaluative property is open to dispute, but both of these assumptions are ones that many philosophers accept. But, then, if perfect goodness involves the inability to will evil, a perfectly good being is not free in the morally significant sense. And then it also seems to follow that a perfectly good being cannot be praised in the moral sense of praise and cannot be good in the moral sense of good. This leads to a third problem. If the concept of perfect goodness is meant to include moral goodness, and yet the concept of perfect goodness is inconsistent with the concept of moral goodness as allegedly demonstrated by the foregoing argument, it seems to follow that the concept of perfect goodness is self-inconsistent.

The Divine Command theory suggests an answer to these three puzzles. According to that theory, God's will and, in fact, God's nature, are prior to morality. What is morally right (or good) is made to be right (or good) by God's will. This theory can resolve the puzzle of the alleged incompatibility between omnipotence and perfect goodness by claiming that God has the power to do anything possible, including the things that are, in fact, evil, but if he were to do such things, they would not be evil. God's freedom is maintained by the same reasoning. God *is* free to do what is in fact evil, but if he were to will these things, they would not be evil. The solution to the third puzzle is to say that whereas God's goodness is moral goodness in a sense, it is not the same sense in which creatures are morally good. God is free to choose anything, good or bad, but there is no evil fixed as evil independent of God's choice, the avoidance of which is a test of God's moral goodness. And this may count as an acceptable way out of the dilemma of God's moral goodness since it does seem to be misguided to think of God's moral goodness as involving the passing of a test independent of himself.

So one of the attractions of Divine Command theory is that it promises answers to the three puzzles of perfect goodness. DC has traditionally faced some significant problems, however. Perhaps the most important one is that it seems to make God's will arbitrary. This is because God cannot have a *moral* reason for willing as he does since his will determines what counts as a moral reason. And it is hard to see how any nonmoral reason could be the right sort of reason or have the right sort of force to ground morality. In addition, DC seems to make the concept of perfect goodness vacuous. That is, there is no content to the property of goodness other than this: goodness is whatever it is that God is, and rightness is whatever it is that God wills.

Besides these three puzzles of perfect goodness, there is one more difficulty, the most intractable of all theological problems: the problem of evil. This problem has a number of forms, but it most directly threatens the concept of perfect goodness by way of the following argument: (1) A perfectly good being would be motivated to eliminate all evil. (2) An omnipotent being would be able to eliminate all evil. (3) If a being is both motivated to eliminate evil and is able to do so, he would do so. (4) So if there were a perfectly good and omnipotent being, evil would not exist. (5) But evil does exist. Therefore, (6) There is no being who is both perfectly good and omnipotent.

Defenses of the compatibility of evil with divine omnipotence and perfect goodness generally focus on modifying either premise (2) or premise (3) of the above argument, or by interpreting them in such a way that (4) does not follow. It is virtually always taken for granted that a perfectly good being is motivated to prevent or to eliminate evil, and so premise (1) is usually accepted by all sides in the dispute. Theists looking for ways out of the dilemma then typically look for reasons why a perfectly good God would permit evil for the sake of some good—often the good of free will or, in general, the good of the world and its creatures. The idea is that a certain kind and amount of evil is a logically or metaphysically necessary prerequisite for obtaining such good.

The Divine Command theory permits a different approach to the problem of evil—the denial of (1) in the sense intended in this dilemma. Since DC theories maintain that what is right or good is determined to be right or good by the will of God, they maintain (1) only in a trivial sense. Since good just *is* what God wills, and since it is trivially true that God is motivated to will what he wills and is not motivated to will what he does not will, then God is motivated to will good and not to will evil. Such an interpretation of (1) does not generate the problem of evil.

Now let us return to motivation-based virtue theory. According to this theory the rightness of human acts and the goodness of states of affairs are derivative from the goodness of human motives, and suppose that what makes human motives good is their similarity to divine motives. Suppose also, as I said above, that God has no will. God's motives could then serve the same function as God's will in a Divine Command theory. God's motivations are an intrinsic feature of his nature and hence good in the primary sense, so good is not something against which the motivations of a perfectly good being are to be measured. Instead, the dependency goes the other way. What is good is good because a perfectly good being is motivated to bring it about. It is not the case that a being is good in part because his motivations are to do or to bring about good. I call this approach Divine Motivation theory.

III. DIVINE MOTIVATION THEORY

The theory I am proposing is structurally like DC, but instead of claiming that what is morally right (or good) is made to be morally right (or good) by God's will, what I propose is that what is right (or good) is made to be right (or good) by God's motives. Like DC, Divine Motivation theory makes God's nature prior to morality. I believe the theory has several advantages over DC without its disadvantages. We already saw that one of the principal objections to DC throughout its history is that it seems to make the divine will arbitrary since there is no natural connection between the divine nature and the divine will when the latter is understood as a faculty of pure choice. A will requires a reason and, according to Aquinas, the will always chooses "under the aspect of good." According to the model used by medieval theologians, then, a reason is understood evaluatively by the intellect and presented to the will for choice. With such a model it appears that either the good to be willed is good prior to its willing, in which case DC is false, or if the will creates the good, there is no ground upon which the choice is made. To say that the ground is the divine nature is not to explain how that provides a reason in the sense of reason required for choice by the will. But the concept of divine motivation serves the purpose of explaining divine agency quite well without the problem of arbitrariness. A motive is psychically more fundamental than the will since a willing is allegedly a way of responding to one's own motives. A willing requires a reason, but a motive *is* a reason. God's motives are clearly not arbitrary and are not only connected with the divine nature but are an intrinsic part of it.

A second advantage of Divine Motivation theory over DC is that DM gives us a unitary theory of all evaluative properties, divine as well as human. Divine Command theory does not. One of the problems facing DC is that there is no way to combine it with a secular ethics. Of course, the theory can be combined with almost *any* theory in a sense. What it would do is to say that the results of that theory yield commands that are ultimately grounded in God's will. But why think there is any such connection? In the case of the varieties of consequentialist or deontological ethics, it takes quite a bit of ingenuity to see any connection at all between the ultimate principles of those theories and anything we would expect to be the product of divine command. The combination of Natural Law theory and Divine Command theory has more promise,[6] since Natural Law theory in its Thomistic form is ultimately grounded in the Eternal Law of God, and the concept of law, as Anscombe has argued, logically requires a lawgiver, a being whose will might plausibly be the basis for the law.[7] But the relation between a motivation-based virtue theory and Divine Motivation theory is natural and straightforward. Having good motivations is partly constitutive of being a good person. Identifying good human persons is problematic for the obvious reason that humans are probably never all good or all bad. If there were such a human person, as Christians believe there actually was in the person of Jesus of Nazareth, the goodness would be obvious, and is something that can even be seen from the vantage point of two millennia. The idea of the imitation of Christ is a central theme in Christian ethics, so the idea of imitating the motives of Christ is presumably an application of a traditional part of Christian moral theory. Given a background theology of one God and the doctrine of the Incarnation, the extension of the theory to the motives of a perfectly good deity links the ethical theory to theology in a way that certainly would be natural for Christian philosophers.[8]

Now let us return to the four puzzles about perfect goodness. Divine Motivation theory has at least as good a way of solving the puzzles as Divine Command theory, and a better way for some of them. First, there is the apparent incompatibility between perfect goodness and omnipotence. To begin with, we might reflect for a moment on the concept of perfection. Problems arise from the idea that perfection is the same as the highest possible degree of any good attribute. But why think that? Even in the case of human properties, more of a good thing is not necessarily a better thing, or even a good thing. Why think that if x is good, the maximal possible degree of x is even better? It is interesting to see how power has traditionally been assumed to be a good, and therefore, absolute power is assumed to be a perfection of the deity. What led to such an idea? Presumably it must turn out that God's will is never under the power of any other possible being. And God's will must never be thwarted. Whatever God attempts to do, God does. Formulating the point in terms of motives rather than the disputable concept of a divine will, the idea would be that whatever God is motivated to do, God is able to do. God never encounters any hindrance to his motives from outside himself. But, of course, there is no reason to think that God is motivated to do any possible thing, or even that it is possible that God is motivated to do any possible thing. A different model of divine power is needed, not because we have encountered a problem in a plausible concept of perfection of power, but because it is not at all clear that power in the extreme is the same as perfection of power.

A plausible source of the idea of divine power is the story of the creation of the world. God controls what is chaotic or arbitrary, which is to say, God's power is *creative*. Divine creativity ought to be considered one of his essential attributes, allied both to his power and to his freedom. When the biblical story says that God created the heavens and the earth and "found them good," we might understand that story as a story of divine creativity expressing itself. The goodness of the universe is derivative from God's own nature; the goodness of God's motivation to create is not derivative from the goodness of the product.[9]

If all moral goodness is defined in terms of the divine motivations, then God's motives are good and their goodness is not explained by their relationship to anything else that is good. The account of good itself precludes the possibility of God's being motivated to do evil. If it is impossible for God to have different motives (understood at a certain level of generality) or to change his motives, then it is impossible for what is good to be evil and what is evil to be good. Many philosophers have the intuition that this is right, and that the denial of it is a counterintuitive result of DC. DM theory does not have that problem. Since God's motivations explain his other attributes, then God is motivated to have knowledge and power, but not the power to have different motives. Omnipotence is power in the highest degree of excellence, which would be defined as power in the manner and degree which God is motivated to possess. Omnipotence cannot conflict with perfect goodness, then, and in fact, it follows from it.

God has lots of choices provided that there is no unique choice that is compatible with his complete set of motives, although choosing evil is not one of them. The second puzzle of perfect goodness was that this is said to prevent God from being "significantly free." But let's look for a moment at the structure of the concepts used in claims of moral goodness. In motivation-based virtue-ethics, good traits, good states of affairs, and right acts are derived from good human motives. Nobody would think that the goodness of motives in such a theory is not moral goodness. But in the complete theory as I am proposing it here, the relation of derivation from the goodness of God's motives is extended to all good things, including the goodness of human motives. God's motives are therefore related to all other goods as good human motives are related to the good states of affairs which are the objects of those motives. This clearly is a moral sense of goodness, not metaphysical or some other sort of goodness. God's goodness is moral goodness in the same way that the root of moral goodness in a virtue theory is moral goodness.

But, it might be objected, does not moral goodness require the ability to do evil? If it does, then there is the third problem described above: (3) The concept of perfect moral goodness is incoherent. The solution to puzzle (3) is the same as to puzzle (2). If God is not motivated to have the freedom to choose evil, then the freedom to choose evil is not a good. God, however, may be motivated for *us* to have such freedom. In any case, we would expect his motivations with regard to us to be different from his motivations with regard to himself. It follows that God is not free in the same sense we are, but this is not yet to say that the sense in which God is free is not the moral sense. Since human motives are morally good by similarity to the divine motives, the divine motives must be morally good, in fact, perfectly morally good.

This approach brings the sense in which God is good much closer to the sense in which humans are good than we get in DC. In the latter theory there is a fundamental difference between the sense in which God's will is good and the sense in which human wills are good since good clearly does not have a dependency upon human wills, whereas it does depend upon the divine will. A unitary account of moral goodness is a desirable feature of a theory, and DM theory is able to provide that.

Finally, let us turn to the problem of evil. Since I have already described a motivation-based approach to the problem of evil elsewhere,[10] I will simply summarize the argument of that essay. On this approach we give up the idea that God aims to create in the world something he independently considers to be good. His motivation cannot be explained by saying that he does something *because* it is good. Instead, God does what he does because he is motivated to do so, and his motives are expressive of his nature. God's actions are like those of the artist who creates works of beauty, but hardly can be said to create these works because they are beautiful. He simply creates out of a desire to create, a desire that expresses the inner beauty or aesthetic value of his own inventive imagination. Similarly, God does not create because his creation is good. It is not as if God sees in thought that such a creation would be good and then goes about creating it. The created universe is good because it is the expression of the motive to create of a perfectly good being whose inventiveness is a component of his omnipotence. It follows that the first premise of the logical problem of evil is false. God is not motivated to choose good and to eliminate evil in the sense intended in the argument.[11]

Divine Motivation theory provides a better way of handling the problem of evil than does Divine Command theory. Both theories deny the first premise of the argument generating the logical form of the problem. That is, both deny that a perfectly good God is motivated to eliminate evil, where evil is taken to be independent of the structure of God's decision-making. DC says that God is motivated to will good and to prevent evil only in the trivial sense that God is motivated to will what he wills and to prevent what he wills to prevent, and good *is* what God wills, and evil *is* what God wills to prevent. The connection between

God's motives and his pure faculty of will is utterly mysterious. In contrast, DM says that the goodness of a perfectly good being is revealed in that being's motives, just as the goodness of ordinary people is revealed in their motives. Since a will is normally thought to be good because of what it wills, not conversely, it takes a difficult reversal of mind to understand that in the case of God's will, the converse relationship holds. No such reversal of the dependency of motive and object need be made in DM. In all cases, divine or human, motives are complex emotional states that are good or bad in themselves, not because of the independent goodness or badness of their objects. The object of a good motive is good because of the goodness of the motive, not conversely. Divine Motivation theory is the same as motivation-based virtue theory, but with the additional claim that, ultimately, the goodness of all motives is grounded in the motives of a single being—a perfectly good God.

In this essay I have proposed a theory I call Divine Motivation theory as the foundation for a comprehensive ethical theory. The theory is structurally parallel to Divine Command theory except that the source of morality is motivating emotional states of God rather than the divine will. I believe that the theory has several advantages over Divine Command theory: (1) It does not have the problem of arbitrariness that DC theory faces. That problem arises because the will is allegedly a faculty independent of reasons and motives but in need of reasons and motives to explain choice. Divine Motivation theory bypasses the need for a theory of the divine will by grounding morality directly in the divine motives. (2) DM can be integrated into a comprehensive ethical theory in which moral concepts are all derived from the concept of a good motive, whether the possessor of the motive is divine or creaturely. DC, on the other hand, completely dissociates the morality of God and his actions from the ethics of human action. (3) DM gives a better answer than Divine Command theory to four conceptual puzzles about the concept of perfect goodness. If the theory has a disadvantage, it is in its nontraditional claim that God has emotions, but, as I have said, I believe the traditional objections to this view can be answered.

The combination of Divine Motivation theory and motivation-based virtue theory has the following general structure: The motivational states of God are ontologically and conceptually the basis for all moral concepts. God's motives are perfectly good and the motives of all other beings are good insofar as they are similar to the divine motives. The concept of a good motive is the foundational concept in this form of virtue theory. A good motive-disposition (a motivation) is the primary component of a good human trait, a virtue. A right (permissible) act is defined in terms of what a virtuous person *might* do in like circumstances. A moral duty is defined in terms of what a virtuous person *would* do in like circumstances. A wrong act is defined in terms of what a virtuous person *would not* do in like circumstances. A good state of affairs is defined as the end of a good motive or, more generally, it is one that is related to certain emotional attitudes of good beings.[12]

NOTES

1. Sometimes the same name applies either to an emotion or to a complex trait (a virtue) of which the emotion is a component.

2. Marcel Sarot examines and defends Thomas's reasons for denying emotion to God in "God, Emotion, and Corporeality," *The Thomist* (January 1994): 61–92. The article also includes an extensive review of the contemporary literature on impassibility.

3. An exception would be the so-called "Cambridge properties" that are of no interest to theology. These are properties such as *being the object of thought by LZ in this essay*.

4. I do not consider some of these states motives. Courage is a complex trait, neither a motive nor an emotion. Sadness is an emotion but may not be motivating.

5. In some writings the will appears to be a faculty of pure pushiness, a pushiness that is independent of the states of emotion and desire. The latter are also pushy, but not purely so.

6. See James G. Hanink and Gary R. Mar, "What Euthyphro Couldn't Have Said," *Faith and Philosophy* 4, no. 3 (July 1987): 241–61.

7. G. E. M. Anscombe, "Modern Moral Philosophy," *Philosophy* 33 (January 1958): 1–19.

8. It is interesting to consider the series of papers on Divine Command Theory by Robert M. Adams. In the final paper in the series, "Divine Command Metaethics Modified Again" (*Journal of Religious Ethics* 7, no. 1, 1979) Adams argues that moral obligations should be identified with the commands of a *loving* God. Adams has imported the kind of emotion state I am arguing should be fundamental into his version of DC theory.

9. We might even get a divine-motivation–based theory of aesthetic value out of reflections on divine creativity.

10. Zagzebski, "An Agent-based Approach to the Problem of Evil," *International Journal for Philosophy of Religion* 39 (June 1996): 127–39.

11. However, there is still the problem of suffering. We expect loving beings to be motivated to prevent their loved ones from suffering.

12. This essay is the second of my Jellema Lectures, delivered at Calvin College, March 12, 1996. The motivation-based virtue theory briefly described here is the topic of the first of my Jellema Lectures, "Making Motivation Primary," delivered on March 11, 1996.

Contributors

Robert Merrihew Adams, Department of Philosophy, Yale University
C. A. J. Coady, Department of Philosophy, University of Melbourne
Charles Crittenden, Department of Philosophy, California State University, Northridge
Thomas P. Flint, Department of Philosophy, University of Notre Dame
Jerome I. Gellman, Department of Philosophy, Ben-Gurion University of the Negev
Philip J. Ivanhoe, Department of Philosophy, Stanford University
Norman Kretzmann, Sage School of Philosophy, Cornell University
Alan Montefiore, Sub-Faculty of Philosophy, Balliol College, University of Oxford
D. Z. Phillips, Religion Program, Claremont Graduate School
Hilary Putnam, Department of Philosophy, Harvard University
Philip L. Quinn, Department of Philosophy, University of Notre Dame
William Rowe, Department of Philosophy, Purdue University
David Shatz, Department of Philosophy, Yeshiva University
Eleonore Stump, Department of Philosophy, St. Louis University
Peter Van Inwagen, Department of Philosophy, University of Notre Dame
Bryan W. Van Norden, Department of Philosophy, Vassar College
Howard Wettstein, Department of Philosophy, University of California, Riverside
Linda Zagzebski, Department of Philosophy, Loyola Marymount University

Peter A. French holds the Cole Chair in Ethics at the University of South Florida. He has taught at the University of Minnesota, Morris, served as Distinguished Research Professor in the Center for the Study of Human Values at the University of Delaware, and most recently served as Lennox Distinguished Professor of Philosophy at Trinity University in San Antonio, Texas. His books include *The Scope of Morality* (1980), *Collective and Corporate Responsibility* (1980), and *Responsibility Matters* (1992). He has published numerous articles in the philosophical journals. **Theodore E. Uehling, Jr.,** is professor of philosophy at the University of Minnesota, Morris. He is the author of *The Notion of Form in Kant's Critique of Aesthetic Judgement* and articles on the philosophy of Kant. He is founder and past vice-president of the North American Kant Society. **Howard K. Wettstein** is chair and professor of philosophy at the University of California, Riverside. He has taught at the University of Notre Dame and the University of Minnesota, Morris, and has served as visiting associate professor of philosophy at the University of Iowa and Stanford University. He is the author of *Has Semantics Rested on a Mistake? and Other Essays* (1992).